VICTORY
1918

VICTORY
1918

ALAN PALMER

GROVE PRESS
New York

First published in Great Britain in 1998 by Weidenfeld & Nicolson
Printed in the United States of America

FIRST GROVE PRESS EDITION

Library of Congress Cataloging-in-Publication Data

Palmer, Alan Warwick.
    Victory, 1918 / Alan Palmer.
        p.   cm.
    Includes bibliographical references and index.
    ISBN 0-8021-3787-3
    1. World War, 1914–1918. I. Title.

    D521.P35 1999
    940.3 21—dc21

                                                                99-045459

Grove Press
841 Broadway
New York, NY 10003

00 01 02 03   10 9 8 7 6 5 4 3 2 1

TO THE MEMORY OF MY PARENTS,
WARWICK LINDLEY PALMER, 1885–1970
EDITH MARY PALMER, 1886–1954

CONTENTS

ILLUSTRATIONS

General Franchet d'Esperey casts a cursory eye at a British Guard of
    Honour[2]
Woodrow Wilson, Visionary of Peace, electioneering[3]

[1] The Camera Press Ltd
[2] The Imperial War Museum
[3] Hulton Getty Picture Collection Ltd

Every effort has been made to trace copyright holders, but if any have been inadvertently
overlooked, the publishers will be pleased to make the necessary arrangements at the first
opportunity.

MAPS

ACKNOWLEDGEMENTS

In writing a wide-ranging narrative of this character my greatest debt must be to the authors of the specialist studies and articles included in the reference notes and bibliography. I have tried to cite them fully, as proper acknowledgement, but I would like also to record my admiration for the recent growth of scholarly research on the First World War; there is a far richer harvest to garner today than thirty years ago. I remain grateful now, as I was then, to the staffs of the London Library, the Bodleian Library and the Public Record Office; it is particularly useful to have so many documents from the PRO available on microfilm in the New Bodleian at Oxford. To Clare Brown, of the Middle East Centre at St Antony's College, Oxford, I owe a double debt: for her advice as archivist at the MEC; and for the encouragement and support which I have received from her and from her husband, Robert, over the past eighteen months – not least when I was feeling very weary in Aleppo.

Many other friends have helped me, too. *The Gardeners of Salonika* in 1964 brought me new contacts with survivors of the campaign and I warmly cherish their fund of reminiscence. Many served in Palestine, too; I especially recall a fascinating conversation with Bernard Livermore, whose published memoirs I am glad to cite. The Salonika Reunion Association was disbanded in 1969, but links with the old theatre of war have been maintained in recent years by Mr and Mrs Philip Barnes of Harrow. It has been an honour to attend the October wreath-laying ceremony at the Cenotaph which they organized. Although it is nine years since I last heard reminiscences from veterans, I have profited on these occasions from talk with kinsfolk of the orginal 'gardeners', including Philip Barnes himself. An unusual light on the Palestine Campaign was shed by Ruth Hummel and Georg Hintlian who entertained me during a visit to Oxford and generously gave me a copy of the Proceedings of the 1995 Symposium on the Austrian

Presence in the Holy Land. For secretarial assistance and advice I am indebted to Lauren Mohammed and also to ADS Services, Woodstock, and Caspian Print, Oxford.

At Orion House it has been particularly gratifying to have the advice and encouragement of Ion Trewin, whom I have known for many years. To my good fortune, another friend with much publishing experience, Linden Lawson, was copy-editor. She was the first person to read the text thoroughly and made many helpful suggestions; it was a pleasure to be working with her again. I am grateful, too, for the editorial assistance of Rachel Leyshon and Francis Gotto. The maps owe their clarity to the cartographic skills of John Gilkes; my thanks to him and to Ian Crane, who compiled the index.

ABBREVIATIONS
USED IN THE TEXT

AEF	American Expeditionary Force
Anzac	Australian and New Zealand Army Corps
BEF	British Expeditionary Force (in France and Flanders)
CIGS	Chief of the Imperial General Staff
DFPS	French Detachment of Palestine and Syria (Army)
EEF	(British) Egyptian Expeditionary Force
GHQ	General Headquarters
GQG	*Grand Quartier Général* (French Military Headquarters)
K-und-K	*Kaiserlich-und-Königlich* (Imperial and Royal); appertaining to the Dual Monarchy of Austria–Hungary
MEF	Mediterranean Expeditionary Force
OHL	*Oberste Heeresleitung* (German Army Supreme Command)
OKL	*Oberste Kriegsleitung* (Central Powers Supreme War Command)
RFC	Royal Flying Corps
SKL	*Seekriegsleitung* (German Navy Supreme Command)
SPD	*Sozialdemokratische Partei Deutschlands* (German Socialist Party)
U-Boat	*Unterseeboot* (German submarine)

PREFACE

The First World War determined the political and social character of the twentieth century. Not surprisingly, it retains a power of awful fascination which continues to generate an industry of writing and historical research. Packed library shelves lead us through half a dozen good general surveys to long lines of memoirs, apologia and official narratives, on to edited eyewitness tales from the trenches and down to coconut-shy anti-hero biographies and the smearing of reputations with Flanders mud. There is an overwhelming concentration on the Western Front, always held to be the decisive theatre of operations, and particularly on the Somme and Passchendaele. But the conflict was a *world* war, fought on three continents and the waters of three oceans and nine seas. 'Sideshows' proliferated, and are frequently forgotten. If remembered at all, their purpose is obscured by tedious and persistent disputes between the inaptly named 'Westerners' and 'Easterners', a distinction first made while the fighting was still in progress. This controversy especially distorts the significance of events in the last year of war, when offensives in the Balkans, the Middle East, Italy and the West all ended victoriously and within a span of seven weeks.

In *Victory 1918* I have tried to bring together the achievements of all these battle fronts; but to do so within the general context of the war as a whole. While concentrating on the later stages of the conflict, especially after the USA became an Associated Power, the book therefore begins with what was, for Britain, the Kitchener era. For to me it is important to recall the occasions when a speedy and early end to the war seemed attainable, and why it was not attained: how very differently a book on final victory in 1915 and its consequences would read! When talking in recent years to young people I have found myself being asked such questions as: 'Why wasn't the war simply with Germany and Austria?'; 'Where does Turkey fit into it?' and 'Why Lawrence *of Arabia* anyhow?'. I hope the book suggests answers to these questions and others, too, at a time when Mesopotamia/Iraq and Serbia and her neighbours are so prominent in our news reports.

The book is dedicated to the memory of my mother and father, who hated the war and all the worry, separation and tragedy it entailed. I was born eight years after the Armistice. The loathsome experience of war was so recent for many people around our home in metropolitan Essex that I passed my childhood under a shadow which had still not lifted when an even deeper blackness enveloped us, and Europe too. My father and four of his brothers had served in the Army; unusually, all survived unscathed, as did a fifth brother in the Merchant Navy; they would talk about those four years, but never glory in them. The prevailing mood was of thankfulness and respect: the two-minute silence was strictly kept each 11 November; and I would never pass the Cenotaph in Whitehall without taking off my school-cap. We had some war souvenirs which I well remember: a German bullet; some twisted inches of aluminium from Zeppelin *LZ-85*; postcards of Salonika and Ismailia; pencilled jottings in tattered diaries, on one of which I thought I could I smell ash from Salonika's Great Fire. Shortly before my seventh birthday my parents took me on holiday to Belgium, crossing from Parkeston Quay to Zeebrugge Mole overnight in the *Archangel*, the ship which brought my father back across the Channel in 1918, feverish with Spanish flu. The days that followed were exciting and, as I now see, mind-broadening. I vividly remember the Mole itself, clambering around what remained of the Kaiser Wilhelm Battery at Knokke, seeing trenches at Hill 60 outside Ypres and my mother searching for familiar names on the Menin Gate; beside her was a woman in black, alone and weeping silently. My boyhood interest in 'the War' I have never shed; and I have seen sectors of every battle front described in this book, except Mesopotamia. Yet if sometimes the drama of the conflict thrills me and I delight too much in feats of arms, there slips into memory's eye the weeping woman of 'Wipers', still in grief fifteen years after it all ended. She remains for me an eloquently silent symbol of why this terrible war, despite its compelling interest, must never become romanticized. Unknown Widow, I would like to think I have been true to your image.

Alan Palmer
Woodstock, Oxfordshire
Mothering Sunday, 1998

PROLOGUE: DOVER,
3 AUGUST 1914

It was a fine August Bank Holiday Monday, sunny enough to tempt people down to the beaches but too hazy to see the French coast, barely twenty miles across the Channel. Europe stood on the brink of war; already German military patrols had penetrated Russian Poland and crossed into France north of the Swiss frontier. For the moment Great Britain, with no formal alliance commitments in Europe, remained at peace, awaiting news from Brussels, for treaty obligations accepted seventy-five years previously bound the government to assist the Belgians repel any invasion of their land. Alongside Dover's Admiralty Pier extension the Calais boat bristled with expectancy, smoke darkening the yellow and blank funnels, preparing to sail at 12.55. Shortly before half past twelve a chauffeur-driven Daimler pulled up on the quayside. From inside the car unfolded the tall figure of Britain's most illustrious soldier, dressed in civilian clothes and ready for a long journey. Field Marshal Earl Kitchener of Khartoum, on leave in England for the past seven weeks, had spent the night at his country home, Broome Park, some ten miles inland, up the road to Canterbury. Now he was returning to Cairo, where since 1911 he had been resident British Agent (governor) and Consul-General for Egypt. A reserved compartment on the 14.50 train from Calais awaited him and his two aides-de-camp. At Marseilles a British cruiser was standing by, to carry them on the three-day crossing to Alexandria.

No one, however, could be certain how long the train journey from Calais to Marseilles would take. In Paris the Minister of War had ordered General Mobilization on the previous Saturday afternoon and, across France, hundreds of special trains were taking reservists to their regiments. Although the War Office in London did not authorize mobilization until an hour before Kitchener reached Dover, there was already congestion on the railways around the capital, partly because of the movement of Territorials from summer camps. Bank Holiday excursions were cancelled at the last moment; regular expresses delayed. Among them was the boat train for Dover, which had not pulled into the Maritime Station by the steamer's scheduled departure time.

Kitchener fumed at the delay. His principal aide, Lieutenant-Colonel Fitzgerald, urged the captain to sail without waiting for the boat train. But that was out of the question. Aboard the packed train were French nationals returning home to serve their country: the steamer was as essential for them as the train to Marseilles for Kitchener's party. As the minutes slipped by, a messenger arrived for Kitchener, relieved to see the Calais boat still at the quayside. Soon after the Field Marshal left Broome, a telephone call had come from Downing Street: Mr Asquith, the Prime Minister, wished Kitchener to postpone his departure for Egypt. He was to return to London for consultation.

Kitchener's first inclination was to ignore the message. He had left Cairo ten days before the murder of Archduke Francis Ferdinand and his wife at Sarajevo, the terrorist act which first conjured up the spectre of war. But for the last four years, ever since making a visit to Constantinople, Kitchener had anticipated a long conflict between Britain and Germany; he believed that Turkey would soon become Germany's ally and threaten Britain's primacy in the Middle East, perhaps even shaking the imperial hold on the Muslim provinces of India. If so, Kitchener was convinced his rightful post was in Egypt, still nominally part of the Sultan's Empire though under British occupation for the past thirty years. Kitchener spoke French fluently; he had his baptism of fire in 1871 as a volunteer private in the army of republican France opposing the German advance on Le Mans; but he knew little of contemporary Europe. His military reputation rested on achievements in Africa and on preparing the overseas Empire for the challenge of wars in which the enemy could as well be France or Russia as Germany. From 1892 until 1900 he was Sirdar (commander) of the Anglo-Egyptian army, finally defeating the Mahdists at Omdurman. His years as Commander-in-Chief in India enhanced his perception of Muslim attitudes. Many other distinguished statesmen and soldiers in London were conscious of the danger posed by pan-Islamic sentiment to British imperial rule, but none perceived so clearly as Kitchener its limitations or knew so well how to exploit its divisions. In 1883, as a junior officer at the start of the Mahdist revolt, he had dressed as an Arab and travelled to desert encampments to contact dissidents angered by Mohammed Ahmed's claims to be Islam's Messiah. Thirty years later he was interested to discover that Sherif Hussein, the Emir of Mecca, sought Arab independence from Ottoman rule. Before returning to England on leave Kitchener and his 'Oriental Secretary', Ronald Storrs, had received the Emir's second son, Abdullah, in Cairo and discussed in general terms the relations between the guardian of Islam's Holy Places and the Sultan-Caliph in distant Constantinople. This was a world in which Kitchener felt at home; Westminster and Whitehall were alien to him.

Yet he cannot have been surprised by the message from Downing Street. On the previous Tuesday and Wednesday he had discussed the mounting crisis with the only member of Asquith's Cabinet who had seen active military service, Winston Churchill, First Lord of the Admiralty. Kitchener emphasized his wish to return to Cairo as soon as possible. 'If war comes, you will not go back to Egypt', Churchill responded bluntly. And the copy of *The Times* delivered at Broome that Monday morning carried an article by its military correspondent urging Asquith to appoint Kitchener Secretary of State for War. With great reluctance the Field Marshal disembarked and motored up to London.

It was still possible that Great Britain would stay out of the war. As Kitchener's car made its way across south London to his temporary home in Belgrave Square it passed close to Kennington Oval where, untroubled by events on the Continent, some 15,000 cricket-lovers were content to watch Jack Hobbs complete a double century for Surrey against Nottinghamshire. From the Pavilion spectators could see, less than a mile away, Big Ben and the Houses of Parliament where, on this holiday afternoon, the Foreign Secretary, Sir Edward Grey, patiently and dispassionately explained the deepening crisis to a crowded Commons, warning the House of a possible German invasion of Belgium and its consequences. 'If we stood aside, our moral position would be such as to have lost us all respect', Grey declared. Yet uncertainty remained in the Commons and the Cabinet, dependent on news from Belgium. And there was uncertainty, too, at 17 Belgrave Square. For, to Kitchener's increasing irritation, after being summoned up from Dover for consultation, no member of the government sought his views; he remained inactive for a whole day. At last, on Tuesday evening, four hours before Britain's ultimatum to Germany was due to expire, Kitchener went to Downing Street with what was, in effect, a personal ultimatum for Asquith: though 'not at all anxious to come into' the government, he was prepared to accept office as Secretary for War; otherwise, as he had already informed the Prime Minister, he would set out again for Egypt on Friday.

Asquith temporized. The Prime Minister had himself been acting as War Secretary for the past four months, an arrangement that clearly

could not continue. But to bring into a Liberal Cabinet a serving Field
Marshal of Tory inclinations with no experience of ministerial politics
was – as Asquith wrote at the time – 'a hazardous experiment'. Grey, and
his chief advisers in the Foreign Office, would have preferred Kitchener
to return to Egypt and shape policy in the Middle East. But popular
feeling, incited and sustained by a press campaign, willed him to the
War Office. By midday on 5 August all was settled; Kitchener would
become Secretary for War on the understanding that 'his place at Cairo
is kept open', ready for him 'when peace comes back'.

It was Margot Asquith, the Prime Minister's wife, who said of
Kitchener's tenure of the War Office, 'He made a great poster'. For over
half a century her comment continued to reflect the general view. K. of
K., forefinger outstretched towards 'YOU', projected such an aura of
infallibility that his prestige raised a New Army of one and three-quarter
million volunteers in eighteen months. Against this unique achievement
were failings which the post-war apologia of Britain's leaders, civilian
and military, readily exposed – for there were, after all, no Kitchener
memoirs to refute them: an inability to delegate; a deep mistrust of
politicians and, even more, of their wives and confidantes; a reluctance
to accept carefully trained Territorials as anything more than 'a town
clerk's army'; a failure, springing allegedly from his days in the Sudan, to
see the need for heavy guns. Above all, Kitchener was assailed for his
autocratic style, for retaining power in his own hands and information
in his own head. He was sixty-four – too old, it was said, for the
responsibilities awaiting him; Churchill was the same age when he
returned to the Admiralty in 1939. There is no doubt that much in the
day-to-day fighting was unfamiliar to him. It did not help Kitchener's
reputation that, over the following months, he remarked 'more than
once' to the Foreign Secretary: 'I don't know what is to be done – this
isn't *war*.' At times, as one reads these comments, it seems a national
misfortune that the Calais boat did not leave Dover on time that Bank
Holiday Monday.

The opening of the archives has softened harsh judgement. In 1914
Kitchener was certainly not the Wellington incarnate of popular faith;
but he did possess a shrewder military understanding and foresight than
his critics admit. Through the mists of war he had some impression of
the peace that must follow final victory; the written testimony of
Cabinet papers shows a statesmanlike vision which he could never
articulate in round-table discussion. In the immediate future he was
determined to give all the aid he could to France, though retaining at
home sufficient troops to meet the threat of invasion and keeping in

reserve, until fully trained, the New Army which he was raising from scratch. Towards Britain's other Entente partner, Russia, he was less accommodating. Suspicion lingered on both sides: less than a year previously over-zealous Russian police had taken a British officer off the train at Warsaw and briefly incarcerated him in punishment cells as a spy; the officer had been an official guest at the Tsar's army manoeuvres. His name was Wavell, and in time he would win a prize cherished in vain by Kitchener in becoming the only Field Marshal to be created Viceroy of India. Yet, despite the Wavell incident and other signs of mistrust, Kitchener was prepared to 'stage demonstrations' in the hope of reducing enemy pressure on weak points in the Russian line. Basically, however, Kitchener never doubted the importance of the Western Front as Germany's chosen arena of battle. 'Sideshows' were welcome and potentially profitable diversions if they employed local levies, backed by imperial forces already serving overseas. If they threatened to draw away troops from France and Flanders, they were unacceptable.

Yet, for all his preoccupation with the Western Front, Kitchener remained at heart a seconded imperial proconsul, deeply aware of the need to consolidate Britain's hold on the Middle East after the war. The long-term general strategy which he sought to impose on his Cabinet colleagues was grimly realistic. If, as he thought, the war would last for not less than three years, he assumed that the great conscript armies of the continental empires – German, Austro-Hungarian and Russian – would exhaust themselves; he even came to believe that Prussian militarism would be destroyed by internal revolution. By his reckoning any combatant who in 1917–18 could put into the field a newly trained and intact army, capable of winning the final victory, might determine the nature of the peace settlement in Europe and in Asia. His reasoning was almost faultless – except for one fundamental miscalculation. He underestimated the drain on the manpower and resources of his own country and of her closest ally, France. No British government could keep in reserve until 1917 the New Armies with which Kitchener believed the war would be won. When, more than two years after his death, victory was celebrated on the Western Front, the arbiter with 'the ships, the men and the money too' was not British, nor even European. He came from the United States of America, an 'Associated Power', free from all inter-Allied commitments. It was President Woodrow Wilson who possessed the strength and authority to offer the world moral guidance and specific proposals for a just and lasting settlement. The spokesmen for Britain and France, Italy, Greece, Serbia and Romania seemed by contrast lesser mortals, mere scrabblers for the fruit of forgotten victories against the fallen props of German power.

CHAPTER I

WIDENING THE WAR

The British people went to war in 1914 with a firm clarity of intent and in expectation of early victory. The immediate occasion of hostilities for Europe as a whole might be an explosion of Balkan nationalism in distant Sarajevo, a protest at Austro-Hungarian 'colonization' of Bosnia, but that affair meant little in London. For the British public the enemy was, quite simply, the German Kaiser; his troops were on the march through 'brave little Belgium'; his High Seas Fleet challenged Britannia's divine right to rule the waves. A small expeditionary force would, it was assumed, cross the Channel and, alongside the armies of France and Belgium, push back the invader while the Royal Navy kept watch over home waters from Orkney to Dover and, more distantly, protected the 'lifelines of Empire' from ocean raiders. In the East the Russian steamroller would press forward relentlessly towards Berlin, and in the Balkans the Serbs could fight their own little war against an empire with whose ruler the British had no quarrel. Not one of fourteen conflicts in mainland Europe over the past hundred years had led to more than eleven months of continuous fighting; in most instances peace came even sooner. There seemed no reason in 1914 why established patterns should change. But it was as well to be cautious. 'It would not be safe to calculate the war lasting less than six months', the Cabinet had been told by the General Staff in a previous crisis. Now, as the armies mobilized, the newly appointed Secretary of State for War warned his colleagues that the struggle might continue for three years. 'That seemed to most of us unlikely, if not incredible', Sir Edward Grey later recalled. 'It will all be over by Christmas', people chose to believe.

But by Christmas the unfolding war made nonsense of such easy assumptions and patterns of expectation. The Russian steamroller became set in reverse gear in Poland; German cruisers, eluding close blockade, emerged from the mists of the North Sea to shell Whitby, Scarborough and Hartlepool; the German Pacific Squadron, not the

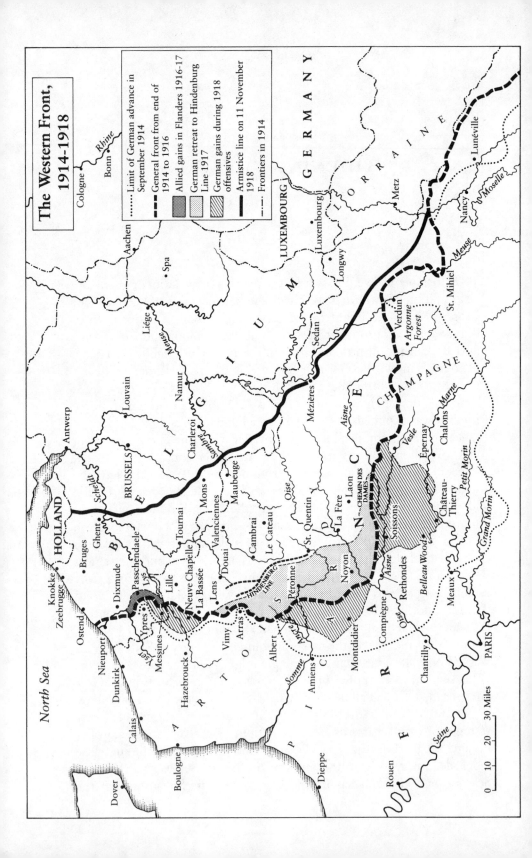

The Western Front, 1914-1918

Limit of German advance in September 1914
General front from end of 1914 to 1916
Allied gains in Flanders 1916-17
German retreat to Hindenburg Line 1917
German gains during 1918 offensives
Armistice line on 11 November 1918
Frontiers in 1914

North Sea

GERMANY

Rhine
Cologne
Bonn
Aachen
Spa
Liége
Meuse
Namur
Louvain
Antwerp
BRUSSELS
Scheldt
Ghent
Bruges
Knokke
Zeebrugge
Ostend
Nieuport
Dunkirk
Calais
Boulogne
Dover
Dixmude
Passchendaele
Lys
Ypres
Messines
Yser
Hazebrouck
Neuve Chapelle
La Bassée
Lille
Tournai
Charleroi
Sambre
Mons
Maubeuge
Valenciennes
Douai
Lens
Vimy
Arras
Albert
Somme
Amiens
Ancre
Cambrai
Le Cateau
HINDENBURG LINE
Péronne
St. Quentin
La Fère
Laon
Noyon
Montdidier
Compiègne
Oise
Rethondes
Soissons
CHEMIN DES DAMES
Aisne
Vesle
Belleau Wood
Château-Thierry
Marne
Epernay
Chalons
Petit Morin
Grand Morin
Meaux
Chantilly
PARIS
Rouen
Seine
Dieppe

HOLLAND
BELGIUM
ARTOIS
PICARDIE
FRANCE
CHAMPAGNE
LUXEMBOURG
Luxembourg
Longwy
Méziéres
Sedan
Argonne Forest
Verdun
St. Mihiel
Meuse
Metz
LORRAINE
Moselle
Nancy
Lunéville

30 Miles
0   10   20

Royal Navy, gained the first victory at sea, a defeat avenged five weeks later but only after two battlecruisers detached from home waters reached the Falklands. But the greatest of shocks came, week after week, from the Western Front. For there the battles proved far more costly than the most pessimistic of forecasts. By the end of August 1914 the French had lost over 300,000 men, killed, wounded or missing as they sought to stem the German advance across Artois and Champagne while also persisting with long-cherished plans for an offensive to liberate Alsace and Lorraine. The momentum of the German thrust was blunted in early September by the series of interrelated actions along a 125-mile front which, by saving Paris, are remembered as the Miracle of the Marne. A British Expeditionary Force, originally comprising 150,000 men, had gone into action at Mons on 23 August. By the second week in November, when the Germans abandoned their first attempt to seize British-held Ypres, the BEF was reeling from the shock of 89,000 casualties in eighty-one days of fighting. As winter closed in on the exhausted armies a continuous static front ran from Belgium's North Sea coast, through flooded fields in Flanders and the shell-pitted Ypres Salient to Armentières and the trenches of the Aisne and along the Chemin des Dames to the Argonne, the Meuse hills and around the Vosges down to the Swiss frontier. Over the next two and a half years this long entrenched line did not move as much as ten miles in either direction.

For Britain the strategic purpose of the war changed during the autumn months as drastically as did the character of the fighting. Hopes of standing aloof from the quarrels of central and eastern Europe were short-lived. The presence of token Austrian contingents along Germany's frontier with France led to declarations of war on Austria–Hungary from London and Paris before mid-August. Within hours of Austria becoming an enemy, however, the Permanent Under-Secretary at the Foreign Office was emphasizing to the Russian ambassador that the defeat of Germany remained the prime task, and 'it would be unfortunate if efforts to this end were diverted to side issues'. And so it long remained. Except for limited naval operations in the Adriatic, there was no direct confrontation between the Western Allies and Austria–Hungary during the remaining months of the year. The Serbs repelled three Austrian invasions of their kingdom; the Montenegrins remained secure in their mountain bastion; and the Russians, though thrown back by the Germans in the great plains of the Vistula basin, were able to reach the Carpathian passes before the snow fell, capturing Lemberg (then the fifth largest city in Austria–Hungary) and threatening Cracow.

As yet there was no need for British or French intervention in eastern Europe.

Briefly in August 1914 it seemed in London possible that the Ottoman Empire might remain at peace, despite the mounting German influence in Constantinople. The military mission led by General Liman von Sanders had for many months been working 'steadfastly and harmoniously for the Germanization of the Turkish army' (as the Kaiser's personal directive insisted), but there were already reports that the Ottoman officer corps resented 'German tyranny'. The British and French were better trading partners for the Ottoman Empire as a whole than were the Germans. Only a fortnight before war was declared on Germany Ottoman bonds went on sale in London to finance further British enterprises on the Bosporus. A week earlier the Turkish Minister of Marine, Ahmed Djemal, was a guest observer at French naval manoeuvres. He then visited the Quai d'Orsay where he assured the French Foreign Minister that 'given the right conditions the Ottoman government "would orientate its policy towards the Triple Entente"'. Although Enver, the Ottoman War Minister, was regarded as a Germanophile, Churchill, as First Lord of the Admiralty, had met him on two occasions and admired his qualities as a leader of the Young Turk reformers; and on 15 August he telegraphed directly to Enver counselling him in 'words of friendship' to safeguard Turkish interests 'by a strict and honest neutrality'. But Enver had already committed Turkey irrevocably to the German side, his final decision having been shaped by the First Lord's own actions; for on 1 August the news broke in Constantinople that Churchill had ordered the seizure and 'temporary' commissioning in the Royal Navy of two Turkish battle-ships newly completed on Tyneside; on 2 August, while the Turkish press railed against this evidence of 'English piracy', Enver secretly concluded an alliance treaty with Germany, providing for eventual action against Russia and guaranteeing Liman von Sanders 'an effective influence on the general direction of the [Ottoman] army'.

Soon the people of the Turkish capital were given visual evidence of German sympathy and support. As dusk fell on 10 August the battlecruiser *Goeben* and the light cruiser *Breslau*, having evaded pursuit by the Royal Navy, entered the Dardanelles. Two days later, as both warships rode at anchor in the Sea of Marmara, they were sold to Turkey, with their German crews still aboard as 'instructors'. On 29 October these two warships and seven Turkish vessels, under German command but flying the Ottoman flag, left the Bosporus for exercises in the Black Sea in the course of which the squadron bombarded

Odessa, Nikolaev and Sebastopol. Russia's response was to declare war on Turkey on 1 November. On that same Sunday two British destroyers sank a Turkish minelayer off Smyrna; on Monday morning, in the headwaters of the Red Sea, a British light cruiser shelled the Turkish fort at Aqaba and a landing-party destroyed the signals stations there; and for ten minutes on the Tuesday afternoon British warships shelled the southernmost forts on either side of the Dardanelles, with conspicuous success. 'We are now frankly at war with Turkey', Asquith casually noted next evening in a letter to his confidante, Venetia Stanley; a formal declaration followed on Thursday morning.

Thus the Entente allies drifted into a second war, parallel to the great conflict in France and Flanders and along Russia's western frontiers, but posing a different set of problems for their governments. If Sultan Mehmed V as Caliph proclaimed a *jihad*, an Islamic holy war against the Infidel, there was a risk of rebellion, not merely in the British Empire and British-occupied Egypt, but in French colonies across North Africa and the Tsar's possessions in central Asia as well. The team of specialist advisers left by Kitchener in Cairo – Ronald Storrs, Captain Gilbert Clayton (head of Military Intelligence), Sir Miles Cheetham (acting Consul-General) – sought to anticipate this danger by reminding their former chief of his contacts with Emir Abdullah, son of the Sherif Hussein of Mecca. Kitchener telegraphed Storrs in the last week of September: he was to send a message to Abdullah asking whether, if Britain went to war with Turkey, 'he and his father and the Arabs of the Hedjaz would be with us or against us?'. But in talks with the Prime Minister and the Foreign Secretary it became clear that Kitchener was not simply thinking of an armed revolt among the Arabs: the Sherif, as head of the Hashemite dynasty, was thirty-seventh in direct descent from the Prophet; this spiritual pedigree was more impressive than any Ottoman sovereign could claim. On 31 October, as the War Secretary was about to travel to Dunkirk for crucial talks with the French High Command over the German threat to the Channel ports, he found time to turn his thoughts to Mecca: 'It may be that an Arab of true race will assume the Khalifate at Mecca or Medina and so good may come by the help of God out of all the evil that is now occurring', Kitchener told Cheetham to let Sherif Hussein know. With such a prospect before him, no guardian of Islam's Holy Cities was likely to wage a religious war for the sake of an Ottoman sultan.

The call to *jihad* came from Constantinople, as predicted; though not until the Ottoman Empire had been at war for a fortnight. It made less

impact than the Allied governments feared. A sultan-caliph did not
enjoy the spiritual authority of a medieval pope: secularists responded
more readily to political and economic inducements; the zealous Shi'ites
of what are today Iran, Iraq, Pakistan and Afghanistan ignored all calls
from a Sunni pretender; and many other strict Muslim communities
hesitated to obey a Caliph who owed his throne to Young Turk
modernizers like Enver and Djemal. Only the Senussi tribesmen along
Egypt's border with Italian-held Libya and ex-Mahdists around Darfur
in the Sudan were ready to answer the call to arms. In Egypt the British
cut the last constitutional link between Constantinople and Cairo by
deposing Mehmed V's subject ruler, Khedive Abbas Hilmi (who had
gone to his palace on the Bosporus at midsummer), and proclaiming his
uncle Hussein Kamil 'Sultan of Egypt'. At the same time Egypt became
a British protectorate: Egyptians were assured that they would not be
compelled to fight in campaigns against the Turks; and a cautiously
phrased undertaking committed Egypt's new protectors to examine
ways of advancing self-government. Of more immediate satisfaction to
Egypt's peasants was a British move to protect the interests of the cotton
producers, for whom war meant a loss of export markets, by purchasing
the cotton crop, while also encouraging cereal production as a much
needed and profitable alternative.

In London every issue concerning Egypt and the Arabs was
automatically referred by Grey to the War Secretary for consideration
and approval – the Middle East remained Kitchener's patch. The
Foreign Office was dutifully informed of military decisions he was about
to impose. No one as yet questioned them. To give his Omdurman
companion-in-arms General Sir John Maxwell command in Egypt
seemed natural. Soon an irreverent junior officer was to observe that
Maxwell took 'the whole job as a splendid joke' and mixed 'a mysterious
gift of prophesying what will happen' with 'a marvellous carelessness
about what might happen', but the General had nearly twenty years'
experience of Egypt and the Egyptians behind him and could write of
problems and places and people in the language which the Secretary of
State readily understood. Kitchener assumed he could also communi-
cate directly with General Beauchamp Duff, Commander-in-Chief in
India; in this command, ten years back, Kitchener had himself created a
fighting force capable of defending the subcontinent and of providing
men and material for expeditions overseas. But, within a few days of
arriving at the War Office, Kitchener found to his surprise that the India
Secretary (Lord Crewe) and the Viceroy (Lord Hardinge) frowned on
such contact. A growl from the Field Marshal to General Duff that 'I do

not think you quite realise in India what the war is going to be' was unlikely to ease mounting friction.

This dispute presaged strategic misunderstanding. British command in the Middle East was divided. The vital defence of the Suez Canal rested with the authorities in Cairo; the defence of Aden and its hinterland, and of the Persian Gulf (with its newly tapped oil resources) was the responsibility of the viceregal authorities in Bombay and of General Duff's headquarters at Simla. The Viceroy deplored any encouragement of rebellion in Ottoman lands, especially along the Tigris and Euphrates; Kitchener and Maxwell, on the other hand, would happily exploit Arab nationalism if it held out a prospect of local levies to discomfort the Turks and their German advisers. Militarily Simla moved faster than Cairo: 'Expeditionary Force D', two brigades from the 6th Indian Division, waited aboard the transport *Dufferin* off Bahrain until the outbreak of the Turkish War; then, escorted by HMS *Ocean*, an ageing battleship from the East Indies Squadron, and smaller vessels of lesser draught, Force D sailed up the Gulf and landed at Fao at the entrance to the Shatt-el-Arab on 6 November to safeguard the oil installations at Abadan. Brushing aside Turkish resistance, the expedition advanced upriver to take Basra within three weeks of the outbreak of war. Thus, with little reference back to London, Force D opened up the longest continuous peripheral campaign of the war. When, almost exactly four years later, the campaign ended in victory amid the oilfields around Mosul, more than 600 miles up the Tigris, 31,000 officers and men of the Mesopotamian Expeditionary Force had perished in battle or from disease or amid the privation of harsh captivity.

In Egypt General Maxwell's first priority was to stand on the defensive and keep the Suez Canal open. Food and oil supplies had to come through to the Mediterranean and, ultimately, home waters. So, too, did the great imperial convoys bringing volunteers from India, Australia and New Zealand to fight (as it was assumed) in France and Belgium. The first Indian troops left Bombay in mid-August and had suffered heavy casualties at Ypres by the end of October. Six more convoys from the subcontinent reached the canal before Christmas, although the last Indian brigade remained in Egypt, 'for training'. That, too, was the fate of the Australian and New Zealand Army Corps, which reached Suez in a convoy of thirty-eight improvised troopships on 1 December and was known by the acronym Anzac well before Christmas. The first line of Turkish outposts lay some 130 miles east of the canal, running inland from Gaza to Beersheba. Behind them lay the historic cities of Jerusalem, Jericho, Damascus and Aleppo, garrisoned by the

Turkish Fourth Army, with 60,000 well trained men. But Maxwell discounted the possibility of a major Turkish offensive to block the canal and reach out towards the Nile, and Kitchener agreed with him. For between the canal and the Sixth Army stretched the waterless undulations of Sinai, a desert barrier to invasion as reliable as the English Channel, or so it seemed. When in London the newly constituted War Council met for the first time on 26 November Kitchener could give sound assurance to the four Cabinet ministers, service chiefs and Opposition spokesman (Arthur Balfour) who were his colleagues; 'At present I feel no anxiety about Egypt and the Suez Canal', he declared.

As in early August, when Germany was the sole enemy, people in England assumed that the war with Turkey could not last long. 'Are there any commissions I can do for you in Aleppo next spring?', 2nd Lieutenant T. E. Lawrence asked a friend in late November, as he was about to set out for Cairo. Optimism lingered even among Cabinet ministers; a War Office report, drawn up in December, predicted that the German army would run short of men within six months, long before the British need commit to battle the New Army Kitchener was raising. Unless the Germans supplied crack troops and munitions from Krupps to their ally no one thought the Turks capable of sustained resistance; in the whole of Turkey there was only one shell-producing factory, at Zeitunlik outside Constantinople, on the European shore of the Sea of Marmara. It was essential for the Allies to secure an effective barrier which could shut off Turkey from Austria–Hungary. The Danube was recognized as an international waterway and a trickle of aid reached landlocked Serbia upstream from Reni, Russia's river-port in the Danube delta. But so long as Serb guns commanded the 200-mile stretch of the middle Danube from Belgrade downstream to the Iron Gates and the Bulgarian border at Radujevac, the waterway was denied to Serbia's enemies; and the only link between Berlin, Vienna and Constantinople remained the railway route through non-belligerent Romania and Bulgaria. A cautious diplomatic offensive was mounted by the Foreign Office to keep Bulgaria and Romania neutral or, better still, to tempt them – and Greece, too – into the war as allies of the Entente.

The most effective way of exposing Turkey's weakness to wavering Balkan states was by emphasizing Allied naval mastery of the eastern Mediterranean. British and French cruisers, and the Russian *Askold*, patrolled the seas off Palestine and Syria virtually unchallenged; Austrian submarines, though a menace in the Adriatic, had limited range; German U-boats did not reach the Aegean until late April 1915;

and not until the following October did they pose a threat in the Mediterranean as a whole. Both Kitchener and Maxwell wished to take advantage of this naval supremacy. They favoured a direct assault on Alexandretta which would cut communications between the Bosporus and both Syria and Mesopotamia. As a preliminary venture a landing-party from the light cruiser HMS *Doris* went ashore north of Alexandretta in mid-December and blew up a bridge, rolling-stock and stores with co-operation from the Turkish soldiery, who were content not to be carried off as prisoners; they watched a locomotive blown sky-high with interest, dutifully lining up the next engine for the big bang with aid from the beams of the *Doris*'s searchlights. In all, the light cruiser lay off Alexandretta for some forty-eight hours, unmolested. 'What kind of Turk is this we are fighting?', naval chiefs wondered in London. The Ottoman Empire seemed so vulnerable that there were hopes of turning the alliance with Turkey into a liability for Germany rather than a strategic gain.

The spread of the war to the eastern Mediterranean and the Aegean opened up a new vista of general strategy. As the year 1914 drew to a close three members of the War Council, independently of each other, searched their minds for some enterprising initiative which would ensure victory to the Allies before the war was twelve months old. Colonel Maurice Hankey, the War Council's acting secretary, developed his ideas in what was remembered as the 'Boxing Day Memorandum'; and on 1 January 1915 the Prime Minister received memoranda from his Chancellor of the Exchequer, Lloyd George, and from Churchill at the Admiralty. Each plan accepted that the decisive theatre of war remained the Western Front; each acknowledged that impregnable defences across Flanders and France had created a war of attrition; each accordingly sought 'some other outlet', where a surprise thrust could strike the enemy. In the first week of December Churchill had (in Asquith's words) wanted 'to organise a heroic adventure against Gallipoli and the Dardanelles' but by Christmas 'his volatile mind' had turned towards the Baltic. Hankey, on the other hand, looked to south-east Europe and beyond: 'Germany can perhaps be struck most effectively and with the most lasting results on the peace of the world through her allies, and particularly through Turkey', he argued. Among his proposals were an attempt to bring the Balkan states united into the war by commitments to 'participate actively in the campaign' and 'the possibility of some co-operation with the Serbian Army against Austria'. But the Ottoman lands were Hankey's chosen field of action: he wanted a sustained land campaign against Turkey, possibly beginning with an invasion of the Syrian coast. 'Is it impossible now to weave a web round Turkey which shall end her career as a European Power?', Hankey asked, with a fine rhetorical flourish. Lloyd George, too, thought Germany might be hit effectively through crippling Turkey, initially by a landing in Syria. But he also proposed carrying the war into Austria–Hungary, perhaps by an amphibious operation in southern Dalmatia, though he preferred to support 'the Serbians, the Roumanians and the Greeks' with 'a great English force' which could 'attack Austria on her most vulnerable frontier'. 'It might be advisable', he added, 'to send an advance force through Salonika, to assist Serbia'. These operations 'would have the common purpose of bringing Germany down by the process of knocking the props under her', he wrote. To that programme of action Lloyd George was to return many times before final victory was achieved.

More than thirty years ago A.J. P. Taylor poured scorn on all such 'cigar butt strategy'. 'Someone', he suggested, 'looked at a map of Europe; pointed to a spot with the end of his cigar; and said "Let us go there".' Yet this picture of amateur strategists playing a Christmas game is, at best, a half-truth. The Prime Minister who studied these memoranda hardly needed to consult an atlas. Asquith always enjoyed travel; he knew the Dalmatian coast; only fifteen months before the outbreak of war he was in Split and Dubrovnik, journeying inland as far as Trebinje and thus seeing for himself the inadequacies of the narrow-gauge railway to Mostar, and ultimately Sarajevo. He was not impressed by his Chancellor's suggestion of a landing in Dalmatia. Yet Lloyd George, too, had some understanding of Europe; he had followed reports from the Balkan Wars in detail, day by day, and was more widely travelled than many Cabinet colleagues, notably the Foreign Secretary. Churchill had made his way up the coast of Asia Minor four years previously, going ashore at Smyrna, and passing through the Dardanelles to spend five days in Constantinople; and he, too, in 1913 visited Split, Dubrovnik and the Austro-Hungarian fleet anchorage in the Gulf of Cattaro. But the best informed of the memoranda writers was Hankey, who had spent five years in Naval Intelligence, mostly in the Mediterranean. He spoke modern Greek as well as French, Italian and German. At the turn of the century he had visited the then Turkish port of Salonika on three occasions, travelling down to the Greek border; and on a fact-finding voyage in 1907 he made a personal survey of harbours and beaches in Syria and Palestine. Twice that summer he sailed through the Dardanelles, carefully observing the forts on the Gallipoli peninsula and the humps of hills behind them from the deck of the battleship *Irresistible* – which was to strike a mine and sink in those same waters eight years later. The War Council respected Hankey's judgements, even though Arthur Balfour, whose acquaintance with Balkan politics went back to 1878, thought it unlikely that the Balkan states could be induced to come together and fight Turkey once more. 'Months of preliminary negotiation would be required to allay passions due to events in the past', he patiently explained.

'We have now a lot of alternative objectives', Asquith informed Venetia Stanley after dining at Admiralty House in the first week of the new year. Churchill was so elated by the search for new war zones that he urged the Prime Minister to convene the War Council daily as 'no topic can be pursued to any fruitful result at weekly intervals'. But Asquith was not to be hurried: though the Council met on Thursday 7 January, to discuss the Western Front, the possibilities of a Southern Front had to wait for assessment until Friday afternoon. By then it was known that the Russians were under great pressure in the Caucasus, where a Turkish offensive seemed likely to overrun Armenia; the Russian commander-in-chief appealed for a diversionary attack, to threaten the Ottoman Empire so gravely that Enver would have to send troops back from the Caucasus. Kitchener thought the Dardanelles 'the most suitable objective', but he continued to press for an attack on Alexandretta to cut 'Turkish communications with Syria' and it was agreed that this possibility should be studied by the Admiralty and the War Office. On the following Monday morning a message was received at the Admiralty from Vice-Admiral Carden, commander of the naval squadron off the Dardanelles for the past sixteen weeks; he sent a detailed plan by which, without any need for troops, a large flotilla of warships would enter the Straits, silence the forts by heavy bombardment, sweep a passage through the minefields and break into the Sea of Marmara, placing the Turkish capital at the mercy of at least four battleships and two battlecruisers – and all this to be achieved before the end of February. Carden's plan, enthusiastically expounded by Churchill to the War Council on Wednesday afternoon, carried the day; it was agreed that the naval force should be augmented by the new super-dreadnought, HMS *Queen Elizabeth*, whose fifteen-inch guns, propelling shells from eight or nine miles out to sea, could be more profitably tested on Turkish forts than on artificial targets in home waters. Asquith, as chairman of the War Council, proposed that the Admiralty should prepare for an expedition, which would 'bombard and take the Gallipoli peninsula' in February and have 'Constantinople as its objective'.

Rather curiously, the significance of this historic decision was not perceived at the time: in the minutes of the Council it holds second place, below instructions to the Admiralty to 'consider promptly . . . action in the Adriatic, at Cattaro, or elsewhere' to bring Italy into the war as a partner and so create a new front, threatening Austria–Hungary from the south-west. It was also accepted that, if the stalemate persisted in France and Flanders throughout the spring, British troops would be sent 'to another theatre of war', preferably Salonika. But, in early February, as preparations were being completed for the naval assault at the Dardanelles, it seemed momentarily as if the initiative in opening up the war had passed to Germany. A plan, prepared in Berlin the previous August, was presented to Djemal soon after he became commanding general of the Fourth Ottoman Army in Damascus in November. The German plan proposed to take advantage of winter rains to send across the central Sinai desert a force of 25,000 Turks, with ten batteries of artillery, pontoons and rafts; the Suez Canal would be crossed between Ismailia and the Great Bitter Lake; it was believed that the Egyptians would then rise against the British. Unusually heavy rain and brilliant staff-work by the Bavarian Colonel Kress von Kressenstein enabled the Turks to fulfil the first stage of the plan, confounding Kitchener and Maxwell's predictions by crossing Sinai successfully in the first days of February 1915.

Fortunately for the canal's defenders, the Turkish presence was spotted by French Nieuport seaplanes, based on Suez and flying for dangerously long hours over the inhospitable desert. When the Turks reached the canal, in the early hours of 3 February, they were met by Indian troops along the west bank covered by warships, which served as floating artillery batteries and pierced the night sky with powerful searchlights. Only one pontoon bridged the canal, and the invading force was soon rounded up. Djemal and Kress withdrew their men, pursued for ten miles by Maxwell's troops. Daylight traffic through the canal was suspended only on invasion day itself; within a week vessels were moving again at night as freely as by day. Yet, though the Turkish attack failed, it made nonsense of any strategic assumption of a desert no-go area protecting Egypt from the east. Colonel Kress remained at Beersheba, occasionally sending out night raiders with mines to block the canal. They claimed only one victim: on 30 June 1915 a Holt Line ship on the India run was sunk in the Little Bitter Lake. At the time, Kress's activities seemed of small value to the Turks; ultimately, however, they were of great significance to the strategy of the war as a whole. A land campaign to clear the Turks from Palestine and Syria became a political necessity for the Allies. More than any other individual, the Bavarian Colonel brought action to the stage of the Egyptian theatre of war. The drama that opened under naval search-lights on the Suez Canal was to end less dramatically three and a half years later with the signing of an armistice aboard a battleship in Mudros harbour.

For the moment, however, in these opening months of 1915 Cabinet ministers and Service chiefs in London still looked for a short cut to victory in the East. Gradually it was realized that the Dardanelles operation, if a spectacular success, would make Italy and the uncommitted Balkan neutrals hasten to join the Allies, in a rush for the spoils of victory; there would be no need for a naval demonstration at Cattaro, nor indeed of bargaining with Greece over Salonika. 'In war words count only so far as they are backed by force and victories', Grey was to write ten years later; and during the last week of February 1915 it seemed as if Britain enjoyed this advantage. The naval bombardment of the outer defences of the Dardanelles began at 8 a.m. on Friday 19 February. Militarily it caused less destruction than had been anticipated; and bad weather, with poor visibility, prevented any further shelling until the next Thursday, to be followed on the Friday by attacks on the second line of forts and the landing of marines, who completed the destruction of batteries on both shores of the Dardanelles with only two casualties before being re-embarked. But it was the political effect of the assault which aroused the intense interest of the Allied governments.

Reports of the bombardment caused a sensation in Constantinople, 150 miles away, at the Golden Horn, where the Sea of Marmara meets the Bosporus. The US ambassador noted a wave of 'fear and panic' in the city and reported that his German colleague had asked whether he could transfer his personal effects to the US embassy if the situation deteriorated. Two trains with steam up stood ready at Haydar Pasha, the capital's Asiatic railway terminus, waiting to take the Sultan, his ministers and the diplomatic corps to Eskishehir in Anatolia, whether the gold reserves had already been evacuated. On the other hand, prayers were being offered up in some mosques for the coming of the British fleet and picnic parties went out to Prinkipo Island south of the capital to watch for the first sign of Allied vessels entering the Sea of Marmara. Further afield, the Bulgarians – who had recently secured a substantial loan from Germany – showed a new interest in any pro-posals British diplomats in Sofia might have to offer; the Greek Prime Minister, Venizelos, offered three divisions for an advance on Constantinople; the Italians opened negotiations in London, ready for

war on the right terms if victory was assured; and the Russians held out
the prospect of an assault on the Bosporus once Allied warships were
inside the Marmara. The bombardment was backed by triumphant
Admiralty communiqués. Though meant to influence wavering neutrals, they inevitably raised expectations at home. 'Peace is almost
in sight', the Prime Minister's daughter, Violet, believed; and she
'indulged in romantic daydreams' in which her brother, her friend
Rupert Brooke and other close companions in the Naval Division were
marching through the streets of Constantinople 'to the sound of silver
trumpets'.

Was such early publicity for the bombardment wise? The lasting
effects could not be verified from ships out at sea. Within the War
Council, there was frequent disquiet over the operation and disconcert-
ing vacillation, particularly over the use of troops to exploit the fleet's
apparent successes. Kitchener and Churchill clashed on several
occasions, most seriously over the War Secretary's reluctance to allow
the 29th Division to sail from England for the Dardanelles; and the
septuagenarian First Sea Lord, Admiral Fisher – who first saw the
Dardanelles as a midshipman at the end of the Crimean War –
increasingly and openly disapproved of the whole project, insisting that
the decisive naval 'theatre of war' remained the North Sea and the
Baltic. Yet there were moments of exhilaration, too, around the Council
table, especially after reports reached the Foreign Office confirming the
deep impression made in neutral capitals by this proof of British
seapower. On 2 March the indefatigable Colonel Hankey circulated a
seven-page memorandum, 'After the Dardanelles, The Next Steps',
which was discussed at the War Council on the following day. He had
no doubt that, once the Royal Navy entered the Sea of Marmara, the
Ottoman Empire would be forced out of the war and he outlined twelve
stages by which this victory could be accomplished and a satisfactory
armistice imposed. Nor did Hankey's vision stop short at Constantinople: he foresaw Germany's map of Europe being rolled back from the
East by a united offensive against Austria–Hungary; Greeks would join
Serbs in penetrating Bosnia and Herzegovina; Romania would come
into the war, linking up with the Russian armies in the Carpathians; and
a British expedition, transported from the Bosporus to harbours in the
Danube delta and supported by a powerful naval flotilla on the river
itself, would form the centre of this Allied Grand Army as it thrust
onwards and upwards through the Fruska Gora highlands to the open
plains of Hungary, following the trail to Vienna blazed (literally) by the
Ottoman armies in the sixteenth and seventeenth centuries.

The Hankey memorandum understandably excited the War Council. For the first time since the start of the war British politicians gave thought to the shape of an eventual peace settlement, though only in the vaguest terms. An end to Turkey in Europe? The Gallipoli peninsula internationalized or handed to Greece? Serbia to have Bosnia–Herzegovina? Bulgaria, if joining the Allies, to recover lost land in Macedonia? And what if the Turks turned about, tempted (as Kitchener suggested) by a proclamation that Great Britain came as 'an ancient friend'? The speculation seemed endless. Churchill, perhaps piqued at being upstaged as a persuasive general strategist, was against making the Danube a main line of advance: British troops should not be used in this theatre of war except 'to induce the Balkan States to march'. But the Admiralty had already shown some interest in the Danube: on 28 January the War Council urged work to begin immediately on twelve shallow-draught gunboats for the Danube; and in early January eight 4.7-inch naval guns, with seaman gunners and Royal Marines, reached Belgrade, apparently with the connivance of Greek port and railway authorities at Salonika. It was a pity that the guns' telescopic sights went missing in transit. After Hankey's memorandum was circulated, the Admiralty issued five pages of 'Notes on the Transport of Military Forces to Serbia' (25 March), to be followed a few days later by a hydrographic survey of the Danube from Budapest to Braila. Rear-Admiral Troubridge was established in Belgrade as head of a naval mission and the War Office sent Captain L.S. Amery – a Harrovian contemporary of Churchill and a Conservative MP for the past four years – to Romania and Serbia for Intelligence assessments of Galatz, Braila, Prahovo and the Iron Gates. The eventual reports of both Troubridge and Amery emphasized logistical problems along the Danube over which Hankey's pen had readily leapt in his enthusiasm to strike at the heart of Europe. By the time they circulated in London they had lost their urgency, for there was no sparkle of victory at the Dardanelles. Three and a half years later they were to prove of value to the Allies, though not to the phantom expeditionary force which Hankey envisaged. Only two battalions of British troops ever reached the banks of the Danube.

It long seemed puzzling that such a discreet observer as Hankey should have written so optimistically of policy 'after the Dardanelles' on 1 March, especially as a fortnight later he was warning Asquith that 'a serious disaster may occur'. The publication by Captain Stephen Roskill in 1970 of passages from Hankey's diary helps to explain the inconsistency. For it is clear that, in the first week of March, Hankey had hopes of success for a secret enterprise which he 'proposed earlier' to his successors in Naval Intelligence at the Admiralty and which would have brought the fleet up to Constantinople unopposed: it was confirmed to him that two British agents were in contact with the former Turkish Finance Minister, Nail Bey, ready with an offer of four million pounds to buy Turkey out of the war (a transaction unauthorized by any member of the Cabinet). The current Finance Minister, Mehemet Talaat, the most influential Young Turk politician in Constantinople itself, was highly interested in the proposal. The agents travelled to the Bulgarian port of Dedeagach and met Turkish representatives, but the talks were protracted. Even as they opened, intercepted wireless messages to Berlin from Constantinople indicated that the Turks were desperately short of shells for the Dardanelles forts and, as soon as he heard of the Dedeagach exchanges, the First Sea Lord ordered the talks to be abruptly broken off: the *Goeben*, Admiral Fisher said, might be worth two million pounds and the *Breslau* one million, 'but nothing else'. The War Secretary, with his long experience of the East, might have treated the strange affair with the seriousness it merited; but the Admiralty was keeping cards close to the chest at that moment in the war, and Kitchener heard nothing of it. There would be later attempts to bribe Turkey into peace, but so good an opportunity never came again.

A more historic missed opportunity was soon to follow. On 15 March Vice-Admiral Carden, who two months previously drew up the plans to force the Dardanelles, collapsed under the strain of command, was put on the sick list with 'atonic indigestion', and returned to England, never again to serve at sea. Carden was succeeded by his deputy, Rear-Admiral John de Robeck. Three days later Robeck led the main naval attack on the Dardanelles. The tragic tale of confusion and hesitancy on that Thursday (18 March) has been recounted many times. The Turkish intermediate batteries were silenced and even the forts at the Narrows; but mobile batteries, hidden in gullies, maintained steady fire on minesweeper trawlers close inshore. But the attack was broken off when success was close at hand (as the Turks subsequently admitted) after three Allied battleships were lost and a battlecruiser badly damaged by Turkish mines unexpectedly laid parallel to the Asiatic shore rather than across the Straits, and therefore missed by the British minesweepers. The War Council expected the naval attack to be resumed after further minesweeping, as indeed Robeck intended. But on the Thursday night a gale blew up from the south-west; there were high seas and squally visibility for the next ten days. Robeck accordingly chose to await the arrival of the expeditionary force, already gathering in Mudros harbour and at Alexandria. But it was the Turks who benefited most from the lull in the fighting. On 24 March Enver entrusted command of the Ottoman Fifth Army, with headquarters in Gallipoli town, to the head of the German military mission, General Liman von Sanders. He had a month in which to prepare plans to safeguard both shores of the Dardanelles from the British, French and Anzac troops whose movements Turkish agents reported without any need for subtle spying. 'The Constantinople Expeditionary Force' could be readily seen encamped in Egypt, with little attempt to conceal its destination, nor its embarkation at Alexandria early in April.

Meanwhile at Westminster the War Council and the Cabinet continued to distribute spoils from a victory not yet won. Kitchener thought the King-Emperor might fittingly take over the protection of Mecca from the Ottoman Sultan – and, indeed, there were many more Muslims who owed allegiance to George V than to Mehmed V. While Kitchener insisted that 'Palestine would be of no value to us whatsoever', Lloyd George thought its annexation would 'give us prestige' and Herbert Samuel, the minister responsible for local government, wanted Palestine brought into the Empire as a Jewish homeland. This particular proposal amused the Prime Minister – 'What an attractive community!', Asquith wrote derisively to Venetia Stanley (herself to convert to Judaism within four months). The India Office coveted Basra, as an outpost of the Viceroy's domain; and on the day Liman von Sanders first travelled down to his Gallipoli headquarters, the Colonial Secretary, Lewis Harcourt, proposed that the British might annex Mesopotamia and solve the traditional Great Power rivalry over the Holy Places of Jerusalem, Nazareth and Bethlehem by placing them under the mandated protection of the United States (whose ambassador Harcourt had not consulted).

This proleptic carving-up of Turkey came abruptly to an end. For soon after dawn on 25 April 30,000 British, Australian and New Zealand troops went ashore at six beaches on the Gallipoli peninsula; five hours later 3,000 Frenchmen landed at Kumkale, on the Asian shore. So intense was the fighting on the peninsula during the first hours that twelve Victoria Crosses were awarded for valour; six were won by the Lancashire Fusiliers who, with 950 officers and men going ashore at the southernmost tip of Teke Burnu at dawn, were reduced to 407 active survivors when they cleared the beach as the full sun broke through. In all, on the first two days of fighting, 20,000 Allied troops were killed or wounded. Not one of the Allied objectives was reached although, as with the naval attack, there were moments when victory came very close. Lack of experience in co-ordinating an amphibious operation; a rigid command structure, ill-prepared for the terrain; ineffectual leadership by Kitchener's own nominees; a shortage of specialist equipment; disdainful dismissal of any possibility of prolonged Turkish resistance – all these weaknesses combined to bring to the Dardanelles the inconclusive futility of fighting on the Western Front, that 'chewing on barbed wire in Flanders' which Churchill, Lloyd George and Hankey deplored.

Widening the war did not bring the promised quick and decisive victory. What started out as a vindication of seapower at 'the centre of world empire' was degenerating into yet another land campaign, rapacious of troops and shells and shipping. Four more divisions were needed at Gallipoli. When the War Council met on Friday 14 May, for the first time in five weeks, Kitchener raised the possibility of abandoning the project. Then, on reflection, he insisted that the moral effect of withdrawal could provoke an anti-British 'rising in the Moslem world': better persevere and push through, he advised, unhelpfully. The reality of war had grimly dispersed the elation of earlier months. No silver trumpets from Violet Asquith's daydream would echo that summer across the waters of the Golden Horn.

CHAPTER 2

PARIS, ATHENS, ROME

Trumpets had sounded down the green valleys of Lorraine ten months before, when in the first days of August 1914, French infantry in scarlet trousers and blue greatcoats followed their white-gloved officers in a rush across the frontier which Bismarck had imposed in 1871 after the Franco-Prussian War. For, with even greater clarity than their British neighbours, the people of France knew precisely why their troops were on the march again; two generations had been told to think of a war of revenge, which would liberate the lost provinces of Alsace and Lorraine. The war would be fought at a time when the republic could count on powerful allies whose armies might lessen the impact of German superiority in numbers. In August 1914 that hour seemed at hand: the Russian masses were under arms; a British fleet was policing the Channel coast; four British divisions were to disembark at Le Havre, with a prospect of new armies following them once training was complete. French reservists mobilized smoothly and expeditiously, while at Marseilles troop transports brought the men of the XIX Army Corps across from Oran and Algiers. Moroccans, Tunisians, Algerians were – like the Foreign Legionnaires – to fight along the upper Moselle and the Meuse. France possessed the second largest colonial empire in the world but, apart from two minor expeditions in West Africa, every military effort would concentrate on defending the homeland – or, better still, on carrying the war into Germany. Unlike 1870 (or 1939), there was no lack of offensive spirit.

Perhaps, indeed, there was too much. At all events there was certainly misjudgement over the strength of the enemy. For no less than a million and a half Germans were thrown into battle along the Western Front. Despite the impetuous courage with which the French thrust forward towards the Rhine, the massed machine-guns and superior artillery fire of the Germans soon sent them reeling back, with far heavier casualties than in 1870, to the long line of another river, the Marne, ominously close to Paris. France was saved on the Marne and its tributary the Ourcq five weeks after the war began by what many contemporaries saw as a miracle: a rash manoeuvre of the German field commander was skilfully exploited by the French High Command at a time when the determination of weary French and British troops to persevere successfully turned a German advance into a great retreat.

The repulse of the invader within twenty miles of Paris made the military reputation of the French Commander-in-Chief, Joseph Césaire Joffre, even though it could be argued that the decisive counter-stroke was inspired by General Galliéni, the military governor of Paris. 'Papa' Joffre was not a great general, skilled in grand strategy; his strength came from supreme imperturbability, a nerveless confidence which ensured that he would resolutely seek to fulfil agreed plans. Like Kitchener – who was two years his senior in age – after receiving his baptism of fire in 1870, he began his military career as an officer of the Engineers and won distinction overseas. When he became commander-in-chief in 1911 he was still remembered especially as head of the valiant column that in 1894 planted the tricolour flag firmly over the waters of the Upper Niger. But in September 1914 this twenty-year-old image changed within days: Joffre of Timbuctoo became 'Joffre of the Marne' by popular acclaim, the first saviour of the republic at war since the days of Bonaparte. Throughout France he enjoyed a similar prestige to Kitchener across the Channel, though it was enhanced by a genuine affection which the Secretary of State for War never aroused.

During the three months which followed his victory on the Marne Joffre possessed another advantage, also denied to Kitchener: he could shape the conduct of the war without daily reference to the politicians. On 26 August the Republican Socialist premier, René Viviani, brought right-wing politicians into his government so as to defy the invaders with a patriotic 'sacred union' coalition. Seven days later the 'sacred union' government, most Deputies and a gaggle of acerbic newspaper-men hurried out of Paris for the safety of Bordeaux. There they remained, well fed and well wined, until mid-December, many weeks after the battle lines receded from the capital; the French parliament was prorogued even longer, with not a sitting held between 5 August and 22 December. This virtual abdication of government had consequences of lasting importance: it turned civilian politicians into figures of ridicule while increasing the prestige and influence of those Deputies who served in the Army and retained their parliamentary seats; and it enabled Joffre to assert and retain 'full liberty of action concerning the direction of operations', originally only in France and Belgium but later overseas, too. Joffre's supreme headquarters, *Grand Quartier General* (GQG) controlled all activities, civil and military, within a huge 'Zone of the Army'. GQG – at Chatillon during the Marne, but in November finally established at Chantilly, twenty-five miles north of Paris – exercised a right to ban all visits to the front line, whether by journalists, civilian Deputies or senators. Only the President of the Republic, Raymond Poincaré, insisted on determining where he should travel, who might accompany him and whom he should meet; and, even then, senior staff officers guided the President's footsteps – for his own protection, it was said.

On 6 October President Poincaré, Prime Minister Viviani and the Minister of War, Alexandre Millerand, travelled to Romigny, an unattractive village north of Reims and headquarters of General Franchet d'Esperey, commander of the Fifth Army. Louis Félix Marie François d'Esperey had already distinguished himself by checking the Germans at Guise in late August and by the ferocious energy with which he led his troops from the Marne to recapture Reims. In character and background Franchet was markedly different from Joffre. He was a dutiful Catholic from an aristocratic family with royalist inclinations, a general with a deep sense of history; he travelled widely, visiting the great Napoleonic battlefields of central Europe. As a colonel in 1911 he spent three months' 'educational leave' in Austria–Hungary and the Balkans, taking a leisurely trip down the Adriatic and then from Athens overland into Albania, across the Thessaly and along what was still the Greco-Turkish frontier. During this tour he met Conrad von Hötzendorf, Austro-Hungarian Chief of Staff, and became well acquainted with senior officers of the Greek Army and the chief administrator of the Greek railway system. It is not surprising that when, during his visit to Romigny, President Poincaré mentioned Turkey's probable entry into the war, Franchet seized the opportunity to project a military vision which lay far beyond the clay-white fields of rain-lashed Champagne around them.

The General spoke impressively, drawing on first-hand knowledge of the Balkans. Greece, he urged, should be encouraged to join the Allies, both to threaten the heart of the Ottoman Empire and to provide bases from which French troops could bring aid to the Serbs on the Danube. A joint offensive in central Europe would penetrate Austria–Hungary and force Germany to withdraw troops from the Western Front to protect the Fatherland from encirclement; such pressure might even make Germany sue for peace. Although the War Minister seems to have shown little interest in all that he heard, the President was attracted by

the proposal; he invited Franchet d'Esperey to present his ideas in detail
on paper.

Over the following five weeks all remained comparatively quiet in
Champagne. A fortnight after Poincaré's visit, Fifth Army headquarters
moved eastwards to Jonchery, on the River Suippe, where they were to
remain for more than three years – a significant instance of the static
character of fighting along the Western Front. Once headquarters
were established in Jonchery, the further development of Franchet's
alternative strategy became a paper exercise for the General and his
most trusted staff officers. There is no evidence that GQG knew of
Franchet's initiative. A detailed assessment of the prospects for a Balkan
Front was taken to Paris on 1 December by a parliamentary Deputy in
Franchet's confidence, Captain Paul Bénazet. The memorandum
anticipated many ideas outlined independently by Hankey and Lloyd
George a month later, though Franchet envisaged a Franco-Serbian
operation without British participation. He proposed sending five army
corps (185,000 men) to Salonika and the smaller harbour of Kavalla; he
acknowledged that the limited capacity of the railway route northwards
through the Vardar–Morava river valleys would make it impossible to
deploy the troops along the Danube for two months after they landed;
but he still believed that an offensive could be launched in the spring of
1915, with Budapest as its principal objective.

President Poincaré took no action on Franchet d'Esperey's proposals
for a month. The delay is hardly surprising: throughout December there
was uncertainty both over the attitude of neutral Greece and over
Serbia's chances of independent survival, for Belgrade fell to the
Austrians on the day after Bénazet brought the plan to Paris. Other
issues, too, were at stake in any projected action at Salonika, a port
which provided a natural stepping-stone for traders seeking a foothold
in Turkish Asia Minor and the Levant. There were doubts in Paris over
the economic wisdom of weakening the Ottoman Empire; significantly,
France never formally declared war on Turkey. In 1914 no other
country had such great financial interests in the Sultan's lands: for the
past twenty years all operations of the Imperial Ottoman Bank were
dependent on financiers in Paris; the Salonika to Constantinople railway
was a French concern, so too were railways around Smyrna and from
Beirut to Damascus; one French company gave Beirut its gas supply,
another French company controlled the waterworks in the Turkish
capital, a third French company supervised the lighthouses around
Turkey's coasts. Greater Syria – including the Lebanon and much of
Palestine – was an area of traditional French interest, partly from four

centuries of French protection given to Catholic Christian communities in the Holy Land. Powerful pressure groups in Paris did not want to see this economic predominance weakened by active fighting. Nor were they worried only by the threat of conflict with the Turk. Wartime allies had recently been old trade rivals; and the Royal Navy's activities off Smyrna and at Alexandretta particularly aroused mistrust, for both ports had long been coveted by French commercial interests.

Other French investors were deeply concerned over the future of Salonika itself, for the modern harbour was a French creation and still controlled by a company registered in Paris while Macedonia was part of the Ottoman Empire. Since Turkey had lost Macedonia to Greece in the Balkan Wars, was it not time for France to cultivate the government in Athens and build up an economic position in the province as strong as in the Lebanon?

With that argument Aristide Briand, a former premier and now Minister of Justice in the 'sacred union' government, was known to have considerable sympathy. In November Briand had even, on his own initiative, sought to interest General Joffre in the military potential of a Macedonian Front, though with no response; France's Serbian allies seemed in full retreat at that time, and Joffre was not going to allow his attention to be diverted from the Western Front by some sideshow thought up by those despised politicians in Bordeaux. But by the New Year the military situation had changed in central Europe. To the surprise of all their allies, the Serbs had thrown back the Austrians along the River Kolubara and recovered Belgrade. Both Franchet d'Esperey's proposals and Briand's interest in Macedonia had greater strategic relevance to the immediate future on the first day of January 1915 than on the first day of December 1914. When, on New Year's Day, President Poincaré at last decided to consider Franchet d'Esperey's proposals he accordingly brought Briand into the discussion with Viviani, and found him extremely interested. It was agreed to make a joint approach to Joffre. On Thursday 7 January, the Commander-in-Chief was summoned from Chantilly to lunch with Poincaré and the ministers at the Elysée, the presidential residence in Paris.

Two other French army commanders, General Galliéni and General de Castelnau, also favoured the opening of a Balkan Front as a way to 'detach . . . Turkey and finally Austria' and so ensure that 'Germany is doomed'; and on the Thursday that Joffre lunched with Poincaré the War Council in London was similarly examining alternatives to the Western Front. But Joffre was adamant. He resented any distraction from his principal military mission: the main army of the chief enemy

had to be destroyed in its chosen arena of battle. Joffre's strategic plan
for the year 1915 required a concentration of the maximum number of
available divisions to serve as battering rams at three points against the
German field fortifications in Artois and Champagne; the British would,
he hoped, take over more of the French lines in Picardy so as to free his
troops for the assault further east. It would be many months before
France had divisions to spare for an enterprise at Salonika, or elsewhere
in the Aegean.

In case the British might doubt Joffre's intentions, the Minister of
War, Millerand, was sent across the Channel to explain the Commander-
in-Chief's ideas and to seek reinforcements. Millerand, who was intensely
loyal to Joffre, dined at Kitchener's London home on 22 January with
Asquith, Lloyd George and Grey as his fellow guests. 'Joffre is anxious
that we should pour all our troops during the next month into his theatre',
Asquith told Venetia Stanley that evening; all three British ministers
emphasized to their French visitor the importance of the Balkans and of
the need to sustain the Serbian army. Millerand asked for four more
divisions to be sent to France. Kitchener acknowledged the importance of
building up the BEF but he, too, insisted on raising the Balkan question.
He was, of course, unaware that Franchet had already put forward a
detailed plan, and he therefore suggested to Millerand that the Ministry
of War might examine the possibility of bringing aid to Serbia by way of
Salonika. But Millerand, like Joffre, refused to be diverted from the
Western Front, nor did he mention what he had heard outlined by
Franchet at Romigny three months previously. As an outstanding legal
advocate, Millerand well appreciated the wisdom of silence. Victor
Augagneur, the Minister of Marine, who came to London two days later,
was more forthcoming; he showed unexpected willingness for a French
flotilla to serve under a British admiral at the Dardanelles. But Augagneur
insisted on one important concession: no naval operations should be
undertaken in the Levant unless sanctioned in Paris. This ruling
effectively vetoed any British landing at Alexandretta.

Through such 'personal interchanges' (as Asquith called them) the
two Western Allies began tentatively to create a co-ordinated general
strategy. Progress, however, was slow, not least because of the suspicion
with which the various factions in Viviani's 'sacred union' coalition
viewed each other's activities. 'Do not tell Briand what he need not
know' was a widespread assumption. When, on 1 February, Lloyd
George travelled to Paris for a meeting of finance ministers he also held
discussions with Briand and Delcassé, the Foreign Minister. To his
indignation he found that Millerand had not let his colleagues know of

Britain's interest in a landing at Salonika. Lloyd George was surprised, and pleased, by Briand's enthusiasm for the project, which he reported to the Foreign Secretary with what the British ambassador in Paris considered some exaggeration. Yet, apart from Millerand, opinion in the French Cabinet did indeed seem to favour a Balkan expedition. A few days after Lloyd George's return, Delcassé became the third member of the French government to cross the Channel in a fortnight; he was able to assure Kitchener that if the British would send a division to Salonika, so too would the French, taken from North Africa rather than the Western Front. On 9 February the War Council agreed that two Anglo-French divisions should go to Salonika in order to open up a Balkan Front, deter Bulgaria from entering the war as Germany's ally and – so Kitchener thought – weaken the morale of Turkish forces defending the Dardanelles.

Salonika, however, was still outside the war zone; it was the second city and second port of a neutral kingdom in which there were deep political divisions. For four and half years the government in Athens had been headed by the former Cretan revolutionary, Eleutherios Venizelos, who sought the creation of a Greater Greece which would include much of Albania, all of Macedonia and Thrace, Constantinople itself, the Turkish littoral from Smyrna to Kuşadasi-Ephesus, some of the hinterland of Anatolia and the islands of the Aegean and the Dodecanese. The Balkan Wars of 1912–13 secured most of Macedonia for Greece, but at the cost of alienating Bulgaria, whose advance troops were less than a day's march from Salonika when, in November 1912, the Greeks accepted surrender of the port from the Turkish commander. Venizelos believed that Greek entry into the war as an ally of the Entente would bring even greater rewards; as early as 23 August 1914 London, Paris and Petrograd were offered an unconditional alliance which would put all of Greece's military and naval resources at the service of the Entente partners. This offer was rejected; the Russians consistently refused to accept any commitments which might assist the Greeks to establish themselves in Constantinople; and the British and French suspected that Venizelos would not be able to persuade his King and the General Staff to follow the policy he advocated. This suspicion was justified: the General Staff, many of whose officers were trained at the German *Kriegsakademie*, respected the Prussian military tradition; and King Constantine I, who was married to the Kaiser's sister, had visited Germany in the late autumn of 1913 and, in an impromptu speech, emphasized the fraternal links binding the officer corps of the two armies. A few weeks later he visited Paris, where he rejected a proposed loan by French bankers, fearing that it would have made Greece too dependent on French political and economic policies – a refusal which increased the hostility felt towards Constantine in Paris during the war. For he was never the convinced Germanophile depicted by allied propagandists: the British minister in Athens reported in February 1915 that the King was showing 'a benevolent neutrality' towards Britain; soon afterwards he allowed the British to use Mudros, the harbour on the island of Lemnos, for a base of operations against the Turks. At the same time a joint appeal by the British and French governments was sent to Athens 'that Greece should go to the assistance of Serbia' and allow British, French and eventually Russian troops to land at Salonika. Venizelos favoured Greek involvement in the Allied expeditions and the King hesitated; but eventually the government in Athens insisted that, before entering the war, Greece needed to be certain that the Romanian Army was mobilized and at war stations along Bulgaria's northern frontier in order to deter King Ferdinand in Sofia from striking at Serbian and Greek Macedonia; and, as the Romanians showed no inclination to enter the war at this particular moment, Greece stayed on the sidelines. Political tension in Athens grew worse when Colonel Metaxas, the acting Chief of the General Staff, warned the King that the army was not yet ready for long campaigns against powerful enemies. Metaxas, a young officer in whom Constantine had great confidence, in effect told the King: 'Either Venizelos goes, or I go'. In the third week of March King Constantine dismissed Venizelos; a minority government was formed, pending a general election later in the year. Meanwhile the King and Metaxas determined all external policy.

With Venizelos's fall, any prospect of Allied forces landing at Salonika and opening up communications with Serbia receded. Over the following three months, in Paris as in London, hopes and fears in the East were concentrated on the fate of the armies landed on the Gallipoli peninsula and on the Asian shore around Kumkale. Even so, the Dardanelles remained for France a sideshow, an enterprise to which the division from North Africa, originally set aside for Salonika, might be diverted, although only to ensure that Viviani's government could speak with greater authority over the eventual fate of Constantinople and the Straits. For in the first week of March the Russian government made it impossible to postpone any longer the formal acceptance by the Western Allies of the territorial objectives sought in Petrograd. Sazonov, the Tsar's Foreign Minister, asked for a secret agreement that Russia would receive Constantinople itself, the western coastline of the

Bosporus, the Sea of Marmara and the Dardanelles, south-eastern Thrace and north-western Anatolia. Within less than a week the British showed a willingness to accept these conditions, provided that there was freedom of commerce in Constantinople, freedom of navigation through the Straits for all merchant vessels, and acceptance of British claims elsewhere in the Ottoman Empire. Viviani and Delcassé reacted more cautiously; French consent to the secret agreement came only on 10 April, and then on the understanding that 'the war be carried to a satisfactory conclusion and that France and England achieve their aims in the Near East and elsewhere'. Once this bargain was struck with Russia inter-departmental committees at the Quai d'Orsay and the Foreign Office began to look at other regions in the Ottoman Empire where a secret understanding between the Allies might define the strategic objectives of future campaigns, especially in the Levant.

The most notorious of all secret treaties made during the war was concluded with Italy in London on 26 April 1915, the day after Allied troops went ashore on the Gallipoli peninsula and at Kumkale. The treaty bound Italy to 'enter the field' alongside Great Britain, France and Russia within a month. The Italians were promised territory carrying the frontier up to the Brenner Pass in the north. Italy would also receive the port of Trieste (Austria–Hungary's third largest city), much of Dalmatia, a protectorate over central Albania, the Dodecanese islands in full sovereignty, a 'just share' of the Mediterranean coast of Turkey around Adalia, and 'equitable compensation' in Africa if the French and British increased their possessions on the continent at Germany's expense. 'The best piece of work we have got through in months', Asquith wrote to Venetia Stanley on the night the treaty was signed. There were high hopes that the Romanians, who in September had reached an agreement with Italy for concerted action, would also come into the war, thus encouraging Greece to fall into line as well. Even if the Romanians continued to play for time – as many experienced Balkan observers rightly suspected – there was much satisfaction with the Treaty of London in Paris and at GQG. On two occasions Napoleon had exposed Austria's vulnerability to any thrust from the south; now it seemed that General Luigi Cadorna, the sixty-five-year-old Italian Chief of Staff, would march northwards on Vienna with an army needing no support from France or from Britain. Cadorna's plans were ambitious: more than 800,000 troops would advance from the Isonzo River, seize Gorizia, bludgeon a path across the uplands of the Carso, and within seven weeks break through the Ljubljana Gap to the central European plain. On paper, Cadorna's army was far larger than any force the Austrians could put into the field. In reality, the Austrians had better heavy artillery, more machine-guns, nearly twice as many aircraft, and troops already experienced in battle.

Although 'patriotic' newspapers orchestrated an interventionist fervour, many Italian politicians had grave doubts over the fighting quality and determination of a conscript army of workers and peasants, confused why they were at war. Less than a year had passed since the 'Red Week' of June 1914, when a general strike across northern Italy threatened to erupt into popular insurrection. Antonio Salandra, the Italian Prime Minister, moved cautiously, unsure of parliamentary support. There was disquiet in London and Paris over the slow response in Rome to Italy's new commitments and a fear that Salandra might become another Venizelos, unable to stay in office. The Treaty of London was signed on 26 April; the Italian parliament seemed hostile as late as 16 May but finally gave Salandra 'war powers' four days later, enabling him to meet the deadline imposed by the treaty. Yet, even so, war was declared on 23 May only on Austria–Hungary. Germany did not become an enemy until late August in 1916, and then in response to strong pressure on Salandra's successor, Boselli, from London and Paris.

A further delay followed Italy's entry into the war, for mobilization did not run as smoothly as in France and revealed alarming shortages of weapons and equipment. Cadorna was unable to send his troops forward along the Isonzo until 23 June. By then the Austrians had good warning of what lay ahead and were able to construct a defensive line across the barren limestone plateau. The heat of midsummer and the inadequate attention given to sanitation and medical support caused outbreaks of typhus and cholera along the river long before the coming of autumn. The first battle led to the capture of the small town and harbour of Monfalcone but ground to a halt on 7 July, with 15,000 Italian casualties. Many deaths were caused by Cadorna's insistence on mounting frontal assaults across a terrain so harsh that exploding shells were made even more lethal by creating a flying splinter shrapnel of their own. A second offensive, launched on 18 July, was even more disastrous. By 3 August when, according to Cadorna's plan, his troops should have been entering Ljubljana, they were still along the Isonzo, having gained no more than a few thousand yards of the Carso plateau – and at a cost of 57,000 casualties, with five times as many lives lost as in the whole campaign of 1866 against Austria. Like Joffre, Cadorna was forced to accept a war of attrition. There was no more talk of a drive on Vienna; even Trieste, a mere seventeen miles along the railway from

Monfalcone, became an unattainable prize. Once again, Allied hopes of a quick, decisive victory away from the long agony of trench warfare receded into the dream world of fantasy strategy.

The war was going badly for the Allies along other fronts. On 9 May Joffre had launched his main offensive: General Pétain's XXXIII Army Corps broke through the German lines in Artois on a six-mile front north of Arras and advanced three miles in less than two hours, but it proved impossible for Pétain to hustle up his reserve troops before the German defence system was reorganized. The battle in Artois continued for another five weeks, but the French could never recover the initiative of that first morning; the casualties were appallingly high, more than 102,000 men lost. The British had gone forward that same day on a two-mile front at Aubers Ridge but, despite an intense bombardment, it was impossible to destroy a trench system held together by five layers of sandbags; more than 11,500 men were lost on that one day. On the Eastern Front the Germans and Austrians, with Turkish support, achieved spectacular successes: the Russians were thrown out of Galicia in May and June, abandoning everything won in the previous autumn; further north, the Germans entered Warsaw on 5 August and by the end of the month had overrun the whole of Poland. There were serious doubts in Paris and London how long Russia would stay in the war.

The only good news in that summer of 1915 came from Athens, for on 13 June the Greek electorate gave Venizelos resounding support, returning his Liberal Party with an overall majority of fifty-eight seats in the new parliament. But this was, to some extent, an empty political triumph, for King Constantine was gravely ill with pneumonia, pleurisy and a blood infection, and for ten weeks after the election he was considered too frail to be troubled with the formation of a new government. Venizelos did not, therefore, actually become Prime Minister again until 23 August. He found familiar problems left unresolved. Among them was the possible use of Salonika as a base to bring aid to Serbia. Five vital months had been lost – five months in which new track could have increased the capacity of the railway northwards at least as far as Skopje (then still generally known by its Turkish name, Üsküb), the principal town in Serbian Macedonia. Time was running out for the Serbs. It was an open secret in Sofia that a delegation of Bulgarian Army officers were in Berlin for talks with General von Falkenhayn, who was both Minister of War and Chief of the General Staff. Bulgaria was ready to become the odd man out in the Balkans by siding with Turkey, Austria–Hungary and Germany against the Entente allies.

There remained of course Gallipoli, where the high hopes of March and April had given way to disillusionment by early May. General Sir Ian Hamilton lost 20,000 men in desperate attempts to reach Kilid Bahr and thus free the Narrows for the passage of ships into the Sea of Marmara. Slowly British and French troops advanced up the peninsula from Cape Helles to the lower slopes of Achi Baba; further north the Anzacs repelled two thrusts by crack Turkish troops, led with almost fanatical determination by Colonel Mustafa Kemal. Yet no one wished to admit defeat and abandon the enterprise. In Britain the newspaper reports of Ellis Ashmead-Bartlett and a wealth of vivid photographs fired the public imagination in a similar fashion to those of William Howard Russell and Roger Fenton during the Crimean War. To anxious news-seeking readers, trying to make sense of the war from far away, the Gallipoli operations possessed one advantage over the terrible battles on other fronts: they had a clear objective. The thought of taking Constantinople carried as great an appeal as had the prospect of levelling Sebastopol to that earlier generation sixty years before. 'Through the Narrows of the Dardanelles and across the ridges of the Gallipoli Peninsula lie some of the shortest paths to a triumphant peace', Churchill could still confidently assert in a speech to his constituents on 5 June, and receive wide applause. Two days later the Dardanelles Committee – as the War Council was now (significantly) renamed – met for the first time; it recommended sending three divisions from Kitchener's New Army to reach the peninsula by mid-July and enable the Mediterranean Expeditionary Force (MEF) to make fresh landings behind the Turkish lines. Kitchener was now backing Gallipoli with the full strength of his personality: did Hamilton wish for a fourth division, even a fifth, he telegraphed? And when Hamilton gave affirmative answers, three of the fastest Atlantic liners – *Aquitania*, *Mauretania* and *Olympic* – were chartered as transports, with two light cruisers fitted with anti-submarine devices assigned to escort them to Aegean waters.

Not that Kitchener had abandoned his conviction that the Western Front should have priority in all strategic thinking. To allow Hamilton's reinforced army to go forward from the peninsula and capture Constantinople was never part of his grand design, as he revealed to Hankey on 19 July in strict confidence. He wished the army to complete the task mismanaged in April by occupying the waist of the peninsula, isolating the 80,000 Turkish troops south of Gallipoli town and allowing the navies to sail into the Sea of Marmara and force Constantinople to surrender, under threat of bombardment. Once the warships were in the Marmara, the MEF could be withdrawn; the five new divisions would return to the homeland, eventually to serve in France or Flanders.

Hamilton launched a new attack on the Turkish positions on Cape Helles in the afternoon of 6 August, pitting 26,000 British infantry and 13,000 French against 40,000 Turks, who were on the alert in well constructed defences in front of the village of Krithia. After nightfall 16,000 Australians and New Zealanders, newly reinforced by fresh arrivals and by an Indian brigade and Gurkhas, moved northwards along the beach of Anzac Cove and struck inland towards the dominating ridge of Sari Bair. Next morning two divisions of Kitchener's New Army went ashore further north at Suvla Bay, making for the high ground around Tekke Tepe. In this sector the Turks were taken by surprise; better leadership, closer co-ordination and a more rapid adjustment to changing conditions on the battlefield could have secured a decisive victory, for there was a real opportunity of straddling the peninsula and cutting off the main Turkish forces around Krithia. But after five days of desperate fighting, the offensive lost its momentum. Already it was feared that the British and Anzac forces had lost 23,000 men; in the first two days' fighting for the ridge known as Lone Pine, 1,700 Australians were killed in pushing the Turks back a mere one hundred yards. The casualty lists made as grim reading as from the Western Front. Nothing could loosen the Turkish hold on the spinal cord of high ground running down the peninsula. By the evening of 14 August Colonel Hankey – who had reached the Dardanelles as an observer on 25 July and remained there for three and a half weeks – telegraphed back to Asquith and Kitchener: 'Regret to report that surprise attack has definitely failed'. By 28 August, when Hankey arrived home in London, opinion in the Dardanelles Committee and in the Cabinet was hardening against any further costly offensives on the peninsula. Asquith told King George V that 47,000 troops were on their way to reinforce Hamilton before the coming of winter. But Hamilton had asked for another 95,000 men, a request Kitchener turned down. With the French demanding British participation in Joffre's autumn offensive, it seemed unlikely that any more divisions would find their way to the MEF.

Yet what exactly did the French want that autumn? The British Cabinet was puzzled by apparent shifts of policy in Paris. On 16 August Kitchener had crossed the Channel to meet Joffre and Millerand. Although he would have preferred to stay on the defensive in France until the spring of 1916, Kitchener accepted Joffre's assertion that a major attack in the West was essential in order to persuade Russia to stay in the war. Kitchener was also uneasy over French morale. In July he had promised substantial reinforcement of the BEF before Christmas; now there was so much disquiet in Paris that Viviani had asked the Chamber for a vote of confidence; a definite commitment from Britain would help preserve the 'sacred union' government from politicians willing to accept German terms for peace. Accordingly, Kitchener agreed that when, in late September, Joffre sent half a million men forward in Champagne and Artois, the British 1 Corps and IV Corps would extend the line northwards and seek a victory amid the fortified slagheaps and mineshafts of the Loos plain. During these conversations Joffre showed no interest in what was happening in the Mediterranean and the Aegean.

A fortnight later, in the afternoon of 31 August, Kitchener was amazed to hear from Paris that Viviani's government had decided to send an army of six divisions to Yukyeri on the Asian approaches to the Dardanelles for an advance on Chanak, provided that Hamilton mount a further assault on the peninsula at the same time. The capture of Chanak would cut supply routes by land and sea to the Turks on the peninsula; it might also provide a base for a further advance around the coast of the Sea of Marmara, threatening the key railways of Ottoman Asia. A similar operation, with Chanak as the objective, had been put before the Dardanelles Committee on 17 June by Lord Curzon ('I am probably the only member of the Committee who has travelled in this part of the world'); but Kitchener brushed the proposal aside – 'cavalierly', Curzon complained: a landing on the Asian shore would require 'at least five divisions'. But in September such strong French backing made the enterprise look promising. For the last time that familiar will-o'-the-wisp, a quick victory over the Turks, flickered in Downing Street.

Within a few days, however, it was clear that there were political strings attached to the French offer. Not unreasonably, the expedition was to be led by a French general; but the chosen commander was Maurice Sarrail, a political maverick, the soldier idol of the Radical Socialist deputies. Although Joffre was an agnostic, most leading French generals were devout Catholics: Foch, Franchet d'Esperey and de Castelnau were educated by Jesuits and Pétain by the Dominicans; they retained their faith and the suspicion of atheistic republicanism which went with it. But Sarrail was different. He was a Freemason, a free thinker and a radical Dreyfusard with a military career shaped not by long years in North Africa or Indo-China, but as guard commandant at the Palais Bourbon, which housed the Chamber of Deputies, followed by command over infantry-training at Saint-Maixent, where good soldierly rankers were turned into good republican officers. When in 1911 his Radical Socialist friend Joseph Caillaux formed a government for the first time, Sarrail was promoted General. He took command of the Third Army in late August 1914, showing a phlegmatic confidence while defending Verdun during the Battle of the Marne. But early in 1915 his political well-wishers secretly championed Sarrail as a replacement for Joffre and on 22 July, after a series of reverses along the Third Army's front, the Commander-in-Chief took the opportunity to dismiss him.

The rumble of indignation among the Deputies threatened a storm which would sweep away the 'sacred union' government. 'The Chamber is in a terrible state of agitation', Viviani warned Poincaré on 23 July. Hastily Sarrail was summoned to meet Viviani and Millerand and was offered the two French divisions serving at the Dardanelles. Such a post Sarrail thought inferior to his rank and reputation; he turned it down. Two days later he was visited by Briand, who urged him to broaden his horizon. On 3 August Sarrail presented his own proposals to Millerand: he demanded four new divisions as well as the two in Gallipoli, and independence of British command; he made it clear that he would not be leaving France until his troops were on their way eastwards. Significantly Sarrail proposed that the force under his command should constitute *L'Armée de l'Orient*, 'the Army of the Orient', an impressive title with Napoleonic undertones. He was invited to prepare a study on objectives in the East, which he submitted on 11 August. His preference was for an advance from Salonika to assist Serbia, but he listed as alternatives three possible landings in Asia; on the Asiatic shore of the Dardanelles for a march on Chanak; or at Alexandretta; or at Smyrna.

These proposals were known at GQG in Chantilly before Kitchener's visit to Paris on 16 August, but Joffre was strongly hostile to them and they were not mentioned in the discussions. Two days later Joffre submitted a damning indictment. No general other than Sarrail would have survived such an onslaught from Chantilly; he hedged away from the Salonika enterprise and, in a further memorandum on 24 August, came down firmly in favour of Chanak. Joffre, however, continued to resist the political pressure. A few months earlier his veto would have scotched the whole affair, but the endless casualty lists in the war of attrition had begun to erode his authority; the elegant lifestyle of Chantilly was discrediting GQG, much as tales of the 'luxury' in

Bordeaux blackened a score of parliamentary reputations after the Miracle of the Marne. Joffre needed support from Britain, at least to deflate Sarrail. Hence the decision on 31 August to let London know of the apparent change of approach in Paris towards the campaign at the Dardanelles.

Not surprisingly, the British Cabinet sought clarification of Joffre's general strategic plan; if four divisions were earmarked for 'the Orient' did he intend to go ahead with the Champagne–Artois–Loos offensive? There was also concern over the advancement of Sarrail, for from the first week in August the British ambassador had kept the Foreign Office well briefed on the political dogfight and on Sarrail's links with the Radical Socialists. On 10 September Kitchener and Hankey crossed to Calais, where next morning they were joined at the Hôtel Terminus by Sir John French (commander of the BEF), General Sir Henry Wilson (his deputy Chief of Staff) and by Joffre, Millerand and Sarrail. The British found Joffre hostile to Sarrail personally and opposed to the Chanak enterprise: nothing must interfere with the autumn offensive on the Western Front; if it succeeded, there would be no need for the troops to go east; if it failed, Joffre conceded that the four divisions might be sent to Marseilles for embarkation, but not until 10 October. For the British it was all highly frustrating. Hankey noted in his diary that the prospects of the promised army ever leaving France were 'not good'; he thought Sarrail 'a bit of a *poseur*'. Kitchener disliked him on sight and was not impressed by the deference which Millerand showed towards a general whom Joffre had sacked seven weeks previously. A proposal by Millerand that General Hamilton be placed under Sarrail's command was sternly rejected. Sarrail, for his part, turned down Kitchener's suggestion that he should visit the Dardanelles over the next few weeks so as to see for himself the problems of fighting the Turk; he could not leave France at such a time, Sarrail explained, with the air of one accustomed to await the call of destiny.

But did Sarrail, through his close links with politicians in Paris, know more about the general situation in the East than anyone else at Calais that Saturday morning? Over the following fortnight he seems to have been playing for time, putting more and more demands on the shopping list he gave Millerand; 100,000 men for the Army of the Orient, please, an Italian division at the Dardanelles? None of these requests could be met at the drop of a *képi*. Increasingly it seemed as if he would not be going to the Dardanelles.

The initiative in the Aegean and the Balkans was slipping away from the Entente allies. For in August Germany decided to give full military support to Turkey. Falkenhayn planned to sweep away the Serbian obstacle along the middle Danube and secure free movement of troops, heavy artillery, munitions and food down the railway route from Berlin to the Bosporus and beyond. Five days before the Hôtel Terminus conference, a Bulgarian mission signed a military convention at German headquarters in Pless: within a month Field Marshal von Mackensen would lead six German and six Austro-Hungarian divisions against Serbia; Bulgaria would then send four divisions into Serbian Macedonia within five days and cut the rail link down the Morava–Vardar valleys to Salonika. As a reward, Bulgaria was given a substantial loan and promised all the land lost to Serbia after the second Balkan War. Should Greece or Romania join the Allies, Bulgaria would recover territory lost to them as well.

For three months warnings of German collusion with Bulgaria had reached London and Paris from the neutral Balkan capitals; by the first week in September there was clear evidence of troop movements through southern Hungary. But Military Intelligence discounted such reports. Grey, at the Foreign Office, still hoped to persuade the Serbs to make such generous concessions over Macedonia that Bulgaria would not simply remain neutral, but enter the war against the traditional Ottoman enemy. A Serbian plea for support in a preventive strike against Bulgaria was, on Grey's insistence, firmly rejected by the British government. The French showed slightly greater realism. It is true that when Poincaré visited Franchet d'Esperey's headquarters at Jonchery on 17 June, the President made little response to the General's renewed championship of a Balkan Front. But on 4 August Joffre did at least agree to a French military mission travelling to Salonika in order to survey harbour installations and the railway facilities. Yet there was no sense of urgency. It was another seven weeks before the mission stepped ashore at Salonika. The officers were ready for preliminary work by 22 September; but that was the Wednesday upon which King Ferdinand in Sofia ordered the mobilization of his army.

Bulgaria's neighbours now had no doubt of Ferdinand's intentions. From Niš, the acting capital of Serbia, a plea was telegraphed to London and Paris for an Allied army of 150,000 men to be shipped at once to Salonika. From Athens Venizelos made a similar appeal; and, with great difficulty, he induced King Constantine to put the Greek Army on a war footing. In London a shrewd 'appreciation of the situation in the Balkans by the General Staff', circulated among the Dardanelles Committee while the Bulgarians were mobilizing, decided that, even

with full support from Greece, there was little possibility of saving
Serbia from the pincer grip of the Central Powers. But, once again, the
French took the initiative. On 24 September Viviani promised the
Greeks 75,000 men and urged the British, as Hankey wrote, 'to do
ditto'. A day later – it was the Saturday upon which the BEF began
the attack on Loos (with poison gas) and Joffre opened his Artois–
Champagne offensive – General Sarrail heard unofficially that he was to
take command at Salonika rather than on the Asian shore of the
Dardanelles. Confirmation of his appointment came on 28 September,
the Tuesday on which Grey pledged (in Parliament) full support to
Serbia and Greece, if it was sought. Kitchener ordered Hamilton to
release the 10th (Irish) Division from Suvla and make certain that it
sailed for Salonika from the island base of Mudros at the same moment
as the French 156th Division. From Athens came unofficial assurances
by Venizelos that the advance party of the Allied force would be
welcomed in Salonika as powerful protectors.

The first transports dropped anchor off the harbour on the morning
of 5 October. Other vessels and a battleship followed later in the day.
The British contingent, mainly two battalions of Irish infantry who had
fought with exemplary courage on the ridge above Suvla in the August
heat eight weeks before, made a poor impression. They were battle-
weary and puzzled by the sudden change; some came with greatcoats,
some in tropical shorts; there were no lorries or wagons with them, not
even a mule. Tents were lugged eastwards along the waterfront and
inland up the rising slopes for three miles. Despite the messages from
Athens, they were greeted with sullen passivity and by the discovery that
the Greek army had requisitioned the buildings recommended by the
British consul and refused to give them up to the city's new protectors.
Next morning the weather broke as a battalion of the Hampshire
Regiment was disembarking and the roads turned to mud. The Greeks
were by now defiantly uncooperative; their newspapers, on that
Wednesday, reported from Athens how, after a protracted audience
with King Constantine, Venizelos had resigned; the King had appointed
as his successor Andrew Zaimis. The new Prime Minister shared the
convictions of his sovereign and the General Staff that intervention in
the war would prove disastrous.

So, no doubt, it seemed to many Greeks in the mainland towns and
villages. For the might of German power, which had thrust back the
Russians earlier in the summer, was now poised to descend on the
Balkans. At daybreak on 6 October Mackensen began his offensive,
sending four Austrian divisions and a German army corps to cross the

Danube and Sava at Belgrade, with two other concentrations crossing the rivers to the east and west. The only Allied military help for Serbia was provided by the few French and British naval guns on the hills around the capital; more enduring support came from the nurses of the Scottish Women's Suffrage Association, sent out from Edinburgh. Belgrade fell on 9 October. More than 400 miles of mountain ranges separated the new battlefield from the token force of British and French troops provisionally encamped outside Salonika.

Bulgaria entered the war on 11 October. Next day General Sarrail reached Salonika. At the last moment before he left France the socialist Deputy, Léon Blum, had suggested that Sarrail should take over the Fifth Army, relieving Franchet d'Esperey, who could then go to Salonika, for he was the one French general who knew the Balkans. But this far-sighted proposal was made by someone who knew little of Chantilly infighting; it was never given serious consideration. Once he was distanced from political intrigue, Sarrail acted with commendable speed. Within a week of stepping ashore, he had moved three battalions of infantry, with supporting field guns, more than fifteen miles along the railway into Serbian Macedonia. The first skirmish between the French and Bulgarians took place on 21 October around Strumica, where the railway station was in Serbia and the town a dozen miles away in Bulgaria itself.

The British commander had little in common with Sarrail. Lieutenant-General Sir Bryan Mahon was a fifty-three-year-old cavalryman who, in South Africa fifteen years before, had won fleeting fame as commander of the flying column which relieved Mafeking. Age and Gallipoli had made Mahon more circumspect. For seventeen days he awaited a clear directive from the War Office, half expecting to be withdrawn now that Venizelos was out of office. But on 22 October he ordered the 10th (Irish) Division up to the wooded slopes of the bleak mountain range along the frontier south of Lake Doiran. Less than five months previously, on 1 June, Kitchener had taken the salute as he reviewed these recruits to his New Army at Basingstoke; eleven weeks later, in tropical heat, they received a baptism of fire at Suvla – which for hundreds became a requiem of fire, too. Around Doiran the survivors found grim conditions which turned from heavy rain into days of thick fog, followed by a week of blinding snow. In December the 'Balkan harriers' (as the 10th were later dubbed) fell back to winter quarters within the entrenched camp around the city. But before they left Doiran the Irish prepared positions which, after them, men from Scotland, Wales and a dozen

English counties held for almost three years, until that late September morning when the still waters of the lake caught the dawn glow of final victory.

CHAPTER 3

'IF WE LOSE EGYPT, WE LOSE THE WAR'

The year 1915, which in London opened with high hopes of a short cut to a victorious peace, was to end in uncertainty and apprehension. On 15 October Kitchener had replaced Sir Ian Hamilton at the head of the MEF with Sir Charles Monro, commander of the Third Army in France; he reached the Dardanelles on 27 October and within four days felt justified in telegraphing back to London a recommendation that the Gallipoli peninsula should be evacuated. Kitchener was shocked at the proposal, and deeply apprehensive. He feared that the army would suffer heavy casualties in seeking to get away from the Gallipoli beaches, and he was alarmed over the loss of imperial prestige which would follow abandonment of the enterprise. On 4 November he left London for Marseilles to embark in a cruiser for the Dardanelles, where he would assess the problems on the spot. Should there be one last attempt by the navy to force the Straits? Or a withdrawal from Suvla followed by a surprise new landing at Bulair, farther north?

Kitchener was convinced, as he confided to a sympathetic French colonel, that to abandon the great enterprise was to court 'a frightful disaster, to be avoided at all costs'; and this mission to the East was an undertaking close to his heart. His ministerial colleagues were glad to see him set out overseas, for they resented his secrecy and lack of candour in Cabinet; they hoped that, once away from England, he could be persuaded that it was his duty to the Empire to remain as his sovereign's representative in Cairo.

The War Secretary broke his journey in Paris, where he found the French afraid that evacuation might encourage a Muslim rising across North Africa. As the French government fell on 25 October he was no longer dealing with Viviani and Millerand; but President Poincaré had kept a 'sacred union' coalition in office, though it was now headed by Briand, who also took over the Foreign Ministry from Delcassé. Rather curiously, at a time when Britain's political leaders were looking at ways

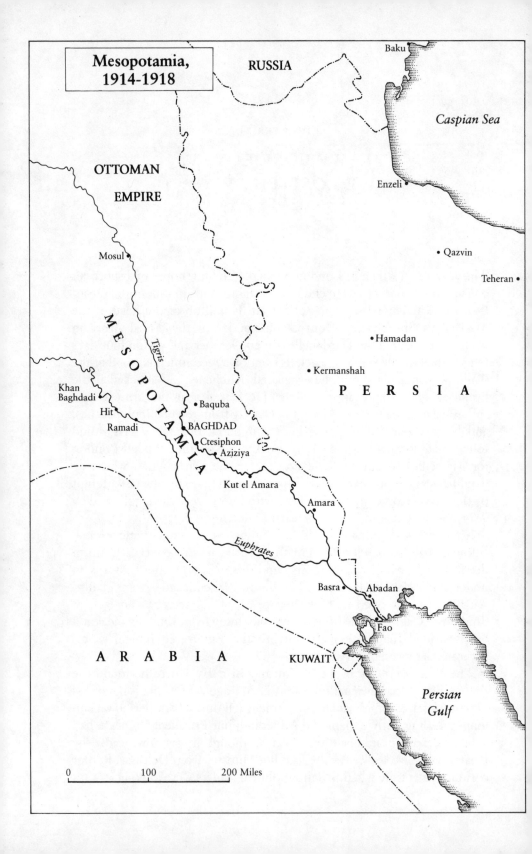

of easing Kitchener out of the War Office, Briand followed the example of Asquith in 1914 and appointed a soldier of distinction as Minister of War: General Galliéni (a sick man, who died within five months) became the first high-ranking officer to hold the post in twenty years. Kitchener found Briand heavily committed to the Salonika expedition, although Galliéni was prepared to divert troops destined for Salonika to Gallipoli in order to make one last thrust.

But Kitchener was a realist, disinclined to defy common sense. Within hours of reaching Mudros on 10 November he held conferences, not only with the army and navy commanders at the Dardanelles, but also with General Maxwell and Sir Henry McMahon, the High Commissioner in Cairo, whom he had summoned from Egypt to consider the implications of withdrawal. There seemed little hope of success at Gallipoli, and reluctantly Kitchener began to contemplate the possibility of evacuation, provided that a new front would be opened against the Turks, so as to offset claims of an Ottoman victory. He welcomed proposals, first put forward by Military Intelligence in Cairo, for a landing in Ayas Bay (north of Alexandretta), whence it would be possible to destroy vital rail links with Syria and Palestine and also with Baghdad and the army in Mesopotamia. Several participants in the conference seem to have looked on the Ayas Bay project as a ruse, a strategic diversion to make the idea of evacuation palatable to Kitchener. In the scheme's favour were the small number of Turkish troops protecting that coastline and the vital strategic importance of the region in Ottoman war-planning. Against the scheme were a naval reluctance to support another landing on an open beach, the General Staff's objection to yet one more 'sideshow', and the likely fury of Briand and his ministers at a British presence astride a vital artery of Syria, a province already regarded as the special preserve of the French colonialists. The Ayas Bay project, like earlier proposals for British activity along Turkey's southern coast, was abandoned within days of being presented to Kitchener.

By 15 November the Field Marshal had visited all three sectors of the Gallipoli Front. With General Monro, he went across to Salonika for a meeting with General Sarrail, who complained of the attitude of the (still non-belligerent) Greek army towards the Allied troops. Then he came back to Mudros before travelling down to Athens, where Kitchener had amicable talks with the King and the Greek Prime Minister, Skouloudis. He also met Colonel Metaxas and other leading members of the General Staff, who warned him that, once fighting ended at the Dardanelles, the Germans and Austrians would support a major Turkish attack on the Suez Canal and Egypt; they surprised their visitor by recommending a landing at Ayas Bay. Kitchener did not doubt that their sympathies were with Germany, but he well knew how extensive were Greek commercial interests in Egypt and he believed the officers were sincere in wishing to keep an Ottoman invading army well away from the Nile Valley and Alexandria. The future of Egypt was being forced more and more to the front of his mind, even when he was considering how Gallipoli might be evacuated with the least loss in men and equipment.

On 20 November, the day on which Kitchener telegraphed an account of his Athens conversations back to London, Asquith proposed that he should go to Cairo and remain there, because of the 'grave problems' facing the country. But Kitchener had no intention of being kicked upstairs into exile; he would return home, recommend a gradual evacuation of the peninsula, and make certain that the needs of imperial defence in Egypt and beyond were not neglected by myopic politicians in London. He travelled by train from Naples, stopping briefly in Rome and at Udine, the Italian headquarters on the Isonzo Front, where he saw for himself the folly of hoping that Italy could spare troops for service in the East.

In Paris, on 29 November, Kitchener gave President Poincaré a clearer exposition of strategic thinking than he had yet made to his colleagues in London. (Did he, one wonders, speak with greater precision, fluency and concentration in carefully acquired French than in the – to him – unnatural English common to his parliamentary colleagues?) He explained to the President that he favoured both the evacuation of Gallipoli and the abandonment of the Salonika expedition so as to concentrate on the defence of the Suez Canal and Egypt. When Poincaré asked if he was not afraid that withdrawal from Salonika would give Germany control of the Balkans from Romania down to southern Greece, he replied: 'That is a political problem. To a soldier it is clear that we cannot stay in Salonika if we want to defend Egypt; and if we lose Egypt, we lose the war.' Subsequently Briand and Galliéni impressed upon Kitchener the French commitment to the Salonika expedition, insisting on the need for the Allies to retain a foothold on the Balkans so as to keep the Serbs in the war and prevent the Germans from establishing a U-boat base in the Aegean. Reluctantly Kitchener began to give ground, though he wished to see Sarrail's army in Macedonia reduced from 150,000 to 60,000 men.

Kitchener reached London on 30 November, surprising Violet Asquith by joining the signatories of the register at her marriage to

Maurice Bonham-Carter in St Margaret's, Westminster; 'we all believed' him 'to be still far away across the seas', she later wrote. There followed a strange fortnight of political tension on both sides of the Channel, with conferences between Allied politicians and generals at Calais, Chantilly and in Paris. The War Committee heard Kitchener's views at a meeting on 1 December. Only Lloyd George and, more hesitantly, Bonar Law favoured the retention of British troops in Macedonia; withdrawal from Salonika would mean the end of all hopes of a unified Balkan Front and would deny the Allies 'any opportunity of touching the Germans except across immensely defended positions', Lloyd George reminded his colleagues. But, with the Serbs in full retreat across Albania and with Sarrail unable to penetrate the mountain barrier along the Greek border, the weight of opinion in the War Committee was against Lloyd George. At the Calais conference Asquith formally let Briand know that 'the military advisers of the British Government' thought 'the retention of the present force of 150,000 men at Salonika . . . dangerous and likely to lead to a great disaster'. But at Chantilly (where only the 'top brass' soldiers came together) spokesmen for the Russian, Italian and Serbian High Commands joined the French in urging the British to remain in Macedonia; and, on French prompting, Tsar Nicholas II sent a telegram to London regretting the decision which Asquith had given in Calais. The unity of the Entente allies seemed at risk. On 9 December Kitchener and Grey went to Paris for further talks. It was agreed that the British and French forces in Macedonia would convert Salonika into a fortified camp, and await decisions over future deployment, which were unlikely to be taken before the spring.

Uncertainty over the Dardanelles campaign was soon resolved. Reports of the appalling blizzard which swept the Gallipoli peninsula at the end of the first week in December, and immobilized some 16,000 men through frostbite and exposure, finally induced the British government to order the evacuation of Suvla and Anzac, a task successfully accomplished five days before Christmas. On 23 December the first Austrian heavy howitzers began shelling the remaining foothold, on Cape Helles – ominous confirmation that the railway supply route linking central Europe to the Ottoman heartlands was already in use. The Cape Helles position was rapidly becoming untenable. Within less than a fortnight more than 35,000 officers and men, 328 vehicles, 130 guns and some 3,700 horses, donkeys and mules were shipped away from the peninsula, without the Turks realizing that a general evacuation was in progress. Since Kitchener had at one time feared the loss of one third of the force, the evacuation was a triumph of meticulous organization. But it was, none the less, an admission of strategic defeat. In eight and a half months the campaign had claimed nearly 50,000 British, Australian, New Zealand, Indian and French lives. Although it is probable that the Turks suffered three times as many casualties, Gallipoli became for the Ottoman soldiery the greatest defensive victory in their empire's history.

During the final months of the campaign Kitchener was desperately seeking ways to offset the imminent loss of prestige throughout the Muslim world. He looked with favour on the mounting signs of disaffection among the Arabs and, in particular, the tenuous contacts with Sherif Hussein of Mecca which he had encouraged on the eve of Turkey's entry into the war. But his Cabinet colleagues had high hopes elsewhere. The Mesopotamian campaign, originally a defensive operation to protect Basra and the oil refineries, seemed by the late autumn of 1915 to promise a striking victory. Reports from the Gulf and from India were encouraging. The Viceroy, Lord Hardinge, and his Commander-in-Chief at Simla, General Duff, spoke highly of General Sir John Nixon, to whom they had given overall command at Basra in the second week of April 1915. Nixon, for his part, admired the initiative of Major-General Townshend, who, making good use of a river flotilla, began to advance up the Tigris on 31 May with the 6th Indian Division. By the end of September Townshend's men were in the fortified township at Kut-al-Amara, with nearly 400 miles of tortuous and winding river between them and their base at Basra. A week later they halted at Aziziya: should they strike now at Baghdad itself, less than a hundred miles upstream? Townshend awaited further orders from Nixon, who sought backing for a further advance both from Duff in distant Simla and the India Office in London.

In reality, Townshend's division was already in grave trouble. Water was short – a cause of distress to men and horses alike. With the temperature at times climbing to 45° C (115° Fahrenheit) it was inevitable that sunstroke and heatstroke cut down some of his British units, notably a battalion of the Hampshire Regiment. Field hospitals were totally inadequate to deal with tropical diseases, or the high incidence of scurvy. Townshend let Nixon know of his problems, but Nixon minimized the difficulties, sending encouraging assessments not only to Simla but also to London. The General's confidence produced a similar response in Downing Street to the earliest reports from the Dardanelles; Baghdad now became the coveted trophy, much as Constantinople had been earlier in the year. The capture of the historic capital of the Abbasid caliphate would rally the Arab peoples to the Allied cause, Grey told his Cabinet colleagues. The prize was tempting; but, significantly, the War Secretary opposed any further advance up the Tigris. Kitchener might well have drawn on his experiences as a young officer in the Sudan, where the over-confident General Gordon was cut off in a greater town than Kut beside an even mightier river, but he concentrated on the strategic implications of seizing Baghdad itself. He did not think that the city could be held for long by the 8,000 or 9,000 troops Townshend might by then be expected to have under his command; they would be 400 miles from their base and totally dependent on river supplies, easily cut by raiding parties. Moreover, the Turks would turn to their most powerful ally for support; no one wished to see a German 'Asia Corps' astride the Euphrates and the Tigris, threatening Persia and ultimately India. At best he thought Townshend might raid Baghdad and destroy accumulated war supplies, but he should not attempt to capture and retain the city.

Twelve months previously his colleagues would have accepted Kitchener's reasoning without dispute. But by now he was no longer infallible; the buffeting of war dented his authority. After ten days of intermittent discussion, the Cabinet sanctioned an advance on Baghdad, with the Secretary of State still a dissentient. What followed became the most protracted of all the harrowing disasters in the war. The Turks rushed reinforcements to the Tigris, strengthening half-hearted Arab units with a leavening of veteran battalions from Anatolia and accepting advice from a German military mission headed by the formidable Field Marshal von der Goltz, with thirty years' experience of the Ottoman Army upon which to draw. Defence lines in depth covered the ancient ruins of Ctesiphon, some thirty miles downstream from Baghdad, while a fortified barrier blocked the river, making it impossible for the gunboats of the naval flotilla to give the infantry light artillery support. After three days of close combat (22–25 November 1915), in which Townshend lost a third of his force, he decided to pull back down the river. By now, however, his troops were weary and in poor health. Three gunboats were lost to Turkish artillery fire along the river-bank before, on 3 December, Townshend reached Kut, where 6,000 Arab refugees were clustered. Within six days the Turks had invested the wretched town, isolating the garrison; the nearest support troops were more than 200 miles away; the Turks could bring an army of 80,000 men southwards from Anatolia.

With great heroism the defenders of Kut-al-Amara held out for twenty weeks; and with matching heroism and endurance relief columns

made their way northwards from Basra. Three attempts to loosen the
Turkish hold on the town during the cold, wet weeks of January 1916
failed twenty miles short of their objective. The relief force came close
to success on 7 March, when 20,000 men penetrated to within two miles
of Kut's defences, only to fall back with one in six of the force left dead
or gravely wounded. A month later the spring floods of the Tigris
turned the desert battle zone into a morass of mud, though the
temperature rose swiftly: 'The air is black with flies', a junior officer,
newly arrived from Cairo, noted in his diary.

Every ruse was attempted. A reconnaissance plane dropped bags of
tinned food into the town, but the amount carried was pitiably slight.
On 24 April a river steamer, loaded with enough supplies to enable
Townshend to hold out for a month, challenged the gauntlet of Turkish
gunfire but ran aground eight miles downstream. On the following
night a message from Kitchener personally confirmed his wish for
immediate action to implement an earlier plan to offer the Turkish
commander a bribe of one million pounds if the garrison was allowed to
go free. Three officers – Colonel Beach (head of Intelligence on the staff
at Basra), Captain Aubrey Herbert and Captain T. E. Lawrence – duly
met Khalil Pasha, the Turkish commander in the field, and tactfully
broached the possibility of monetary 'compensation', and a guarantee
that none of the men freed would be sent to fight the Turk again so long
as the war continued. Khalil would strike no bargain. On 29 April over
11,500 British and Indian troops surrendered. Never before in Britain's
past – not even at Yorktown in the American War of Independence –
had so many soldiers capitulated. Like the even greater number of men
who surrendered at Singapore in 1942, the captives were treated with
callous brutality, as much by the Iraqi Arabs as by their Turkish
overlords. The rank and file fared worst: 1,750 British soldiers and 2,500
Indians perished on a death march north to prisoner of war camps in
Anatolia. By contrast General Townshend was taken by train from
Mosul to Constantinople and held in 'honoured detention' at an island
villa in the Sea of Marmara.

The news that Kut had fallen broke in London during the weekend
after the Easter Rising in Dublin, when the press was responding to
public indignation with those Sinn Fein republicans who hailed
Germany as a 'gallant ally' while their countrymen in the 16th Irish
Division were resisting with stoic courage a German gas attack on their
trenches near Loos. But a *Sunday Times* leader concentrated on Kut,
saluting the defenders' commander under the heading '*Ave* Townshend'. The article praised his 'heroic band' for adding 'another glory to

the greatness and prestige of the British name'. Readers were assured that the surrender was 'not fraught with high military importance', nor was it a 'total failure': 'At its inception the coming invasion of Egypt was being trumpeted far and wide and the fact that today the idea of such an invasion is a chimera of the past is due in considerable measure to the stand made by General Townshend'. Such reasoning was far from convincing in 1916 and seems even stranger in retrospect. But the emphasis is significant: Kut-al-Amara had saved Egypt; and for the general public, as for Kitchener, the safety of Egypt and passage through the Suez Canal stood second in importance only to the safety of the United Kingdom itself.

By the beginning of 1916 more than a quarter of a million men from Great Britain, India and Australasia were concentrated in Egypt; some defended the western border from incursions by Senussi tribesmen, but most were quartered around Cairo, Alexandria or along the canal. It was feared that Djemal had an even larger force in Syria and Palestine; the completion of a railway from the coast at Jaffa to Beersheba and the building of a metalled road westwards from the railhead would ease the problems of crossing the central Sinai desert, posing a more serious threat than during Kress's attack the previous February. But the danger was exaggerated for, though a single-track line existed, there was throughout Turkey a shortage of locomotives and waggons; supplies were slow to come through from Anatolia; and coastal transport was gravely restricted by the close naval blockade. All remained quiet along the Sinai Front throughout the first quarter of the year.

The respite enabled the British authorities to take stock of military and diplomatic problems in the Levant. General Sir William Robertson had become Chief of the Imperial General Staff (CIGS) in December 1915, with control over the strategic conduct of the war on land, an appointment which marked a significant diminution in Kitchener's authority as War Secretary. He was a firm believer in the need to defeat Germany on the Western Front and in February 1916 he urged Asquith, on military grounds, to consider the possibilities of a negotiated peace with Turkey and Bulgaria. When the Cabinet rejected this proposal as inopportune, Robertson insisted on bringing back to France surplus divisions from the East, despite Kitchener's misgivings. Among these men were seventy-eight battalions of well trained Anzacs, together with fifty Anzac squadrons of cavalry, for whom there was far more scope in the East than in France. No less than nine of the fourteen divisions in Egypt were transferred to the Western Front between January and June 1916, bringing the total strength of the BEF (now led by Haig) up to 1,400,000 men by midsummer, the eve of the Battle of the Somme.

Robertson also insisted on reforming the command structure overseas as an essential preliminary to any concerted bid for final victory. Kitchener welcomed the first change: from February 1916 responsibility for Mesopotamia passed from Indian Army headquarters at Simla to the War Office, a move which came far too late to help the unfortunate garrison besieged in Kut. But Kitchener disliked Robertson's proposal to send his predecessor as CIGS, General Sir Archibald Murray, to Cairo with enlarged powers as Commander-in-Chief of an Imperial Strategic Reserve covering the whole of the Levant as well as of the Egyptian Expeditionary Force (EEF). As a compromise Murray was sent to Ismailia, in command of the armies along the canal, while Kitchener's trusted nominee Maxwell remained in Cairo to handle the military problems of Egypt as a whole, including the western border. Within a few weeks even Kitchener admitted that this arrangement was unworkable, and in March Maxwell was brought back to England and Murray assumed unified command against the Ottoman armies. There was, however, one serious anomaly: General Mahon's troops in Macedonia continued to be dependent administratively on the Levant Command, even though as the crow flies Salonika was nearer to London than to Cairo. Unfamiliarity with Balkan conditions led to tiresome delays in providing supplies: a request for woollen underclothing to give protection against the bitter winter was not met until early summer, as there were no stocks of such necessities in Alexandria; this delay was followed by a long correspondence on why the same troops needed sun helmets in July and August, when the temperature climbed to over 90° Fahrenheit; and, in answer to another urgent request from GHQ Salonika, by an astonished 'Why are fire extinguishers required?'. Neither Robertson nor Murray believed that the five divisions landed at Salonika by mid-January were there to stay.

Nor indeed, at first, did Kitchener. On 27 March – at a time when, after five weeks of fierce assault, the fate of Verdun lay in the balance – the Allied leaders met in conference in Paris. The prime ministers of France, Britain, Italy, Belgium and Serbia, together with military representatives from Russia and Japan, stressed the need for unity and a general world strategy. In separate talks with Joffre and a Russian general, Kitchener sought a phased withdrawal of the British force of 118,000 men from Salonika, beginning with the immediate transfer of one division to France. In supporting Kitchener, General Robertson suggested that this withdrawal should be followed by a steady reduction commensurate with the arrival of Serbian troops, who were to be brought by sea from Corfu, where the survivors of the retreat through Albania had received treatment in French hospitals and were being re-equipped; the first Serb regiments were expected at Salonika early in April. But Joffre insisted that no troops ought to leave Macedonia at this stage, when he was hoping Sarrail would soon go over to the offensive. Briand, as warmly committed as ever to the Salonika expedition, inevitably backed Joffre. The five British divisions remained in Macedonia.

Both Robertson and Kitchener were dismayed by the French attitude. There was a 'great deal of Finance as well as Politics mixed up in the French enterprise', the CIGS complained to Murray a week later; and an irritated and peeved Kitchener told Haig that French persistence with the Salonika venture confirmed his suspicion that they were more interested in realizing imperial ambitions in the eastern Mediterranean than in fighting the Germans actively on the Western Front. This seems an extraordinary remark at the height of the battle for Verdun; it is possible that Kitchener had heard of the collapse in morale of the French 29th Division while he was in Paris, but not of the subsequent heroic response of other French units along the left bank of the Meuse to a week of relentless German attacks. He had certainly heard from a senior liaison officer in Paris of the French Prime Minister's love-affair with the young Princess George of Greece (born Marie Bonaparte, great-great-niece of the Emperor, and living in Saint Cloud); current political gossip maintained that Briand's plans for Greece included making his mistress Queen in Athens by deposing the King in favour of his brother, George. Such far-fetched speculation would feed Kitchener's mistrust of statesmen who allowed wives or mistresses to meddle in politics.

Kitchener had already told his Cabinet colleagues that he believed the French were using the war as a cloak for imperial expansion in the East. On this occasion, however, he was concerned with the Levant rather than with Greece and in particular with French opposition to an Arab rebellion. For the past eight months a series of letters had been exchanged between Sir Henry McMahon, the High Commissioner in Cairo, and Sherif Hussein of Mecca, developing further Kitchener's concept of an independent Arab state, which would include the Muslim Holy Places and much of the Arabian peninsula from Aqaba southwards to the Yemen. But proposals from Hussein in August 1915 had gone far beyond these limits: in return for leading a rebellion against Ottoman rule he sought assurances that he would be accorded sovereignty over

Syria and Mesopotamia as well as in the peninsula. McMahon at first dismissed Hussein's terms as 'exaggerated . . . pretensions', but in the second week of September 1915 a deserter from the Ottoman army in Gallipoli, Lieutenant Muhammad al-Faruqi, arrived in Cairo with details of an extensive pan-Arab secret society which was supported by Arab officers in Damascus, Aleppo and northern Mesopotamia and was in touch with Hussein of Mecca. Although the officers in Syria were suspicious of French aspirations, Faruqi said that they would back a rebellion under British auspices in return for guarantees of Arab independence within an area corresponding closely to Hussein's ambitious claims; support from a landing at Alexandretta would be welcome.

These developments were referred back to the Foreign Office and the War Office in London. Grey authorized McMahon 'to give assurances that will prevent the Arabs from being alienated', but he said there was 'not time to discuss an exact formula'. Kitchener, by contrast, pressed for a definite alliance to 'prevent any alienation of the traditional loyalty of the Arabs to England'. McMahon was in no position to conclude a formal alliance, but on 24 October 1915 he did send a letter which pledged good intent: if there was a sustained Arab revolt, most of Hussein's demands would be met. Certain areas, considered non-Arab, were excluded from any future independent state; these included Alexandretta in the north and a region defined as 'those portions of Syria lying to the west of the districts of Damascus, Hama, Homs and Aleppo'. Hussein was told that the British would expect to give an independent Arab state advice and assistance and would exercise 'special measures of administrative control' over the Baghdad and Basra regions in Mesopotamia. He was also reminded that any British promise could relate only 'to those portions of territory wherein Great Britain is free to act without detriment to her ally, France'. McMahon saw the letter as a message of encouragement, not a binding agreement; there seemed in it no grounds for long controversy.

Both Grey and Kitchener recognized the need for an understanding with France, especially when the future of Syria was in doubt. On 21 October Grey invited the French to appoint a representative who would define the areas of particular interest to them. Briand enthusiastically backed a recommendation from Paul Cambon, the ambassador in London, that their delegate should be François Georges-Picot, the pre-war consul-general in Beirut, who was now serving as First Secretary at the embassy and was a leading member of an influential pressure group, the *Comité de l'Asie Française*. Briand was content for Picot to draft his own instructions, accepting them without amendment. From his first discussions at the Foreign Office on 23 November 1915 it was clear that Picot ruled out almost every claim put forward by Hussein and Faruqi. 'The French must of course have the whole of Syria and Palestine', he insisted, with a southern border along 'the present Egypto-Turkish frontier'; and Cilicia and Mosul (Faruqi's birthplace) should also be under French control. 'Syria', he asserted, 'was very near the heart of the French', who would 'never consent to offer independence to the Arabs'. Picot dismissed the pan-Arab movement; it was 'much exaggerated by the Cairo authorities' and 'had little or no strength or following'.

There was a shortage of experts on the Levant in London at that moment. But a fortnight later Lieutenant-Colonel Sir Mark Sykes, the thirty-six-year old Conservative MP for Hull, returned from a three-month fact-finding mission in the Middle East, during which he had discussed Arab insurgency with Faruqi in Cairo and kept abreast of McMahon's exchanges with Hussein. Although much of Sykes's knowledge was superficial, he was at once given the responsibility of handling Picot. Remarkably, in three days the two men reached a compromise, generally known as the Sykes–Picot Memorandum, though sometimes called the 'Arab Proposals' (3 January 1916). An Arab confederation was to be established which would be ruled by 'an Arabian prince' and extended southwards from Mosul, Diarbekir and Adana to include the Arabian peninsula; the coast would be 'protected' by Britain and France, who would provide administrative advisers for the confederation and receive 'especial facilities in matters of enterprise and industrial development'. An accompanying map was at variance with several of these provisions: it provided for direct French administration of the Mediterranean littoral from north of Alexandretta through Syria and Lebanon to Haifa and Acre, which were to be British-administered, as also were the districts of Baghdad and Basra; Jerusalem and the Holy Places would be administered by an international commission; a French zone of influence would include Damascus, Aleppo and Mosul; a British zone would have Gaza, Aqaba, Amman, wide areas of desert, and central Mesopotamia. The map and memorandum were circulated to government departments in London and, with tighter restriction, in Paris, too. Briand frankly made it clear to the ambassador in London that he wanted the agreement ratified 'rapidement', before the British changed their minds, even though he envisaged trouble with the extreme 'colonialists' in the Chamber for allowing the British trade concessions at Haifa and Acre. The Arab specialists at

Cairo were not informed of the Sykes–Picot talks until March (unofficially), with the terms only formally conveyed to them in April. The British government declined to ratify the agreement until Sykes and Picot had travelled to Petrograd and established what parts of Kurdistan and Armenia the Russians wished to acquire. The definitive Sykes–Picot Agreement (16 May 1916) in essentials confirmed January's 'Arab Proposals', while recognizing that Russia would have a free hand after the war to settle the fate of northern Kurdistan as well as of Erzerum (which fell to the Tsar's troops on 15 February) and the surrounding regions of Turkish Armenia.

Sykes later asserted that the compromise with Picot was worked out 'along Lord Kitchener's lines', by detailed consultation 'nightly' with his chief aide, Colonel Fitzgerald; 'I acted, Fitzgerald spoke, he inspired', Sykes (almost) explained. It seems curious that Kitchener, who a year earlier argued strongly in favour of the acquisition of Alexandretta and Mesopotamia, should approve an agreement which so clearly condemned Great Britain to second-class status in the Levant and distorted the aspirations of the 'Arab nation' he had encouraged for many months. There would seem to be three reasons for his change of approach: a belated desire to emphasize the importance of concentrating on defeating the Germans, and thus discourage the French from 'sideshows' promoting post-war commercial gains; a realization that, with each passing week of inactivity in Sinai, the risks of 'losing Egypt' to an invading army became more and more remote; and a suspicion that Faruqi's prediction of imminent mutiny by Arab officers in Djemal's Syrian army was wide of the mark. The Foreign Secretary told his colleagues as early as 23 March that he regarded the arrangements for a protected Arab confederation as largely hypothetical, for he did not believe that Husein's proposed uprising, upon which all plans of partition depended, would ever take place. Kitchener, despite his initiative in encouraging the Arabs, did not dissent.

Yet, at that moment, Sherif Hussein and his family still had hopes of a concerted rebellion: Hussein's third son, Feisal, would travel to Damascus and encourage an Arab rising in northern Syria, preferably with British naval support at Alexandretta or further south; his eldest son, Ali, would cut the railway north of Medina. But Djemal struck first. Early in May, while Feisal was in Damascus, the Turks seized and executed twenty-one Syrian nationalists and he was lucky to escape capture. Hussein decided to act, without waiting to complete his preparations. On 5 June 1916 he fired a symbolic rifle shot at the Ottoman barracks in Mecca. At the same time he issued a proclamation, condemning the impiety of the Young Turk officers who had imposed restraint on the Sultan-Caliph's prerogatives and 'taken the religion of God as an amusement and a sport'. Arab nationalism, though disguised under a cloak of Islamic purity and falling far short of general rebellion, was the latest recruit to the Entente cause.

Kitchener, who had first encouraged Hussein to cherish hopes of the caliphate, never heard the news. A few hours after the symbolic gesture outside Mecca on that Monday the cruiser HMS *Hampshire* struck a mine laid by the German submarine *U-35* off the Orkneys and sank in heavy seas. Aboard the cruiser was the Secretary of State for War and his staff answering a call for advice from Tsar Nicholas II. The awesome autocrat, who conjured up national armies from a people who abhorred soldiering, and who read the French military mind with a clarity his colleagues never perceived, perished on a mission to bring cohesion to yet another ally's war effort. Even though within the Cabinet his standing and authority had diminished, to the country as a whole his death seemed a disaster. 'Kitchener Drowned – Official' ran the heavy print of billboards selling *The Star* in London streets on Tuesday afternoon. 'Brutally abrupt, laconically cruel', an onlooker commented next morning, 'Groups formed round each purchaser of a paper, and as the news sank in faces visibly paled and voices fell to a pained hush'. But the deep-rooted faith in Kitchener of the public 'created a single rumour born of hope – "Kitchener is saved". It ran like wildfire throughout London.' The rumour was false. There were only twelve survivors, members of *Hampshire*'s crew carried ashore on rafts swept from the deck as the cruiser went down. But such was Kitchener's world prestige that it was not only in Britain that people scorned acceptance of his mortality. In the lands which the Field Marshal knew best of all, Sir Mark Sykes broke the news to an Arab sheikh – and received the simple reply, 'Lord Kitchener can never die'.

CHAPTER 4

ORGIES OF SLAUGHTER

Within three weeks of Kitchener's death more than 400 heavy guns began a bombardment of German trenches along twenty miles of the River Somme, north and east of the town of Albert. The countryside around the new battlefield was reminiscent of southern England, little more than a hundred miles away, beyond the Channel: chalk hills sloping up in gentle ridges from the willows and rushes of a sluggish river; occasional beech woods; apple trees around clusters of villages on downland never more than 300 feet above sea-level, though steep at Thiepval, above the Somme's tributary, the Ancre. Many trees and copses still stood at the edge of the long fields when the bombardment began, for there had been little fighting along this sector of the Western Front since the first autumn of the war. It remains questionable why there should have been a battle there at any time. A victory on the Somme would bring no grand strategic advantage, as at Verdun (to either protagonist) or in Flanders, where the Germans might be forced back from the Belgian coast, losing the U-boat havens of Ostend and Zeebrugge. At best, a breakthrough in the line could enable cavalry to create a more open and mobile form of fighting; but that was true of many other points along the Front, sectors where the enemy had not constructed dugouts thirty feet deep, with armoured machine-gun nests covering dense entanglements of barbed wire. The Somme was a set-piece in Joffre's war of attrition with which, in essentials, Haig and Robertson agreed. Originally it was planned to relieve pressure on the French at Verdun, although, to emphasize and maintain Allied solidarity, the attacks north of the Somme were undertaken by fourteen British and two French divisions, while another three French divisions went forward south of the river. Behind the decision to mount this great summer offensive of 1916 at the centre of the Western Front lay a familiar fallacy: inflict each month on the German enemy 150,000 casualties killed, captured or seriously wounded and shortage of manpower will force the Kaiser to sue for peace before the year is ended.

The preliminary bombardment continued for seven days, longer than any of its predecessors. No less than 1,700,000 shells fell on the German lines, with another 600,000 shells fired on the morning of 1 July, the opening day of the battle, reaching a crescendo of fifty-six shells a second along a twenty-five-mile front soon after dawn. Yet the heavy guns failed to cut the German wire or knock out well concealed German batteries; nor did ten powerful landmines, exploded under the German lines two minutes before the attack began, destroy the deep dugouts. And by assuming that the infantry, though laden with sixty-six-pound packs on a blazing summer's day, could advance rapidly, the barrage crept ahead of the assault troops a hundred yards at a time, enabling the Germans to emerge from cover and defend the trenches before the British reached their parapet. Of some 140,000 British infantrymen who went 'over the top' that morning, 57,470 were casualties by nightfall, over a third of them fatal; of the Newfoundland Battalion only one in eight soldiers was fit to continue the battle on its second day. Never before or since have so many British troops perished in a single day's fighting. But the Somme battle was to continue for another four and a half months, ending in the slush of mid-November snow. By then 95,675 British and Empire soldiers had been killed, together with 50,729 French. German casualties were even higher. The invader had been expelled from a devastated strip of the French countryside, almost thirty miles long and, at one point south of the river, seven miles deep; but no town of importance and no strategic railway junction changed hands.

The Somme, which Liddell Hart once described as 'both the glory and the grave of Kitchener's Army', began at a time when there was no Secretary of State to head the War Office, for political infighting left the post vacant for a month after the sinking of the *Hampshire*. During the last weeks of his life Kitchener had studied details of the proposed summer offensive with mounting misgiving. He did not think it possible to break the German line by a frontal assault of this nature; he feared the attack would wipe out carefully trained young officers in the New Armies which he hoped would, in a year's time, prove strong enough to end a war whose earliest combatants were exhausted. Several members of the War Committee shared at least some of his doubts, Lloyd George among them. Privately, in a diary entry as early as 2 May, Hankey expressed a fear that 'the Army want a regular orgy of slaughter this summer and . . . plan . . . a great offensive . . . which no member of the

Cabinet and none of the regimental soldiers who will have to carry it out believe in'. This bitter comment may reflect Hankey's dismay that the offensive was to open before the first 'caterpillars' (i.e. tanks) were ready to go into action and smash their way through barbed wire, but it was also consistent with the views he had long held on the folly of seeking a decisive victory through trench-storming. When the earliest details of the first day's fighting on the Somme reached London, the maverick amateur strategist Lloyd George reminded Hankey sympathetically of his Boxing Day Memorandum in 1914, with its insistence that 'victory was only to be obtained in the eastern theatre of operations'. Four days later, on 7 July 1916, Lloyd George took office as Secretary of State for War.

It was from the East that the best news came during those midsummer days. On 4 June the Russians surprised their Austro-Hungarian enemy by launching a major offensive from the Pripet Marshes southwards to the rivers Dniester and Pruth, a region from which nine divisions had recently been withdrawn by the Austrians for service on the Italian Front. Little progress was made in the north of this long front but the southern sector held promise of a striking victory. 'Brusilov's Offensive', as history remembers this last epic of Russia's imperial armies, established a corridor 200 miles wide and in places sixty miles deep, bringing the Tsar's troops back to the eastern Carpathians and threatening a descent to the Hungarian plain. The Foreign Office in London heard that three leading Hungarian magnates wanted peace, and there was said to be an anti-war mood among politicians in Berlin. Fifteen German divisions were rushed eastwards, thus easing the pressure on Verdun, and a Turkish army corps was sent by train to Galicia. But on the Eastern Front, too, reckless deeds conjured up an 'orgy of slaughter'. After suffering over a million casualties, and hopelessly starved of shells by an incompetent administration, Brusilov's South-West Army Group ran out of energy in late September on the forested beech slopes of the Bukovina.

Brusilov's initial advance stirred the Romanian government to a flurry of secret diplomacy. In Bucharest there were mass demonstrations in favour of a march westwards to 'liberate' the three million Romanians living within Hungarian Transylvania; there must be no more of that hesitancy which had kept Romania neutral in the spring of 1915 when the Italians struck their bargain with the Entente. Now it could be seen in Bucharest that Italy, too, had cause for celebration: for a counter-offensive in the Trentino pushed the Austrians back into the mountains while, on the Isonzo in early August, Cadorna's troops at last captured

Gorizia. With Russia and Italy striking such blows against their common enemy and with great Magyar landowners favouring peace talks with the West, Ionel Bratianu – Romania's strongman Prime Minister – moved decisively: Austria–Hungary must not go out of the war before Romania staked a claim to the spoils. On 4 July 1916 Bratianu told the French Minister in Bucharest that Romania was prepared to join the Allies if suitable terms could be agreed. Otherwise, so he warned the French, he might have to resign office and a pro-German government would come to power. Among his conditions were the eventual cession to Romania of Transylvania and much of the Hungarian plain, as well as the Bukovina, and equal status at the peace conference with the four Great Power allies – Italy, Russia, France and Britain. The proposed territorial demands would double the size of Romania and give the kingdom substantial minorities of Hungarians, Ukrainians, Serbs and families of German descent. Bratianu also sought military guarantees: the Russians would continue an offensive along 'the whole Austrian front'; they would send troops to help the Romanians defend the Dobruja; and Sarrail would launch an attack in Macedonia so as to prevent the Bulgarians from moving troops northwards and invading southern Romania.

The prospect of sending Romania's army of some 400,000 front-line troops into action in the Danube basin and, at the same time, depriving the enemy of Romanian oil and grain induced the British and French governments to look favourably on Bratianu's exorbitant demands. Three days after Lloyd George became War Secretary Briand and Joffre were told that, if Romania signed a military convention to enter the war by a specific date, British troops in Macedonia would co-operate in an offensive 'on a scale commensurate with the strength and equipment of their force'. By now there were some 400,000 troops from five nations in and around Salonika, for the original French and British expeditions were joined by a re-equipped Serbian army of 122,000 men during May, by a brigade of Russians in late July, and by an Italian division in the second week of August. Tension was at times high between General Sarrail and the individual national commanders. General Mahon, who had come with the 10th Division from Gallipoli in October 1915, left Salonika in May for Egypt, and was invalided home soon afterwards. He was succeeded by a forty-nine-year-old artilleryman from Aberdeen, Major-General George Milne, who was a veteran of Omdurman (where his battery scored a direct hit on the Mahdi's tomb), and a friend of the CIGS, Sir William Robertson, since staff college days at Camberley. Milne had fought on the Marne, the Aisne and in Flanders before coming out to Macedonia as a corps commander in January 1916. During the summer months his work had been hampered, not only by a high incidence of malaria among his men, but also by uncertainty over London's attitude towards the *Armée de l'Orient* and its commander's desire to abandon passive defence for attack.

As late as 3 June Milne was ordered by the CIGS not to participate in any combined assault on the Bulgarians, even though it was clear that Sarrail was preparing plans for an early offensive. Only on 23 July was he told to support Sarrail, 'by engaging the maximum of Bulgar forces' so as 'to cover the mobilization and concentration of the Romanian army as well as its action in the direction of Austria and Hungary against an enemy offensive on its Southern front'. This ambitious directive was followed by private messages from General Robertson emphasizing that Milne should 'guard against being committed for any serious action' until it was certain that Romania was entering the war. Bratianu was still inclined to raise his price, and their experience of Greek vacillation in the previous year made the Western Allies wary. But after the habitual frustrations which accompanied all Balkan diplomacy, a secret 'Bucharest Convention' was signed on 17 August: Romania would go to war on 28 August in return for assurances by the Allies that they accepted all of Bratianu's original demands.

It is sometimes hard to tell whom London distrusted more, the haggler statesman Bratianu or the political general, Sarrail? British suspicion of Sarrail's intentions in Greece had revived in early June when, with backing from Briand, the General used alleged collaboration between the commandant of a Greek frontier fortress and the Bulgarians as an excuse for proclaiming a state of siege in Salonika. At the same time the French took control of all railway, telegraph and postal services and Sarrail even sent a naval squadron, with a French brigade in support, to threaten the government in Athens. The British noted, with disapproval, Sarrail's social links with local entrepreneurs and the extent to which he encouraged the foundation of French schools. Sarrail believed it was his duty to look ahead: 'We ought to prepare for after the war by immediately imposing our products and trademarks on places regained by our armies', he wrote to Briand on 3 August, two days after setting up a 'Commercial Bureau for French Importations' in Salonika; and close contact was established with French chambers of commerce, particularly at Lyons, Dijon, Grenoble and Marseilles. The prospect of British competition did not especially worry Sarrail, but he was left uneasy by the arrival of an Italian division and kept close tags on its commander, General Pettiti – who was in

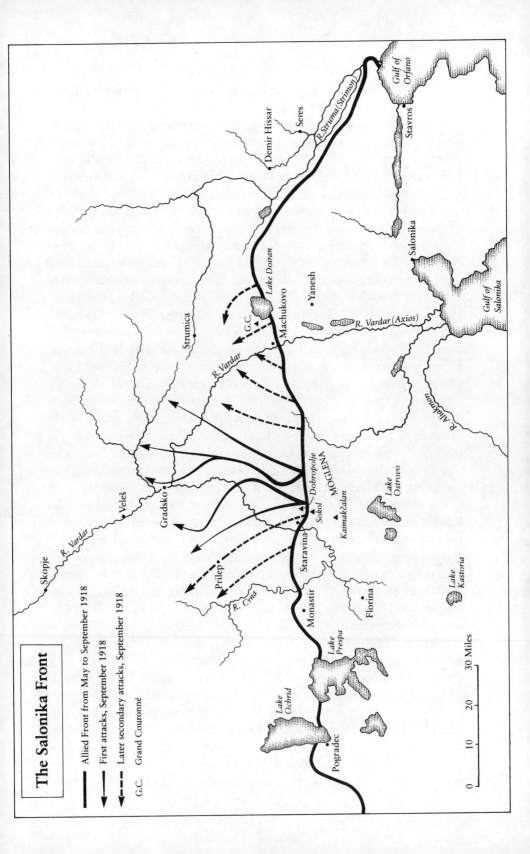

The Salonika Front

— Allied Front from May to September 1918

→ First attacks, September 1918

⇢ Later secondary attacks, September 1918

G.C. Grand Couronné

Gulf of Orfano

Stavros

R. Struma (Strimon)

Demir Hissar

Seres

Salonika

Lake Doiran

Machukovo

Yanesh

G.C.

Strumica

R. Vardar (Axios)

Gulf of Salonika

R. Vardar

R. Aliakmon

Veleš

Gradsko

Dobropolje

MOGLENA

Sokol

Kaimakčalan

Lake Ostrovo

Skopje

R. Vardar

Staravina

Prilep

Lake Kastoria

R. Crna

Monastir

Florina

Lake Prespa

Lake Ochrid

Pogradec

0   10   20   30 Miles

fact no travelling salesman but a courageous soldier, through and through.

Not that Sarrail was lacking in professional dedication: 'A strong man with big ideas and outlook with great brain power but of a conceited, excitable, impetuous and unscrupulous nature', wrote Milne to Robertson in a personal letter on 20 July, 'Possibly a good strategist but not a great tactician. . . . His mental calibre far and away above his Staff.' On paper the plans for Sarrail's offensive looked admirable: a Serbian thrust on the mountainous western sector of the Front towards Florina and Monastir; a British advance in the east across the River Struma; a French advance up the Vardar valley along the traditional route northwards; Russians, Italians and the most recently arrived Serbs to be held in reserve. But there could be no chance of taking the enemy by surprise. The Allied armies were stretched along a front of over 170 miles; it was impossible to conceal the movement from base camps to forward positions from the local peasantry, many of them hostile to the French and Serbs and ready to feed information to the Bulgarians. Sofia, and ultimately Berlin, had no doubt that an attack was pending. And on 17 August – the morning on which the Romanians signed their military convention – the Bulgarians struck first, attacking both flanks of the Salonika army. In the centre of the line, astride the River Vardar and that vital single-track railway artery to the heart of Europe, were two German divisions of nine battalions each, moved to the Balkans from the Vosges, the quietest sector of the Western Front.

For a week the Bulgarians had the ball at their feet. The port of Kavalla was occupied in the east, while in the west the Serbs were forced back to within seventy miles of Salonika. But, to his credit, Sarrail refused to abandon his plans for an offensive. Troops from the reserve plugged the gaps in the western mountains while the British infantry held a ninety-mile line along the lower Struma, in the east. By 28 August, the day on which Romania declared war, the fighting had died away. Sarrail revised his plans, so as to avoid the German defences in the Vardar, and moved extra troops into the area where the Bulgarians gained their most striking successes. Beyond the mountain chain – the pre-war Greek-Serbian frontier – was Monastir and beyond Monastir were two valleys leading to the upper Vardar: penetrate either of these valleys and the German defences on the railway trunk route would be turned. The great obstacle on the frontier itself was the Kajmakcalan ('butter churn'), a twin-peaked mountain rising 2,480 metres above sea level, with Bulgarian observation posts on the summit, controlling artillery on the lower slopes. General Zivojin Mišić, commanding

Serbia's First Army, assured Sarrail that his troops would scale the Kajmakcalan.

He kept his word. At six in the morning of 12 September Serbian and French heavy guns around Lake Ostrovo threw down the opening barrage of Sarrail's autumn offensive and Mišić's infantrymen surprised the Bulgarians in their forward trenches below the 'butter churn'. It took them a week to fight their way to the top, struggling first up precipitous tracks, then into beech forest and finally across the sun-baked rock face, where each gully or cleft became a natural, rock-hewn trench. And even when the Kajmakcalan was in Serbian hands, the Bulgarians counter-attacked, disputing possession of the mile-long ridge between the mountain's twin peaks for a further eleven days. To the left of the Serbs two French divisions and a Russian brigade had also gone forward on 12 September, following a narrow valley along which a railway ran north-westwards to the small town of Florina, the frontier at Kenali, and eventually to Monastir fourteen miles due north and 107 miles from Salonika. Although Sarrail anticipated stiff resistance on Kajmakcalan, he was furious at the slow progress made up the Kenali valley, failing to realize that the Bulgarian gunners were ensconced in a Greek Orthodox monastery high above Florina and that the Bulgarian commander, General Boyadief, had taken advantage of a sandstone ridge east of the village of Brod, where under German supervision his infantry prepared a trench system with as much care as in Flanders or along the Somme. Further east the British launched attacks in the Struma valley, north of the malarial marshes, and probed the defences east of the River Vardar, suffering heavy casualties around the village of Machukovo, where a crack German regiment had, once again, dug into well planned positions on the crest of a hill. By early October it was clear that, as on the Gallipoli peninsula and in the Italian Carso, the terrain favoured defence. The possible 'Balkan breakthrough' seemed a chimera. The battle for Monastir, like the struggles on the Western Front, unexpectedly dragged on for many weeks. Not until 19 November did French, Serbian and Russian troops capture the town, by then deep in snow and slush. Despite the long delay and reversals of fortune, this success on a largely forgotten front was a fine achievement; Sarrail could claim that his *Armée de l'Orient* had won the first victory for French arms since the Marne, twenty-six months before.

At first Sarrail's offensive aroused little interest among the paladins of German Supreme Headquarters at Pless. Field Marshal von Hindenburg, who became Chief of the General Staff on the day Romania entered the war, and his deputy, First Quartermaster-General Ludendorff, rated Macedonia as the least important war front in Europe, a region where the fighting could safely be left to the Bulgarians. On the other hand, the Romanians could bring war and devastation to the granary of central Europe. When in the last days of August the enemy crossed into Transylvania, Hindenburg declared: 'The last man who can be spared from the East and West must be sent against Romania'. But he (and the Kaiser, too) overreacted to the news. The German and Austro-Hungarian High Commands had long anticipated Romania's intervention. On 3 September General Mackensen led a combined German, Bulgarian and Turkish force northwards in the Dobruja. Within two days Tutrukan, a fortress town on the Danube, capitulated, enabling Mackensen to capture more than a hundred guns and 25,000 men; and later in the month General Falkenhayn threw the Romanians back across the Transylvanian Alps and began to move on the oilfields at Ploesti and on Bucharest itself. Bratianu appealed for Russian aid to help defend the Dobruja, as promised in the Military Convention, but received only 20,000 largely untrained troops, many of them Czechs and Croat volunteers from prisoner of war camps, who if captured were shot as deserters from the Austro-Hungarian armies. By October Romania was fast becoming a liability to the Entente rather than an asset.

But at this moment Mackensen was forced temporarily to slow down his advance. Unwelcome news came from the Bulgarian First Army in Macedonia, where the weather had broken and heavy rain was flooding the trenches around Brod: a crack battalion, exuberant during the advance in August, had mutinied, and disaffection was spreading rapidly among other units. Sarrail heard the rumour from interrogation of prisoners and, over in the Struma valley, British Intelligence, too, detected a sharp falling-away of Bulgarian morale now that winter was approaching. In Sofia urgent pleas were sent to Mackensen for the return of a German regiment he had moved northwards in August for the Dobruja offensive. The matter was referred to Hindenburg in Pless, where in the second week of September the Kaiser had entertained King Ferdinand and Crown Prince Boris of Bulgaria, together with the Bulgarian Commander-in-Chief, General Jekov, and the Turkish Generals Enver and Zekki. The visiting dignitaries accepted the creation of a Supreme War Command (*Oberste Kriegsleitung* – OKL) to be exercised by Hindenburg over the armies of the four Central Powers. So confident had been the assertions of joint purpose that Hindenburg scoffed at these tales of falling Bulgarian morale. All that was needed, he thought, was better organization under good, firm, German leadership: General von Below must set up Army Group Headquarters for the whole Macedonian Front at Skopje. Below was told to content himself with existing forces until Mackensen and Falkenhayn had beaten the Romanians, 'when the Balkan Question will be as good as solved and the Bulgarian troops would liquidate Sarrail easily enough'.

But though Below brought German reserves across from the Vardar section, he could see that the Bulgarians were at the end of their tether. From Skopje Below telegraphed directly to Pless, and the Hindenburg–Ludendorff partnership recognized the reality of the crisis. Individual, detached battalions were found in Champagne, in Poland and in the Vosges to be sent by train through Belgrade and Niš to hold the Balkan Front; heavy guns were even moved eastwards from the Meuse hills around Verdun, where in its ninth month the appalling battle that cost 700,000 lives was nearing its end. The prospect of relief by German forces seems to have checked disaffection among the Bulgarians, but to Below's dismay almost 1,000 German troops were taken prisoner by Serb and French colonial troops (Zouaves) in the second week of November; and Allied Intelligence interrogators in Salonika found many of these new prisoners were Western Front veterans, angered by lack of support from their Bulgarian ally. Other German relief forces, all from the West, found the icy route through the Babuna Pass south of the railhead impassable. They did not reach the battle front until Monastir had fallen and Sarrail was ordered by Joffre to 'suspend all operations' until the snows melted in the spring.

To Sarrail it seemed as if Bulgaria was close to collapse in late October, and his confidence encouraged speculation at Chantilly and in London: what happens if Berlin's links with Constantinople are severed by a Bulgarian withdrawal from the war, the CIGS wondered? General Milne, shrewd Scotsman as he was, did not share Sarrail's optimism, believing, as he wrote to Robertson on 5 November, that 'Germany will fight desperately to retain Bulgaria'. In the early autumn of 1918 a similar offensive on a larger scale caused a comparable collapse in Bulgarian morale; on that occasion the spirit of mutiny spread and sparked off rebellion which did, indeed, take the kingdom out of the war. But the general situation in 1916 was markedly different. The war had as yet made little difference to life within Bulgaria and, though the troops in the western Macedonian mountains were battle-weary, the regiments serving under Mackensen were counting on a speedy victory and good pickings in the Dobruja. Significantly, the German High Command preferred to draw on troops from the Western Front than from the two armies in Romania.

Mackensen resumed his advance long before Below's difficulties were eased at Skopje. The port of Constanta was in German hands by the end of October, a success duly celebrated in Sofia; and an Austro-Hungarian pontoon unit threw a bridge across the Danube near Zimnicea three weeks later, enabling Mackensen to head towards the capital. Falkenhayn, too, moved swiftly once clear of the Transylvanian Alps. The grain fields of Wallachia were overrun. Bucharest had been bombed by Bulgarian aeroplanes early in the war, in a much publicized raid; on 25 November the government was evacuated to Jassy and on 6 December the Germans entered the city, which the Romanians left undefended. A day later Falkenhayn's army reached Ploesti oilfields, only to find the immediate effectiveness of the oilfield weakened through acts of sabotage which were supervised by Colonel Norton Griffiths, the Conservative MP for Wednesbury. Despite this rebuff, pessimists in London reckoned that Germany had probably acquired enough oil and grain by the invasion to meet the needs of the Central Powers for two more years. Mackensen and Falkenhayn had gained a striking victory against the Entente's newest recruit. Two days before Christmas Falkenhayn accepted the surrender of 10,000 Romanian troops; three-quarters of their country was by now under enemy occupation. Only in Moldavia to the east of the River Sereth did the rump of the Romanian army continue stubbornly to resist.

Joffre calculated that, with the scaling-down of their operations in Romania, the Germans would have 40,000 troops available for service elsewhere, most probably in Macedonia; but neither he nor Robertson would countenance the despatch of reinforcements to Salonika. Theoretically Sarrail could now call on an army of 20,000 Greek 'volunteers', willing to fight in defence of land won from the Turks, and denied to the Bulgars, during the Balkan Wars. On 27 August an officer in the Royal Army Medical Corps at Salonika, Captain Dudden, had noted in his diary: 'Another scorching day, but we forget the heat in the excitement of the revolution'. For, with Sarrail's benevolent encouragement, on that Sunday a local hero of the Balkan campaigns, Colonel Zymbrakakis, led a crowd of supporters to Allied headquarters and pledged support to the Entente cause. As a gesture of revolutionary intent Zymbrakakis established a 'Committee of Public Safety' in August and undertook to create a 'National Army', which would fight for the honour of the Greek people, in contrast to those royalist officers who shamefully surrendered key positions in eastern Macedonia to the advancing Bulgarians.

Outside Salonika, however, Zymbrakakis was little known, and to many northern Greeks it looked as if he were Sarrail's puppet. But on 27

August the demonstrators had shouted, not only '*Zito Ghallia*' ('Long Live France') but '*Zito Venizelos*' as well, and on 25 September the best known of Greece's political leaders escaped from Athens in a car with a French tricolour on the bonnet. French patrol boats escorted Venizelos's vessel from Phaleron Bay, whence he embarked to his native Crete, where he put himself at the head of the National Movement: 'Save what may still be saved', Venizelos urged the Greek people. In Canea he was joined by two widely respected veterans, General Danglis and Admiral Koundouriotis, as well as by three Greek warships and by armed supporters who had backed him in the struggles of the past twenty years. The islands of the Sporades followed the example of Crete; and by 9 October, when General Sarrail was at the quayside to welcome him to Salonika, Venizelos had behind him a genuine national following, wider in hopes and vision than Zymbrakakis could ever inspire.

Venizelos's movements and intentions were misunderstood at the time and have been misrepresented by later commentators. They ignore the week spent in Crete and write as though he fled directly to Salonika, 'with Sarrail's connivance'. In reality, in both 1916 and 1917, Venizelos astutely exploited Sarrail and the French connection. He sensed the danger for Greece of the General's ambitions and constantly sought to remain independent of him. There was also marked suspicion between Venizelos and Briand – whose mistress was the wife of his old political enemy in Crete, Prince George. When Venizelos set up a Provisional Government in Salonika he entrusted the handling of commercial affairs to a leading shipowner, Constantine Embeirikos, who took advantage of Sarrail's 'Commercial Bureau' but had no intention of weakening his own position for the benefit of his shipping rivals at Marseilles. Venizelos personally encouraged closer military links with the British than with the French; three battalions of his National Army were serving on the Struma Front by the third week in November 1916; they took part in attacks on a farmhouse that had been seized and fortified by Bulgarian invaders. A few days later Venizelos formally notified Sarrail, as Commander-in-Chief, that more than 23,000 volunteers had enlisted in the National Army, and a steady flow of recruits could be expected to arrive from the Greek islands.

General Milne wished to see 'the Venizelos people' integrated with the British Salonika Force. But, in a private letter from Robertson, he was told: 'It is no good you asking for all the Greeks to come definitely under you because that has been decided against . . . You are expected to help them'. 'We have *got* to get on with the Greeks, the French and all those other allies the best way you can', the CIGS reminded him. Milne's doubts over Sarrail's intentions deepened as the Monastir offensive came to an end. He thought a protracted civil war in Greece probable and was dismayed, but not surprised, by the tragic and confused episode in Athens on 1 December 1916 when a landing-force of French soldiers and British marines, seeking to compel the handing-over by King Constantine of ten batteries of mountain artillery, was fired on by Greek royalist troops, with 212 casualties. The British government still hoped for reconciliation between the Greek factions in the capital and in Salonika because they believed that a monarchical Greece would be less under the influence of the French in the post-war world than would a republic. Even so, on 21 December London and Paris both gave formal recognition to the Provisional Government in Salonika and prepared to send accredited diplomatic envoys to the city.

That Christmas fortunate families in Britain and France and Italy received from their loved ones serving in Salonika an attractive festive card, printed on stretched silk. It brought greetings (in French) from *L'Armée de l'Orient* and bore no religious symbolism. The card was brightened by a colourful cluster of flags, representing the six nations whose troops were serving on the Macedonian Front. They were draped around the centrepiece – which was, predictably, a portrait of General Maurice Sarrail.

CHAPTER 5

A VICTORY WHILE YOU WAIT

The final quarter of 1916 saw changes of leadership among both the Central Powers and the Entente allies. The creation of OKL confirmed the ascendancy of Hindenburg and Ludendorff as decision-makers for the Central Powers, with armies of 6,000,000 men at their disposal. The Kaiser remained All Highest War Lord within Germany, but only on sufferance. When Emperor King Charles (who succeeded Francis Joseph on 21 November) wished to show Austria–Hungary's independence of German policies, he and his commanders were called sharply to heel by OKL at Kreuznach, the Rhineland town whither headquarters moved from Pless in February 1917. German officers determined the disposition of Bulgarian regiments; and in the Ottoman Empire, Enver welcomed the appointment of General von Falkenhayn, Hindenburg's predecessor, to command an army group at Aleppo, though the overbearing manner of OKL's nominees infuriated Djemal and the most successful of Turkey's generals, Mustafa Kemal.

In Great Britain the change of leadership was political. A demand for 'more energetic conduct of the war' and fears that the nation was close to economic collapse led to the downfall of Asquith's coalition, with Lloyd George becoming Prime Minister on 7 December and setting up a new War Cabinet of ministers who held no departmental responsibilities. Significantly, the first War Cabinet consisted of Lloyd George himself, three Tories (Bonar Law, Curzon, Milner) and one Labour spokesman (Arthur Henderson), with the indispensable Maurice Hankey as secretary. Balfour succeeded Grey as Foreign Secretary; Lord Derby – a favourite 'malleable' politician of the Western Front generals – became War Secretary. Both ministers might 'attend' War Cabinet meetings, but were not usually present. There was no place for Churchill, still the political scapegoat for failure at the Dardanelles. Before winning Conservative support, Lloyd George had been forced to give the Tory leaders an assurance that Churchill would not be invited to join the new team.

It seemed probable that the French, too, would soon change their government. The strain of Verdun and dismay at the failure to dent the German defensive system in the war of attrition threatened to topple Briand during the closing weeks of the year. But, after a series of secret sessions in parliament, Briand acted decisively, desperately clinging to office by overhauling the military machine: the title 'Marshal of France', never previously conferred under the republic, was revived in mid-December to honour Joffre, who took no further part in shaping policy. Henceforth there would be no commander-in-chief of all the French armies; GQG at Chantilly ceased to exist and overall responsibility for France's military effort was assumed by General Lyautey at the Ministry of War in the Rue St Dominique, Paris. The new Commander-in-Chief of the French armies on the Western Front was General Robert Nivelle, who had shown initiative at the head of the Second Army in the last phase of the battle at Verdun and was largely responsible for the morale-bolstering recapture of Fort Douaumont. Nivelle was a cadet of the prestigious cavalry school at Saumur, but chose to become an artillery-man, whereas Joffre had been an engineer; and in December 1916 Nivelle brought with him a gunner's solution for breaking through the German defences on the Aisne. He favoured a massive bombardment on limited objectives, launched with complete surprise, to be followed by a deep, creeping barrage, as the infantry went forward to capture the defence line in a single day and so 'rupture' (his word) the enemy. Although Nivelle could not project Joffre's aura of authority, he was self-confident, persuasive and fluent in English, his mother's native tongue. He asked for the British to take over another twenty miles of the French line and to mount an attack on Cambrai from Arras, designed to draw in German reserves ahead of the proposed French breakthrough on the Aisne. Haig (newly promoted Field Marshal) was hesitant and in no hurry to mount the offensive; but, as Hankey observed, Nivelle 'made a very favourable impression on the War Cabinet', even if Lloyd George, with his habitual suspicion of 'Westerners', felt he overstated his case.

'L.G. wants a victory quickly, a victory while you wait', the CIGS noted a few days before Christmas, 'He does not care where.' Robertson's comment was perceptive; it showed a sound understanding of the new Prime Minister's character. For, like Churchill, and unlike Asquith or Grey, Lloyd George remained receptive to the public mood. In his first speech to the Commons as head of government he was prepared to take the nation into his confidence:

I must paint a stern picture, because that accurately represents the fact . . .
A good many of our misunderstandings have arisen from exaggerated
views which have been taken about successes and from a disposition to
treat as trifling real setbacks . . . Britain has never shown at its best
except when it was confronted with a real danger and understood it.

But, despite the stern words, he was conscious that after twenty-eight
months of war and unprecedented casualties there had as yet been few
British successes to celebrate. Many victories seemed incomplete. Thus,
although Jutland ultimately proved a strategic naval triumph, twice as
many British seamen perished during the battle as German, and the
Royal Navy lost fourteen warships to the High Seas Fleet's ten. 'Were
we celebrating a glorious naval victory or lamenting an ignominious
defeat?', Nurse Vera Brittain was later to recall, 'We hardly knew.' And,
contrary to expectations, there was still a battle front in Africa, rapacious
of men and supplies; for though German South-West Africa, Togoland
and the Cameroons were swiftly overrun and in East Africa General
Smuts controlled the central railway from Dar-es-Salaam to Ujiji,
bush warfare in Tanganyika continued with the German commander,
Lettow-Vorbeck, emerging as the most persistent and elusive of guerrilla leaders. Small wonder if a new prime minister wished to confirm
and strengthen his ascendancy by giving the nation 'a victory while you
wait'.

Unexpectedly, the victory came in Mesopotamia – a theatre of war
from which the British were contemplating complete withdrawal only
a few months previously. In July 1916 General Sir Stanley Maude,
who had successfully evacuated 13th Division from Gallipoli, arrived
on the Tigris, taking command of the Mesopotamia Expeditionary
Force a month later. He convinced the War Office and the India
Office that, with careful preparation, a determined thrust could avenge
the humiliation of Kut-al-Amara and secure a permanent foothold
between the two great rivers of Asia Minor. The CIGS regarded
Mesopotamia as the worst of all 'sideshows' and grudged Maude every
shipload of supplies. But the possibility that the Russians might break
through the Turkish positions in the Caucasus and sweep down on the
oilfields from the north was an incentive for swift action, especially to
the 'Indian lobby' in London, with its concern for the post-war
balance of power. Maude began an advance six days after Lloyd
George formed his government. Some 10,500 Indian and 60,000
British troops moved steadily upriver, backed by bombing raids from
the RFC and constant support from the flotilla of six river gunboats.

Elaborate schemes of deception and enterprising work on a pontoon bridge enabled Maude to take Kut on 24 February 1917. In another fifteen days his army covered one hundred miles, reaching Baghdad on 11 March, after one last night march. 'We had none of us washed or shaved for three days (and some not for a fortnight)', wrote Major Crowdy of the 15th Indian Division to his wife. 'We were white with dust, thirsty, hungry and bone weary, and gazed at the sacred city through bloodshot eyes. Men lay down and went to sleep where they halted.' Yet if the entry itself was no triumphant victory march, news of Baghdad's capture lifted morale at home. To Lloyd George it came as 'a stroke which at once rehabilitated our prestige in the East and cheered our people . . . The name of Baghdad counted throughout the Mussulman world'. And, as Hindenburg was to admit some years later, 'The loss of the old city of the Caliphs' was 'painful to us' in Germany 'and to all thinking Turks'.

Yet, while Lloyd George exploited the good news from the Tigris, his main military concern in these first weeks of office was with the war in Europe. Although experience had begun to blunt his earlier support for the Salonika expedition and he 'recognized the West as the principal theatre' of war, the appalling lesson of the Somme reinforced old doubts whether it 'was possible to defeat the Germans' in France, 'at any rate, not next year' (1917). But what of the Italian Front? In the last days of 1916 he proposed that a top-level Allied conference should be held in Rome. He would offer the Italians heavy guns and shells in the hope of persuading them to launch a spring offensive which would capture Trieste, break through to the Ljubljana plain and open up the route to Vienna and Budapest. At the same time the Allied commanders at Salonika, Sarrail and Milne, would be summoned to Rome for consultation over Greek affairs and with the conviction that a Balkan offensive would also help 'to knock away Germany's props'. On 2 January 1917 Lloyd George, Lord Milner, Robertson, Hankey and four senior civil servants crossed the Channel and on the following night travelled down to Rome in the same train as Briand, Lyautey and the French delegation. Milne and Sarrail arrived, independently of each other, next day.

The Rome Conference achieved little. General Cadorna, whose armies had already suffered more than 300,000 casualties in nine battles along the River Isonzo, was highly suspicious of Lloyd George's proposal that, because spring came earlier south of the Alps, Italy should launch the first offensive of the year. Could he be certain of support from other fronts? He was afraid that the heavy artillery, promised 'on loan' by Lloyd George, would be withdrawn for service on the Western Front before the Italians had reached their objectives – a possibility which appears to have been suggested to him by Robertson who, convinced of the need to concentrate military power in France, wished to trim Lloyd George's broader strategy. It was agreed to prepare contingency plans for a rapid movement of troops from the West to northern Italy should they be required. Briand urged reinforcements for Salonika, but neither the British nor the Italians were prepared to send further divisions east. The Italians, with a foothold established south of Valona in Albania, had no wish to see powerful French or British interests supporting post-war Greece. Lloyd George and Briand did, however, persuade the Italians to begin work on a road from southern Albania to Monastir. When completed, this route would enable Brindisi to develop as a ferry port, thus shortening the journey to Salonika and avoiding the U-boat-infested waters of the Aegean.

Unexpectedly, both Lloyd George and Hankey were impressed by General Sarrail. 'A man of quite exceptional charm', wrote Hankey in his diary; and the Prime Minister told his personal secretary (and mistress) that Sarrail was 'a remarkable, fascinating character, handsome, impulsive, full of fire'. He rejected the General's proposal that the authorities in London and Paris might 'shut their eyes or turn their heads for a fortnight' while he dealt with the Greek royalists in Athens; such drastic action, Lloyd George explained, would harm the Allied cause with neutrals, and especially with the United States. But he saw no reason why the royalists should not be required to quit Athens and withdraw into the Peloponnese. He told Sarrail that he could count on 'fair play' from the British government – at which point the two men shook hands. Sarrail was at last officially confirmed as 'Commander-in-Chief of the Allied Army of the Orient', with each national contingent accepting his operational orders, though with a right of reference back to its own government.

Poor Milne was 'cross-questioned' by Lloyd George and Milner soon after his arrival and then virtually ignored, although on the second morning he did exchange sympathetic grumbles with his old friend, Robertson, whom he found 'much put out' by a conference at which 'we soldiers do nothing'. The official French record of the conference forgot to mention Milne as a participant. When he arrived at the station to take the train down to Taranto, high-ranking Italians were grouped on the platform; but, as Milne drily noted in his diary, 'they show little desire to see us off'; the officers had turned out to honour a traveller in another coach, for to Cadorna there seemed little doubt that, however much the Italians might distrust him, Maurice Sarrail was Soldier of the Hour.

Belatedly, when Milne reached Salonika, he found his status raised from a 'General Officer Commanding' to 'Commander-in-Chief of the Salonika Army'. No infantry reinforcements reached him, only three batteries of heavy artillery, although 60th (London) Division had arrived from France in the second week of December, to form a strategic reserve. Sarrail, on the other hand, received two colonial divisions in December and two more in January. As he was now confident of backing from London as well as from Paris, he began preparations for an offensive which, with preliminary attacks in mid-March, was to reach a climax a month later. A five-pronged attack would, he hoped, break the mountain defence line and ensure a victorious march into Sofia by midsummer. The will to victory was certainly there, both at GHQ and among the national contingents, including the two Russian brigades. Preparations went ahead despite appalling weather: constant rain throughout late January and February, with icy winds clawing into the French, Italian, Russian and Serb troops in the mountains west of the Vardar. Farther east, in Milne's sector, road traffic was impossible, so that over the last fourteen miles supplies for the 10th Division in the Struma valley were carried by mules, driven slipping and slithering along a serpentine track to the waterlogged trenches below.

Then, on the eve of preliminary skirmishes for the offensive, came the great Vardar Blizzard. Ominously, on 28 February, Colonel Warde-Aldham of the 20th London Regiment – veterans of 'minnie' (*Minenwerfer*, mine-canister throwers) attacks on their trenches at Vimy Ridge – spotted two wolves who had come down from the mountains to seek food and cover in the foothills beyond his battalion's tents at Mihilova, between the Vardar and Lake Doiran. Within a few hours the blizzard struck. 'We were expecting a Bulgar attack', wrote one of his riflemen, Bernard Livermore; instead,

> With amazing and surprising ferocity came . . . mighty blasts of wind bringing torrents of rain and stinging hailstones . . . followed by snow and sleet. Icy water swept under us and penetrated every inch of our clothing. The intense shock of this snow water seeping through our trousers and slowly creeping up our spines to the shoulders was a torture one would never forget . . . Our Sergeant . . . dished out a generous dose of rum . . . with tears freezing on his unshaven cheeks. When the minnies were falling at Vimy there was no time for prayer – only time to dodge round a corner,

if one were lucky. In this cursed Blizzard we had nothing to do, save to try to continue to exist. To remain alive and try to wriggle our toes.

They survived 'that ghastly night'. Early spring sunshine came out next morning. 'The sun was hot and our wet clothes started to dry. A mist of steam surrounded every man.' Arduous training resumed, for everyone knew that an attack on 'Johnny Bulgar' was pending – once 'this 'ere French chap . . . from his Salonika hotel' could make up his 'ruddy mind'.

So it might seem to English riflemen encamped in the Balkan foothills. But the final decisions over grand strategy did not rest with General Sarrail. He had certainly achieved a personal success at Rome, but Lloyd George had travelled to Italy, not so much to size up Sarrail as to galvanize Cadorna; the thunder of heavy gunfire rolling up the valleys from the Isonzo would, he hoped, provide the overture to 1917's concerted offensive. Cadorna's obduracy deeply disappointed him; there could now be no joint assault from Venetia and from Macedonia, striking northwards into Austria–Hungary. Inevitably, Salonika was sidelined; the defeat of Bulgaria was less pressing; it was the 'knockout blow' against the Central German Powers that mattered most. On returning from Rome Lloyd George began to reassess Nivelle's proposals for an offensive on the Western Front early in April: here was a plan which, with its emphasis on surprise, might succeed; and – an important consideration for any British prime minister – the plan assigned a subsidiary role to Haig's divisions, leaving the principal task of breaking through the German Front on the Aisne to Nivelle's massed twenty-seven French divisions. Haig, however, wished the offensive to be delayed until May, complaining that the poor state of the French railways made it impossible for him to complete his preparations earlier. Such apparent dilatoriness angered the Prime Minister. He was prepared to accept French proposals to place Haig and the BEF under Nivelle's command, in much the same way as Milne was now subordinate to Sarrail. During a stormy two-day conference in Calais at the end of February it seemed likely that Haig, Robertson and Derby (the War Secretary) would resign, since, as Hankey's diary records, 'Ll.G. . . . really seemed rather to like the French scheme'. A compromise, put forward by Hankey, subordinated Haig and the British armies to Nivelle only until the end of the proposed offensive, and allowed Haig a right to appeal to the War Cabinet if he thought Nivelle's operational orders endangered the survival of his army. So great was the dispute over command in France that a further item on the agenda – the unfolding war in Macedonia – was only raised shortly before lunch on the final day. 'What next in Salonika?', the top brass pondered – but not too deeply. 'That vexatious problem was not allowed to keep them long from the hors d'oeuvres', the liaison officer, Major Spears, records. 'For the present, the decisive defeat of the Bulgarian Army is not a practical objective', the conference decided, 'The mission of the allied forces at Salonika is to keep in the front the enemy forces now there, and to take advantage of striking at the enemy if opportunity offers'.

The CIGS and Lloyd George returned to London on 28 February, the eve of the Vardar Blizzard. No one telegraphed the conference's decision to Salonika until 4 March; and then the message came only in the form of a general instruction from Robertson to Milne. He went at once to Sarrail's headquarters only to find that, though Sarrail had told Lyautey he wished to send French troops forward in the first probing attack on 11 March, he knew nothing of the Calais meeting. An immediate request to Paris for clarification went unanswered for five days. Eventually, on 9 March, Sarrail was given details of the decision, together with an assurance that he had 'full liberty to begin operations when you think the moment is favourable'. It was clear that neither London nor Paris believed in Sarrail's projected march on Sofia. The map of the Balkans no longer commanded attention.

This is hardly surprising. For in retrospect the months of February and March in 1917 stand out as a historical climacteric in the war. Great issues posed urgent questions. For the British government the gravest problem was the threat to food supplies from German U-boats. On 1 February the Germany Navy began unrestricted submarine warfare, with attacks on any ship trading with British ports, calculating that a fleet of over a hundred operational U-boats could force Britain to sue for peace by August. The losses inflicted by the U-boats did indeed rise dramatically, to reach a disastrous peak of 860,334 tons of world shipping during April; only nine of 105 U-boats were sunk during these three months, two of them destroyed by German-sown mines. When the United States of America went to war with Germany on 6 April 1917 (a momentous decision, which is examined in the following chapter) the principal American liaison officer in London was warned by the Admiralty that unless the destruction of merchant ships could be checked, the British would have to accept German peace terms within a few months. Inevitably the need for effective countermeasures in the war at sea figured prominently in the almost daily sessions of the War Cabinet that spring.

Imperial statesmen, too, were consulted. For in March and April leading members of the governments of Australia, Canada, New Zealand, Newfoundland and South Africa and a maharaja representing the Indian princely states held fifteen meetings in London, as well as attending the War Cabinet, in order to discuss general strategy, the problem of supplies, manpower needs and the future peace settlement; 'The British Empire' so Lloyd George told his guests on 20 March, 'will easily then be the first Power in the world'. Not all his listeners were impressed by the speech: 'Platform bunkum', one noted in his diary, 'Mostly rather tosh'. Optimism did not come readily at such a time.

One challenger to world power was by now clearly out of the race. On both sides of the Channel there was doubt over what was happening in Petrograd. From 25 January to 20 February 1917 Lord Milner was in Russia at the head of an inter-Allied mission to assess the will of the Russian people to stay in the war and 'fight to a finish'. Back in London on 6 March, Milner told the War Cabinet that there was political unrest, a possible descent into anarchy through sheer maladministration, dismay over German influences at Court, but no threat of imminent revolution. His judgement was at fault. Within ten days the Tsarist system collapsed and Britain and France hastily gave recognition to a new Provisional Government. In both countries there was, at first, a certain relief: 'England hails the new Russia with a higher hope and a surer confidence in the future not only of this war but of the world', a leading article in the *Manchester Guardian* concluded on 16 March; and in Paris the principal radical Opposition newspaper, Clemenceau's *L'Homme Enchaîné*, for four days welcomed the revolution as a sign that Russia's war effort, under new leaders, would become vigorous and sustained, an example to the people of France. By the end of March, however, doubts over the mounting appeal of the peace party in Petrograd began to influence policies in the West. It seemed essential to strike a decisive blow in France while there was still an Eastern Front on which the Russians could tie down 139 German and Austro-Hungarian divisions.

The edition of the *Manchester Guardian* which hailed the overthrow of Tsardom also carried welcome news from France. A report described how the Germans were 'in retreat before the British on the Ancre–Somme front' and a French communiqué announced that they were also pulling back on the Oise. But was this desirable? There had been extensive activity behind the German trenches for five weeks; one French commander, General Franchet d'Esperey, urged Nivelle to allow his Army Group North to seize the initiative and take the Germans by surprise, but Nivelle refused to modify his long-term plan.

On 15 March French and British troops moved cautiously forward, to find empty trenches before them often mined and only evacuated after booby-traps had been set. Felled poplars blocked the main roads, orchards were destroyed, fields turned into wasteland, water supplies contaminated, villages and some small towns gutted. For this was not, as the press reporters supposed, a retreat; it was a planned retirement, a voluntary withdrawal to carefully constructed and well fortified defences, in some places twenty-five miles behind the old trench system. From 18 March the Germans could await their attackers along a shortened line which would enable OKL to create a mobile reserve of some thirteen or fourteen divisions, which could be employed elsewhere on the Western Front, most profitably around the Ypres Salient. The Germans called their new defences the Siegfried Line, but to the Allies they constituted the Hindenburg Line, an obstacle as solid and formidable as the eponymous Field Marshal himself – though, in fact, the fortifications were the brainchild of Ludendorff.

Nivelle originally intended his offensive to begin on 1 April. Friction with Haig, mainly over the movement of troops, postponed the start by a week and the German withdrawal to the Hindenburg Line required further modifications to the plan. For a fortnight it seemed probable that the whole project would be abandoned. For on 19–20 March two of Nivelle's leading political supporters left office: General Lyautey stalked out of the Chamber of Deputies in a huff and promptly resigned; and his War Minister's departure made it impossible for Briand to preserve the coalition he had held together for seventeen months. The new Prime Minister, the seventy-five-year-old conservative republican, Alexandre Ribot, had no grasp of strategy, leaving such matters to Lyautey's successor as War Minister, Paul Painlevé, who feared that Nivelle was recklessly over-confident. Only after President Poincaré chaired a Council of War on 6 April and Nivelle threatened to resign was the Commander-in-Chief given the go-ahead. Even then General Pétain, of Army Group Centre, continued to protest that the assault on the new defences would entail terrible casualties. But Nivelle still believed he could rupture the enemy, with a breakthrough of ten miles on the first day; his recipe for a final, decisive victory was 'Laon in twenty-four hours, and then the pursuit'.

When propounding his earliest plans, five months previously, Nivelle spoke of a surprise attack; and the proposal was welcomed by the politicians. Unfortunately, Nivelle had gone on speaking of his coming surprise attack, indiscreetly, in Paris and in London, where he came once more on 15 March. By then the Germans were fully on their guard.

Interrogation of prisoners taken in trench raids revealed the build-up of British forces around Arras, even though full use was made of the city's cellars to conceal the final concentration; and captured documents gave a clear impression of French intentions along the Aisne. Interception of wireless messages, decoded by the French and with the British cipher easy to break, enabled the Germans to anticipate adjustments during the course of the battles.

General Allenby, a cavalryman through and through, commanded the Third Army south of Arras and was responsible for detailed planning of the battle as a whole. He proposed a concentrated forty-eight-hour barrage in place of the habitual five-day bombardment but was overruled by Haig and the top artillerymen. His heavy guns were already pounding away while Poincaré's Council of War was meeting. But rain and sleet postponed the Easter Day opening assault by twenty-four hours, and it was not until 9 April that Allenby's troops went forward, a whole week before Nivelle intended to make his bid for total victory.

Unlike the Somme, the first day of the Battle of Arras held a promise of success. The weather worsened during the morning, but despite squalls of snow the First Army covered three and a half miles north-east of Arras before dusk. The epic assault of that Easter Monday was the capture by the four Canadian divisions of Vimy Ridge, the low eminence which had resisted French and British attacks in the spring of 1915. To take and hold the two miles of German positions commanding the Ridge cost the lives of 3,598 Canadian troops. On the far south of Arras Anzac veterans from Gallipoli attacked the village of Bullecourt, though it was another three days before the imaginative use of seven tanks cut a way for the Anzacs through wire and over trenches. In the centre Allenby's infantry moved steadily forward behind a further innovation, a 'rolling' barrage of bursting shells fired at targets which were adjusted so as to 'advance' ahead of the assault troops. Although not all objectives were reached, Allenby issued an encouraging Order of the Day: 'The Third Army is pursuing a defeated enemy'. But the following days showed that the final line of German defence was impenetrable. When at Haig's bidding Allenby sent his cavalry towards an apparent gap in the wire, horses and men were cut down by machine-gun fire. There would be no cavalry pursuit of an enemy who, despite the confident forecasts, showed little sign of defeat. By Thursday, 12 April, the whole attack was losing momentum. Haig despatched amended orders which, with a ghastly confusion reminiscent of Balaklava, Allenby misinterpreted; and he mounted a succession of infantry assaults against newly arrived German troops in strongly prepared defences. The losses, especially among the Scottish riflemen, the 5th Cameronians, were appalling. Before dawn on Sunday 15 April, Haig called a halt to all operations around Arras. Vimy Ridge remained in Canadian hands, 13,000 Germans were on their way to prisoner of war camps and 200 guns were captured, but during less than a week of battle Haig's troops sustained over 40,000 casualties. And Nivelle's long-heralded offensive, to which Arras was to have served as a prelude, had still not begun.

Next morning, from his headquarters at Compiègne, Nivelle issued an Order of the Day: 'Soldiers! The hour has come! Courage. Confidence. *Vive la France!*' At 06.00 on 16 April, some seventy miles south-east of the BEF's battlefields, whistles blew in Nivelle's advance trenches and the *poilus* in their *horizon bleu* uniform went forward with that impetuous exhilaration which had carried the red-trousered infantrymen across the frontier of Lorraine in the opening days of the war. Far less enthusiastic were the khaki-clad colonial regiments, especially the Senegalese, many of whom were so numbed by the cold that the fingers of hands clasping rifles were rendered useless. For half a mile all seemed to go well for the *poilus*, but then they came under the crossfire of thousands of machine-guns, well concealed behind unbroken barbed wire. In sudden disillusionment the survivors sought what cover they could find, waiting for fresh orders or waiting for stretchers, as a bitter wind blew sleet and snow across the huddled bodies, and French guns, losing their targets in the eerie light, sent shells falling on their own infantry. Tanks, used by the French for the first time, proved ineffectual: thirty-two were lost on that Monday. Medical provision for the wounded was hopelessly inadequate: 10,000 wounded for the whole offensive, Nivelle had predicted. Yet on the first day alone there may have been as many as 120,000 casualties. 'Courage' remained an essential requisite for those who fought on; but 'confidence' was gone. On 23 April Haig resumed his attacks south of Arras, at Monchy-le-Preux, to take pressure off Nivelle. The French quest for victory in the West degenerated into yet one more costly drama of a war of attrition. It became a battle to seize the Chemin des Dames, that almost forgotten royal road on a ridge beyond the Aisne, laid to ease the buffeting of princesses' carriages journeying from palace to hunting-lodge before the great Revolution.

On the evening of the third day of Nivelle's offensive Lloyd George arrived in Paris. Already there was a sense of failure among his French hosts. Hankey noted that 'Painlevé, the new Minister of War . . . was very down-hearted', in contrast to his visitor, who remained elated by the capture of Vimy Ridge. But Lloyd George was less concerned with the Western Front than with broader projects. He wished to discuss with Ribot the prospects of knocking away Germany's chief 'prop', in taking Austria–Hungary out of the war by a separate peace. Ribot had already been contacted by the Austrian Emperor's brother-in-law, Prince Sixte of Bourbon-Parma, and while in Paris Lloyd George met the Prince for conversations so confidential that not even the Foreign Office was informed. There had been some evidence earlier in the year that Emperor Charles favoured peace, but Sixte misrepresented his brother-in-law's attitude and it appears that both the British and French prime ministers exaggerated the extent of war-weariness in Vienna. They realized, however, that any concessions Austria–Hungary might offer were unlikely to meet the territorial demands conceded in the (still secret) Treaty of London. There was an obvious need for talks with the Italian Foreign Minister, Baron Sonnino, though both Lloyd George and Ribot were determined to say nothing of Prince Sixte's mission. They travelled together overnight in a special train to St Jean-de-Maurienne, in Savoy, near Mont Cenis. Sonnino came from across the frontier; and on 19–20 April talks were held aboard the train, in a railway siding.

Only fifteen weeks had passed since the Rome Conference. Lloyd George still hoped for greater activity on the Italian Front, though the snow around his train showed the folly of having believed there might be an early spring offensive in this theatre of operations. He made one more bid to induce the Italians to march on Trieste; as chief port and third largest city in the Habsburg lands it was a prize worth seizing if pressure were to be put on the government in Vienna. But Sonnino was in no position to commit Cadorna to military operations. The Italians were, however, tempted by the prospect of receiving (as Hankey wrote) a 'cut off the joint of Turkey'; if refused Istria and Dalmatia by the Austrians, their land hunger might be satisfied in the East by gaining the seaports of Smyrna and Adalia and the Ottoman provincial capital of Konya, some 150 miles inland. As yet, however, their operations against the Turks had been limited to protection of pre-war gains in Libya and the Dodecanese. 'L.G.', as Hankey's diary records, 'spoke very straight to Sonnino' on the need for a greater military effort against their combined enemies. He seems to have known nothing of General Foch's journey to Vicenza eleven days previously, when the Italian Commander-in-Chief seemed so fearful of German intervention on the Isonzo that he convinced his French visitor of the need for detailed inter-Allied staff-work on contingency plans to rush troop reinforcements from the West if the Germans attacked in strength.

Salonika, so high on the agenda at the Rome Conference, was passed over rapidly at St Jean-de-Maurienne. Sarrail had still not mounted the offensive agreed three months previously, though even as the Allied leaders met in their train General Maitland Wilson's XII Corps were digging the last support trenches for a night attack on Bulgarian fortifications above Lake Doiran. But with no 'victory while you wait' coming from Salonika, Lloyd George was disenchanted with the Balkans; he had lost patience with Sarrail, that 'impulsive character full of fire' who had so charmed him in January. Salonika, the CIGS told the War Cabinet in the first week of April, 'had no military justification and had been a failure from the first'; Milne's men were 'likely to contribute far more to winning the war' in Palestine. With some reservations, the Prime Minister for once agreed with him.

For, while no successes had been telegraphed back from Salonika, the prospects looked good for Sir Archibald Murray's Egyptian Expeditionary Force, now cast for a greater role than guardians of the Suez Canal. Methodically through the last months of 1916 the EEF had cleared Turkish outposts from the Sinai desert and, using a virtually conscripted Egyptian labour corps, prepared a land route for the march northwards into Syria. A railway, a water pipeline, an improvised road through the desert made of wire netting and pegged down by the engineers, crept steadily forward until, with the capture of the Turkish base at El Arish four days before Christmas in 1916, Australians and New Zealanders were less than twenty miles from the border. A fortnight later they were fighting in Palestine itself, taking some 1,500 Turks prisoner at Rafah.

Murray seemed almost to be following the tracks of Bonaparte in 1799. On that occasion the Turks had surprised the French by holding out at El Arish for eleven days, but they then surrendered the ancient city of Gaza, fifty miles to the north, without a shot being fired. There was no hope of such an easy success now for, though only seven Turkish battalions were garrisoning Gaza, they were supported by Austrian and German artillery, and a squadron of German aircraft patrolled the skies over the city and the coastal plain. Murray could not avoid an attack on Gaza, for he did not have sufficient men or heavy guns to march northwards, leaving the city besieged. He completed his preparations in the last week of March, encouraged by the news from Mesopotamia, where Maude's entry into Baghdad suggested a falling-away of the Turkish will to resist.

But the first battle for Gaza, which began on Monday 26 March 1917, saw victory thrown aside. A sea mist throughout much of the Monday morning delayed the infantry assault on a vital ridge south of the city, but enabled Anzac light cavalry to complete an encircling movement without being spotted by German aircraft. By dusk the ridge was in British hands, the Turks forced back into the town itself, and the Australians and New Zealanders, with support from British yeomanry, were well placed to cut off any relief force that Kress von Kressenstein might bring southwards from headquarters at Beersheba. But poor staff-work failed to co-ordinate the operation; the cavalry commander believed that the attack on the ridge had failed and needed to water his horses. Accordingly, rather than waiting until daybreak on Tuesday, when it would have been possible to enter Gaza from both north and south, the horsemen fell back. This apparent retreat was identified by the holders of the ridge who, believing that the assault was called off, duly abandoned the line they had captured. Tuesday brought clear skies, German reconnaissance planes, a hot sun, shortage of water and a series of abortive attempts to recover what had been lost during the night. Enfilade fire from Turkish, Austrian and German batteries caused heavy casualties. By sunset on Tuesday the survivors of the attack were sheltering in Wadi Ghazze, a dried-up river-bed six miles short of their objective.

Murray's report of these two confused days showed such tact of omission that the War Office in London confidently assumed that one resolute push would clear the city and allow an advance on Jerusalem. Robertson therefore ordered Murray to mount a second assault, which began on 17 April and was still in progress while Lloyd George was at St Jean-de-Maurienne, seeking to strike his bargain with Sonnino. In this second battle the EEF infantry were backed by guns of a French warship, by eight light tanks and, for the first time in the Middle East, by poison gas. But the Turks had strengthened the outer defences of Gaza and were content to watch the tanks get into mechanical difficulties and the gas concentrations dispersed by a strong wind. Surprisingly, Murray held back the cavalry, perhaps conscious of inadequate water supplies. Infantry attacks up the ridge where the Turks were defending the Gaza–Beersheba road met a crossfire as deadly as that on the Chemin des Dames.

By 23 April, when Lloyd George was home in London, it was clear that Murray had failed; there was to be no quick victory in the Holy Land to celebrate in early summer. Nor, indeed, were the prospects brighter on any other Front. At the end of March the Russian

Commander-in-Chief, General Alexiev, let Paris and London know that ill-discipline in his armies ruled out any possible offensive on the Eastern Front or in the Caucasus until midsummer at the earliest. Two days after the Prime Minister's return news came from Salonika that Milne's long-delayed assault on the Bulgarian positions around Lake Doiran had begun, with the expected night attack by the British 26th Division on the Petit Couronné and the Grand Couronné, the hills that served as the enemy's main defence line, with supporting attacks to the east of the Vardar by the 22nd Division and the 60th Division. Austrian howitzers and German naval guns pounded the British trenches, which were illuminated by a concentration of thirty-three searchlights. The night attack failed, with heavy losses among the shire infantry battalions (9th Gloucesters; 11th Worcesters; 7th Royal Berks; 10th Devons). A similar attack a fortnight later achieved more, until the Bulgarians higher up the mountain began another heavy bombardment of an easy target beneath their guns. These two assaults on the Bulgarian defences left over 5,000 men dead or seriously wounded – one quarter of all the British casualties in Macedonia throughout the three years of conflict – and not a single soldier came within two miles of the key central position in the Bulgarian defence line. Greater success came to the British XVI Corps in the mosquito-infested Struma Valley, where the terrain was more familiar – open fields, often marshy but sometimes covered with high crops of corn and maize; here the Bulgarians were pushed back towards the mountains. But on the left of the line, sixty miles to the west of the Doiran battlefield, the weather remained too bad for Sarrail to launch his offensive until 9 May. It then made little headway, and after eleven days of steady bombardment from well sited German and Austro-Hungarian artillery, Sarrail called a halt. In all, there were 14,000 Allied casualties during this belated and brief 'Spring Offensive in the Orient', and only pitiable gains: outposts taken and held in three separate sections of the Front. The experience confirmed the CIGS's repeated doubts over the value of Salonika.

Yet it was to Paris that Britain's leaders looked most anxiously, even if the gravity of the situation in France during this summer of 1917 was never fully recognized in London. On his journey back from St Jean-de-Maurienne in late April, Lloyd George met Nivelle again in Paris. It was obvious that by now the General who had so impressed the War Cabinet four months previously no longer enjoyed the confidence of his political masters; for they would not otherwise have summoned him to the capital, away from a battlefield where he had launched an offensive less than a week ago. For the moment Nivelle retained his command

and fighting continued, both along the Chemin des Dames and in the British sector around Monchy, but within a few days General Pétain, the strongest critic of his strategy, was made Chief of Staff at the Ministry of War; he became Commander-in-Chief on 15 May, when Nivelle was sent to North Africa. By then war-weariness had sapped the morale of many of France's finest regiments. Mutiny spread rapidly, until at the start of June a sober estimate suggested that among fifty-six divisions within a hundred miles of the capital there were only two upon whose loyalty GHQ could absolutely count. Unlike the first disturbances in Russia there was no murder of officers, though news from Petrograd encouraged the disaffected. Neither Haig nor Robertson realized the extent of disaffection. Remarkably, all the mutinies were successfully concealed from German Intelligence, too.

Haig, though aware that 'all was not well' with the French, convinced himself that he could win the war in Flanders before the coming of winter. This illusion was as disastrous as any held by Nivelle; it led, after four and a half months of battle, to the quagmire which had once been Passchendaele village. Pétain knew better. Patiently he stood on the defensive, insisting on a strict postal censorship but improving food supplies, leisure facilities and opportunities for leave among the troops under his command. Never again, he assured them, would they be called upon to throw away their lives in a reckless offensive. The New World and new weapons would come to their aid. 'We must wait for the Americans and the tanks', Pétain told the divisions he visited in the aftermath of mutiny. It was an unheroic programme of inaction but, as the war headed towards a fourth year, a soberly realistic one.

CHAPTER 6

ASSOCIATED POWER

On the last Monday in March 1917 Hans Vandermade, a Dutch resident in New York, dined so well at a restaurant in Asbury Park, New Jersey, that his table talk became loud and injudicious: he criticized the American attitude to the war and 'reviled' the flag of the United States. Thereupon the cook, one Wilhelm Gelman, 'sallied forth from the kitchen in his apron' and, having 'yanked' Vandermade into the street, 'shook' him 'till his teeth rattled and demanded that he doff his hat to the flag' above the door. When 'the Hollander refused' Gelman felled him with a punch in the face. Next morning Vandermade was up in court. He could not remember 'what had occurred', he said, but 'something must have happened to his nose'; he was duly fined five dollars. Gelman, by contrast, became a local hero; his response to a national insult won warm approval from the *New York Tribune*, under the revealing headline, 'German Teaches Patriotism'. On the facing page the *Tribune* reported; 'Enlistment Campaign Goes on Briskly All over City'; 'Half of Army's Recruits Are Of Foreign Birth'.

The two news stories, printed exactly a week before President Woodrow Wilson asked Congress to declare war on Germany, recall both the intensity and the uncertainty of public sentiment in an America which, for two and three-quarter years, had observed events in Europe with an interest which was often highly emotional. Most Americans were English-speaking, and ties of law, political tradition and custom bound them more closely to British institutions than to the ways of other peoples. Sympathy with France ran deeply, too, as from one great republic to another, with historical associations dating back to the era of revolution: the Statue of Liberty – that 'lamp beside the golden door' welcoming 'huddled masses yearning to be free' – had arrived in New York as a gift from the French people to mark the centennial of American independence. But German links were strong in many states, though they sometimes perpetuated a liberal tradition stifled by

Prussian militarism. The twelfth most populous city, Milwaukee in Wisconsin, had been greatly influenced by German immigrants who left their homes after the failure of the 1848 revolutions; similarly Cincinatti in Ohio (thirteenth in population, by the 1910 census) owed its transformation from a town of abattoirs into a manufacturing city largely to German-American enterprise, and still had two German-language newspapers. There were large German communities in Minneapolis, Detroit, Chicago and central Texas as well as isolated pockets down the eastern and western seaboards, even in California. The brewing industry was dominated by Milwaukee families of German origin, an association increasingly 'exposed' by the rapidly growing band of prohibitionists once war fever spread through the larger cities. No doubt Cook Gelman's show of prandial fisticuffs came as a welcome assertion of loyalty to the most scrutinized of 'hyphenated American' communities that spring.

By now many such families were second- or third-generation Americans; but the 1910 census still found 13.3 million US citizens – one in seven of the population – to have been born abroad. Of these newcomers, 2.5 million were from Germany; 1.6 million from Austria–Hungary; 1.3 million from Ireland, often arriving with a grievance against rule from London; and only 1.2 million from England, Scotland and Wales. There were also 1.6 million born in Russia, for the most part strongly hostile to Tsarist autocracy; and 1.3 million Italians who, unlike the Russians, remained in close touch with their kinsfolk in Europe and shared their national aspirations. Yet though some 200,000 'tempest-tost' Italians continued to land in New York each year, during the decade immediately before the outbreak of war the greatest number of immigrants came from the Slav lands of Austria–Hungary or from Russian Poland and the Ukraine; many were Jewish, with no wish to become embroiled once more in the power politics of a continent which rejected them. The wisest approach for the government of such a heterogeneous nation was vigilant neutrality; and this course President Wilson sought to pursue from the first days of the great conflict. Between August and November 1914 he issued no less than ten proclamations of neutrality: American citizens were forbidden to enter into 'the service of any foreign prince or state'.

But as newspaper reports described the effects of invasion on the peoples of Belgium and France, an emotional upsurge of sympathy for Germany's victims enveloped urban America. 'The Sack of Louvain' – the deliberate firing of the Belgian university city of Leuven by German soldiers on 25 August 1914 – deeply shocked a people who knew little of the horrors and hatreds of war (though there were folk in their seventies who could recall Atlanta in flames and Sherman's 'march to the sea'). Leuven and its aftermath led several thousand volunteers to defy the ban on enlistment. Some enrolled in the Canadian Army. More than a hundred joined the French Foreign Legion in the first months of war, several going into action on the Western Front as early as November 1914. During the following winter some wealthy young Americans raised the 'Lafayette Squadron', a force which from April 1916 was attached to the French 'air army'. Over the following twenty months 180 American pilots gained war experience, although fifty-one were killed in action; the squadron claimed 200 German aircraft shot down. At that time there was still only one squadron of primitive aeroplanes in the US Army as a whole.

Letters home from France, often summarized in local newspapers, heightened the prevailing mood of support for the two Western Allies. Some of Woodrow Wilson's political opponents – notably the Nobel Peace Prize winner and ex-President Theodore Roosevelt – were urging military intervention even before German submarine warfare threatened American cargoes and American lives. President Wilson, on the other hand, hoped to achieve a negotiated peace before war enveloped the nation. He sent his closest adviser, the Texan Democrat 'Colonel' Edward M. House, to London, Berlin and Paris on a peace mission in February 1915, at the moment when U-boat warfare intensified. House was still in London on 7 May when the British liner *Lusitania* was torpedoed off the Irish coast, with 128 American passengers among the 1,198 people drowned that day. A mood of anger swept the United States: 'We shall be at war within a month', Colonel House predicted.

Yet even Colonel House, who understood the working of the President's mind as well as anybody, was mistaken. 'There is such a thing as a man being too proud to fight', the President declared. He had cast himself in the role of mediator, bringing about a lasting peace without any protagonist being able to boast of victory, and this task he pursued relentlessly. When Britain imposed a strict blockade, preventing food supplies reaching Germany even in neutral ships, the President protested to London. When, as with Cunard's *Lusitania* and the White Star line's *Arabic*, German U-boats sank passenger vessels without warning, Wilson protested to Berlin even more forcibly, prompting his Secretary of State, the war-loathing idealist William Jennings Bryan, to resign office. The President's firm persistence was backed by Bryan's successor, the international jurist Robert Lansing, and seemed to pay dividends when, on 1 September 1915, Germany announced that the submarine strategic offensive of sinking vessels on sight without warning was at an end.

Throughout his political career Wilson possessed the facility for reconciling a high-principled academic's aloofness towards expediency with convictions which enhanced America's best interests. In 1915–16 he was sure that total victory for either the Central Powers or the Entente allies would result in a humiliating peace, imposing a settlement so fragile that it could scarcely benefit America's developing business and commercial interests. On 6 January 1916 Colonel House was again in London on his way to Paris and Berlin, putting forward the President's idea of a conference to secure a negotiated peace – one to be guaranteed by disarmament and 'a league of nations to secure each nation against aggression and maintain absolute freedom of the seas'. But House's mission was not a success. Although the Kaiser personally was glad that 'peace can be discussed' and 'exceedingly optimistic' over the American attitude, the British and French thought Wilson's approach vague and simplistic. Asquith and Balfour dismissed House's intervention as 'humbug and a manoeuvre of American politics', while the British ambassador in Paris scoffed at this 'sheep-faced but fox-minded gentleman . . . out on an electioneering mission for the President'. The Kaiser told his principal naval aide it was clear that in England House found as much hostility against America as 'against ourselves'. This was wishful thinking; Grey (then still Foreign Secretary) trusted Wilson's emissary and accepted that there might come a time when mediation by a president of the United States would pave the way for a negotiated peace. He did not, however, believe that this time had yet arrived. Nor was he convinced that, when the moment did come, Woodrow Wilson would still be President.

It was inevitable that throughout the year 1916 American policy, and the reaction of the belligerent governments to it, should be influenced by the forthcoming presidential election. The Republican Party, more openly in sympathy with the Entente, selected Charles Evans Hughes, ex-Governor of New York and Supreme Court Justice, as candidate; and all the early skirmishing in the primaries went Hughes's way. Wilson personally was content to fight the campaign on largely domestic issues – two good years of social legislation, including workmen's compensation, farm loans, an eight-hour day for railway workers, and checks on child labour. Ex-Governor Glynn, of New York, who made the keynote speech at the Democratic Party Convention in St Louis on 14 June, found that the warmest cheers greeted his long list of occasions when the President had refused to be provoked out of neutrality. Glynn's peroration set, in carefully measured cadence, the tone of the campaign: 'Sons of America will fight when Reason primes the rifle, when Honour drapes the flag, when Justice breathes a blessing on the standards they uphold'. Significantly, the campaign slogan, 'He Kept Us Out of War', was added to the final draft of the Democratic platform at the last moment. But Wilson affirmed his position as the peace candidate in a speech in New Jersey on 30 September: a Republican victory might mean war, he warned America's voters.

The election became the closest contest for twenty years. Early editions of papers on the eastern seaboard showed Hughes taking such Europe-conscious states as New York and New Jersey. By 10 p.m. on election day itself Hughes had secured 247 electoral college votes, and only needed nineteen more to be certain of victory; the *New York Times* took it for granted that Hughes must win. But throughout the following day returns from the Midwest and the Pacific seaboard backed Wilson. By nightfall it was clear that all depended on the count in California, where there was an enthusiastic German relief fund among expatriates in the largest city, San Francisco. The Democrats won California by a mere 4,000 popular votes. That was enough to ensure Wilson's majority in the electoral college (Wilson 277; Hughes 254). Wilson was indebted to former 'progressives' more concerned with his reform record than with a distant war in Europe, but many German-Americans voted for the Democrats as the lesser of two evils. Whatever the reason, the final returns show that in 1916 three million more American voters backed their high-minded President than in 1912. 'There will be no war', he assured House on the eve of his second term, 'This country does not intend to become involved in war. It would be a crime against civilization for us to go into it.'

Wilson remained a convinced peace-broker. A week before Christmas he declared himself 'the friend of all nations engaged in the present struggle': let the belligerent powers make public their war aims, he asked, so that differences might be settled; the objective of each side was 'virtually the same', he asserted, rather curiously; future peace could be guaranteed through 'the intelligent organisation of the common interest of mankind'. Neither set of belligerents welcomed this initiative. But on 10 January 1917 the Entente did at least list some war aims: restoration of Belgium, Serbia, Montenegro; liberation of Italians, Slavs (*sic*), Romanians, Czecho-Slovaks; 'the liberation of the populations subject to the bloody tyranny of the Turk and the eviction from Europe of the Ottoman Empire'. Such a spirited response was, in a sense, a rebuff. But on 22 January Wilson could still speak out nobly for a 'peace without victors and vanquished' and for a settlement 'without annexations or indemnities', since 'only a peace between equals can last'. As yet the rulers of the darkness of this world had failed to dent his breastplate of righteousness.

But if Wilson sensed the enormity of war he was never at heart a pacifist. As early as April 1914 he had sent a fleet and a landing-force to seize Vera Cruz, the stronghold of Mexican insurgents who had captured and held several US marines; and in July 1915 he ordered the military policing of Haiti, where prolonged anarchy threatened US investments. He was aware, too, that America might be forced into the greater war, which he so deplored. Twelve months before his second election, he accordingly embarked on a precautionary programme of military preparedness. A National Defense Bill was drafted to allow the regular US Army to double in size, eventually reaching a strength of 220,000 men, and there were proposals for the 'citizen soldiers' of the National Guard (70,000 men, enlisted by the forty-eight states) to become integrated within a federal defence system.

It was, however, painfully obvious that the US Army was not ready to fight any European power. Apart from a project for invading Canada – drawn up in 1912–13 as a centennial exercise – offensive plans did not exist; the defence of continental America was entrusted to the US Navy, with bases along the Atlantic seaboard and contingency plans for challenging a German invasion fleet in the Caribbean. The Army's weapons and training were obsolete and the command structure based on a regimental system rather than on divisions. Notions of inter-service co-operation and staff planning were rudimentary. In 1903 a joint Army and Navy Board had been set up, under the presidency of Admiral of the Navy George Dewey, the captor of Manila in 1898; but the main purpose of the Board was to give the Navy an opportunity to tell the Army how it wished its bases defended, principally against the mounting threat from Japan. Also in 1903 the War Department authorized the establishment of a General Staff in Washington, but the Chief of Staff was not permitted to have with him in peacetime more than eighteen officers, for fear that 'militarism' in Washington DC might intimidate the nation's elected Congress. There was an ingrained pacifism among many Americans.

This mood, however, was fast changing, not least as a consequence of the political turmoil which spread across Mexico from 1910 onwards and showed the vulnerability of America's southern border. Early in 1916 a raid on Columbus, New Mexico, by Pancho Villa, the demagogic revolutionary and bandit chief, together with Villa's execution of sixteen

American mineworkers taken from an ambushed train, challenged the US Army to cross the border in pursuit. Twelve thousand American soldiers were assigned to a punitive expedition, commanded by Brigadier General John Pershing, which spent a year gaining field service experience in 'hot pursuit' of the elusive bandit force. That the expedition failed to capture Villa was of little consequence, especially as his bases were destroyed; what mattered was the publicity accorded to the force and to its commander. General Pershing became, almost overnight, a newspaper idol. As the threat of war with Germany intensified early in 1917, the American public believed they had found their own Missouri-reared Kitchener, a general in whom they could place their trust. He did not let them down.

'Black Jack' Pershing was, in fact, born ten years after Kitchener, with whom he had little in common except for a certain masterful taciturnity. When Kitchener began building up the Anglo-Egyptian Army to recover the Sudan, Pershing was pursuing 'native American' Sioux warriors across the plains of North Dakota; and when General Kitchener won Omdurman, Captain Pershing was fighting, with astounding courage, against the Spanish in Cuba. There followed a command against insurgents in the Philippines, a term as observer of Japan's war against Russia in Manchuria, and seven years as military governor of Mindanao. Pershing's wife and young daughters perished in a fire at the Presidio, army headquarters in San Francisco, in August 1915, and this personal tragedy intensified the natural reserve of a personality as austere as that of his President. Pershing's greatest qualities were self-discipline, an obstinate independence, persistence in seeking total fulfilment of any training programme, and skill in organization. Although his father-in-law was a leading Senator, he remained uninterested in politics. He was not, however, lacking in military ambition.

Late on Wednesday 31 January 1917 the State Department was notified that, from the following day, German submarines would sink any merchant vessel within a war zone encompassing the British Isles and the Mediterranean. After several months of resistance, the Kaiser and his Chancellor had given way to pressure by the admirals and the High Command and authorized a policy which they knew would almost certainly bring America into the war against Germany. This risk they were prepared to take, never doubting that unrestricted U-boat warfare would force Britain to sue for peace within five months, long before America could send any forces to Europe; if Britain contemplated withdrawing from the war, her allies would speedily seek terms from

Berlin. As Germany anticipated, the USA responded to the submarine threat by breaking off diplomatic relations on Saturday 3 February.

Already precautions were being taken by the US War Department. The harriers of Pancho Villa had been pulled out of Mexico that week. As early as Monday 5 February, General Pershing himself was welcomed back in Texas. To a group of newspapermen he confided: 'We have broken with Germany. That means we will send an expedition abroad. I'd like to command it.' He hoped they would help him achieve his goal. But events moved more slowly than Pershing envisaged. The press reported several instances of industrial magnates and business tycoons offering their services to the government and there were numerous patriotic demonstrations: 'Ten thousand Navajo Indians are ready to go to war and fight to the death against Germany', declared one telegram from Utah to the White House. Yet the President still stopped short of seeking a declaration of war from the Congress; he was content to warn Germany that if US vessels were sunk and American lives lost, active steps would be taken. On Friday 23 February, British Naval Intelligence handed over to the American ambassador in London a deciphered version of the famous intercepted telegram sent by the German Foreign Minister, Arthur Zimmermann, to the embassy in Washington on 19 January for transmission to Eckhardt, Germany's envoy in Mexico City. In the telegram Zimmermann proposed that, if the USA declared war on Germany, Eckhardt should seek an alliance: he should tell Mexico's President Carranza that, in return for 'generous financial support' from Berlin, the Mexicans would be required to invade the United States; and, as part of the peace settlement, Germany would insist on the cession to Mexico of 'lost territory' in Texas, New Mexico and Arizona. President Carranza was also to seek Japan's adhesion to the alliance, by serving as mediator between Berlin and Tokyo and inducing the Japanese to change sides. The telegram was so improbable that it read like the synopsis of a 'When William Came' scare novel; small wonder that the American press fell into the habit of referring to the whole affair as the Prussian Invasion Plot.

It is, too, hardly surprising that when the German proposals were made public by President Wilson on 1 March, even many Anglophiles thought the telegram must be a forgery. Doubts, however, were soon allayed, for Herr Zimmermann was proud of such ingenious match-making; he considered his enterprise a perfectly legitimate exercise in preparatory diplomacy. On 3 March he summoned a press conference in Berlin. 'Of course Your Excellency will deny this story?', the correspondent of the (anti-British) Hearst newspapers dutifully asked.

'I cannot deny it', snapped Zimmermann, 'It is true.' His admission was in the New York papers before nightfall that Saturday. 'The Mexican revelations have aroused the public more than anything since the outbreak of the war', the British people could read with satisfaction in *The Times* on Monday.

Yet still Wilson seemed to linger, though in reality he was hampered by filibustering in the Senate, led by Robert La Follette of Wisconsin. News from Petrograd that autocracy was overthrown and Russia moving towards a democratic republic removed one objection to siding with the Allies. The loss to U-boats of three American ships, sunk without warning on the same day (Sunday 18 March), hardened feeling in Wilson's Cabinet. On Tuesday there was a unanimous vote in favour of a declaration of war, only the President refusing to commit himself. But on Wednesday morning he summoned Congress for a special session on 2 April. There could no longer be any doubt over his purpose.

The War Department had been considering its options for the previous six weeks, though with an almost Zimmermannesque unreality, it would seem. One early plan opted for a Mediterranean expeditionary force which would rally support from the Greeks for an invasion of Bulgaria – though, in fact, the United States never went to war with either Bulgaria or Turkey. Another plan looked for alliance with the Netherlands: American troops would join the Dutch in falling on the German flank in Belgium, and thus force a decision on the Western Front. Not until America actually entered the war was it accepted that four infantry regiments should be shipped to France as soon as possible, as a vanguard to the divisions that would follow once they were raised, trained and equipped. In weighing up the dangers of provoking America to fight, the German High Command had assessed the military strength of the United States by totting up cavalry brigades and infantry regiments; and on that score the Germans ranked it alongside the Swiss, Danish and Dutch armies. However, in a memorandum drawn up for Ludendorff by a Major Wetzell six months after America entered the war the High Command was belatedly reminded of the extraordinary skill shown by the federalist administration during the Civil War in raising an army of millions within a short time. Germany never understood the potential power of the USA in providing troops, arms and munitions – or in finding the money, which had until recently been the chief contribution of the City of London to sustaining the wars of the righteous.

The US Navy was almost as strong as the Royal Navy and Admiral

William Benson, the chief of naval operations, was better prepared for war than General Hugh Scott, the Army's Chief of Staff. Benson, by no means sympathetic to the British, accepted the need for close co-operation in the Atlantic. While Wilson awaited the special session of Congress, Benson chose the Canadian-born commandant of the Naval War College, Rear-Admiral William Sims, to go to London and establish contact with the Admiralty. Sims and a personal aide, both in civilian clothes and under false names, sailed for Liverpool aboard the American liner *New York* on 31 March. As the *New York* approached the English coast on 9 April she was damaged by a mine laid by the German submarine *UC-65*; the passengers had to take to boats. Sims therefore arrived in London for talks with his old friend Admiral Jellicoe on 10 April with personal knowledge of the dangers that lurked in the grey coastal waters.

Eight days before their meeting, President Wilson delivered his war message to the US Congress. Pacifists tried to besiege the Capitol during that Monday morning; mounted cavalry were called out to guard the route from the White House, and it was not until twenty minutes to nine in the evening that the President sought the joint resolution from the Senate and the House declaring war on Germany. 'We have no selfish ends to serve. We desire no conquest, no dominion', he asserted, speaking sternly and with no rhetorical gestures. 'The world must be made safe for democracy', he declared in a phrase so famous that one forgets its context. Even now, however, he had to wait four days before Congress completed its deliberations. In the Senate, the war resolution was debated for thirteen hours, but when the vote was taken on 5 April only six of the ninety-six Senators opposed entry into the war: three were Democrats (Lane of Oregon; Stone of Missouri; Vardeman of Mississippi); and three Republicans (La Follette of Wisconsin; Gronna of North Dakota; Norris of Nebraska). The House of Representatives backed Wilson by 371 votes to fifty. Among those voting against the war were two convinced pacifists: the only Congresswoman, Jeannette Rankin from Montana, and Charles Lindbergh Snr from Minnesota, whose son was to outstrip him in fame ten years later, with the first solo flight across the Atlantic. In the small hours of 6 April, Good Friday, the resolution was finally carried, and the United States went to war with Germany.

Wilson, more fortunate than Lincoln on an earlier Good Friday, risked a theatre visit in Washington while the resolution was under debate and he received a rapturous reception, with the orchestra striking up 'The Star-Spangled Banner' in his honour. And at Westminster on 4

April MPs cheered when his name was mentioned in the House of
Commons. Yet no other national leader took his country into the war
with so heavy a heart nor with so many restraints imposed upon him by
conscience and conviction. Political leaders in London and Paris did not
realize that Wilson genuinely believed he was waging a separate war
against Germany. In the last days of April Arthur Balfour became the
first British Foreign Secretary to travel to Washington for consultations
with an American administration. He made the journey in the hope of
discovering how much help might be expected from America and how
soon US troops would be plugging gaps on the Western Front.
Portugal, by tradition 'England's oldest ally', had gone to war with
Germany on 9 March 1916 and raised an expeditionary force of 50,000
men who reached France on the day America broke off diplomatic
relations with Germany; the Portuguese had been placed under Haig's
command, and were virtually to lose all national identity by the time
they went into action in Flanders that summer. The British realized that
they would not be able to treat the Americans with such cavalier disdain
as the unfortunate Portuguese; but they assumed that, because of their
common language, the two armies would work closely together, with a
US commander having a similar relationship to Haig as Milne to Sarrail
(though, one hoped, a more felicitous one). The French, too, were
curious over American military plans. They saw no reason for there to
be any links with the BEF; and Marshal Joffre was duly sent out to
Washington to offer practical advice to the US Army Department. Both
the Foreign Secretary and the Marshal found that President Wilson had
no intention of becoming a formal ally. An American Expeditionary
Force would cross to Europe when it was fully trained and properly
equipped and would remain responsible to the President of the United
States in his executive capacity as commander-in-chief. On 7 May
General Pershing found his ambition fulfilled: he was told he would
command American forces in France and should be prepared to cross
the Atlantic 'as soon as possible'. The basic orders handed to him that
day, by War Secretary Newton D. Baker, clearly defined his relationship
with the French and British: 'You are directed to cooperate with the
other countries', Pershing was told, 'but in so doing the underlying idea
must be kept in view that the forces of the United States are a separate
and distinct component of the combined forces, the identity of which
must be preserved'. Pershing fully agreed with the principles behind
that 'underlying idea' and, despite intense pressure in March 1918, over
the following eighteen months sought strictly to fulfil that order.

During his visit to Washington, Balfour found wide differences between the American and Entente approach to peace objectives. The divergence did not take him by surprise, for Wilson's pronouncements over the previous two years showed deep disapproval of multi-nation states and of territorial 'imperialism', and a desire for 'freedom of the seas' which posed as much a challenge to the naval policies of his would-be allies as to the enemy. 'No peace can last, or ought to last, which does not recognise and accept the principle that governments derive all their just powers from the consent of the governed', the President told Congress on 22 January 1917; 'No right anywhere exists to hand peoples about from sovereignty to sovereignty as if they were property'. There was little doubt that Wilson would abhor the commitments of the 'secret treaties' with Russia, Italy and Romania or the provisions of the Sykes–Picot Agreement, and Balfour was reticent in his discussions. When asked what precisely was implied by the term 'a sphere of influence', the US diplomatic documents record that the Foreign Secretary's reply was 'not altogether clear'. After Balfour's return to London, the Lloyd George government (as Dr David French has recently observed) 'embarked upon the delicate task of extracting the greatest possible quantity of manpower and resources from the USA, while making the fewest possible concessions to those parts of Wilson's programme which ran contrary to British interests'.

Pershing sailed from New York for Liverpool in the liner *Baltic* on 29 May – at the height of the French army mutinies – bringing with him to Europe fifty-nine officers, sixty-seven other ranks and thirty-three clerks. He landed safely at Liverpool on 8 June, to learn next day that fifteen other vessels had been sunk around Britain's coasts while he was at sea. On 10 June the General was received in audience at Buckingham Palace by the great-great-grandson of the sovereign against whose rule the American colonists had rebelled. To his embarrassment, General Pershing found that King George V exaggerated the immediate strength of the United States, confusing potential with actuality. Others in London, too, totted up America's manpower and resources and were convinced by what they wished to believe. Much was expected of the United States. It was a sombre Pershing who, on 13 June, stepped ashore in Boulogne. That evening, however, he received a hero's welcome in Paris, when Marshal Joffre and the Minister of War, the Garde Républicaine and thousands of cheering onlookers greeted him at the Gare du Nord. He was designated a saviour of France in anticipation, within five hours of setting foot in the country for the first time.

Long before Pershing's rapturous reception, Admiral Sims had succeeded in coaxing a reluctant Navy Department into giving the British prompt assistance in the crucial war against the U-boats. Six of America's newest destroyers reached Queenstown (now Cobh) in Ireland on 4 May and, working closely with the Royal Navy, were on their first patrol west of Ireland on 8 May, four and a half weeks after the USA entered the war. By the end of June there were twenty-eight US destroyers based at Queenstown. Commander Joseph K. Taussig, who brought the first six destroyers across from Boston, had been told 'to assist naval operations of Entente Powers in every way possible'. The presence of the American warships, and Admiral Sim's support for the convoy system adopted by the British Admiralty in May, helped to cut the losses from submarine attack, which had reached the disastrous level of 860,334 tons in April 1917. But by early July the Navy Department was, like the Army, insisting on putting America's interests first: Sims was reminded by Navy Secretary Daniels that his 'paramount duty' was to ensure that the destroyers protected American troop transports; 'everything is secondary' to assigning escorts to the convoys of the Expeditionary Force, he was told. That, of course, was the right policy in terms of grand strategy. In Berlin the State Secretary responsible for naval affairs, Admiral von Capelle, assured the Reichstag that no sizeable American army could be expected in Europe for another eighteen months, adding, 'And they won't come, either, because our U-boats will sink them!' Arguably, Capelle's boast was based upon the greatest military miscalculation of the century, an error comparable to Hitler's decision to attack the Soviet Union twenty-four years later. For only one troopship was torpedoed – the *Tuscania*, in February 1918 – and, although 210 men were lost on that occasion, 2,187 were picked up by other vessels in the convoy. By the time that Capelle's 'eighteen months' expired more than 1.1 million American troops had crossed safely to Europe; and for Germany the war was lost.

The vanguard of the American Expeditionary Force (AEF) landed at St Nazaire on 26 June, some 14,000 men from four infantry regiments forming the 1st American Division, later called 'The Big Red One'. No one could describe the large contingent as first-rate material; many were recent volunteers who had hardly completed basic initiation, for the War Department retained many regular soldiers to help raise and train the half-million recruits who would be drafted under the new Select Service bill, rushed through Congress in May. Before they were ready to go into the front line the 1st Division would need months of arduous instruction; they would have to discover for themselves the new techniques of trench-digging and trench-raiding, of how to deal with gas attacks, how to use grenades rather than rifles, and how to find shelter from relentless bombardment. From St Nazaire the newcomers were brought by rail to the villages around Dijon and Troyes, a pleasant countryside in which to learn this strange business of war.

But, to bolster morale, it was essential that the Americans should not be hidden away. Was it entirely coincidental that German prisoners of war should have been on the quayside at St Nazaire on the day the 1st Division disembarked? President Poincaré and Prime Minister Ribot wished to exploit to the full the presence of American troops in the European theatre of war. Accordingly it was decided that, to celebrate Independence Day, Pershing and his men would honour the memory of the Marquis de Lafayette, aristocrat champion of the rights of man on both sides of the Atlantic, comrade-in-arms of George Washington during both the grim winter of Valley Forge and the decisive victory at Yorktown. On 4 July a battalion from the 16th Infantry Regiment, chosen as the troops most likely to march smartly in step, paraded through eastern Paris, crossing the Place de la Nation on their way to the small cemetery of Picpus, where Lafayette's tomb is set in earth brought from Maryland, at the Marquis's request. In a brief ceremony, as wreaths were laid at the tomb, General Pershing made a speech suitable for the place and occasion: 'I hope, and I would like to say it, that here on the soil of France and in the school of French heroes, our American soldiers may learn to battle and to vanquish for the liberty of the world'. These were admirable sentiments, but Pershing's speech never hit the headlines. What captured the imagination of the pressmen was a salutation from the division's Quartermaster, Colonel Charles Stanton: 'Lafayette, we are here', the Colonel said. From kindness or respect to the American commander – or from sheer confusion – the reporters seized on Stanton's four words and turned them into the most telling affirmation General Pershing never uttered. 'Lafayette, we are here' became the first legend of America's war.

CHAPTER 7

A BULL AMID THE CAMELS

While Pershing was still in Washington, discussing the composition of the division to be shipped to France, Robertson's staff in London completed an assessment of the military assistance which might be expected from the United States. They decided, like the German High Command, that the Americans could make little impact on the Western Front until the following year. A month later, after the CIGS had met Pershing in London and the Balfour mission arrived home, the General Staff were even more pessimistic: by their reckoning, six American divisions in France by January 1918 seemed likely, and probably only eighteen by the following Christmas. Across the Channel, Pétain had decided that the only way to save France from military and domestic collapse was to remain on the defensive on the Western Front throughout the year and wait for American support, a source of strength in which he placed far more confidence than did the British generals. Lloyd George himself was at first inclined to agree with Pétain, and could never reconcile himself to the Flanders offensive, which Haig had advocated for many months and to which his Cabinet colleagues were attracted. Despite his inconclusive talks with Sonnino at St Jean-de-Maurienne, the Prime Minister continued to press for more support for the Italians. He still had hopes of inducing Emperor Charles to break with the Germans. A successful campaign by Cadorna's thirty-eight divisions on the Isonzo Front might tip the balance in favour of a separate peace.

Cadorna, for his part, had every intention of honouring Italy's undertaking to contribute to the Entente's series of spring offensives as soon as the weather made possible an assault on the Austrian positions. On 12 May 1917, for the tenth time and with no modification in operational plans or tactics, the Italians duly went forward, from the wooded heights around Plave down to Monfalcone and the Gulf of Trieste, some thirty miles to the south. In ten days they suffered

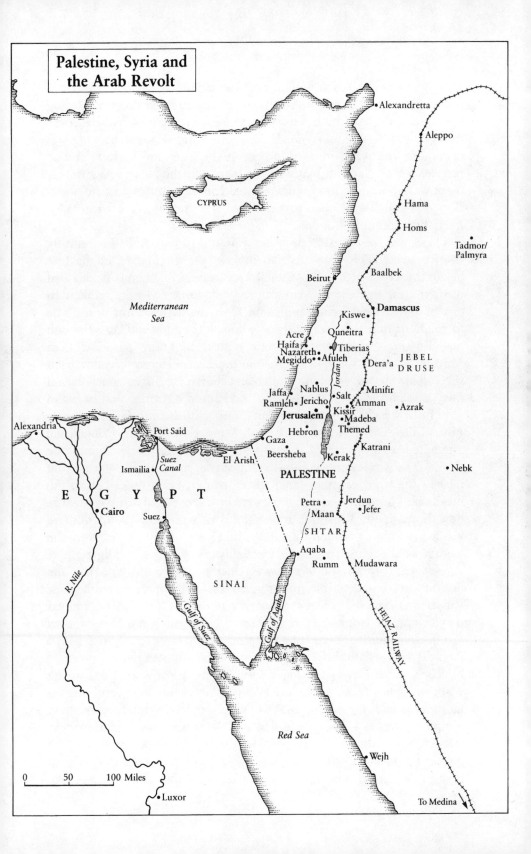

Palestine, Syria and the Arab Revolt

Alexandretta

Aleppo

CYPRUS

Hama

Homs

Tadmor/
Palmyra

*Mediterranean
Sea*

Beirut

Baalbek

Damascus

Kiswe

Acre

Haifa

Nazareth

Megiddo

Afuleh

Tiberias

Quneitra

Dera'a

JEBEL
DRUSE

Jaffa

Ramleh

Nablus

Jericho

Salt

Minifir

Amman

Azrak

Jerusalem

Kissir

Madeba

Hebron

Themed

Alexandria

Port Said

Gaza

Beersheba

Katrani

Ismailia

*Suez
Canal*

El Arish

Kerak

Nebk

E G Y P T

PALESTINE

Cairo

Suez

Petra

Maan

Jerdun

Jefer

SHTAR

Aqaba

Rumm

Mudawara

S I N A I

Gulf of Suez

Gulf of Aqaba

R. Nile

Jordan

HEJAZ RAILWAY

Red Sea

Wejh

0   50   100 Miles

Luxor

To Medina

157,000 casualties and at no point penetrated more than two miles into the Austrian trench system. A subsequent enquiry revealed that, during April's build-up to the offensive, 2,137 Italian soldiers had deserted, though these figures were not known until long after the fighting was over. Cadorna was willing to attack in the Trentino in June and to prepare for an eleventh battle of the Isonzo in the heat of August, for there was no diminution in his personal commitment to press forward. But, after the tenth Isonzo battle, Lloyd George found few backers for his Italian option in London.

There was, of course, one other Entente partner still theoretically able to strike a blow at Austrian morale. On 26 March, in the first uncertain weeks of the Provisional Government, General Alexiev had made it clear that the Russian armies he commanded were unlikely to mount an offensive before midsummer, at the earliest. But in the first fortnight of June there was still some hope in London and Paris that the new Russia – where the energetic radical Kerensky was now War Minister – would spring a surprise in the East. General Brusilov, who succeeded Alexiev as Commander-in-Chief on 4 June, concentrated forty-three divisions of the Seventh and Eleventh Armies along a forty-mile front west of Tarnopol for yet another thrust into Galicia during July, while General Kornilov's Eighth Army, backed by the Romanians, attempted a turning flank movement between the Dniester and the Pruth. The strategy was soundly conceived, and the Eleventh Army pushed the tired Austrian troops back some twenty miles before the inevitable German counter-attacks fatally exposed Russian war-weariness. At that point Brusilov's army simply withered away. Though there was heavy fighting around Riga in the first week of September, from the beginning of August 1917 Russia virtually ceased to be a belligerent.

Even earlier that summer it was clear that Great Britain had the deciding voice in determining the general strategy of the Entente allies. Russia was crippled, the French Army mutinous, the Italians pinned down along the Isonzo and in the Trentino, the American Army not yet an effective fighting force. The initiative should have rested with Lloyd George, but his authority was dented by the support he had given to Nivelle's disastrous plans, and he was forced to bow at times to the wishes of senior colleagues in the War Cabinet, while still promoting, so far as he could, the 'sideshows' which others derided. Three of these peripheral fronts – Italy, Palestine and Mesopotamia – continued to interest him. But the fourth – Salonika – he was prepared, for the moment, to leave to the French, giving them a free hand to deal with royalist Athens. It was under French pressure that King Constantine went into exile on 15 June; and his second-born son, Alexander, was graciously permitted to accede, provided that Venizelos was recognized as Prime Minister of a united Greek kingdom at war with the Central Powers. Some observers in London were shocked by events in Greece: 'The forcible deposition', Hankey wrote in his diary, was a 'horrid breach of faith . . . by the French'; and he noted that Lord Robert Cecil – Minister of Blockade and, as son of the great Lord Salisbury, a Tory peer of influence – was furiously indignant. But Lloyd George thought otherwise, showing positive 'delight at the whole thing', as Hankey wrote disapprovingly. The Prime Minister was relieved that the French had resolved an embarrassing political problem, one made especially awkward in London by King George V's readiness to criticize the 'bullying spirit' shown towards his royal first cousin in Athens by the Entente allies.

Lloyd George was himself politically in a difficult position. For, lacking any power base within the Liberal Party, he was to some extent a Prime Minister on sufferance, dependent on the goodwill of former Tory enemies who could find no natural leader from within their own ranks. He never possessed that firm hold on the supreme shaping of policy enjoyed by Churchill throughout most of the Second World War. To safeguard his position after the Nivelle disaster, he accepted the creation of an advisory War Policy Committee consisting of himself, Lords Milner and Curzon and General Smuts (with Hankey as secretary). The Committee came into being on 11 June 1917. Over the next five weeks it met sixteen times to consider future strategy. But it was never convened in August or during the first three weeks of September, despite successive crises on the Western Front.

There was little doubt that the gravest threat to Britain's survival was still posed by German U-boats, despite the adoption of convoy systems in May and the spread of minefields to limit submarine access to the main shipping lines. Military and naval needs therefore greatly influenced the War Policy Committee's strategic thinking. Curzon, Milner and, after some hesitation, Smuts were all attracted by Haig's proposals for breaking out of the Ypres Salient and heading for the Ostend–Bruges–Zeebrugge triangle of U-boat bases, a plan which also appealed strongly to Admiral Jellicoe, the First Sea Lord. Memoranda from Haig on the value of a step-by-step advance in Flanders held the Committee's attention throughout the first ten days of its existence. Rather oddly, it failed to recommend naval support by attacks on Ostend and Zeebrugge; inter-service co-operation remained as un-familiar a concept as at the Dardanelles.

In later years Haig deluded himself (and others) with claims that he had been asked to mount an offensive by Pétain in order to take pressure off the French. From the diaries of the day it is clear that, on the contrary, he pressed for support from Pétain, with the French taking over a section of the BEF's line in Artois, so that his main force could concentrate in Flanders between the Messines Ridge and the Yser Canal. Personally he remained certain that a German defeat in Belgium would not simply clear the North Sea coast but also convince Berlin that it was essential to end the war. 'He was quite sure that another 6 weeks fighting & the heart of the Bosches would be broken', General Wilson (then chief liaison officer with the French) noted in his diary on 5 June, after dining with Haig.

The War Policy Committee did not agree to the Flanders offensive until 16 July. Even then it insisted that the attack must not degenerate into a drawn-out battle of the Somme type. Two days later the War Cabinet endorsed the Committee's decision, but Lloyd George was reluctant to give firm support to Haig's plans: he feared heavy casualties for limited gains; he foresaw demoralization on the home front if the newspapers carried long casualty lists again in the autumn; and he knew there was little prospect of a surprise breakthrough, for Haig could not attack until late July, and already the enemy seemed certain that Flanders was his chosen arena of battle. If sure of his position as head of the government, Lloyd George should have insisted on vetoing the Flanders offensive. Instead, he hoped for the best of both worlds: Haig to succeed in removing all threat from Germany in the West without distracting the Cabinet from larger objectives and greater material rewards in other continents. For the Prime Minister felt it was essential to secure a commanding position in the Middle East before peace broke out. Within south-west Asia Britain should create an annexe of empire – though not necessarily an empire of annexations.

'For me [Palestine] was the one really interesting part of the war', Lloyd George told the British Zionist leader, Chaim Weizmann. Welsh Nonconformist origins made him more familiar than most British politicians with biblical place names and the appeal of the Holy Land 'to the imagination of the people as a whole'. And there were more tangible attractions, too. Curzon might think Palestine a barren and unrewarding stretch of land compared with the fertile crescent farther north, while others complained (as had Kitchener) that there was no decent harbour anywhere on the Palestinian coast; but to Lloyd George, and such 'servants of empire' as Milner and Leo Amery, Palestine was the first span in a land bridge linking the Mediterranean and the Persian

Gulf – and, in effect, the African sphere of the British Empire with the Indian. Such ambitions were, of course, likely to fan the embers of old disputes with the French. The Prime Minister had never liked the agreements worked out by Sykes, Picot and the Russians in 1916 by which Palestine was to be placed under international control at the end of the war and, with the collapse of Tsardom, he considered all such understandings invalid. The colonialist pressure groups in Paris regarded Lloyd George's extra-European interests with mounting suspicion. When General Murray led the EEF out of Sinai and on to Gaza, the 'Syria lobby' of French Deputies became seriously alarmed. Picot himself, writing from the London embassy, warned the Foreign Minister in Paris, 'London now looks upon our agreements as a dead letter, English troops will enter Syria from the south and disperse our supporters'. The French government had already let their ally know that, if the army in Egypt crossed into Palestine, they would expect a French representative to be attached to Murray's staff. Now, almost inevitably, they selected François Georges-Picot for that post.

To have Picot politicking east of Cairo was most unwelcome for the Foreign Office; someone who knew the Arab world and the French mind would have to keep an eye on him. It was decided that Sir Mark Sykes, who had been assisting Hankey as Political Secretary to the War Cabinet for the past four months, should lead a British political mission to Murray's GHQ. Sykes, who was by no means unsympathetic to the French, was given the delicate task of working alongside his old companion, Picot, so as to preserve what London considered a proper balance of Allied interests. He was summoned to 10 Downing Street on 3 April for instructions from the Prime Minister and Curzon: nothing should be done to worsen relations with France and no pledges given to rebellious Bedouins which might prejudice future British policy, especially in Palestine, where it was probable that the Zionist movement would develop 'under British auspices'. Lloyd George himself favoured the recruitment of specifically Jewish military units, though there was a fear that open encouragement of Jewish dissidents within Ottoman Syria would lead to the persecution of the Jewish minority, with Arabs assisting their Turkish rulers. All in all, Sykes's instructions were curiously cautionary and negative, but the principal objective of government policy was firmly stated, with a clarity which was lacking in other theatres of war: 'The Prime Minister laid stress on the importance, if possible, of securing the addition of Palestine to the British area in the postwar Middle East', the notes of the Downing Street meeting record.

Sykes and Picot travelled out to Egypt together and reached Cairo
three days after Murray's second failure to take Gaza. This rebuff
convinced both Lloyd George and the CIGS that a new commander with
fresh ideas was needed for any advance into Palestine. The Prime
Minister's first choice was General Smuts, the South African Defence
Minister, who made a great impression on his colleagues in the Imperial
War Cabinet during March and stayed on in London. Smuts was
respected as an astute judge of political niceties, and in East Africa he
had recently confirmed his reputation as an imaginative and fast-moving
soldier. After consulting General Botha, South Africa's Prime Minister,
on 28–9 May, Smuts seemed ready to accept the command, provided the
whole enterprise would be treated 'as a first-class campaign in men and
guns'. That was Lloyd George's intention. But when Smuts sought
assurances from Robertson, the CIGS dismissed Palestine as a personal
obsession of the Prime Minister: it was a 'sideshow'; whoever
commanded it could expect no troops or equipment released from the
Western Front. This warning alerted Smuts. He was too shrewd a
politician to be pushed off centre stage. Without support from the War
Office, Smuts would not commit himself to a field command over
unfamiliar divisions in unknown terrain. But for the rest of the war he
retained great interest in Palestine. Though he favoured the Flanders
offensive in 1917, he backed Lloyd George in later disputes with the
generals.

When Smuts refused the offer, Robertson proposed General Sir
Edmund Allenby, commander of the Third Army in France. Allenby's
fine earlier record in command of the BEF cavalry during the retreat
from Mons was now offset by doubts over his handling of the later
stages of the Battle of Arras and apparent misinterpretation of Haig's
orders. Friction between the two generals intensified during May, with
Allenby scarcely concealing his mistrust for Haig's proposed offensive
along the Ypres Salient, where he had commanded an army corps during
the German attacks in the spring of 1915, when gas was first used; he
thought the ground too easily waterlogged for the movement of tanks or
heavy guns. The recall of Murray gave Haig the opportunity to rid
himself of a subordinate as critical of his plans as Pétain of Nivelle's a
few weeks earlier. For Allenby was too good a general to be given a
home command; the bovine aggression that, long before the war, made
him feared and respected as 'The Bull' stamped him as a formidable
adversary in the field. Allenby was summoned back to London on 6
June, knowing that Cairo awaited him.

Soon after his arrival the General accompanied Robertson to 10

Downing Street for a meeting with the Prime Minister, who wished to emphasize the importance he attached to the Palestine theatre of war. Lloyd George, ignoring the hostility of the CIGS to any build-up of forces against Turkey, undertook to ensure that Allenby would receive the men, guns and supplies he needed for a successful offensive, with Jerusalem as his first and principal objective. The capture of the city was to provide 'a Christmas present for the British nation', the Prime Minister emphasized. Allenby had less than a fortnight to discover all that he could about conditions in Palestine. The Middle East was a region new to him. His pre-war military career had been spent in England, Ireland or southern Africa. Unlike many of his brother officers he never soldiered in India or served in Egypt, though with his wife he visited the country briefly six years before the war. His knowledge of the terrain in Palestine came from a good grounding in the Old Testament and from the works of the Scottish Presbyterian minister, Sir George Adam Smith, especially his *Historical Geography of the Holy Land* (1894) and his two more recent volumes on Jerusalem itself. Allenby left London on 21 June, travelled by train across France and down Italy to Brindisi and boarded a cruiser for the forty-hour crossing to Alexandria, where he disembarked on Wednesday 27 June. He assumed command of the EEF at midnight on Thursday.

His main striking force comprised four under-strength infantry divisions and three cavalry divisions in the field, with an additional division promised from Salonika; the 75th Division was in reserve awaiting further battalions from India. Effectively the EEF numbered some 90,000 men, more than twice the size of the Ottoman Eighth Army facing it, although the Turks could call on reserves in Syria. On the Thursday that Allenby reached Cairo there were still 180 days to go before Christmas, and Jerusalem lay little more than seventy miles from advanced field headquarters. With such an advantage in man-power, there seemed no reason why Allenby should not be able to let Lloyd George give the nation 'Jerusalem by Christmas'. But Allenby would not be rushed into premature attack. He went forward to the Front soon after his arrival and was well briefed by Chetwode, the cavalry General whose light horsemen had almost encircled Gaza in March. Chetwode believed the terrain favoured a war of movement rather than a static concentration with the bombardment and infantry assault of trench positions, as in France, Italy and on Gallipoli. Crucial to all planning was the search for water. The Turkish defenders, supported by German and Austro-Hungarian units, were spread over a wide area, though with strong fortified lines around Gaza itself. Inland, the opposing lines were sometimes from five to nine miles apart in many places, eventually trailing off into desert or the barren hills of southern Judaea. If it was possible to find water for the horses and go forward in the autumn, after the summer heat but before the rains of November, Chetwode recommended an enveloping movement to outflank Gaza. Allenby accepted many of Chetwode's proposals; but he wanted strong support from the air. He told the CIGS he needed three squadrons of aircraft and two additional divisions, with full artillery support, for he was concerned over possible counter-attacks once he had broken through to the Judaean Hills. Seven thousand camels, essential for a water convoy system into the desert, could be purchased locally.

Reluctantly Robertson agreed to meet most of Allenby's needs. An Australian air squadron was raised in Egypt, and Allenby was promised some of the most versatile fighter aircraft (Bristol F2Bs) and some De Havilland 4 bombers, but there was little prospect of their arrival until October. Although the CIGS could not spare heavy guns from the Western Front, a brigade of South African field artillery was brought northwards from Durban and some mountain howitzers from India. For the most part, however, Robertson drew heavily on Milne's army in Macedonia. The 60th (London) Division, which had seen heavy fighting around Machukovo in late April, was already outside Salonika awaiting troopships when Allenby took up his command; and the 10th (Irish) Division was pulled back from the Struma sector in mid-August. The Irish, who had arrived in Salonika amid widespread confusion nearly two years before, were also unfortunate in the timing of their departure. For they reached their transit camp from the Struma during the weekend of Salonika's Great Fire: half the city was destroyed in a sixty-hour blaze which started on 18 August in the narrow streets of tinder-dry wooden houses of the upper town and spread down to British headquarters on the waterfront. Yet while shortage of shipping kept the 60th Division waiting three weeks for transport, the 10th Division was shifted more speedily; most were ashore at Alexandria by the beginning of September. These newcomers were, however, so weakened by malaria that they remained encamped between the Nile and the Suez Canal for six weeks before going forward to field headquarters at Rafah. Even more frustrating to Allenby's staff planners was the need for ships to sail in escorted convoys across the Mediterranean, a necessary precaution but a cause of delay in the arrival of stores and equipment. General Allenby had hoped to mount the first attacks before the end of September and thus take full advantage of temperate weather conditions, but he was forced to postpone the projected offensive for another month.

There was, of course, always the danger that the Turks might strike first. For the fall of Baghdad and the tightening British hold on the upper Tigris struck a serious blow at the ambitions of both German and Ottoman expansionists: the invasion route to Persia and India was cut. Their response threatened Maude's hard-won victory. The German High Command created an *Asienkorps* (Asia Corps) which, though comprising no more than three battalions of élite infantry, was well equipped with machine-guns, four squadrons of aircraft, light artillery, cavalry and motorized transport. The Asia Corps was given specialist training at Neuhammer, in the deep forests of Silesia, ready to set off for the Euphrates in the early autumn. At the same time General Falkenhayn, fresh from his successes in Romania, was appointed to command Turkish, German and Austro-Hungarian troops in Army Group F, known to the Turks as the *Yildirim* (Lightning) army. To the satisfaction of Enver – who, as War Minister, remained Turkey's principal neo-imperialist – *Yildirim* was intended to strike directly at Baghdad. Ulimately the army group would invade Persia, which Enver envisaged as forming a future tributary state in a resilient Ottoman Empire.

But before Falkenhayn could assume command, Enver faced opposition from his own generals. On 20 June – the eve of Allenby's departure from London – Enver was in Aleppo whither he had summoned the Turkish commanders in the Caucasus, eastern Anatolia, Syria and Mesopotamia to co-ordinate plans for an offensive down the Euphrates. But Djemal, who was still the Sultan's virtual viceroy and commander in Greater Syria, insisted on reinforcements in order to hold the Gaza–Beersheba line, where he knew he was outnumbered by the British. The Djemal–Enver dispute over the best strategic objective for *Yildirim* continued until Falkenhayn arrived in Syria in early September.

After visiting southern Palestine Falkenhayn decided that the British concentration posed such a threat that it needed to be eliminated before any lightning strike could be made in the East. His concern was not simply with the fate of Jerusalem or of Damascus, but with an eventual Entente advance on Aleppo, the pivotal point of Ottoman strategy. 'An enemy break-through would bring them into Syria and cut off our Baghdad Army from all its communications', wrote Major von Papen, the aide who accompanied Falkenhayn on his tour of inspection. The defences in the southern Judaean Hills were to be strengthened on Falkenhayn's orders, but he knew he could not hope to launch an offensive himself before the end of the year. He seems to have been surprised by the logistical complexities awaiting him; for a vital section of the Baghdad railway (changing at Aleppo for Damascus and cities south) was unlikely to be completed until the summer of the following year, at the earliest. Falkenhayn found he had to leave the train at Karapunar in the Taurus Mountains, transfer into a narrow-gauge improvized railway and then back to a standard-gauge carriage for the journey across the Adana plain. Every soldier, gun, item of food or equipment, can of petrol or bag of fodder destined for the Ottoman armies in Syria, Arabia or on the Euphrates was required to be moved slowly across the Taurus in this way.

Falkenhayn's worries were intensified by a disaster at Haydar Pasha, the railway terminus on the Asian shore of the Bosporus. For on 6 September, two days after Falkenhayn set out by train from Constantinople for Aleppo, Haydar Pasha was wrecked by an explosion in an ammunition train at the sidings outside the station. Locomotives, rolling-stock, stores and munitions were destroyed, and the departure for Syria of the German Asia Corps was delayed. When, in the last days of October, the EEF stood ready to march on Jerusalem, the German advance party was still in Aleppo, 400 miles to the north of the battle front, while the main body of troops and equipment had not yet set out from the ruined station beside the Bosporus.

Even today it is not clear if the explosion at Haydar Pasha was accidental or due to sabotage. London claimed it as the work of 'British agents'. If so, the agents were probably Armenians, a people treated atrociously by the Turkish soldiery over the previous two years, and indeed for at least two decades. But the saboteurs may well have been Jewish, for a group of Palestinian Jews had received instruction in blowing up railways from British engineer officers in Cyprus that summer; two of these agents were landed south of Haifa, with explosives to blow up a section of the railway from the coast to Deraa and ultimately Damascus. At the same time, Arab guerrillas were attacking the Hejaz railway at several points north of Amman and south of Maan.

Few images of war stand out so vividly to later generations as the blowing-up of trains along the pilgrim railway from Damascus to Medina, 750 miles to the south. This campaign of destruction is integral to the 'Lawrence of Arabia' epic, a legend inflated by film and early admirers but scorned by anti-hero detractors. It is an association which distorts both the purpose of the Arab Revolt and its significance for later years. When Allenby took up his command, Lawrence had been attached to Sherif Hussein's army for eight months and the revolt was a year old. As yet it had achieved little. For the fuse of rebellion laid by Kitchener's Cairo 'kindergarten' – Storrs and Clayton especially – failed to ignite. Hussein was supported by Bedouin tribesmen in the Hejaz and by a handful of Arab defectors; there was, however, no sign of the 100,000 warriors who his son, the Emir Feisal, predicted would rally to the Arab cause. The Turks were cleared from Mecca, but continued to hold a fort in neighbouring Taif and their position in the second Holy City, Medina, seemed unassailable. On 13 June 1916 Jidda – the Red Sea port fifty-four miles from Mecca – had been seized by the Arabs, with covering fire from the Royal Navy. Jidda became the principal Allied base, housing a British mission headed originally by Colonel Watson (later by Colonel Stewart Newcombe), and, from late September, a French mission under Colonel Brémond. Naval support allowed the Arabs to take and hold Yenbo and Rabegh further north; but by December 1916 Ottoman counter-attacks, supported by aircraft, had made Feisal's situation so critical that he was forced to ask if General Murray could mount a diversion in Syria. This nadir of the Arab cause was a sorry reversal of roles, for the original strategic purpose of the insurrection had been to pin down Turkish troops, thereby relieving pressure on the EEF as it waited to go forward into Palestine.

Early in 1917 Arab fortunes began to improve. Another joint operation with the Royal Navy led to the capture of Wejh, a small town and anchorage 150 miles north of Yenbo. From Wejh there was a route inland to Wadi Ais, along which Arab forces could mount assaults on the Hejaz railway. Even so there still seemed little possibility of linking the rebellion among the Bedouin of western Arabia with an eventual campaign in Syria. Mutual support could be given only if the British or the Arabs seized Aqaba, the ancient port of Aila, at the northern tip of the eastern gulf leading to the Red Sea (with Suez, 160 miles across the Sinai peninsula, at the northern tip of the western Gulf). Proposals for a naval assault on Aqaba were considered during the summer of 1916, but rejected. It was easy enough to silence Aqaba's protective fort and put a raiding-party ashore; but to consolidate and exploit a landing by an advance northwards was another matter. For the Turks could speedily bring infantry and field guns down from Maan, forty-five miles away, and hold Wadi Ytem, a gorge which runs between the mountains that overlook Aqaba and provide natural parapets as readily defensible as the heights on Gallipoli. A plan, vigorously put forward by Colonel Brémond in January 1917, to land French colonial troops at Aqaba alarmed the British, for although in this instance they thought little of the prospects of success, they had no wish to see their Entente partner looking for a foothold anywhere in the region.

Nor indeed did Emir Feisal who, without knowing the details of the Sykes–Picot Agreement, could see that the French were hostile to any nationalist movement which might spread to Syria. Feisal, whom the British regarded as effective leader of the Arab Army, favoured a succession of combined operations with the Royal Navy which would give his followers outposts along 240 miles of Red Sea coast north of Wejh, until they finally reached Aqaba. This project was strongly opposed by Lawrence, the best informed of Feisal's advisers, who had visited Aqaba in February 1914 while mapping the region for an official survey. Lawrence emphasized the menace the Turks would continue to pose so long as they commanded the mountain ridges above the port. Feisal's proposals were also politically unwelcome to the British authorities. General Clayton – once Kitchener's head of Military Intelligence in Egypt and since February 1916 director of the 'Arab Bureau' at Cairo – was especially hostile: 'We don't want Arabs claiming Akaba after the war', he commented, 'Akaba may be of considerable importance to the future defence scheme of Egypt. It is thus essential that Akaba should remain in British hands after the war.'

Clayton preferred a second proposal put forward by Feisal: the 'Mecca Arabs' (as Clayton called them) might seek support from the desert peoples of the north-east and 'establish a forward base at Tadmor which is only 300 miles from Baghdad'. Such a project would link the Arab insurrection more closely with Maude on the Euphrates than with Allenby. Politically it would steer the Arabs away from the proposed French sphere of influence. But was the plan realistic? The oasis of Tadmor – the historic city of Palmyra – was 130 miles beyond Damascus and some 600 miles from Wejh; could Sherif Hussein of Mecca count on the loyalty of the Bedouin so far north? It seemed doubtful after the frustrations of the past year. Several expert advisers were already in low spirits. Colonel Newcombe had accompanied several Arab raids on the Hejaz railway; he thought little of their discipline under fire or practical achievements. 'I have no hope of doing anything of material damage to the Turk', he reported. At that moment he reckoned that only six people in the forces at his disposal were actively harming the enemy.

On 9 May, four days after Newcombe wrote so despondently, one of his fighting six, Captain Lawrence, set out inland from Wejh with fifty Arabs, much explosive and even more gold sovereigns. In discussion with Emir Feisal and Sheikh Auda abu Tayi (chief of the Howeitat

Bedouins, around Maan) Lawrence had decided to support an enterprise which he believed could transform the Arab Revolt, though would not refer detailed plans back to Cairo for fear of formal disapproval. Auda had convinced him that Aqaba could be captured by troops sweeping down on the port from the north. He therefore proposed to lead his raiders from Wejh to Maan, occupy Wadi Ytem so as to deny its defences to the Turks, and overwhelm the Aqaba garrison from the rear. His party went deep into the desert, taking ten days to reach the Hejaz railway (dynamiting the track as they crossed) and finally established a base at Nebk oasis. While Arab sheiks enlisted recruits at Nebk, Lawrence and a small group of Arab raiders turned north; they kept well to the east of the Jebel Druse and on 9 June reached El Ain Barida, twenty-four miles west of Palmyra-Tadmor, where the desert roads eastwards from Homs and Damascus converged. There Lawrence found local Bedouin prepared to join the revolt. With them he made a surprise attack on the railway fifty miles *north* of Damascus. The damage was slight, but the presence of a raiding-force on the border of Lebanon prompted a rapid redeployment of Turkish troops. Lawrence even had a secret meeting with the pro-Arab Mayor of Damascus, Ali Riza Rikhabi. Then after further reconnaissance around Maan, he rejoined his main force at Nebk, after a journey of some 300 miles. The improvised Arab army was now strong enough to fulfil Auda's plan. It surprised the Turkish outpost in Wadi Ytem, commanding the route down to the Gulf. On 6 July, eight weeks after their camels left Wejh and having ridden across 450 miles of desert, the Arabs swept into Aqaba; they had little difficulty in capturing the fort, whose guns faced seawards. Lawrence at once set out across the Sinai peninsula for Suez, Ismailia and ultimately the Arab Bureau in Cairo. There, on 10 July, he astonished General Clayton with news that Aqaba was in Arab hands.

The event itself, and its coincidental timing, made a deeper impact on the history of the next eighty years than anyone envisaged. The fall of Aqaba attached a seal of accomplishment to Hussein's proclamations: henceforth Hashemite rule was no longer confined to the Arabian peninsula. Without the capture of Aqaba there would have been no Transjordan between the wars and no Hashemite Kingdom of Jordan in the second half of the century. The immediate military effects were also of great consequence. For the Arab victory was the first good news received by Allenby since his arrival in Egypt; he sent for Captain Lawrence on 12 July, a fortnight after becoming Commander-in-Chief. The two men – a bull beside a bantam – were totally different in character, though they shared an interest in natural history and a

common sense of the Crusader past. Allenby, the most intimidating of
inspector generals, was nevertheless sympathetic to young officers with
initiative and courage, however unorthodox. It was not only the capture
of Aqaba that interested him. Lawrence's reconnaissance of the
Damascus–Baalbek–Palmyra triangle opened up possibilities of comparative freedom of movement east of the River Jordan, provided an
army of desert irregulars could be given support from aircraft, armoured
cars, signals units and light artillery. Allenby readily understood the
military value of the Arab attacks on the Hejaz railway, for experience
with the Boers made him acutely aware of the threat posed by sabotage
and guerrilla raids on communications in apparently 'safe' areas.

But Allenby could not risk giving the Arabs free range to conduct a
rebellion of their own. Independent action might be followed by
separate bargains with individual Turkish leaders which could put his
own plans in jeopardy. Arab operations needed to be closely co-
ordinated within the general strategy of his campaign. It was desirable
that the Sherifian forces in the field should continue to be led by Emir
Feisal, but serving as a subordinate commander willing to accept the
plans of GHQ. Lawrence travelled back to Jidda where, on 28–29 July, he
met Sherif Hussein for the first time. He found the Sherif highly
suspicious of French aspirations – for he had given an audience to
Georges-Picot in May, with Sykes in attendance – but he was fully
prepared for his troops to form part of a combined Allied army against
the Turks under British leadership. From early August 1917 Allenby's
operational plans assumed that he could count on Feisal providing a
mobile scouting-force of Arab camelry or horsemen beyond the right
flank of the EEF, capable of striking the enemy well behind the lines.
The Bedouin fighting spirit was always present even if, occasionally, the
British found fulfilment falling short of expectation.

CHAPTER 8

JERUSALEM BEFORE CHRISTMAS

On 29 July 1917, the day on which Sherif Hussein in Jidda confided to Lawrence his suspicions of French policy, Lieutenant Michael Allenby MC was killed by a shell-splinter on the Yser Canal near Nieuport on the eve of the offensive which his father had so strongly deplored earlier that summer. The telegram which broke the terrible news of his only child's death to General Allenby was received in Cairo on 31 July; it was the Tuesday on which the battle in Flanders began in earnest, with nine British and six French divisions moving forward along fifteen miles of the Ypres Salient. No previous attack had been preceded by such a great ten-day bombardment and none so well advertised, for it was impossible to conceal from German aircraft the massing of troops over 300 square miles of featureless Flanders plain, where the only extensive ridge – Passchendaele itself – was held by the enemy as part of a deep defensive system. Although substantial gains were made on the first morning, within twelve hours of the initial assault heavy rain swept across the shell-cratered wasteland, soon flooding fields where there was no surface drainage. For most of the following month the rain continued to fall, giving the Flanders plain two and a half times the average rainfall for August. Tanks, which even on the first day wallowed like stricken whales in the mud, were death traps and by the second week of the offensive eighteen-pounder field guns were almost as useless, having to be pulled clear of the churned-up clay by gun crews exposed to fire from enemy pillboxes. Despite Haig's assurances to the War Policy Committee, the third battle of Ypres became a 'slogging-match' as ghastly as the Somme. On 21 August Haig claimed that, though territorial gains might be reckoned in thousands of yards rather than in miles, the enemy must have lost 100,000 men and were close to final collapse. 'One more hard thrust will crumple up his defences', the commander of the Fifth Army assured his officers. But, before the end of the month, the offensive had claimed the lives of some 74,000 Allied troops and there was no sign of a German collapse.

'Blood and mud, blood and mud – they can think of nothing better', Lloyd George complained of Haig and his senior commanders. By the end of the third week in August he was convinced that, even if Haig did not realize it, his strategy was essentially a variation on the theme of attrition; he would never break through in Flanders. The Prime Minister wished to switch every effort to helping Italy knock Austria–Hungary out of the war. For on 18 August Cadorna began the eleventh battle of the Isonzo, with a night attack by General Capello's Second Army on the Bainsizza plateau which threw the Austrians back five miles along a ten-mile front. Although the Third Army – downriver in the more heavily defended Carso region – made no progress, this was the best news received from Italy in the last twelve months. Reports of Capello's success were so inflated by editors eager for victory headlines that Lloyd George wanted 300 guns sent at once from the Western Front to pound the Austrians and maintain the momentum of the Italian attack. He believed the Emperor Charles was anxious for peace; if Austria–Hungary was faced with defeat and invasion from beyond the Julian Alps an armistice would soon follow.

Lloyd George's reasoning was basically fallacious. For Emperor Charles sought not a *separate* peace, but a *general* peace. Defeat in the field was unlikely to improve the prospects for a negotiated settlement, because a major setback would intensify Austria–Hungary's military dependence on Germany. The Prime Minister also thought that Cadorna would persist with his offensive for several weeks. But the CIGS better understood Italy's position. After visiting Cadorna's GHQ earlier in the year and seeing that the Italian Army was short of heavy guns, Robertson arranged for the despatch of fifty-two batteries of six-inch howitzers; most of them were in action along the Isonzo by August. Now the CIGS refused to be hustled. Lloyd George might have a 'crazy' enthusiasm 'to send the whole Army to Italy' (as Leo Amery noted in his diary for 29 August), but the CIGS remained level-headed. He was annoyed when, on 3 September, Lloyd George summoned Haig across from Flanders to discuss Italy rather than the Ypres Salient. Eventually a compromise was put forward, which Robertson may well have been convinced Cadorna would reject: the Italians were to be told that the BEF would part with such a mass of artillery only if it was certain that 'a really great victory could be won . . . on the Italian front', without aid from British troops. In agreement with the French, one hundred heavy guns were immediately made ready for the railway journey through the Mont Cenis tunnel.

Cadorna could give no such assurance. The eleventh battle of the Isonzo ended as early as 12 September, partly from exhaustion, partly from a fear that German troops released from the Eastern Front would soon arrive in support of their ally and make a thrust southwards, to take the Italians in the rear. The British and French were told that it was unlikely Cadorna could attack again before the end of the year. They were also reminded, somewhat testily, that it was for the government in Rome to decide when and where Italy's armies should take the offensive. The immediate British response was to hold back the guns intended for the Isonzo. The French were far more accommodating.

Meanwhile the Flanders offensive continued, at appalling cost in casualties to attackers and defenders alike. The assault on Passchendaele, which began nineteen days before the Italian advance in Bainsizza, was still in progress eight and a half weeks after a relative quiet returned to the Isonzo. Ironically the wettest August anyone could remember in Flanders gave way to the driest September for many years, with two weeks of almost cloudless sky – until, that is, dusk on 19 September when, as British and Australian troops moved up for a fresh attack on the Menin Road, drizzle began, followed by heavy rain and mist. The next day's fighting was, however, reckoned a success: the Allied line was advanced half a mile; some 3,000 enemy prisoners were taken; the Allies and the Germans each lost about 22,000 men dead or seriously wounded. Haig was satisfied by the day's advance. After similar small gains later in the week Haig wrote in his diary, 'The enemy is tottering'. But within a fortnight new attacks were called off because of more rain and heavy mud. On 10 November Canadians at last entered Passchendaele. The battle took the lives of 62,000 Allied soldiers. Five months later the ridge was once more in German hands.

Publicly Lloyd George continued throughout September to show every confidence in the Flanders offensive; in private he was left 'despondent' by the news from the Salient and the ever-mounting casualty lists. Once again his thoughts turned to ways of 'knocking away the props'. If nothing could be done in Italy or the Balkans, he was still hopeful of Allenby in Palestine. 'Lloyd George . . . rediscussed military policy. He wants to abandon all activity on the Western Front and to concentrate our efforts against Turkey', Hankey noted in his diary for 16 September. But motives for the change were not entirely military. Claims by agents in Switzerland – high-placed armaments dealers – that they were in contact with Enver and Talaat encouraged the Prime

Minister to believe that a substantial bribe from 'moneybags' (an interesting code name for the British government) would secure Ottoman withdrawal from the war. But, as with Italy and Emperor Charles's apparent wish for peace, Lloyd George thought that a good, firm military thump on the 'prop' would encourage the politicians to make up their minds. In this belief the Prime Minister was, yet again, deluding himself; bargains could be struck after long, patient haggling but never under pressure. These highly secret exchanges with Turkish contacts in Switzerland continued intermittently throughout the winter. The generals in the field knew nothing of them.

For the moment, the immediate task was to ensure that Allenby had the troops, guns and aircraft to give the British public the victory which it craved. For though the sight of Americans marching through London lifted spirits in mid-August, morale fell again over the following two months when German bombers from airfields in Belgium took advantage of the 'harvest moon' to attack the capital and towns on the Thames Estuary on ten nights. 'Jerusalem before Christmas', put forward as a desirable objective in June, was by now a necessity. The War Policy Committee was reconvened: the guns promised to Cadorna must be transported immediately across the Mediterranean for Allenby's army, it decided. And two divisions should be prepared to leave the Western Front for Egypt as a general reserve. If Allenby did not need them, they could give support to Maude in Mesopotamia – where, on 28 September, Anglo-Indian troops captured Ramadieh, a river-port on the Euphrates, eighty miles west of Baghdad. But it was Palestine which continued to fascinate the Prime Minister. He told the War Cabinet in this last week of September that it was essential to give Allenby 'overwhelming forces to make sure of one offensive being successful'. Three weeks later he was insisting that 'a Palestine campaign is the only operation to undertake'. Robertson, unsure of his position now that the Flanders offensive was under political attack, caught the mood of the moment and duly let Allenby know on 5 October that the War Cabinet wished Turkey 'eliminated' from the war at a single blow. Allenby was assured that, should he need further support, new British divisions would be sent out to Egypt 'at the rate of one every sixteen days'. Not since June 1915, when Kitchener promised Hamilton at the Dardanelles fresh troops by fast transatlantic liners, had the War Office offered a sideshow such encouragement.

Fortunately the plans of Allenby and his staff were too well advanced to be affected by a gush of latter-day enthusiasm unlikely to survive the next round of London's political infighting. He would, he told the CIGS, welcome another thirteen divisions; but the orders of attack which he prepared were based upon the resources at his disposal. What mattered most to him was the early capture of Beersheba, some twenty-five miles inland, at the foot of the Judaean Hills. The defenders must be taken by surprise, before they could destroy the wells and pumps which made the town a natural base. A fast-moving campaign could only be sustained if there were adequate water supplies for men and beasts. Elaborate preparations were made to overcome this difficulty. Surveys by archaeologists before the war showed that thirteen miles south-west of the town lay the site of the Greek city of Eleusa, where it was assumed there must be water. If hidden wells were found they could be developed by pumping-units from the Royal Engineers. By now the specially constructed pipelines, introduced to the region by General Murray, could bring (cleansed) drinking water from the Nile over 140 miles eastwards to rock basin stores at Shellal; and there the quartermaster responsible for the Imperial Camel Brigade calculated that 2,000 water-container-carrying camels could be loaded with two and a half gallons each in one hour. Troop training conditioned the men 'to the minimum needed to sustain the body', but as an infantryman in the 60th Division wrote, 'there were very many days when even that small quantity did not reach us. An unlucky hit from a shell might wipe out a couple of camels; that meant a reduction of our water ration.'

The most effective way to achieve surprise is to plant false information in advance. Allenby was determined to deceive the enemy over the nature and timing of the initial assault. Here he was unexpectedly helped by the Turks' newly arrived German advisers. 'I had myself fought against Allenby's divisions at Vimy Ridge (sic) and had little doubt that he would employ the methods used in France of preceding his attack by an overwhelming artillery barrage', Major von Papen admitted in his memoirs a third of a century later. The Turks made this useful item of information widely known, as the British discovered by an intercepted signal. British Intelligence took a famous initiative on 10 October when Colonel Richard Meinertzhagen, reconnoitring No Man's Land, deliberately attracted fire from a Turkish patrol; he feigned injury and in making his escape seemed accidentally to drop field glasses and a haversack, which the Turks duly seized. The haversack contained personal letters and money as well as a pocketbook containing notes of staff conferences; these notes showed that Gaza would be Allenby's main objective, with a feint towards Beersheba and a landing from the sea north of the city. The Turks saw no reason to doubt the authenticity of this information. And on the

morning of 27 October the predicted artillery bombardment of Gaza
began. Next day, from a misty sea the guns of seven British and French
warships gave support, the flotilla moving northwards as though
towards an agreed invasion beach. A feint embarkation in motor
launches was made further down the coast and was duly spotted from
distant Turkish observations posts. At headquarters in Huleiwat, some
fourteen miles behind the front line, General Kress von Kressenstein,
now field commander of the Ottoman Eighth Army, assessed these
reports. There was no doubt in his mind that Gaza was Allenby's
immediate objective. 'General Kress . . . relied on Meinertzhagen's
pocket book', a Turkish colonel later complained.

Before daybreak on 30 October the crunch of shells falling on Gaza,
twenty miles away, could be heard by the infantry waiting to go forward
on Turkish positions above two wadis outside Beersheba. Allenby had
concentrated 40,000 men at that point of the line, relying primarily on
the Australian and New Zealand horsemen in the Desert Mounted
Corps who enveloped the town from the east. The thirty-three-year-old
Turkish corps commander, Colonel Ismet – who as Ismet Inönü was
Turkey's President from 1938 to 1950 – soon perceived the seriousness
of the attack and sought reinforcements from Kress, who refused to
believe him. A cavalry charge by the 4th Australian Light Horse,
wielding sharpened bayonets as if they were swords, bore down on the
Turks at full gallop, forcing them in panic to shoot wildly. Some
Australian horsemen maintained the impetus of the charge and broke
through into the town itself. Colonel Ismet was forced to head
northwards on foot, narrowly escaping capture. Beersheba, and its
water wells, were securely in Allenby's hands by nightfall. Gaza held out
for a whole week of bombardment. Finally, almost cut off from the
north by fast-moving horsemen and ruined by gunfire from land and
sea, fortress and town were evacuated on 6 November on Falkenhayn's
personal orders. But not before a German U-boat had surprised the
naval flotilla and sunk a British monitor and the destroyer HMS *Staunch*.

The Germans and Turks remained puzzled by Allenby's intentions.
Now that Gaza had fallen, would he follow Bonaparte's route, up the
coast towards Ramleh, Jaffa and Haifa, or would he strike inland,
following the metalled road through the Judaean Hills to Jerusalem?
Their greatest immediate worry was caused by what a senior German
officer called 'a hostile patrol of camelry about seventy strong' which
approached the town of Hebron, more than halfway between Beersheba
and Jerusalem; it seemed ominous that these 'splendid riding animals,
specially trained by the Bedouin for long-distances' came 'from the

direction of the Dead Sea'. Were they the first signs on the main battlefield of an Arab rising in the east, a threat from beyond the Jordan to the Turkish left flank? It was not quite so; for 'the camelry' comprised Arabian scouts, Sudanese camel-handlers and British Lewis machine-gunners led by Colonel Newcombe, who by his reckoning had found a better way of causing 'material damage to the Turk' than in blowing up the railway to Medina. Newcombe, whose pre-war surveys gave him a passing acquaintance with every wadi north of Aqaba, brought his force rapidly and secretly through dried-up valleys east of Beersheba to attack the metalled road near Hebron. He had hoped to raise rebellion among the Arabs of the region, but found them as yet too cautious to commit themselves. His detachment held out against a hundred German specialist troops and two companies of Turkish infantry for some forty hours and caused a redeployment of Turkish forces so as to guard all approaches from the east. On 2 November Newcombe was taken prisoner. His friend and colleague, Lawrence, was on that day far to the north-east, deep in Syria and hoping to destroy a vital railway viaduct west of Deraa. This raid was betrayed and frustrated, but if – as the reports of Lawrence 'sightings' suggested to the Turks – parties of Feisal's Arabs could move so freely between the River Jordan and the Jebel Druse there seemed good reason for the Ottoman authorities to fear the imminence of a general Arab rising. Troops remained deployed at strategic points in the east throughout the following months.

Briefly it seemed possible that a New Zealand mounted division might reach Newcombe on the road to Hebron before 'the camelry' were overwhelmed. But, in the hills, the Turks rapidly regrouped after losing Beersheba; and German and Austro-Hungarian units fell back in an orderly fashion up the railway route from Gaza to Ramleh and Jerusalem. On 8 November the Worcestershire and Warwickshire Yeomanry battalions in the Desert Mounted Division charged German and Austrian gunners on a ridge near Huj; but, despite the careful preparations, water shortage slowed down the army's general advance. The captured wells were drier than anticipated because of drought earlier in the year. But at least Allenby saw his insistence on the importance of air power vindicated. Bombing raids by some twenty RFC planes destroyed enemy airfields and storage depots. New techniques of machine-gunning retreating columns were perfected. While horses and their riders might be desperate for water, there was no shortage of fuel for the Bristol fighters.

On 15 November Australians entered Ramleh and Lydda. Next morning the New Zealanders were in Jaffa. Links between Jerusalem and the coast were cut. Such rapid gains caused disquiet in the War Cabinet. There was some uneasiness over the movements of the German Asia Corps, as yet uncommitted. Might Allenby prove to be a Townshend rather than a Maude, a general who reached out for the prize so eagerly that it never came within his grasp? These fears were groundless. The Bull had far greater perception than Townshend. Moreover, he was served both at field headquarters and in Cairo by staff officers of considerable breadth of understanding and rare perspicacity, among them – as political liaison officer – Lieutenant-Colonel Wavell. The Mounted Yeomanry persisted with attempts to cut the Nablus road out of Jerusalem, and on 25 November the 75th Division stormed and held the ridge of Nebi Samwil, a height commanding the city from the north. But Allenby was then prepared to pause, take stock, and bring up reserves before making the final assault on Jerusalem.

Perhaps the climate gave him little option. For suddenly, as earlier in the year at Salonika and in Italy and Flanders, the weather turned against the attackers. Now that the 60th Division had moved from Macedonia to Palestine, veterans of the Vardar Blizzard in March found themselves caught by the coming of an exceptionally severe winter to the Judaean Hills. 'We were still wearing thin drill tunics and shorts; torrents of rain soaked us to the skin, and it was bitterly cold in our bivvies at night', wrote Rifleman Bernard Livermore. 'We slogged along through heavy rain and sleet. We had to sleep in wet clothes every night.' Despite fierce Turkish counter-attacks to the north-east of Jerusalem in the last days of November, it was almost inevitable that for a fortnight after the capture of Nebi Samwil there should be a lull in the British offensive.

The respite coincided with a period of intense political concern. On the day Allenby opened his attack on Beersheba the War Cabinet in London accepted proposals first put forward by Balfour, the Foreign Secretary, in July that the British government should make clear its sympathy 'with Jewish Zionist aspirations' and designate Palestine as 'the national home of the Jewish people'. This decision was embodied in the Balfour Declaration, a letter from the Foreign Secretary to Lord Rothschild, the most distinguished member of British Jewry, dated 2 November – coincidentally, the Friday on which a US infantry battalion was in action for the first time on the Western Front, against a Bavarian raiding-party in the French sector at Barthelémont in Lorraine. But the Balfour Declaration was not intended directly to win backing for Britain from Jewish communities in America (most of whom remained indifferent to Zionism), nor was it even necessary to encourage the

Jewish settlers of Palestine, many of whom were already working openly or clandestinely against the Turk. Balfour's original hope was that his declaration would influence the Jewish people of Russia, bolstering their resistance to anti-war sentiment in Petrograd and Moscow. But, rather curiously, publication of the letter in London was held over for seven days, so that it could appear simultaneously in the weekly *Jewish Chronicle* and *The Times* of 9 November. The impact of the Balfour Declaration was thus diminished; for by that Friday, in Petrograd, Red Guards had stormed the Winter Palace and a Bolshevik government, headed by Lenin as Chairman of the Council of People's Commissars, was ready to take Russia out of the war and plunge Europe and Asia into revolution.

Both of these events had immediate consequences for the campaign in Palestine. The Balfour Declaration made it essential for the British authorities to strike a careful balance between Arabs and Jews in the towns and villages occupied by the army. There was already widespread admiration for the courageous work of the Intelligence agency and saboteur group organized by Aaron Aaronsohn, and Jewish persistence had won over to the Zionist cause such earlier doubters as Meinertzhagen and Sykes. But others in the Arab Bureau at Cairo were seriously alarmed. The Declaration, General Clayton warned Sykes at the end of November, 'has made a profound impression on both Christians and Moslems who view with little short of dismay the prospect of seeing Palestine and even eventually Syria in the hands of the Jews, whose superior intelligence and commercial abilities are feared'. Hussein and Feisal's commitments to the Entente cause were thin. There was a danger that the Turks would use the Declaration to discredit the British with the Arab nationalists; and Lenin's revolution provided Ottoman propagandists with supplementary material. For within a fortnight of overthrowing the Provisional Government the Bolsheviks had published and repudiated the text of 'imperialist secret treaties' found in the Foreign Ministry archives. The Sykes–Picot Agreement and other pledges were printed in newspapers in Europe, the USA and across the Middle East during the second half of November. Urgent exchanges between London and Cairo followed these revelations. For if at such a time of brooding crisis and mistrust Turkish rule was about to end at last in Jerusalem, what prospect was there of finding a stable administration to take its place?

'Jerusalem is built as a city that is at unity in itself', Psalm 122 declared; 'Peace be within thy walls and plenteousness within thy palaces'. Sadly, three thousand years of history had long made a

mockery of this ideal. The Jerusalem that awaited Allenby's army was a
Holy City of three great religions suspicious of each other and divided
among themselves. The population remained overwhelmingly Muslim,
though far from sympathetic to the Turks and desperately short of the
essential staples of life. Two waves of locusts had swept through
southern Palestine in 1915, drastically cutting food supplies. A shortage
of manpower caused neglect in the water distribution system and there
were local epidemics of typhus and cholera. Conditions in the city were
made even worse because, on the outbreak of war, Christian and Jewish
families living along the coast were considered likely 'spies'; they were
hurriedly moved inland, swelling the population of Jerusalem itself. The
administration of Djemal, military commander over Syria as a whole,
was harsh in every town, although alone among the Young Turk
generals he was well disposed towards the Armenians who elsewhere in
the Ottoman Empire fell victims to an organized genocide. The Jewish
population had greatly decreased, partly through famine and disease,
but also because of Djemal's systematic policies of deportation. Latin
Christian bishops, priests and pastors, Catholic and Protestant, were
hustled from the city in the third week of November, some to Nazareth
though most to Damascus, 130 miles to the north. But the Armenian
quarter within the walled city was spared further affliction; and the
Armenian bishop there, Mesrop Neshanian, kept a vivid diary of the last
days of Ottoman rule.

General Falkenhayn, who only reached Jerusalem from Damascus on
the evening of 5 November, seems to have contemplated a series of
counter-attacks, to be followed if necessary by a steady defence of the
city; he assumed that Allenby's army would be reluctant to bombard
Jerusalem. He counted on the arrival of the German Asia Corps and
other *Yildirim* detachments to bolster his defences during the winter
weather. But he was soon to realize that shortages of food and water
made siege resistance impossible. On 13 November Enver came to
Jerusalem for consultation; he agreed with Falkenhayn that troops
should be withdrawn rather than face a siege; not yet, however. Next
morning the Turks placed sticks of dynamite in several historic sites.
But such destruction was not in Germany's interests. 'Falkenhayn had
them removed', Bishop Nashanian recorded in his diary. On Monday 19
November, the General decided to quit Jerusalem, moving headquarters
to Nablus, some thirty-two miles to the north. The Turkish corps
commander Ali Fuad was left to defend Jerusalem for as long as possible
with tired Ottoman troops. For a fortnight they held on, as if hoping for
relief. But some measures taken in Ali's name make strange reading.

Thus on 3 December his orders required the remaining dignitaries to provide 'carpets for the soldiers fighting in the trenches'. Bishop Nashanian had less than twenty-four hours to collect a hundred pieces from his Armenians. When next morning his carpets were delivered to police headquarters, 'forty were returned as unsuitable'. The location of the carpet-lined trenches remains unknown; trucks and lorries were heading north throughout that Tuesday.

Detailed directives from the War Office on the future conduct of operations reached Allenby on 21 November. Further guidance from the government followed over the next fortnight, for he was being asked to handle the prickliest political nettle in the world. Military restraints included a ban on the bombardment of Bethlehem or any of the sacred places within Jerusalem revered by Christians or Muslims or Jews. Casualties, civilian as well as military, were to be kept as low as possible. When victory was won there must be no display of triumph in the Holy City; no imperial exclusiveness to annoy Britain's allies; nothing to offend the Islamic susceptibilities of the Arabs, or of 140 million Muslims in the Empire.

To avoid inflicting damage on the sacred sites Allenby's staff again perfected an enveloping movement, as at Gaza. The Anzac forces in the Desert Mounted Corps were on the coastal plain, pursuing the Ottoman Eighth Army towards Haifa. For Jerusalem itself the final orders were issued on 5 December by General Sir Philip Chetwode, commander of the British XX Corps: Londoners of the 60th Division would come from the north-western suburbs beside the Nablus road; the (predominantly Welsh) 53rd Division from the south-west through Bethlehem; the Worcestershire Yeomanry would pass east of the city and turn back along the Jericho road, south of the Mount of Olives. General Chetwode insisted that the XX Corps should be ready to press forward on Saturday 8 December, even though rain and sleet swept down from the hills on the Friday afternoon and evening.

'At midnight heavy fog on Jerusalem, till 7 a.m.', noted Bishop Nashanian next day. Outside the city conditions were far worse. Horses slipped on the treacherous surface, toppling to the side of the roads the field guns they were hauling; camels fell with splayed legs and had to be destroyed; several Egyptian camel drivers died from hypothermia. Long before the main assault began the infantry were cold, wet and weary. Yet in the morning the 60th Division stormed Turkish positions set in rocks above the approach roads. By midday fog and rain obscured the way ahead and in mid-afternoon Chetwode accepted that the main attack on the city would have to be postponed until Sunday. But the constant pressure had proved too intense for the Turks. On Saturday evening, unknown to the attacking force, they evacuated the city. Under cover of another dark and wet night, they sought to join the main body of the Ottoman Seventh Army south of Nablus. Isolated units continued to hold some high points around the city, most menacingly on the Mount of Olives.

Early on Sunday morning, 9 December, the rain ceased. In a valley some three miles north-west of Jerusalem Private Church and Private Andrews, mess-cooks in the Queen's Own, 20th Battalion of the London Regiment, ventured out in search of a freshwater well, or more probably of a hen and her eggs. They lost their way, and at about half past five were astonished to encounter the Mayor of Jerusalem, a Turkish officer with a white flag and a group of some dozen dignitaries who explained in English that they wished to hand over the keys of the city in token of surrender. Such a responsibility the mess-cooks declined. So, some time later, did Sergeants Hurcomb and Sedgwick of another battalion of the London Regiment, whom the Mayor's party approached while they were on outpost duty; by now it was light enough for a group photograph, with the sergeants looking incongruous in regulation shorts as they stood beside the Mayor, in his thick overcoat. Undeterred by these rebuffs, the mayoral party continued to hawk around their offer of surrender, the soldiers they accosted rising steadily in rank; two artillery majors, looking for a site for their batteries to engage the Turkish rearguard, courteously undertook to telephone back the Mayor's offer as soon as possible. Eventually, three and a half hours after meeting the two mess-cooks, the Mayor had some success: a brigade commander in the Royal Field Artillery, Lieutenant-Colonel Bayley, agreed to remain with the white flag party while his companion, Major F. G. Price, telegraphed divisional headquarters the news that Jerusalem had surrendered and that the civic authorities 'were awaiting any General Officer to take over the city'. A brigadier-general now joined the party, with an escort of twelve gunners. The group then rode down to the walls and entered the city through the special gate made in 1898 for the Kaiser's excessively ceremonial visit. The newest captors of Jerusalem 'were greeted by some American ladies, overjoyed at their arrival'. Two companies from the 60th Division and some dragoons from the 53rd Division mounted guard over the gates later that Sunday morning. 'Never have I seen more joyful faces than had those Londoners', Colonel Bayley was to recall some years afterwards.

The War Cabinet, though alert for most eventualities, never envisaged so tame a fall of Jerusalem. Nor indeed did the Comman-

der-in-Chief. On that Sunday Allenby was still in advanced headquarters under canvas at Es Suafir el Gharbiye, on the Gaza railway
across the coastal plain, some thirty miles south-west of Jerusalem, and
slightly nearer to Jaffa. In Allenby's absence, and with no prescribed
instructions from London, it was left to General Chetwode to ensure
that peace reigned within the walls of Jerusalem, at least until a regular
administration could take over the whole region. The inner city was put
out of bounds, though not before some eager sightseers from the two
advanced British divisions had managed to slip through the gates.

General Sir Edmund Allenby made his formal entry at noon on
Wednesday 11 December, conforming closely to his orders from
London or, as one of the participants wrote, 'to the catholic imagination
of Mark Sykes'. For the first time the capture of one of the world's
greatest cities was to be filmed by a camera crew, under War Office
auspices. Guards representing every unit which had fought in the EEF
were drawn up at the Jaffa Gate; twenty Frenchmen of all ranks, and
twenty Italians were also present. Allenby stepped out of his staff car and
walked through the gate, preceded by two junior aides and followed by
his military secretary, Lord Dalmeny, and by Colonel Wavell. Among
sixteen other officers in the procession which made its way from the
Jaffa Gate to the citadel was the head of the Arab Bureau, General
Clayton who, with Allenby's personal approval, had beside him as an
aide the newly promoted Major T. E. Lawrence. Also in the procession
was the egregious Georges-Picot, in uniform as a staff officer attached
to the French military mission, but ready to assume the role of a High
Commissioner determined to emphasize his country's historic traditions in the region. When the procession reached the citadel, a
proclamation was read in seven languages, placing the city under
martial law but pledging protection for shrines and endowments
associated with all three religions. No Allied flags were flown over the
newly captured city. Guards were mounted at each of the Holy Places,
with Indian Muslim troops assigned to the El Aska Mosque. Never,
before or since, has the captor of a city shown such sustained political
tact.

Illness robbed Lloyd George of the satisfaction of announcing
Jerusalem's fall to the Commons, a Christmas present for the nation.
Instead, the news was broken with total lack of theatricality by Bonar
Law, the stoical Leader of the House, who had lost two sons killed in
action that year, the elder in Murray's assault on Gaza in April. As the
Prime Minister had long anticipated, reaction to the news inside and
outside Parliament was enthusiastic. Victories in the Holy Land

captured the public imagination at such a time of year: church bells pealed in victory celebration; newspapers reported *Te Deums* sung by the best choirs; apposite topicality refreshed Advent sermons; well into the New Year the illustrated weekly press carried photographs of the campaign and any prints of the 'bible lands' they could find. By mid-January picture houses and a few theatres were advertising the film of 'General Allenby's Entry into Jerusalem'. The news made splendid propaganda to brighten a winter of dismay.

Yet in a broader sense the Prime Minister was disappointed. The fall of Jerusalem did not precipitate the collapse of the Ottoman Empire, as he had hoped. It did not even serve as a springboard for further victories. Three days after Allenby walked through the Jaffa Gate a telegram to the CIGS made it clear that he thought a winter offensive out of the question: 'Any advance northwards during the next two months can only be made step by step. Owing to badness of roads I must depend on the progress of my railway.' If there was no heavy rain and no flooding, the best of labour corps might, by hard work and sustained effort, lay half a mile of railway track in a single day. Repairs to bridges destroyed by a retreating enemy on existing tracks would take even longer. Damascus was still 130 miles from Jerusalem. And from Damascus it was another 245 miles up to Aleppo, pivotal city of Ottoman communications in the Levant. The prospect of a speedy victory in the Middle East during the coming year began to look remote.

CHAPTER 9

CAPORETTO AND AFTER

The fourth and coldest winter of war hung heavily over Europe's capital cities long before Christmas 1917. In Berlin official optimism at the collapse of Russia was offset by long casualty lists from the Western Front and by everyday frustrations – tight rationing of meat, which sold at artificially inflated prices; bread loaves held together by the addition of swedes and potatoes; soap rationed to one small bar a month; a shortage of warm clothing and footwear, and many other privations. In Vienna, a city swollen with refugees from the war zones, conditions were even worse: 'Many workers seem to be living mainly off sour cucumbers', a parliamentarian with a comfortable home in suburban Grinzing noted in his diary; food riots followed in several towns during January. In Russia Petrograd remained a nominal capital throughout the winter, as a Revolutionary executive, meeting in the former convent school of Smolny, sought to give a people desperately short of fuel and electricity the 'peace and bread' which Lenin had promised them.

In Paris, too, homes were wretchedly cold, for nearly half of France's coalmines were in the northern war zone. Food, however, was more plentiful; even if butchers were required to close their shops two days each week, the only serious deprivation was a lack of coffee beans. A brittle surface frivolity prevailed; but Deputies remained the figures of scorn they had been since the flight to Bordeaux and rumours of treason created a deep mistrust of ministerial office-holders. President Poincaré, aware of the disquiet around him, reluctantly felt he must unleash Georges Clemenceau, the 'unsullied' tiger who had mauled successive governments. 'This devil of a man has every patriot on his side, and if I do not call on him his legendary strength will make any other cabinet weak', Poincaré commented. When on 16 November he appointed the seventy-six-year-old Clemenceau Prime Minister the republic gained, in effect, a neo-Jacobin dictator. One political journal, looking uncertainly ahead, consoled itself with the thought, 'At least he

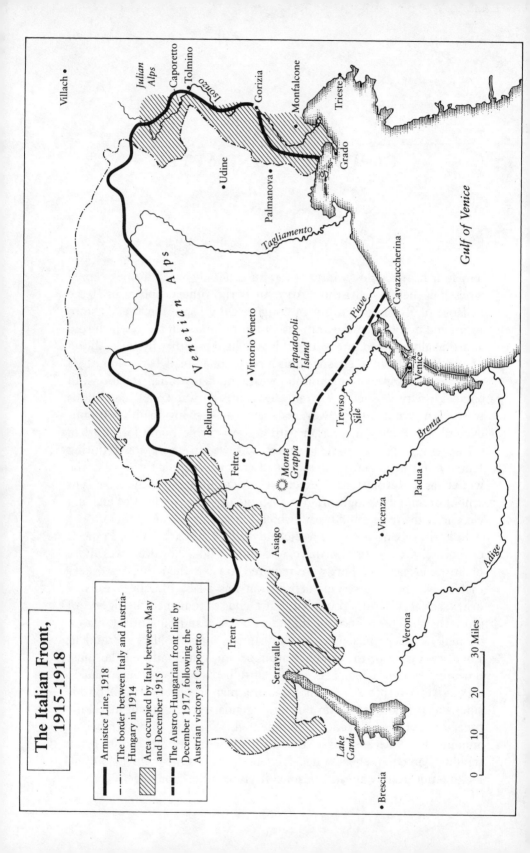

The Italian Front,
1915-1918

Armistice Line, 1918

The border between Italy and Austria-Hungary in 1914

Area occupied by Italy between May and December 1915

The Austro-Hungarian front line by December 1917, following the Austrian victory at Caporetto

Villach

Julian Alps

Caporetto
Tolmino
Gorizia
Monfalcone
Trieste
Grado

Udine

Palmanova

Gulf of Venice

Tagliamento

Cavazuccherina

V e n e t i a n   A l p s

Vittorio Veneto

Papadopoli Island

Piave

Venice

Belluno

Treviso
Sile

Brenta

Feltre

Monte Grappa

Padua

Vicenza

Trent

Asiago

Verona

Adige

Serravalle

Lake Garda

Brescia

0   10   20   30 Miles

will not have M. Clemenceau against him'. Soon, with battles still waging, the feared tiger would become a trusted lion, the '*Père-La-Victoire*'.

Across the Channel political life ran more calmly, with no real challenge to Lloyd George's leadership and as yet no formal rationing (though it was to come – for flour, fats, meat and sugar – on 30 January 1918). In London, where the first incendiary bombs fell on Hallowe'en and three nights of air raids darkened the run-up to Christmas, a stoic perseverance persisted, even if family nerves were occasionally weakened by the scramble to find food and a cumulative burden of more than three years of anxiety. The great need, as surviving letters emphasize, was to 'keep going', to stifle despondency with thoughts of what will happen next spring and summer, once America 'really comes in'. But it proved to be a winter in which, all too often, sudden hopes were speedily dashed.

Even before news came of Allenby's entry into Jerusalem, church bells had rung out on one occasion, the first victory peals of the war. For on 21 November the papers reported that, in France on the previous day, the Third Army achieved the breakthrough on the Western Front which had eluded Haig for so many months. On the chalk downs southwest of Cambrai some 380 tanks led almost a quarter of a million British and Canadian troops forward in a frontal assault on a six-mile sector of the Hindenburg Line. The Germans were taken completely by surprise, as there was no artillery overture to the attack. Tanks penetrated three lines of defence, to a depth of from three to four miles. Many carried bundles of fascines which, dropped over trenches, opened a way for the infantry through the wire entanglements which the machines had crushed. In six hours more ground was won than in four months around Ypres. Some 8,000 Germans were taken prisoner.

But London's victory peals were premature. The first day's successes were greater than Haig or Sir Julian Byng, the Third Army commander, thought possible. No plans were ready to offer guidance on exploiting the initial gains; the infantry could not maintain the momentum of the assault; the tanks, too, ran into difficulties, partly with mechanical failures but also because canals crossing the plain posed problems. The first tank to cross a bridge over the Scheldt Canal brought the structure down, and was left on its side in the water. More than half the tanks were out of action by nightfall, although after the Passchendaele experience, casualties seemed relatively light. Inexplicably, two cavalry divisions waiting to take up the assault on the first day never received the order to go forward, perhaps because enemy artillery fire remained steady and accurate. By the second day a fresh German division, hurried west by rail, held the line of the St Quentin Canal, and General Byng would not risk his horsemen in open country covered by newly arrived machine-gunners. The inevitable German counter-attack came nine days later and the month of November ended with the loss of all the ground gained apart from two ruined villages. If, as Britain's tank enthusiasts believed, Cambrai was a portent of more flexible warfare, it served also as a warning. More than any earlier operation on the Western Front, Cambrai showed the need for co-ordinated, far-sighted planning and for joint training if trench-bound infantry were to fight effectively alongside the new land battleships.

The gravest news that winter came from eastern Europe. The Entente governments had long anticipated that Russia would collapse; but the general public was taken by surprise when, on 15 December 1917, Soviet delegates concluded an armistice with the German High Command. How long would it be before German divisions from the East could bolster the Hindenburg Line, or Ottoman troops from the Caucasus turn southwards and, under German leadership, head for Persia, the Gulf and even India? Yet, despite those ominous newcomers who defended the St Quentin Canal, these fears were much exaggerated. Peace talks between the Bolsheviks and the Central Powers opened at Brest-Litovsk five days before Christmas, with more than 300 military or civilian delegates present – Russian, German, Austrian, Turkish, Bulgarian. The chief Soviet representatives, Joffe and later Trotsky, were skilled debaters who played for time, hoping that the fuse of revolution would fire Berlin and Vienna. In mid-February 1918 OHL grew impatient and broke off the talks. Technically the war resumed; but not for long. A treaty was signed on 3 March 1918 and ratified by the German and Soviet governments at the end of the month. Poland, Lithuania, Latvia, Estonia, Finland, the Ukraine, Bessarabia and the Caucasus were lost to Russia. Never before had a defeated European great power surrendered so much territory.

But throughout the long wrangling at Brest-Litovsk, German, Austro-Hungarian and Turkish divisions remained deployed in the East, ready to occupy and police Russia's lost lands. Moreover, both Ludendorff at OHL and Enver had ambitious dreams of eastward expansion. Armies were kept in the old Russian Empire for so long that, when efforts were made to move them to the West, disaffection spread after fraternization with the Red Guards. At least ten per cent of the soldiery deserted during the train journeys. The Allies, especially the British, were much concerned over the fate of Russia's Baltic Fleet and

Black Sea Fleet. The treaty stipulated that the Baltic warships should remain in Russian hands, but the British feared that the German admirals would seize them. They need not have worried. Admiral von Capelle was so committed to U-boat warfare that he did not want to find crews for the Baltic Fleet. Attempts were made to hand over the Black Sea Fleet to Germany's puppet creation, the independent Ukraine. But the Red Navy sailors preferred to scuttle most vessels, though one Black Sea dreadnought, the *Volya*, flew the German Imperial Naval ensign for a fortnight in Sebastopol harbour. She never put to sea under German command.

The collapse of Russia also meant the withdrawal from the war of Romania. After the fall of Bucharest the Romanian army continued to fight valiantly in Moldavia for eleven months, but the Soviet–German armistice left the Romanians isolated in a remote corner of eastern Europe. On 17 December Romania concluded an armistice with the Central Powers, eventually signing a peace treaty in May 1918. Territorially the Romanians fared better than they had feared. The southern Dobruja became Bulgarian again, the northern Dobruja was jointly administered by Germany, Austria, Turkey and Bulgaria, pending a final settlement; and Hungary gained from a frontier rectification across the border of Transylvania. But the Germans raised no objection to the union of Romania and Bessarabia, for the Central Powers were more concerned with exploiting Romania's natural resources than in any redrawing of frontiers. Germany, however, insisted on complete economic control of the country. The prospect of petroleum from Ploesti and cereals from the Romanian plains travelling westwards across central Europe angered the Entente allies – although the German and Austrian railway systems were so overextended and undermanned that the economic gains from imposing peace on Romania never matched Hindenburg and Ludendorff's expectations.

The defection of Russia and Romania – and, indeed, the formation of the Clemenceau government – was preceded by a disaster on a remote sector of the Italian Front, a lost battle in the mountains which threatened to take another ally out of the war. The coastal plains inland from the north-western shores of the Adriatic up to the escarpment of the Alps are cut by a succession of furiously falling mountain streams which become rivers as they meander across limestone beds to end in broad estuaries of muddy shallows and mere. From classical times they have provided invasion routes into northern Italy from beyond the Alps. The Isonzo in the east is backed by the Tagliamento, the Livenza and the Piave, which cuts in narrow defiles through Cadore and Longarone to linger among the foothills between Belluno and Feltre before cutting an almost straight path south-eastwards to the Adriatic some twenty miles short of Venice. Further west come the Sile, almost a canal linking Venice lagoon with Treviso, and the (strategically important) Brenta and its tributary, the Bacchiglione, running from the Asiago plateau to serve Vicenza and Padua. And some thirty miles west of the Brenta is the Adige, the river of Verona, which in Napoleon's opinion constituted 'the best defensive line in Italy'. It was these routes down from the Trentino to the plains that seemed to Cadorna and the Italian *Comando Supremo* to pose the greatest threat if German troops backed a new Austrian offensive; and defence works were constructed, to cover the Asiago plateau in particular. By Cadorna's reckoning, however, the main arena of battle was still along the lower Isonzo. He was not especially concerned with the upper Isonzo; for if the Germans and Austrians intended to use mountain regiments, it seemed more likely they would deploy them in the Trentino, for a thrust on Vicenza, or even Verona, rather than deploy them in the Julian Alps. A change in the Austro-Hungarian command structure seemed significant; on 1 March 1917 Emperor Charles replaced Field Marshal Conrad von Hötzendorf, the long-serving Chief of the Imperial and Royal General Staff in Vienna, by General Arz von Straussenburg; Conrad was given command of the Tyrol Army Group, with headquarters at Bolzano. When Kaiser Wilhelm dismissed Falkenhayn, the fallen German Chief of Staff was given crucial commands in Romania and the Ottoman Empire. Would Conrad's transference to Bolzano be followed by a forward thrust from the Trentino, over a region which it was known had long interested him?

But Arz had different ideas. He was more concerned with defeating the main Italian army in the field than in taking place names steeped in history. Like Cadorna, he wanted a decision on the Isonzo. His principal objective was to push the line of battle back to the Tagliamento. But not, however, by familiar strokes of strategy and tactics. The 1911 edition of Baedeker's *Austria–Hungary* describes the small town of Karfreit, at the head of the Isonzo valley, some 800 feet above sea level, with a mountain backcloth leading to the Predil Pass in the Julian Alps. Around Karfreit were 'smiling valleys', 'picturesque villages' and 'prettily situated market towns'. Travellers were advised to take the 'twice daily diligence' from Tarvis, the nearest station on the Vienna–Venice railway, thirty-two miles to the north; anyone from Berlin, Dresden or Prague could book through carriages on the Karawanken railway to Trieste, alighting at Tolmein (Tolmino); they must then walk a mile to the village of Santa Lucia whence a carriage would take them to Karfreit, fourteen miles to the north-west ('fine view of the mountains of the upper Val Isonzo'). No great armies had ever brought war to these high Alpine valleys, for Bonaparte took care to avoid them in 1797, moving further eastwards on his advance from Gorizia to Villach. Only a reference to 'fortified defiles' in the vicinity warned Baedeker readers that frontiers drawn in 1866 left much of this magnificent scenery within a sensitive military area. Today the Austrian overgrown village of Karfreit is known as Kobarid and lies within an independent Slovenia; but it is by the Italian name of Caporetto that history remembers the town.

Caporetto, some six miles across the pre-war border, was taken by General Capello's Italian Second Army in 1916 with deceptive ease, though Tolmino to the south remained in Austrian hands and was well fortified. There was little fighting so high up the Isonzo and, in order to concentrate his best troops on low-lying land further downriver, Capello stationed on this sector 'punishment battalions' of munition workers from Turin, who had been called to the colours in August 1917 after a socialist strike. They reached the trenches with little training and no desire to fight the enemy. From late September Italian Intelligence reports indicated that a long-expected Austro-German offensive would soon begin; and from observation of railway movements it seemed likely that the attackers would include some of the best German and Austrian mountain troops. The obvious region in which to deploy such specialists was the Trentino, either in the high peaks above Lake Garda or, more probably, east of the River Adige towards the Asiago plateau and the plain of Vicenza, forty miles west of Venice. Already in May 1916 the Austrians had gained local successes between Trent and Asiago. Sixteen months later the *Comando Supremo* at Padua feared that a determined thrust on this sector, followed by an advance from the Isonzo, would cut off the main Italian armies. By late October three officers from 'subject nationalities' – a Czech, and two Romanians from Hungarian Transylvania – had gone over to the Italians and made it clear to Cadorna's Intelligence officers that an offensive was imminent around Tolmino; but the deserters did not know if there was to be a parallel attack from the Trentino. Cadorna accordingly kept troops in reserve which could be sent, if needed, to the Asiago plateau or to the Carso. From assessing the Intelligence reports he thought the main Austro-German attack would strike at the Duke of Aosta's Third Army in the sector southwards from Tolmino to Gorizia; and he strengthened the Third Army with machine-guns and artillery. In fact, his staff misread all the portents; the Austro-German Fourteenth Army was to pivot at a point some twenty miles *north* of Tolmino, around the town of Caporetto itself.

The commander of the Fourteenth Army, General Otto von Below, was 'a simple, kindly old gentleman of the same type as Hindenburg', noted the chief of the Kaiser's naval office; he had fought with distinction at Tannenberg and served on the Eastern Front before being sent in 1916 to Skopje. His plans owed much to his Chief of Staff, General Krafft von Delminsingen, lately commanding officer of the German Alpine Corps. The immediate objective of the offensive was to dislodge the Italians from the ground they had won in the eleven earlier battles of the Isonzo; they would thus, as Arz intended, be forced back to the Tagliamento, halfway to Venice. Krafft, however, looked much further ahead; he hoped it would be possible to cross the Tagliamento, the Piave and the Adige, driving a broken enemy westwards into the Lombard plain. The Fourteenth Army would then advance along the coast into southern France – thus putting the young Bonaparte's historic Italian campaign into reverse gear. Krafft's ambition was to be on hand when Below triumphantly entered France's second city, Lyons. No doubt this was a fantasy strategy; but it was at least an attempt to carry into western Europe the mobility of movement which had proved so decisive on the Eastern Front.

Below and Krafft's approach plans showed masterly concealment: the movement southwards through Austria in little more than a month of some 2,400 trainloads of men, ordnance and equipment for the four corps of the Fourteenth Army could hardly be kept secret. But the final concentration was well hidden. The twenty-six-year-old Württemberg company commander *Oberleutnant* Erwin Rommel found that his *Alpenkorps* battalion had to march for three days across the mountains from Carinthia, travelling only after dark. They were ordered to conceal themselves from reconnaissance aircraft in daylight hours. As they moved into assault positions they had to avoid Italian searchlights on the mountain heights, with beams that 'made us lie motionless for minutes at a time'. Even so when, after six hours of bombardment, Rommel moved forwards on the morning of 24 October towards a ridge of mountains around Matajur his company took the Italians by surprise. So, too, did other German and Austrian troops making their attacks further south, on a sixteen-mile front.

Along the whole length of the Isonzo the Germans and Austrians massed thirty-five divisions against the Italians' thirty-four; but Below's Fourteenth Army comprised only seven German and three Austro-

Hungarian front-line divisions. The 12th German soon encircled Caporetto town, taking prisoner a major-general and his staff. Before dusk the Germans advanced fifteen miles, capturing 15,000 men and a hundred guns. Deserters had given Cadorna twelve hours' warning of the enemy bombardment and of the likely use of gas. But Cadorna observed heavy rain driven by a strong wind, noted that the barometer was falling, and felt sure the attack would be postponed. The cumulative effect of all these errors – from placing punishment battalions in the front line down to faulty weather forecasting – led to a retreat which, over the next few days, became a rout. Not least among Italy's misfortunes was the plight of the Second Army's highly competent commander General Capello who, after weeks of illness, collapsed on the second day of the battle and was carried off to hospital. During crucial hours his headquarters was thrown into confusion.

The earliest reports of Caporetto reached Paris and London on 26 October. General Foch, the French Chief of the General Staff, had conferred with Cadorna at Vicenza in April and attended a conference in London early in August to consider Italy's military needs; he therefore at once perceived the gravity of the disaster. He immediately ordered two French divisions to be sent to Italy, though it would be a fortnight before they were ready for the front line. A personal appeal for help from Cadorna prompted Foch to alert four more divisions, as well as some heavy artillery units; and on Sunday 28 October Foch himself set out from Paris, crossing into Italy the following night. When he reached the *Comando Supremo* at Treviso on Tuesday morning he was not impressed to find Cadorna asleep in bed and disinclined to begin work before nine o'clock. Foch remained in Italy for the next three critical weeks, strengthening the Italian resolve to stay in the war. He had studied the historic Italian campaigns in some detail, partly because his maternal grandfather, Romain Dupré, had been a junior officer in the *Armée d'Italie*; Citizen Dupré's bravery won him a personal citation from General Bonaparte, and he later fought against the Austrians at Austerlitz. Foch's sympathetic affinity with the Italians in 1917–18 has been overlooked by commentators more concerned with his contribution to victory on the Western Front.

In London the extent of the defeat only became clear after telephone calls from Paris on Saturday 27 October. Hankey broke the news to the Prime Minister at Walton Heath golf links in Surrey, and Lloyd George sent a message to the CIGS to 'have two divisions ready' for Italy. His golfing party, which included Churchill, then completed a round of the course, 'playing appallingly badly', Hankey noted, 'everyone's mind

being preoccupied with the Italian affair'. For Lloyd George the bad
news had a double significance. In his general policy the Italian Front
had long been much more than a sideshow, and he wished it kept in
being. But he was determined to use this latest crisis to support his
advocacy of a Supreme War Council, a body which would co-ordinate
military strategy and bring cohesion to a higher direction of the war.
Such a council was regarded with deep suspicion and hostility by Haig
and by Robertson, though not by General Sir Henry Wilson, who was
rapidly becoming the Prime Minister's closest military confidant. Lloyd
George accordingly welcomed French proposals for an immediate
inter-Allied conference to bolster Italy, where the Sicilian Vittorio
Orlando was hastily forming a new government. An Italian suggestion
that Nervi, near Genoa, might be a suitable place for a conference
was, to the relief of those who spoke English, abandoned in favour of
Rapallo, further down the Ligurian coast. Lloyd George, accompanied by General Smuts, Hankey, Sir Henry Wilson and his private
secretaries, left London at midday on 3 November. In Paris next
morning Lloyd George held a long conversation with General Pershing,
urging him to come to Rapallo for the sake of Allied co-operation. But
Pershing, conscious of President Wilson's insistence on America's
status as an 'associate' rather than an 'ally', felt unable to attend the
conference, even as an observer, without sanction from Washington.
The British team reached Rapallo on the evening of 5 November. There
they met the French and Italian delegations and were joined by Foch
and by Robertson, who had arrived at Treviso a day after his French
colleague.

Rapallo was a curious conference, totally without precedent but with
a significant impact on Allied policy for the remainder of the war. Two
powerful partners, who had induced the host country to enter the
conflict two and a half years previously and who were themselves war-
weary, were now seeking to stave off an Italian collapse by minimizing
the effects of a defeat which everyone could see was culminating in a
breakdown of discipline and order. While they were at Treviso Foch
drafted a memorandum, with which Robertson agreed, emphasizing to
Cadorna that only one of Italy's four armies had suffered a defeat and
urging him to call for resolute defence along the Tagliamento and
Piave. Foch and Robertson then travelled to Padua, where they gave a
similar message to Italy's new Prime Minister – who broke to them the
news that the enemy was already across the Tagliamento. Italy,
however, would fight on, Orlando declared, even if it meant abandoning
the peninsula and crossing to Sicily. 'There is no question of retreating

to Sicily', Foch interposed, 'You must stand on the Piave'. At Rapallo Foch gave the same advice but he found his audience, including the Italian delegates, pessimistic. If the Piave was crossed, the Germans would be in Venice within a couple of days. To lose Venice would deprive the Italian Navy of any base higher up the Adriatic than Brindisi and would thus expose the east coast of the peninsula to raids or bombardment by the powerful Austro-Hungarian fleet. Moreover the first estimates suggested that 200,000 Italians were on their way to prisoner of war camps and that Below's army had captured 2,000 guns. Although Foch had encouraged Cadorna with the reflection that only one of Italy's armies had been defeated, it was now clear that the Duke of Aosta's Third Army, in the lower Isonzo, was also far below strength, having lost half its heavy artillery and a quarter of its field guns. Orlando told the conference that Italy needed fifteen French or British divisions to help hold the Piave line and check Conrad's long-awaited invasion from the Trentino.

Lloyd George insisted that, before any further aid came from the West, Cadorna would have to go; a younger general, less unpopular with the troops, must become Italy's commander-in-chief. At the same time he argued that one of the lessons of Caporetto was the need for a Supreme War Council, with a permanent military staff. For the moment he gained all that he wished, the only dissentient being the CIGS, Robertson. The first meeting of the Supreme War Council was convened in the New Casino Hotel at Rapallo on 7 November. It agreed that the Council members should be the prime ministers of Britain, France and Italy, each of whom would nominate a Permanent Military Representative: the French chose Foch; the British chose Henry Wilson; and the Italians – at Hankey's suggestion – chose Cadorna, as a means of easing him away from the *Comando Supremo*. Headquarters for the Supreme War Council would be at the Trianon Palace in Versailles. Subsequently, in early December, Clemenceau insisted on replacing Foch as France's representative by his faithful 'shadow' and Chief of Staff, General Maxime Weygand; and President Wilson agreed that General Tasker H. Bliss could speak for the Associated Power.

Hankey thought the Supreme War Council could become 'the germ of the real League of Nations'. But the immediate task was to complete the rescue of Italy. The British and French Military Representatives travelled to Peschiera to meet Victor Emmanuel III, who agreed to the removal of Cadorna. But he rejected on dynastic grounds a proposal that the Duke of Aosta, the King's first cousin, should become commander-in-chief; if the Duke failed to stop the invasion, the people's anger would turn against the monarchy. Cadorna was replaced by General Armando Diaz, a Neapolitan eleven years his junior. Diaz was given the help of two deputies: the ex-Minister of War, General Giardini, responsible for broad strategy and liaison with Orlando in Rome; and General Pietro Badoglio (at forty-six the youngest general in the Army), with the taxing task of combating defeatism and restoring morale.

Lloyd George returned to London on 13 November well satisfied with Rapallo. In the Supreme War Council he had created a machine through which he might bypass the limited plans of Haig and Robertson and impose his own general war strategy on the Allies. The Council was established at a time when British political authority was in the ascendancy: Orlando was new to high office; Clemenceau – whom Lloyd George shrewdly sought out for half an hour's private talk on his way through Paris – still stood on the threshold of government; and across the Atlantic Woodrow Wilson remained aloofly oracular. The only immediate threat to Lloyd George's primacy in Allied counsels came from the French General Staff, but the Prime Minister found Foch more biddable than Pétain and with a far wider range of vision than Joffre ever showed earlier in the war. There was a strong feeling in the Commons, and several newspapers, that the growth of the Supreme War Council might put British soldiers on the Western Front under foreign command; Lloyd George stilled these fears with vigorous assertions of his total opposition to the concept of a generalissimo. He would have liked to rid himself of Haig and Robertson by finding for each of them a powerless post of vacuous dignity. But before such blissful elevation could be achieved there were three obstacles to overcome: the hostility of the Tory press and the War Minister, Lord Derby; the difficulty of finding a successor to Haig; and the firm backing Haig invariably received from King George. For the moment, nothing changed. Yet after Rapallo Robertson could see his days as CIGS were numbered and in Henry Wilson he recognized a likely successor.

The total losses suffered by the Italians during the fortnight after Caporetto were even greater than Foch had reported. Before the retreat ended, at the line of the Piave, 40,000 Italian soldiers were dead or gravely wounded and 280,000 taken prisoner. A further 350,000 became stragglers or deserters. Cadorna told the King and Orlando – and, indeed, Foch and Robertson – that the *Comando Supremo* had been betrayed by troops infected with insidious socialist defeatism. He insisted that a creeping Bolshevism could be seen at work in the *Viva Lenin* slogans daubed in red on factory walls across much of northern

Italy. The legend of a Red betrayal was embellished during the fascist era, although in 1917 the discharged wounded sergeant, Benito Mussolini, placed the main responsibility on the failure of the officers to provide effective leadership. The Russian example – though only rarely in a Bolshevik form – had already manifested itself in the mutinies of May and June in France; and from Salonika in late July General Sarrail reported mutinous outbursts in three French regiments, though no shots were fired. But the grievance most common to would-be mutineers in France, Italy and Macedonia was unrelated to the doctrines of Marx or of Lenin: it was an absence of home leave. When the Italian Second Army disintegrated in the last days of October, troops hurrying back from the Front simply continued their flight until they reached the towns and villages they knew.

By mid-November, however, stragglers were reporting back to the military authorities; life back home was impossible, for their families could not draw rations or claim benefits. Some stragglers were intimidated by threats of summary execution, implemented by the more brutal senior commanders: thus General Andrea Graziani had thirty-four alleged deserters shot by his personal guards without the formalities of court martial during the month of November. For loyal soldiers who remained with their units conditions speedily improved: a promise of ten additional days' leave; increased rations; more relaxation permitted during rest periods away from the front line; welfare supervision of soldiers and their families by a new Ministry in Rome, particularly attentive to pensions for the war-bereaved and wounded. Already, in late July 1917, the first élite troops – *Arditi* – had been raised, though only in small numbers. Badoglio encouraged their growth, with smart uniforms, better pay, better conditions, and more leave; and companies of *Arditi* were assigned to each army corps, to serve as exemplars of the ideal soldiery of the future. It was, in many respects, an ominous development. Significantly Mussolini, editing in Milan *Il Popolo d'Italia* (with a British subsidy), could write in December 1917 of the men serving along Italy's battle fronts as 'the aristocracy of tomorrow'.

For the moment, however, they remained the plebeians of the trenches. Six French and five British divisions from the Western Front were on hand to strengthen the resolve of the Italians not to fall back any further, but the fifty-mile line along the Piave – far shorter than the old Isonzo position – was already holding steady before the first troops from France went into battle in the second week of November. To the north of the Piave, Cadorna had prepared a series of small forts around Monte

Grappa, which he envisaged as a key position to halt the advance on
Venice from the Trentino that he had for so long anticipated. Elsewhere
the Italians improvised new defences, often with ingenuity. To help
deflect the attacks on Venice along the shores of the Adriatic two
battalions were raised from officers and ratings at the naval base,
gradually expanding to form the Naval Infantry Regiment, which was
supported by its own artillery. Sandbags stuffed with seaweed protected
the treasure churches of the *Serenissima*. Large tracts of marshland
between the Venice Lagoon and the Piave were flooded, so as to bring
additional protection to the city. Even so, on 16 November a Hungarian
division captured the small coastal resort of Cavazuccherine, within
sight of Torcello's red-brick Romanesque campanile and only sixteen
miles from the heart of Venice.

But Cavazuccherine proved to be the limit of advance along the coast.
Heavy fighting continued north-west of the upper Piave, around Monte
Melette, throughout November and flared up again in mid-December.
Conrad von Hötzendorf, commanding the Tyrol Army Group,
launched determined and costly attacks, using gas bombardments in
the mountains north of Feltre. 'Venice by Christmas' became Conrad's
objective. Leaflets found by the Italians on captured Tyroleans sought
to boost morale with an assurance that good Catholics would hear Mass
in St Mark's Cathedral on the great Feast of the Nativity. Yet, in twelve
centuries of history, no enemy has ever captured Venice by assault. And
so it was to be in 1917. For though Conrad's Army Group pushed
relentlessly towards the edge of the Alpine escarpment, the Italian
defences held firm. On 21 December, with eight inches of snow in the
mountains and constant sleet in the valleys, the fighting died away; and
for several months only stray bursts of gunfire broke the winter
standstill amid the mudbanks and reeds of the lagoon's swollen waters.

CHAPTER 10

PLANS FOR PEACE AND FOR WAR

A week before Christmas in 1917 a British traveller with a passport in the name of Ashworth arrived at the Hôtel de Russie in Geneva to claim a room booked, a shade unimaginatively, for a 'Mr Smith'. To any guests who had recently been in Rapallo Ashworth/Smith may have looked uncommonly like the khaki-clad General, Jan Smuts, seen six weeks ago in the New Casino Hotel. But it is unlikely they would have known the identity of the aristocratic visitor who arrived in Geneva that same Monday evening from Vienna to meet him. Count Albert von Mensdorff-Pouilly, Francis Joseph's ambassador in London for ten years before the war, came with instructions from Czernin, the Austro-Hungarian Foreign Minister, to discover if the British envoy had proposals for a negotiated peace with the Central Powers. Smuts, a member of the War Cabinet, had gone to Geneva after telegrams to the Foreign Office from the Minister in Berne, Sir Horace Rumbold, made it clear that Czernin wished to contact a senior British official. There remained, however, some basic confusion, for during the subsequent talks each protagonist believed it was the other who wished them to take place; and the British, who always shrouded such meetings in secrecy, never realized that Czernin had let his German ally know of Mensdorff's mission.

For eight months hopes for a negotiated peace had flickered faintly in Berne. It was through Switzerland that Prince Sixte of Bourbon-Parma, an officer in the Belgian Army, travelled to Laxenburg for meetings with his brother-in-law, Emperor Charles. Twice in the spring Prince Sixte had brought messages from Vienna to Paris and London; on 23 May he was even received by King George V at Buckingham Palace. But this strange flurry of dynastic diplomacy achieved nothing, partly because the Italian demands were more than Vienna would concede, and Sixte's activities left Lloyd George with the unwarranted conviction that Charles was putting out feelers for a separate peace, whereas in reality the young Emperor saw himself as a beneficent mediator promoting a general settlement. In the same week of April that Sixte was in Paris with Charles's first letter, Count Mensdorff paid a private visit to Geneva. While there, he called on an old friend, Mrs Victoria Barton, widow of a British consul-general and a granddaughter of Sir Robert Peel. Mensdorff made it clear to Mrs Barton that he thought the war in the West a stalemate and saw no reason why the conflict should continue; he would, he indicated, welcome a chance to talk to the British Minister. Mrs Barton told Rumbold of Mensdorff's visit and the Minister sent a report to London which was circulated to the War Cabinet. It was natural that when Mensdorff's name was mentioned again in November, Lloyd George should link the new initiative with the exchanges Sixte had encouraged in the spring.

By December, despite the Austro-German victory at Caporetto, the British were convinced that Austria–Hungary was close to disintegration. In the last week of November Count Mihály Károlyi, one of Hungary's richest landed magnates and leader of the radical Independence Party in Budapest, had come to Berne seeking to make contact with Entente representatives in order, as he said, 'to bring about, in conjunction with the Western Powers, action against Germany'. Characteristically, the Count's immediate programme was imprecise; Károlyi seems to have hoped for joint Magyar, Czech and southern Slav collaboration within the Dual Monarchy so as to neutralize the German-Austrian hold on affairs and introduce democratic government. But, however vague Károlyi's plans might be, the British were impressed by his message. He was known to have told Emperor-King Charles earlier in the year that continuation of the war would leave Austria–Hungary dependent on Germany and unable to counter Entente backing for Serbia and Romania.

Smuts prepared a memorandum in which he outlined the proposals he intended to put to Mensdorff; he submitted it to the Foreign Office three days before setting out for Geneva (and after the report of Károlyi's views reached London). With Russia gone, a stable Europe would need a reconstituted Habsburg Monarchy to act as a counterweight to Germany. Austria–Hungary must shake off German domination. Once that was achieved he would recommend enlarging the Monarchy so as to contain an autonomous Poland and an autonomous southern Slav state, which might include Serbia. Smuts put nothing on paper about the future of the western Slavs (Czechs and Slovaks), nor about the likely frontier with Italy in the mountains and the war-ravaged lands west of Trieste.

Mensdorff and Smuts met at a villa on the outskirts of Geneva three times on 18 December and briefly on 19 December. Mensdorff wished to clarify the statement on the Entente's war aims sent to President Wilson on 10 January 1917 which, in championing the principle of nationality, seemed to threaten the existence of both the Habsburg and Ottoman Empires. Smuts denied that the statement indicated a wish to break up Austria–Hungary; 'our object', he explained, is 'to assist Austria to give the greatest Freedom and autonomy to her subject nationalities'. He assured the ex-ambassador of the continued friendly feelings of the British people towards the Habsburg Monarchy; and he promised help in economic reconstruction once Austria was 'emancipated from German domination'. At this point, however, Mensdorff fell back on his instructions from Czernin: there could be no break with Germany 'so long as the war lasted', he insisted; was Britain prepared to discuss peace terms with Germany? Smuts made it clear that London was in no mood to temporize with Berlin. Mensdorff tried again, regretting the demise of Europe and the passing of economic and financial power to America and Japan. 'Why', he wished to know, 'were we going on fighting? . . . If another year of this destruction had to pass, the position of Europe and civilisation, already so pitiable, would be beyond repair.' It was a powerful and percipient plea; and Smuts duly reported Mensdorff's exact words to the Cabinet. But he could take no action. The British, he sought to explain before he left Geneva, were acutely conscious of 'the dangers to the future political system of Europe, if Germany survived as a sort of military dictator'. The door remained ajar for further meetings in the New Year.

Smuts was accompanied to Switzerland by Philip Kerr, a leading member of Lloyd George's secretariat, who became better known in the 1930s as Lord Lothian, Liberal statesman and ambassador in Washington. While Smuts was with Mensdorff Kerr went on from Geneva to Berne, where Turkish dissidents had frequently contacted Rumbold. Kerr's remarks to Turkish emissaries closely followed Smuts's comments to Mensdorff. The Turks, too, were assured of financial and economic aid if they broke with Germany and made an immediate peace: they would be allowed to keep Constantinople, would lose both Arabia and Armenia and would have to pull back from Mesopotamia, Syria and Palestine, though these provinces might be left under nominal Ottoman suzerainty but with no executive power in Turkish hands. Kerr's contacts lacked the standing of Mensdorff or the backing of any important figure; and the obvious gains to Turkey from the collapse of Russia meant that nobody in Constantinople was especially interested in what the West proposed to dispose. Kerr's remarks were only useful for filing away.

Once back in London the two envoys emphasized that, from their experience of these talks, 'it would be very useful if the Allies would restate their war aims'. That possibility had been under consideration in the Entente capitals for the past month, and in Washington for even longer; the exchanges with President Wilson before the USA entered the war had not gone far enough; and the disappearance of Tsarist Russia posed new questions over future boundaries in Asia and in Europe. What was to happen to Russia's assigned spheres of influence within the Ottoman Empire, for example? And, most pressingly, what of Poland? A fortnight after the Tsar's fall, the Russian Provisional Government issued a proclamation which 'removed in the name of the highest principle of equity, the chains which weighed down the Polish nation'. A Polish National Council, headed by the democrat Roman Dmowski, was duly established in Paris, and a Polish Corps recruited by the French to fight beside the Allies. But the outstanding national leader, General Josef Pilsudski, had commanded a Polish Corps in the Austro-Hungarian Army since the first week of war and was encouraged by the Austrians to set up a Supreme National Committee of Poland in Cracow. Did Dmowski speak for the real Poland? Or Pilsudski? Or the patriot pianist Paderewski, ever active in America? There was urgent need for guidance from the Western capitals on who would ensure that the world was 'made safe for democracy'; and when.

Over such matters the Bolsheviks set the pace. Lenin's 'Decree of Peace' of 8 November called on 'all warring peoples' to 'seek a just and democratic peace' on the basis of 'no annexations, no indemnities, and the right of self-determination'. The Decree was soon followed by the texts of the secret treaties, published by Trotsky to discredit the bourgeois governments and their imperialist ambitions. This exposure of recent bargains discredited 'secret diplomacy', although censorship of the press limited the information available to the general public in the Entente countries. But the word 'peace' was never a Bolshevik copyright. In Great Britain democratic socialists, Gladstonian liberals and many pragmatic Tories, too, wished to find acceptable ways of ending the fighting. The Labour Party set up its own Advisory Committee on International Questions, almost a Foreign-Office-in-waiting, which was to produce a statement on war aims before the end of the year. On 29 November the *Daily Telegraph* published a letter from Lord Lansdowne (rejected by *The Times*) in which the former Unionist Foreign Secretary argued in favour of a negotiated peace: a programme of war aims should be formulated, although he did not wish them too precise and recommended 'a suspension of judgment' on the rearrangement of national boundaries across the map of Europe; the warring nations should not have to wait for peace until Prussian militarism made way for democracy. This was a direct challenge to the British government's insistence that peace with Germany could only be achieved when Berlin was prepared to satisfy such fundamental objectives as the restoration of Belgian independence and the return 'of provinces formerly torn from the allies by force or against the wishes of their inhabitants'.

On the Thursday the 'Peace Letter' was published Lloyd George, Balfour, Milner and Hankey were in Paris, preparing for the first full-scale session of the Supreme War Council to be held at Versailles on Saturday. They were hardly surprised by Lansdowne's views, for he had sent a not dissimilar private memorandum to the Cabinet twelve months previously. But in Paris they could see for themselves the consternation the letter aroused among their French and Italian allies. Assurances were given that there would be no lessening in Britain's commitment to a Continental land war. Although over the following days most discussions concerned military strategy, Lloyd George – and, to a lesser extent, Clemenceau – recognized the need for agreement on war aims. At a meeting in the Quai d'Orsay (also attended by Sonnino, the Italian Foreign Minister, and by Colonel House) hurried attempts were made to produce a joint statement. Lloyd George drafted three versions; Sonnino and House one each; the French, well versed in the subtleties of diplomacy by conference, abstained. For it was, of course, impossible speedily to reconcile the interests of the countries. In private talks, however, some progress was made. Lloyd George found Clemenceau so totally committed to expelling the German army from France that he had no interest in building up a French colonial empire in the Levant. If France acquired a protectorate over Syria, so much the better because it would satisfy some of 'the reactionaries' in Paris, he said, but personally he did not attach importance to the issue; Lloyd George could have a free hand to propose any terms which he thought acceptable on the Turks. And the Italian Finance Minister, Francesco Nitti, told Lloyd George two days later that if, owing to the recent 'unfortunate changes in the military situation', it proved impossible to acquire the Trentino and Trieste, the Italian people would be satisfied with guarantees of proper protection for their kinsfolk living in those regions under Austrian rule.

In 1914 a proclamation of war aims could appear boldly comprehensive while, in practical terms, remaining mercifully imprecise. 'We shall not sheathe the sword . . . until the rights of the smaller nationalities of Europe are placed on an unassailable foundation', Asquith had declared at the Guildhall in London on 9 November 1914. But such simplicity of purpose could not last. Within ten weeks of his speech Asquith was plunged deeply into unfamiliar ground when he invited to lunch Frano Supilo, a Dalmatian journalist who was the chief promoter of the Yugoslav ideal. Supilo explained 'at great length' – with the aid of maps – 'the ambitions and hopes' of two of the least known smaller nationalities, 'the Croats and Slovenes'. Over the next two years the activities of exiles like Supilo (who was to die in September 1917) and his chief colleague, Ante Trumbić, proliferated. By August 1916, when Asquith invited the Foreign Office to prepare a memorandum on a possible basis for a peace settlement, notice had to be taken not only of Trumbić's 'Yugoslav Committee' but also of Czech émigrés like Thomas Masaryk in London and Dr Beneš in Paris, Dmowski's Poles, and the obligations given to the Italian and Romanian governments. By the end of the year the fate of the Ottoman subject peoples, too, came high on any agenda – Arabs and especially Armenians, for news of the genocide inflicted on this long-suffering Christian nation in 1915 by Turkish soldiery aroused deep passions on both sides of the Atlantic.

It was the Versailles meeting of the Supreme War Council which first clearly showed the full breadth of Allied commitments. Spokesmen for every cause seemed present. Amery's diary for 27 November 1917 says there were 109 people bound for the conference on the 8.25 boat train from Charing Cross that morning, but as he includes 'half the US Navy' and 'half the Jap Army and diplomatic service' it is, perhaps, safer to settle for Hankey's restrained 'enormous crowd . . . some 60 persons in all'. Among them were (as Amery noted), 'Venizelos and Co.'; and four days later the Greek Prime Minister took the opportunity to remind the Entente leaders that King Alexander's Greece was now an Allied Power, capable of raising another twelve divisions for a Balkan campaign 'if they can be fed'. Serb spokesmen were also at Versailles, to emphasize the importance of the Pact of Corfu of July 1917, by which Trumbić committed the Yugoslav Committee to support a post-war Kingdom of the Serbs, Croats and Slovenes. Stefanik, the Slovak aviator, was present with Dr Beneš to press, in vain, for formal recognition of Czecho-Slovak nationalism. Tempers at times became strained. Thus when Colonel House backed a proposal by the new French Foreign Minister, Stéphane Pichon, for recognition of Polish independence, Lloyd George complained that the moment was 'unpropitious' for assuming new obligations in eastern Europe. He could, he said, 'understand the United States asking for some such action' because they had a large Polish population, but he asked 'Was the United States prepared to send an army to Poland?' Great skill and tact would be needed in preparing a programme on war aims to satisfy such varied interests.

Pichon made the first attempt, speaking for France on 27 December, emphasizing the need to recover Alsace-Lorraine, showing sympathy with the Czechs and giving positive support for Poland. 'We do not separate her case from ours', he declared, 'We want her one, independent, indivisible.' In London next day a special meeting of the Labour Party and the Trade Union Congress approved the Advisory Committee's definitive statement on war aims: a sweeping away of old diplomacy; reconciliation with a democratic Germany; the establishment of a League of Nations; German withdrawal from Belgium, with compensation; the peoples of Alsace-Lorraine and contested regions in the Balkans to have the right to settle their own future; Italy to receive the parts of Austria in which Italians were in a majority; all colonies in Africa and Asia, including British and French possessions, to be placed under international trusteeship so as to prevent imperialist exploitation. On the previous night, in a propaganda exercise designed to cause embarrassment to their enemies, the Germans announced they had accepted a request from Trotsky for an adjournment of the Brest-Litovsk peace talks in order to give the Entente and the Americans an opportunity to participate in them. London, Paris, Rome and Washington were given until 4 January to decide if they wished to negotiate a general peace.

They did not. But something decisive had to be said speedily to calm the mounting unease of those who thought the war would never end. The War Cabinet discussed the British programme for peace at a series of sessions before and after Christmas. As the House of Commons was in recess Lloyd George decided to announce the Government's war aims in a speech on 5 January to some of his most persistent critics, trade unionists meeting at Caxton Hall, Westminster, across the road from Parliament. He spoke with authoritative clarity of purpose, without the flights of imaginative rhetoric which came so readily to him. Britain was fighting a war of self-defence on behalf of the sanctity of treaties, he emphasized. 'The settlement of the new Europe must be based on such grounds of reason and justice as will give some promise of stability. Therefore we feel that government with the consent of the governed must be the basis of any territorial settlement in this war.'

Some specific proposals were common to most programmes of war aims, but others were defined with significant reservation. Belgium, occupied France, Serbia, Montenegro and Romania would have to be evacuated; Alsace-Lorraine must go back to France; 'Arabia, Armenia, Mesopotamia, Syria and Palestine' would 'not be restored to their former sovereignty' and merited 'recognition of their separate national condition'; the Straits were to be internationalized and neutralized, the future of Germany's colonies left to a peace conference to decide; and an international organization would be established in order to maintain the peace. Despite his doubts over Poland five weeks previously, Lloyd George now asserted that 'An independent Poland, comprising all those genuinely Polish elements who desire to form part of it, is an urgent necessity for the stability of Eastern Europe'. In the speech there was also an echo of Smuts's message to Mensdorff: 'The break-up of Austria–Hungary is no part of our war aims', Lloyd George said; but a lasting peace would require a grant of 'genuine self-government on true democratic principles to those Austro-Hungarian nationalities which have long desired it'. He skated over promises to Italy and Romania in the secret treaties: 'We regard as vital the satisfaction of the legitimate claims of the Italians for union with those of their own race and tongue . . . We also mean to press that justice must be done to men of Romanian blood and speech in their legitimate aspirations.'

One curious ambiguity remains unexplained. The text printed in the United Kingdom gave an assurance from the Prime Minister that British troops were not fighting 'to deprive Turkey of its capital or of the rich and renowned lands of Thrace, which are predominantly Turkish in race'. But the version handed to the Americans and retained in the State Department omitted the comma after 'Thrace' and included a significant addition. The end of the sentence in the American version reads: '. . . rich and renowned lands of Asia Minor and Thrace which are predominantly Turkish in race'. The difference in meaning is, of course, considerable. It is probable that the revised version, which is favourable to Greek aspirations, is a more accurate reflection of Lloyd George's views, formed at a time when he remained much impressed by his first meetings with Venizelos.

As so often in a Lloyd George speech, the omissions are significant: no mention of 'self-determination' – a principle unwelcome to the 'servants of Empire' in his government; no direct reference to Serb or Czech aspirations; no insistence on imposing a more democratic constitution on Germany, but rather an acknowledgement that the German people should decide such a fundamental issue themselves. To a greater extent than the British newspaper editors appreciated at the time, the speech reflected the willingness of the government to conclude a negotiated peace with Germany's partners if they so desired. The War Cabinet minutes show that the Prime Minister, so far from 'knocking away' the Austrian 'prop' for all time, wished the Monarchy to remain in being, but as a pillar of stability in the post-war world rather than in support of German power. The Cabinet had given serious thought to a positive statement that a strong Austria was desirable, but the Prime Minister explained that 'his main object was to give a clear indication to Austria that we did not wish to destroy her'; he wanted 'to make her people lukewarm in the war, thus deterring her from using her strength actively against us'.

Lloyd George's speech momentarily exasperated President Wilson. Some months earlier Colonel House, on the President's instructions, had formed a small research group to prepare, not simply an outline of agreed war aims, but 'a programme of the world's peace'. The group, which was headed by House's brother-in-law, Sidney Mezes, completed its report in the first days of January 1918; and around their recommendations Wilson drafted an address to Congress which would proclaim liberal democracy's answer to the simplistic appeal of Bolshevik peace propaganda. After reading Lloyd George's speech he considered scrapping his carefully prepared words, fearing that they would be treated merely as one more variation on a well known theme. His advisers urged him to go ahead, but the final decision was long delayed; on 8 January Senators and Representatives were given only half an hour's notice that their presence was required on Capitol Hill to hear their President.

Wilson's lofty idealism elevated his programme to a nobler plane, one which accepted that 'the day of conquest and aggrandizement is gone by; so also is the day of secret covenants entered into in the interest of particular governments'. There were many specific points which corresponded closely to Lloyd George's programme: the future of Belgium and Alsace-Lorraine; autonomous development for non-Turkish nationalities in the Ottoman Empire; the readjustment of Italian frontiers on lines of nationality. Like the British, the Americans did not envisage the destruction of Austria–Hungary (against whom – as 'the vassal of the German government' – Congress had voted to declare war on 4 December); but Wilson emphasized that 'the peoples of Austria–Hungary . . . should be accorded the freest opportunity of autonomous development'. The famous Fourteenth Point, with its plea for the formation of 'a general association of nations', echoed British backing for a league to guarantee the maintenance of peace. But where

Wilson's programme went beyond all others was in the radical changes put forward in the first five points. He insisted that peace should be determined through 'open covenants, openly arrived at', and there should be absolute freedom of the seas in peace and in war, the removal of economic barriers, the reduction of armaments and an adjustment of colonial claims in the interests of subject peoples. Behind all the President's ideas was the concept of self-determination – 'not a mere phrase', he explained in February 1918, but 'an imperative principle of action which statesmen would thereafter disregard at their peril'. This repeated affirmation that in the post-war world the territorial limits of a government's authority must rest on the consent of the governed rekindled dampened flames of idealism, at least among families spared the horrors of front-line carnage. Nor was it only to the Entente peoples that Wilson's words made an appeal. The final section of the speech, a call to Germany 'to associate herself with us and the other peace-loving nations of the world in covenants of justice and law and fair dealing', was remembered along the Rhine and in Berlin ten months later when, as the Western Allies celebrated victory, the Fourteen Points stood out to the defeated as a charter of sane peace.

As early as 24 January Czernin declared publicly in Vienna that he was ready to accept some of Wilson's proposals 'with great pleasure', although on the same day the German Chancellor, Georg von Hertling, refused to give any assurances over the future of Belgium and ruled out any changes of status for Alsace-Lorraine. Briefly there was talk, even in the War Cabinet, of a meeting in Switzerland between Lloyd George and Czernin, but the contacts gradually weakened. In early March Philip Kerr again visited Berne, hoping that Czernin would come to meet Smuts, but the Austrians left a professional diplomat, Alexander Skrzynski, to deal with the British envoys; and no progress could be made. Ironically, within five years Skrzynski was to become Foreign Minister – and later Prime Minister – of Poland, a great beneficiary from the Allies' war aims programme. By early March Lloyd George had given up hope that the Austrian prop would topple over. It needed to be pushed militarily – and psychologically. Lloyd George accordingly appointed the press magnate, Lord Northcliffe, to supervise an Enemy Propaganda Department, with headquarters at Crewe House, London. Specifically Northcliffe was to use expert assistance to encourage disaffection among the subject nationalities of the Dual Monarchy. There was to be no positive call made for an end to Habsburg rule across central Europe; but denials that 'the break up of Austria–Hungary is not an allied war aim' ceased forthwith.

Despite his Foreign Minister's speech in late December, Clemenceau remained much less concerned with programmes for peace than did Lloyd George and Wilson. Soon after coming to power he announced that he had one 'very simple' war aim – victory. Significantly he decided to govern France, not from the prime ministerial offices at the Hôtel Matignon but from the Ministry of War in the Rue St Dominique. His immediate task was to lift morale by getting rid of political corruption and defeatism. An iron hand fell on those Radical Socialists believed to have had contact with the Germans. Joseph Caillaux, head of the government in 1911–12, came under particular suspicion, not least because he advocated a compromise peace. Police searches found hundreds of letters from Caillaux to men who were discovered to be German agents. His parliamentary immunity from arrest was suspended by the Chamber of Deputies on 22 December and a month later he was charged with 'plotting against the interests of the state'. Louis Malvy, Minister of the Interior since the start of the war, was accused of protecting traitors and defeatists rather than pursuing a vigorous campaign to expose them.

The British ambassador thought Caillaux would be shot and Malvy fortunate to escape a similar fate. In fact, though both politicians spent long periods in detention, lack of evidence of treason allowed them to escape lightly. But at the time of their arrest, all their associates came under close suspicion, not least among them the Allied Commander-in-Chief at Salonika; for Maurice Sarrail owed his early promotion to the rank of general to Caillaux and his knowledge of political infighting during 1915 to his close friend, Malvy. On 10 December Clemenceau telegraphed Sarrail: 'I have the honour to inform you that, acting in the general interest, the Government has decided to order your recall to France'. Next day a felicitously phrased press release in Paris acknowledged that 'General Sarrail has had to contend with serious difficulties and has rendered great services'. He left Salonika on the day Caillaux was deprived of his political immunity. By the time Caillaux was charged with plotting against the state, the General was at his home in Montauban, well content to keep out of the public eye and begin writing his memoirs.

The fate of Sarrail and his independent forays in Balkan diplomacy were among the earliest topics raised in the Supreme War Council at Versailles. Since the spring, there had been little activity in Macedonia, though the British made some successful night raids against the Bulgarian lines around Lake Doiran. But in September Sarrail ordered General Jacquemot to lead a hurriedly improvised force to take the small town of Pogradec, on a wooded spur overlooking Lake Ochrid and south-eastern Albania. Jacquemot's surprise move gained a swift victory with few losses, and he reported the capture of more than four hundred Austrians and Bulgarians and considerable equipment. But, like so much of Sarrail's generalship, this success carried political overtones. For in ordering an advance to Pogradec, Sarrail was strengthening French influence in Albania, long seen by Italy as their God-given foothold in the Balkans. Sarrail had even gone so far as to recognize one of the most dubious Albanian leaders, Essad Bey Pasha (ex-Turkish general), as 'President of the Albanian Government'. By this action he succeeded in infuriating three of the four Allies whose contingents were serving in his multinational Army of the Orient: the Italians looked on Essad as a bandit; the Greeks knew he had ambitions in Ioanina, where much of the population was ethnically Albanian; and the Serbs were so mistrustful of all the activities around Pogradec and Lake Ochrid that Pašić, their Prime Minister, came in person to Sarrail's headquarters to make a forthright protest. When the name 'Sarrail' was raised at the Supreme War Council it provoked predictable reactions from Venizelos and from the Serb and Italian representatives. There must be no more jockeying for influence in such a sensitive region.

For Clemenceau the problem was, who should replace Sarrail? President Poincaré had no doubt of the answer. It was exactly three years since Franchet d'Esperey's staff had presented the President with their general's plan to carry the war from Salonika to the Danube. Since then Franchet d'Esperey had boosted his reputation as an energetic commander by a series of successes in the Army Group of the North; but he remained the one French general with the strategic vision to see that the Balkans looked inwards on central Europe and that Salonika was not simply a staging-post for the Levant. Both Foch, as Chief of the General Staff, and Pétain, as Commander-in-Chief in France, grudged the imminent removal of so skilled a general from the Western Front; but with Poincaré's backing, Clemenceau instructed Pétain to offer Franchet the Salonika command.

To Clemenceau's displeasure, after two days of deliberation Franchet d'Esperey turned down the offer. He did not give detailed reasons at the time; but it is clear from the record of his conversations that his refusal was shaped by both political and military considerations. He was known as a right-wing Catholic: if he removed from office Sarrail's camp-followers – an urgent task incumbent on any successor – the radical Deputies in the Chamber would denounce him as a reactionary, and the label would stick for the rest of his career. Moreover, like Smuts when offered command in Egypt, Franchet doubted whether he could count on support for such a forgotten sideshow from the Ministry of War. If the Germans threatened Paris again, was there anyone in the Rue St Dominique who would even think of sparing an artillery battery or a battalion for distant Salonika? In December 1914 a Balkan command had looked an attractive prospect; but in December 1917 Franchet d'Esperey was convinced he could give France greater service by remaining with the *Armées du Nord*.

Clemenceau thought of ordering Franchet out to Salonika, but he gave way to the combined opposition of Foch and Pétain. They recommended as Sarrail's successor the commander of the Second Army, with headquarters at Verdun, General Marie-Louis Guillaumat. He was an infantryman, seven years younger than Sarrail and Franchet; he had long experience of colonial regiments (who formed nearly half the French contingent in Macedonia); and he was a totally dedicated soldier, with no taste for politics whatsoever. Guillaumat reached Salonika before Christmas. 'A fat little man, says nothing', was General Milne's first impression on being introduced to him by Sarrail, sullen and superseded. But within a month Milne was full of praise for Guillaumat's professionalism and tact. Most skilfully Guillaumat helped to heal the old rifts between Venizelists and royalists which had prevented the Greeks from mobilizing some of their best fighting troops. King Alexander of Greece visited Salonika, personally intervened to deal with munities in two anti-Venizelist regiments at Lamia and Larissa, and established good relations with all the Allied commanders in the second city of his kingdom.

Guillaumat knew he could hardly expect new divisions spared from the Western Front or Italy; but soon after his arrival he did receive reinforcements from a source hitherto untapped. During the brief period that Kerensky was in power in Petrograd he allowed ex-prisoners of war who had formed a 'Serb Volunteer Division' in the Tsar's army to seek transference to the Macedonian Front. Ten thousand of these volunteers – mostly Croats, but some Slovenes and Serbs whose homes were within Austria–Hungary – sailed from Archangel to Cherbourg and reached Salonika in the first days of the New Year. The Bolshevik Revolution prevented a second division from finding transport to Archangel. Some of this force remained in Russia and joined the Red Army. But the majority – over six thousand tough veterans – made their way slowly along the Trans-Siberian and Chinese Eastern railways to Port Arthur (then in Japanese hands) and, by way of Hong Kong and

Port Said, eventually reached Salonika on 29 March 1918. This contingent, almost entirely from Bosnia and Herzegovina, travelled 14,000 miles in eleven weeks in its determination to fight as a composite Yugoslav division within the Serbian Army. By April they were ready to attack the Bulgars, Austrians and Germans in the mountains west of the Vardar should Guillaumat and the Serb Chief of Staff, General Bojović, wish to press forward in the spring.

But in the opening weeks of 1918 it seemed more likely that the armies in Macedonia would stand on the defensive for much of the year. There was even a possibility that most French, British and Italian troops would be withdrawn entirely, if the Greek Army could be brought up to strength. Haig suggested in the last week of January that all British and French divisions should be brought back to the Western Front at the earliest opportunity. Clemenceau would not take so drastic a step as this, but he had long been hostile to the whole Macedonian enterprise. Two years earlier, when he was a trenchant critic of Briand's policies, the Tiger poured scorn on an army that, by his reckoning, was wasting its time constructing an entrenched camp around a Balkan seaport while German invaders were on the Oise, barely sixty miles from Paris. His newspaper, *L'Homme Enchaîné*, dubbed Sarrail's troops 'the gardeners of Salonika', and he never relented. All his instincts were against any large-scale commitments east of the Adriatic. But he was a realist. If Guillaumat could tie down German troops on the edge of the Balkans, without drawing on reserves in France, so much the better.

Much of January was spent in discussions at Versailles and in London over the general strategy for the year. Haig would have welcomed an opportunity to strike once again in the Ypres Salient if he could have another 650,000 men, ready to take the offensive when the weather made progress possible. All the evidence suggested, however, that Ludendorff was preparing for a grand attack in the West and the Military Representatives at Versailles preferred to recommend standing on the defensive in Flanders, France and Italy, until the Germans had exhausted their powers of assault. 'Joint Note 12', of 21 January 1918, urged maintenance of the existing numerical strength of the British and French armies on the Western Front, construction of defences in depth, a steady increase in tanks, guns and aircraft, and, allowing for the arrival of two American divisions each month, achievement of such preponderance in front-line troops and equipment that it would be possible to mount the decisive offensive against Germany in 1919. The Joint Note, which seems to have been pushed forward by General Wilson from draft recommendations by Colonel Amery, echoed many of Lloyd George's expressed views on general strategy, for it backed proposals to destroy the Ottoman armies in Palestine and Syria on the assumption that the loss of Damascus and Aleppo would make the Turk break with the Germans and conclude a separate peace.

The War Cabinet gave formal approval to Joint Note 12 on 25 January. When, however, the Supreme War Council met at Versailles a week later the proposed campaign against Turkey ran into heavy criticism from Clemenceau, Foch and Pétain, and also from Haig and Robertson (who was still CIGS). Clemenceau agreed on the need to hold on, throughout 1918, until American assistance came in full force. But he was alarmed by easy assumptions that an enemy attack in the West must blunt itself on successive lines of fortifications, giving the Germans only limited gains of a few miles and at heavy cost. He did not see how the British could contemplate 'embarking on this eastern adventure' without starving the Western Front of reinforcements and material. Eventually, after two days' discussion, the Council accepted a compromise: the general strategy for the year would derive from Joint Note 12, but with a proviso: in the Middle East, Britain would concentrate on making effective use of troops already in that theatre of war rather than take forces away from France. Even then, Robertson continued to oppose a Turkish offensive. He shared Clemenceau's concern for the safety of the Western Front. A few days later Robertson clashed with the War Cabinet because he thought – as also did Foch – that two divisions rushed to Italy after Caporetto should be summoned back to the Western Front now that the Austro-German invasion was checked.

On 2 February Robertson informed Allenby of the Supreme War Council's decision. Allenby was told not only that he was expected to advance on Damascus and Aleppo, but that the War Cabinet was sending General Smuts to Cairo immediately to discuss strategy and manpower needs. In his letter, however, Robertson made no attempt to conceal his hostility to a campaign which he believed could bring little advantage to the Allies: Allenby was to remember in his talks with Smuts that the Western Front must have priority: 'very heavy fighting' was expected shortly in France or Flanders; his plans should therefore be so flexible as to allow for a cut in men and resources at short notice.

The message was hardly a recipe for victory. But Allenby pressed ahead with plans he had already drawn up at the end of the year. On 19 February the 60th Division went forward from positions in the hills thirteen miles north-east of Jerusalem, crossing bleak country on the edge of the biblical 'wilderness'. Two days later the 1st Light Horse

Brigade captured Jericho, on the last escarpment of the Judaean Hills, six miles north of the Dead Sea. At the same time New Zealand yeomanry scrambled down the rocky cliffs from beyond Bethlehem to the Dead Sea, hoping in vain to cut off the retreating Turks.

Allenby was not present when these operations began. On 11 February Smuts arrived in Cairo, accompanied by Colonel Amery and two senior staff officers from the War Office; they were joined by General Gillman, Chief of Staff in Mesopotamia. After visiting Jerusalem with Allenby on 15 February, the whole party returned to Egypt. Much of the following week was spent in revising war plans in accordance with the compromise agreed by the Supreme War Council. Several of Allenby's best staff officers – including Wavell – doubted the Prime Minister's conviction that defeat in Syria would induce the government in Constantinople to seek a separate peace; they were impressed by the morale of captured Turkish officers and their conviction that their German ally would soon be gaining victories in France. Allenby himself was cautious, once again emphasizing the logistical problems that hampered any rapid movement northwards. Final decisions were only taken after the whole party, including specialist advisers, moved up the Nile to Luxor which, though as far from the battle lines in the Judaean Hills as Whitehall from the Wilhelmstrasse, was free from suspected enemy agents. The ageless tranquillity of the temples, thought Amery, made one look at this war in perspective. 'After tea, concocted a plan for a cavalry raid up the Jordan valley', he noted in his diary for 18 February.

At Luxor it was agreed that all efforts against Turkey would concentrate in Palestine. The army in Mesopotamia – where General Maude had died from cholera in November 1917 – would stand on the defensive. An Indian division had already reached Suez from the Gulf; it would be followed by two more divisions and a cavalry brigade from Mesopotamia, while an Indian cavalry division, for which there were few opportunities on the Western Front, would be brought from France as soon as possible. Allenby would then have ten infantry divisions and four mounted divisions with which to advance on Beirut and Damascus. He would have liked at least one more division: in the end he received one less, for the War Cabinet decided not to weaken the force on the Tigris until the fate of Mosul was clear. The EEF would seek protection for its eastern flank by crossing the Jordan, raiding Amman and removing all threats from the Hejaz railway. It would then secure a line from Tiberias westwards to Haifa and move northwards along the sea, securing successively Tyre, Sidon and Beirut before swinging inland to

Homs, thus isolating Damascus, which would be threatened from the south by smaller columns advancing from Deraa. This general plan coincided with Allenby's intentions. Smuts also agreed with his insistence on continuing the construction of a railway to bring up supplies from Egypt to Haifa. Two battalions of Canadian railway engineers were to be sent to Alexandria as soon as shipping permitted.

In all these arrangements there was no prospect of total early victory; the main effort was to be a long, slow and hard push up the coast. On paper the strategy looked as cautious as any operational directive put out by Murray before Gaza. Horses and camels were to be used only beyond the Jordan, in collaboration with the Arabs. But the overall character of the Luxor plan seems to have been regarded by Allenby as a programme of minimum achievement, something to be taken back to London by Smuts to satisfy the War Office. He hoped for greater and more rapid success, attained – as in the assault on Beersheba – by surprise and innovation. Meanwhile he continued with his own preparations. Ten days after the Luxor meeting, Major T.E. Lawrence was summoned to a conference of Allenby's corps commanders at GHQ in what had been a German school at Bir Salem, ouside Ramleh. There it was agreed that Lawrence should receive 700 additional camels from the Egyptian Camel Transport Company, which would enable his Arabs to raid more deeply along the Hejaz railway. Approval was given for a plan to seize Maan, while Allenby's regular troops were to launch the projected raid across the Jordan on the hillside town of Es Salt and eventually on Amman. The Bull would charge if conditions were ripe.

Increasingly, Allenby was impressed by the value of aircraft in the Middle East: for reconnaissance; for bombing; and for attacking columns of troops. When, at the start of the last week in February, news reached GHQ that Robertson had resigned as CIGS to be replaced by Sir Henry Wilson, a fresh attempt was made to secure more squadrons of modern planes for Palestine. But although Henry Wilson was more sympathetically inclined to Palestine's needs than his predecessor, the first telegram from the new CIGS, received on 7 March, was not encouraging: the War Cabinet wanted Allenby to continue his 'operations against the Turks with all energy'; it was important to 'cut the Hejaz railway as already planned'; and they wished to know when he could 'be ready to make a northwards advance'. But over the RFC, the CIGS was adamant: 'As regards aircraft, at present the requirements of France must have precedence', Allenby was told. It was a response he would hear repeatedly over men, munitions and machines in the months ahead.

Allenby selected 21 March as the day when his Anzacs and Londoners would cross the Jordan and head towards Es Salt and Amman. He would have preferred 19 March, if only the rains had stopped on schedule. The River Jordan itself was swollen after what seemed like unending downpours, the waters rising nine feet during the night before the attack began. But the assault went ahead and was sustained for eleven days. Both towns were entered, but the vital railway viaduct outside Amman was not destroyed and the offensive could not be maintained. It was not merely that the weather, as so often, was appalling and the tracks in the hills of Moab virtually impassable. The decisive reason came from two thousand miles away, for another offensive had also begun on 21 March, the long-expected German drive for victory in the West. On 23 March, before his troops had even entered Es Salt, Allenby received the first order to put a division on standby for embarkation and transport to France. Four days later his general directive to prepare a northwards advance was formally cancelled: the EEF was to remain on 'active defence'; last month's Grand Design became Luxor's newest relic. Before the end of May 60,000 officers and men had left Palestine for the Western Front. In London there was no longer any talk of securing a decision that year in *some* theatre of war. By the spring of 1918 the drama in the West was becoming far too tense for sideshows.

CHAPTER 11

THE EMPEROR'S BATTLE

For many months the British and French anticipated that the Germans would launch a major offensive during the spring of 1918, striking in the West before the American Expeditionary Force (AEF) was fully trained and equipped. Haig awaited the assault with a self-confidence bordering on complacency. His staff had learnt much from the German defences which frustrated them in the Ypres Salient during the autumn: by now the British trench system had an advanced outpost line, protected by wire, about a mile ahead of the main network of trenches and supporting alleys, which in some places reached back two and a half miles. Machine-gun fire and artillery would, it was assumed, cut down the attackers before they could dent the defences. Smuts and Hankey visited the Western Front in late January at Lloyd George's request to inspect defences and look for an alternative younger commander to replace Haig. Hankey was impressed by the defences, though not all were yet complete, particularly behind the Fifth Army's line in the south. There was, he felt, an air of 'steady but subdued optimism'. But the talent spotters found no likely successor to Haig. 'The army is tired of the war, and there is a general feeling that peace is not very distant', Hankey wrote privately to Lloyd George.

On paper, Haig had 155 divisions spread along a front line of 126 miles; another eight divisions were held in reserve. This figure was not so impressive as it appeared. Nominally each division should have comprised 12,000 men, divided into twelve battalions, but the high casualty rate over the previous year had cut the manpower by some twenty-five per cent; and from 23 January 1918 each division was reduced to nine (often under-strength) battalions, an administrative reorganization that caused vexation during the six weeks before it was completed. Doubts remain over the number of combatant troops available to Haig: probably about 1,236,000 men but certainly less than in March 1917, perhaps by more than 50,000.. At the same time his zonal responsibilities became greater; at the end of 1917 the British line was extended further beyond St Quentin to join the French Sixth Army at Barcis, south of the Oise. Yet Haig was sure he could meet the German challenge 'if it comes'. During the second half of January he inspected three of the four armies under his command; on 2 March he told his generals he was so impressed that his only fear was that the Germans would now hesitate before launching an attack on them. If Ludendorff did strike in March he would, it was thought, make his main effort against General Horne's First Army – fourteen divisions, defending the thirty-three miles between Armentières and Arras – and General Byng's Third Army, which also comprised fourteen divisions and covered the twenty-eight miles from Arras southwards to the Somme.

Perhaps because of his own earlier plans to push the enemy back from the Belgian coast, Haig believed the ultimate objective would be the Channel ports, Calais and Boulogne. General Gough, commanding the Fifth Army further south, disagreed. From prisoners brought in by patrols, and from studying a French analysis of recent German tactics at Riga on the Eastern Front and at Caporetto, Gough maintained that Ludendorff would strike at the point where his army flanked the French. General von Hutier, who broke the Russians at Riga by sheer strength of artillery, was still commanding the German Eighteenth Army, facing Gough. If Hutier's firepower forced a wedge between the British and French forces the Germans could head for Amiens or even Paris, barely seventy miles to the south-west. Gough knew this was the weakest point of the whole Front; the Fifth Army's sector covered forty-two miles; his defences in depth were still unfinished and he had under his command only twelve infantry and three cavalry divisions. Plans to plug any gap, agreed by Haig and Pétain, were never finally settled. Haig remained so convinced the German blow would fall further north that he kept six reserve divisions covering Calais and Boulogne, while assigning Gough's Fifth Army only two. It was anticipated that Nature would strengthen the Fifth Army's defences. During February and early March for the past three years the rains had left the River Oise in flood; GHQ was certain that when the rains came in 1918 the flooding would provide the Fifth Army with twelve miles of defensive moat. Unfortunately, with that meteorological perversity which pervaded this whole war, the rains which had been so constant in the late summer and autumn failed to fill the dykes in February. Instead of a broad moat there was a muddy plain, too soft for the tanks which Gough sought to use as mobile batteries or weapon carriers, but firm enough to support the specially chosen

German storm troops as they bore down on the weary British veterans, most of whom had fought at Passchendaele and were now to be outnumbered four to one.

On Saturday 16 March, an Intelligence report at Haig's GHQ in Montreuil, forty miles back from the nearest trenches, gave a confident assurance that no sustained attack was 'to be expected south of the Bapaume–Cambrai road'. Ludendorff's support troops were still well behind the Front; perhaps they were not going to strike at the British after all? Pétain anxiously moved his reserves eastwards, to cover Reims, and even Verdun. That Saturday night no less than forty-seven German divisions were on the march, like the troops before Caporetto moving under cover of darkness, plodding on for twenty miles at a time and bringing with them 2,600 heavy guns and 4,010 field guns to strengthen twenty-eight German divisions already in the trenches. The marches continued each night until Wednesday. The British had no idea of the strength being massed against them. There was no week-long preliminary bombardment. At four in the morning of Thursday 21 March, 6,000 guns began intensive shelling between Arras and St Quentin with high explosive and mustard gas. Since midnight there had been thick fog, muffling the sounds of preparation. The fog lingered all the morning, trapping the deadly gas, and making it impossible to see the storm troops until they loomed up fifty yards ahead. The Fifth Army's forward zone was overrun before, around noon, the fog lifted. Under spring sunshine the German storm troopers swept relentlessly forward. Before dusk, in the vital southern sector, the attackers had broken through three zones of defence, and open country lay ahead of them. Their forward troops had advanced almost five miles. That night Gough, seeking to keep what remained of his army together, ordered a retreat on his extreme right, behind the Crozat Canal some seven miles back, a regrouping that opened the dreaded gap with the French. Further north, along the Bapaume–Cambrai road, the Third Army also suffered considerably during the morning fog but were able to check the advance during the afternoon.

Ludendorff had staked everything on this offensive in the West. He was, at that moment, the most powerful man in the German Empire for, though Hindenburg was nominally his superior at OHL, it was the archetypal Prussian general who settled tactics. When in August 1916, under pressure from the Army chiefs, Kaiser William II reluctantly gave the Supreme Command to Field Marshal von Hindenburg, with General Ludendorff as First Quartermaster-General, he was heard to remark that he might just as well abdicate. Thereafter the sovereign's powers were fettered by the military leaders. He retained royal and imperial prerogatives: it was in the Kaiser's name that Theobald von Bethmann-Hollweg was succeeded as Chancellor in July 1917 by an unknown 'God-fearing Prussian', Georg Michaelis; and it was also in his name that, sixteen weeks later, Michaelis made way for Count von Hertling, a seventy-four-year-old Bavarian Catholic. But Bethmann's fall was determined by Hindenburg and Ludendorff and, though Hertling had parliamentary backing behind him, as soon as he attempted to coax his sovereign into a political initiative it was vetoed by OHL. 'Even a decision of His Majesty cannot relieve the generals from the dictates of their conscience', Ludendorff wrote. His Majesty was allowed to stomp the battle fronts, believing that he lifted morale by his presence. He visited his allies: the Sultan in Constantinople; King 'Foxy' Ferdinand in Sofia and on the Bulgarian-occupied plain of Philippi; and, with Emperor-King Charles, he saw newly won Gorizia and Monfalcone. But, despite the pomp and ceremonial with which he was greeted, there was little doubt William remained a puppet of the High Command. Three days before Christmas in 1917 the Kaiser was in France, visiting Crown Prince Rupert of Bavaria's army group near Cambrai. The troops were drawn up on parade; he inspected them; and then announced that he brought commendation and 'greetings from the Field Marshal'. It alarmed Rupert that the All Highest War Lord should come before his men as Hindenburg's messenger: subjects should be a mouthpiece for their sovereign, not the other way about, Crown Prince Rupert maintained.

But now in the spring of 1918 there had come a moment when, by courtesy of General Ludendorff, the Kaiser's falling prestige might receive a boost. As the last attack divisions completed their march into Picardy, William II spent the night on the imperial train in Belgium. He was received by Hindenburg at OHL's advanced headquarters in Avesnes, fifteen miles south of the Franco-Belgian frontier, as the storm troops were tightening their hold on Gough's forward positions. The Kaiser remained at Avesnes for some nine hours, assessing the reports that reached Ludendorff from the front line, forty miles to the south. And, though he slept and dined in the train, for the next ten days he was beside Hindenburg, on several occasions going down to the line and seeing for himself the scars of battle. His presence sealed a bond between OHL and the monarchy. William once again assumed the trappings of All Highest War Lord, the dignity in which he had swaggered through a quarter of a century of make-believe war games and manoeuvres. The General Staff's first war communiqués from

Avesnes took on a new tone: the great battle in the West was 'under the personal leadership of His Majesty the Emperor', the German people were told. In the Rhineland next day's *Kölnische Zeitung* called the offensive *Die Kaiserschlacht* (the Emperor's Battle), a name soon taken up by other publications, daily and weekly. At once, the stakes in Ludendorff's gamble were raised. More now was in the balance than the continued power of OHL. Victories by his generals would redound to the Kaiser's credit; but what if there were defeats? Over the next seven months the fate of the armies in the West and the prestige of the House of Hohenzollern became as closely linked for the German public as the *Grande Armée* and Napoleon for the French after the retreat from Moscow.

Admiral von Müller, who was with the Kaiser on the imperial train, noted in his diary for Friday 22 March that 'the mood at breakfast was low'. The offensive had been checked on the first day, it was felt; for, despite Gough's well justified fears, the pivot of Ludendorff's plan was not intended to be Hutier's Eighteenth Army, but the Seventeenth Army further north. There its commander, General von Below – the victor of Caporetto – had failed to break through the British Third Army's defence system and so begin the wheeling movement to cut off Arras, which was Ludendorff's first objective. At London breakfast tables on that Friday there was concern over the 'bulges' in the Fifth Army's sector, but as yet no real sense of alarm. During that Friday the news from Gough's army became worse: a 'retirement' was becoming a retreat back to the Somme, at least thirteen miles behind Thursday morning's line. By Saturday morning there were even fears that the retreat would turn into a rout.

In retrospect it is clear that this weekend of 23–25 March 1918 was, for the British, the most dangerous moment of the land war. Haig himself appears to have remained sanguine until the Saturday morning (23 March), when he visited Gough's headquarters at Villers-Breton-neux and found it was proving impossible to hold the line of the Somme; the Germans were thrusting forward over bridges which, in the haste of evacuation, no engineers had destroyed. There was already a gap some forty miles wide in the Allied line and Haig thought that Amiens, the nub of the railway system for the BEF, was in danger. That afternoon he met Pétain and asked for French support to prevent the two armies being separated. One French division, with limited ammunition, is known to have joined Gough's tattered force that day. But Haig wanted twenty French divisions to be concentrated 'about Amiens astride the Somme'. This aid Pétain refused to provide; he believed the German attack on the British positions to be merely a preliminary for an even more devastating offensive in Champagne, aimed directly at the capital. Haig thought Pétain 'much upset, almost unbalanced and most anxious'. The first shells had fallen on Paris during Saturday morning, one in the Quai de la Seine on the Île de la Cîté only 500 yards from Notre Dame and another outside the Gare de l'Est. There was consternation in the city. When Paris was bombarded in January 1871 the German guns were five miles away; how close was the enemy now, it was wondered? Had the censors concealed a German breakthrough in the past few days? There had been no shelling in 1914 during the crisis on the Marne. The 'Paris gun' was in fact firing from Crépy, near Laon, more than seventy-five miles away; but it took some time to identify the site. And even when the firing position was verified, the report brought Pétain little comfort, for Laon stood in the centre of the sector from where he was expecting Ludendorff to launch his next assault.

Fortunately for Haig and Pétain, Ludendorff was puzzled over his immediate moves; he was disappointed that Below had not made more impression on Byng's Third Army, and he failed to realize how far Hutier's Eighteenth Army had advanced towards Amiens. He dissipated German strength with limited attacks on three different sectors rather than concentrating on a single objective. This hesitancy gave the Entente allies an opportunity for top-level consultation, meetings where it would be possible to counter Pétain's defeatist despair. On Tuesday 26 March Clemenceau and Lord Milner took the initiative at a joint conference in Doullens; they secured the acceptance of Foch as Allied 'co-ordinator' on the Western Front, in effect a generalissimo to whom Haig and Pétain were 'requested to furnish . . . all necessary information'. Eight days later at a further conference, on this occasion in Beauvais, representatives of the British, French and US governments gave Foch 'the strategic direction of military operations'; and on 14 April his position was finally clarified, when he was made 'General-in-Chief of the Allied Armies'. Thus, by an ironic twist, Germany's 'Emperor's Battle', so far from enhancing the military reputation of the Kaiser, ensured that after forty-four months of war his enemies at last attained a unity of command in the West.

There was, too, a further irony in these early German successes. One of the field gun officers in Hutier's Eighteenth Army, Lieutenant Herbert Sulzbach, noted in his diary how delighted were his men on that first Saturday of the advance at finding such fine rations abandoned by the Fifth Army in its precipitate retreat – not merely tins of corned beef, or bacon and cheese and jam, but oats for the horses – delighted, that is, until his more hard-bitten veterans began to reflect that, if Britain's front-line troops had such abundance of supplies, then the U-boats could hardly have brought 'England' to the verge of starvation, as German propagandists maintained. But in this fourth week of March there was little time for introspection. Although Foch was prepared to use his reserves to plug the gap between the Allied armies, the German offensive retained its impetus. Hutier's advance troops were still pushing ahead; nine miles on 26 March; ten miles on 27 March, carrying them well south of Montdidier and cutting an important railway linking the British sector of the old front line with Paris. But German hopes that Below's army would break into open country in the west, lower down the Somme, and reach the Channel coast were checked by Byng's Third Army. General von der Marwitz's Second Army suffered an even greater setback; they attacked between Arras and Albert on 28 March, but were held by some of the finest troops under Haig's command, including the Guards Division and the Canadian 3rd Division. Not a single German objective was attained that day. Hutier regrouped his Eighteenth Army for a further thrust south-west in the first days of April, belatedly threatening Amiens; and his tired troops came within ten miles of the city, exposing the main Calais–Boulogne–Paris railway to shellfire. But on 5 April Ludendorff conceded that the resistance of the Allied armies 'is beyond our strength'. The sixteen-day battle in Picardy came to an end, with more than 70,000 prisoners, seven shell-battered French towns and 1,250 square miles of once fertile countryside passing into German hands. Captain Gerhard Ritter – one of Germany's most distinguished military historians this century – served with Hutier's shock troops throughout the battle. Writing some forty years later, after what he called 'the upheavals in soul and mind of the Second World War', Ritter could still remember the sense of 'crushing disappointment' in failing to fulfil March 1918's high hopes of victory.

General Gough was relieved of his command as early as 28 March, becoming the scapegoat for an offensive which he had foreseen but was denied the reinforcements to resist. What remained of his Fifth Army was reconstituted as the Fourth Army, under General Sir Henry Rawlinson (who had, in fact, been Gough's predecessor in the Fifth Army, before the 1917 Flanders offensive). In his diary Rawlinson wrote two days previously: 'With our backs to the wall, we shall, I know, give a good account of ourselves. The Boche reserves are not unlimited.'

Mood and metaphor may well have crossed with Rawlinson to France; upper lips needed stiffening over the next fortnight. For, only four days after calling a halt in the southern sector of the Front, Ludendorff sent twelve divisions of top-grade troops, with two weary and under-strength divisions in support, against the (predominantly) British First Army on a ten-mile front along the River Lys from south of Armentières to La Gorgues-Estaires. Later attacks, over the old Belgian frontier on either side of Ypres, were against the British Second Army. The immediate objective was Hazebrouck, an important railway junction, from where in peacetime it was possible to take a train twenty miles up the line to Ypres or forty-six miles down the line to Arras. Ominously, there were also railways from Hazebrouck to Dunkirk (twenty-five miles), Calais (thirty-seven miles) or Boulogne (fifty-two miles). Ludendorff seems to have considered wheeling on Hazebrouck, turning northwards to take Poperinghe and so cut off the obstinate BEF defenders of Ypres. But, more pressing for Haig, the 'Battle of the River Lys' posed once again the problem of safeguarding the Channel ports. To disrupt British operations in France and Flanders it was not even necessary for the Germans to occupy the French ports. If the Germans established themselves around Hazebrouck or St Omer, constructing emplacements for Krupps' twenty-one-centimetre long-range guns similar to the four used to bombard Paris, cross-Channel shelling would be possible, with the key English embarkation ports of Dover and Folkestone coming under fire.

The first assault wave on 9 April broke on flat, marshy country north of Givenchy, between the La Bassée Canal and the upper waters of the River Lys. The sector was held by a Portuguese division, weary of being treated as mercenary cannon fodder and due for relief that week after a long turn of duty in a hitherto quiet part of the line. The 'pork-and-beans', as they were nicknamed by their British comrades, had no particular quarrel with Germany and no particular war aim, except to get away as soon as possible from mud-caked Flanders fields and return to the green hills and sun-baked plains of the homeland whence they had been uprooted fiteen months before. The German bombardment is said to have speeded them on their way: 'I don't believe that some of them have stopped running yet', a junior officer in their neighbours, the Northamptonshire Regiment, wrote from hospital to his sister six weeks later; others claim to have last seen them pedalling stolen bicycles in the direction of Le Havre. But such tales may well be based on the conduct of one particular battalion within the three Portuguese brigades. Some 6,000 Portuguese went into German prisoner of war camps after the battle; and, as one in seven of their expeditionary force perished on the Western Front and this was their grimmest day of fighting, Portuguese casualties from the initial attack on the trenches on 9 April must have been heavy. The assault by the Germans carried such impetus that the Scottish Highland Division, coming to relieve the Portuguese, could only blunt its ferocity. The 7th Battalion Gordon Highlanders (nominally 1,000 strong) lost more than 700 officers and men during that Tuesday.

The Portuguese flight created a dangerous salient; and next day the Germans widened the battle northwards from Armentières to the Messines Ridge. Mustard gas and phosgene shelling wore down the resistance and, once the Highland Division had moved into the line, the British had no reinforcements to rush to newly threatened sectors. Less than a fortnight previously Haig had willingly subordinated himself to French leadership for the sake of Allied unity. Now, to Haig's surprise and lasting resentment, Foch held back French reserves, waiting to see where the main German thrust came and hoping to mount counter-attacks. 'I found Foch most selfish and obstinate', Haig wrote in his diary after the two commanders met on Tuesday 9 April; not until ten o'clock on Wednesday night did Foch agree, after another visit to Haig's field headquarters, that he would put 'a large force of French troops ready to take part in the battle'. But when would the French reach the salient where they were needed? Hazebrouck was already in danger of falling. This uncertainty prompted Haig, on Thursday morning, to write out by hand his famous Order of the Day:

> 'Many amongst us are tired. To those I would say that
> Victory will belong to the side which holds out the
> longest. The French Army is moving rapidly and in
> great force to our support. There is no other course open
> to us but to fight it out. Every position must be
> held to the last man. There must be no retirement.
> With our backs to the wall and believing in the justice
> of our cause each one of us might fight on to the end. The
> safety of our homes and the Freedom of mankind alike depend
> upon the conduct of each one of us at this critical moment.'

This message was not 'a despairing cry', as an eminent British historian wrote half a century later; it was both an alarm bell and a rallying call, the dour Haig's best attempt to strike a Harry the Fifth attitude (Agincourt was just down the road from GHQ). But the danger was not, in fact, so acute as three weeks previously. The Royal Air Force, in its first fortnight of independent existence, attacked German positions and bombed the approach roads steadily throughout Friday 12 April. The German infantry storm troops, though achieving tactical triumphs in the first days of battle, were unprepared for regrouping once they had made the initial breakthrough; and by 14 April many units had become cut off. Three days later Ludendorff's attempt to inflict on the Belgians north of Ypres a defeat similar to that of the Portuguese was parried with resolute defence. Both British and Germans were desperately weary and many were caked with mud and 'filthy from lack of baths – none of us having had our clothes off for twenty odd days', as one brigade commander wrote. On the morning after reading Haig's Order of the Day, Brigadier-General Freyberg visited the Hampshire Regiment outside Bailleul an hour before dawn and 'found the whole battalion asleep, lying in every kind of position'. But later on that Friday, as he visited another 'snoring' company, 'something unexpected happened about midnight': exhausted Germans, including a sergeant, wandered into the British lines and surrendered; another German drove a cart into the British outposts while fast asleep. For the British this development was more heartening than the Order of the Day; the will of the Germans to fight was being worn down by their generals' persistence in keeping the offensive going, something the British Tommies had experienced at Ypres the previous autumn and the French *poilus* under Nivelle. But the fighting continued, especially in the north of the sector around the hillocks known as the Flanders Heights. And on 24 April there was a tactical innovation further south, almost a trailer for the drama of 1940 in that same countryside: thirteen experimental German heavy tanks moved towards Amiens, only to be met by thirteen British tanks, supported by an Australian brigade. After a final bombardment with gas shells and explosive and an assault by seven German divisions on the hillocks south of Ypres, Hindenburg and Ludendorff agreed that their forces needed a pause for regrouping and a reassessment of objectives. The second phase of the Emperor's Battle had failed to change the strategic balance in the West.

On 2 May, for the first time in forty days, no shells from the long-range guns fell on Paris. The Supreme War Council met at Abbeville that Tuesday, with Lloyd George, Milner, the military chiefs and the First Sea Lord (Admiral Wemyss) discussing the threat to the Channel ports with Clemenceau, Foch and Pétain: should the Allied armies separate, enabling the British to defend Boulogne and Calais, or should the British and French fall back together, south of the Somme? Foch was reluctant to give his support for either plan. When pressed, he said the armies should retire together; but he insisted 'it would never' come to that: 'Never, never, never', a 'phrase repeated again and again in half-bantering tones . . . *Jamais, jamais, jamais*', Hankey recorded. Foch was right. By 2 May the Channel ports were safe, Ypres was safe, Amiens was safe. Though Foch believed Ludendorff would soon strike again elsewhere, a lull in the spring offensive would bring relief to both sides.

For the British, however, there remained great worries, particularly over manpower. On 21 April, when the German attacks were a month old, Sir Henry Wilson, as CIGS, telegraphed a candid report to Allenby in Palestine. In four weeks, he admitted, the British had lost 225,000 men on the Western Front, about one in five of the BEF's combatant troops. Although Haig had received 180,000 reinforcements, hurried to France, the CIGS would only be able to supply him with 23,000 men a month during the summer. Many of the new arrivals in France were very young and incompletely trained. Allenby therefore had to accept the loss of seasoned veterans and would have to modify his plans so as eventually to accommodate more troops from India and the dominions. On the same day Wilson telegraphed to Milne in Salonika, stressing the need to get as many battalions from overseas to France 'as a matter of the greatest urgency'; but Guillaumat was extremely reluctant to spare any men while he was seeking to fulfil Foch's orders for an offensive in the Balkans 'at an early date'. By the end of May it was agreed that some 10,000 British troops, and another 10,000 French, were to leave Salonika for France. From the Italian Front, Haig received two British divisions in March; several battalions were in action in Flanders on 12 April. Other British and French units soon followed them; and three months later General Diaz even spared some Italian brigades for the Western Front, where they helped the French to check the Germans along the upper Marne.

Potentially the greatest source of support for all the Allies was, of course, the United States. 'Peace awaits Wilson's armies', an Italian parliamentarian remarked on 9 January, after the Fourteen Points speech was reported in Rome's newspapers. By that week some 200,000 American soldiers had sailed from the eastern seaboard for Europe. But the President and his chief military advisers were determined to retain, so far as possible, the 'associate power' concept. General Pershing believed it was essential for the Americans to build up an independent army, with a command structure capable of determining the scope and nature of operations in which US troops took part. Accordingly, an unusually high number of the early American arrivals in Europe were non-combatants. Of troops in France at the time of the President's great speech only 58,000 (twenty-nine per cent) were front-line infantry or machine-gunners. The men who paraded at Lafayette's tomb on 4 July 1917 had completed their intensive training by the end of October and provided the battalion which relieved some French infantry at Barthelémont in Lorraine on 2 November; within twelve hours of entering the trenches a corporal and two privates were killed and twelve Americans made prisoners by a Bavarian raiding-party. But this was an isolated and costly experiment. Not until 18 January 1918 did the US 1st Division take over a sector of the Front on the Meuse, around St Mihiel, with orders to remain on the defensive and gain experience.

American artillerymen needed particularly long periods of training, for they had to accustom themselves to French guns: the standard thirty-year-old seventy-five-millimetre field gun, with an effective range of five miles; and the 155 Grande Puissance howitzer, with a range of eleven miles. Thus the artillery brigade of the US 2nd Division had worked up at Camp Robinson, Wisconsin, for several months before crossing the Atlantic. The brigade landed at Brest on 27 December, spent six days travelling across France by train to Valdahon, the French artillery range near Besançon, and was finally ready for a 'quiet sector . . . south of Verdun'; the brigade reached Rupt-en-Woëvre on that ominous Thursday, 21 March, twelve weeks after setting foot in France. But another ten weeks were to pass before the division felt the full heat of battle.

Lloyd George grew impatient at the delay in bringing the Americans into action on a large scale. He thought the US War Department too insistent on equipping each shipment of men with transport and other supporting services. On 23 March he telegraphed Lord Reading, the British ambassador in Washington, asking him to see the President and press him to 'send over infantry as fast as possible without transport or other encumbrances'. When Lord Reading was received at the White House he found the President sympathetic, and prepared to consider sending an order to Pershing for American units already in France to be 'brigaded with British and French troops'. Some 500 Americans helped defend the higher ground west of Ypres in April and 2,000, many of them engineers, joined in the defence of Amiens. But Pershing was still extremely reluctant to accept integration: the Portuguese experience was not a happy precedent. 'When the war ends, our position will be stronger if our army acting as such shall have played a distinct and definite part', he patiently explained to the US Secretary for War. At the Supreme War Council meeting in Abbeville on 2 May Pershing was 'very obstinate', refusing to allow Foch a free hand in disposing the American divisions along the Front. 'Are you willing to risk the Allies

TOP The making of a legend. Lord Kitchener before becoming 'a great poster'.

MIDDLE In search of 'quick and decisive victory'. Australians go forward at Gallipoli, 1915.

BOTTOM A Turkish shell bursts beside a pier at Cape Helles on the eve of evacuation of the Gallipoli peninsula, January 1916.

General Maurice Sarrail takes the salute at a British parade in
Salonika. In the centre, General Sir Bryan Mahon, April 1916.

Italian troops arrive at Salonika. Contingents from seven Allied armies served under Sarrail in 1916.

'Over the top' on the first day of the Somme. A still from an official film of 1916. But where are the heavy packs which photographs show the infantry carrying?

The harsh terrain of the lower Isonzo Front. Italian troops move along a communications trench.

TOP Arab horsemen mass for the attack on Aqaba, July 1917.

MIDDLE Sergeants Hurcomb and Sedgwick, with the Mayor of Jerusalem and other dignitaries, pose for the camera before not accepting the surrender of the city, 9 December 1917.

LEFT At the Jaffa Gate, Jerusalem, 11 December 1917. General Sir Edmund Allenby listens as the proclamation pledging protection for the city is read out in seven languages. On Allenby's right is Colonel Piépapé of France and on his left the Italian, Major Agostino. Behind the reader of the proclamation is General Sir Philip Chetwoode and on his right, Colonel Wavell. On the right of the second row, looking away from the camera, is Major T.E. Lawrence; to his left is Brigadier-General Clayton; second from Lawrence's right is Georges-Picot.

ABOVE Germany's military paladins. Hindenburg shows the Kaiser a position on the map, with Ludendorff in attendance.

LEFT General Sir George Milne's first meeting with General Franchet d'Esperey at Salonika, 18 June 1918. 'A smart looking little man', Milne noted in his diary.

BELOW Balkan Front, 29 September 1918. The Moroccan Spahis of Jouinot-Gambetta's Brigade who on that Sunday completed their epic march on Skopje.

RIGHT Western Front, 29 September 1918. The Staffordshire Territorials rest on the slopes of the Canal de St Quentin after their victory at Bellenglise. Some still wear life-belts brought from the cross-channel leave boats at Boulogne.

OPPOSITE

ABOVE The forest clearing where the Armistice was signed in November 1918. The German delegates' venerable carriages on the left; Marshal Foch's converted Wagon-Lits on the right.

BELOW 'A crowd of Londoners and servicemen on leave filled Trafalgar Square', 11 November 1918

ABOVE A Bulgarian fortified observation post stormed by the Serbs high above Monastir.

BELOW Baghdad celebrates news of the Mudros Armistice with Turkey.

Admiral Beatty's Day,
21 November 1918.
His flagship, *HMS
Queen Elizabeth*, leads
the way to the surren-
der of the
High Seas Fleet.

Scapa Flow,
21 June 1919. The
scuttled battleship
Bayern sinks slowly
by the stern.

The Bull and Uncle George. Generals Allenby and Milne in Constantinople, 1919.

General Franchet d'Esperey casts a cursory eye at a British Guard of Honour, in Constantinople 1919; General Sir Henry Maitland Wilson follows.

Woodrow Wilson, Visionary of Peace, electioneering.

being forced back to the river Loire for want of your reinforcements?', Foch asked dramatically. Pershing said that he accepted that risk. The Supreme War Council confirmed that it sought the formation of an independent American Army in France at the earliest opportunity. As an emergency measure, for the month of May, Pershing agreed to the temporary attachment of some units for active service, as well as training, with the British and French. The shipment of American infantry and machine-gunners was speeded up: 80,000 Americans crossed the Atlantic in March; 118,000 in April; 245,000 in May. By early September half a million American combatants were in action on the Western Front and by a month later there were 1.2 million. 'America thus became the decisive Power in the war', Ludendorff wrote in his memoirs, a couple of years later.

This newly strengthened mailed fist of his enemy first parried Ludendorff's blows when Paris seemed once more within Germany's grasp. The bombardment of the capital was resumed on Monday 27 May, and over the next sixteen days more than eighty shells hit the centre of the city. Of far greater military significance was the bombardment, with gas and high explosive, which began from 4,000 guns and trench mortars before dawn on this same Monday. The shells fell along a twenty-four-mile front on the Chemin des Dames held by the French Sixth Army, to which five battle-scarred British divisions were attached while 'resting' from Flanders. This third assault by Ludendorff's troops in ten weeks took Foch and Pétain by surprise. General Duchêne, the commander of the Sixth Army, massed his infantry into the front line, instead of preparing and manning deep defences back to the River Aisne as the commander-in-chief had proposed. In packed trenches the troops suffered appallingly under the customary heavy barrage from the Germans. Once again fog favoured the attackers. The rapid advance of picked storm troops overwhelmed four French divisions in the western sector, while further to the east the Germans broke through to the River Aisne, virtually brushing aside eight more French or British divisions. By Tuesday night a salient, forty miles across and fifteen miles deep, was poised menacingly over Paris on the war maps.

During that Tuesday an American brigade seized and held the village of Cantigny, the first specifically American victory in Europe: 'Bravo, the young Americans!', the *Evening News* declared in London, a shade patronizingly. 'Nothing in today's battle narrative from the front is more exhilarating than the account of their fight at Cantigny'. But the 'exhilaration' had been bought at a cost of 200 American lives; and it did not prevent the Germans sweeping forwards south of the Aisne. Soissons fell next day, and by Wednesday night 50,000 French soldiers had been taken prisoner. By Thursday the Germans were back on the Marne, covering a twenty-mile stretch of the river east of Château-Thierry; by Friday 1 June, they were within forty miles of Paris. Pershing, seeing for himself the plight of the Allied armies, loosened his grip on the AEF; Foch was told he might have five US divisions, for service as he saw fit along the Marne.

By then Duchêne's Sixth Army was a broken reed, its survivors hardly more reliable than Cadorna's men after Caporetto. As the US 3rd Division hurried forward to the south bank of the Marne they met fleeing *poilus* who sent them into battle with derisive shouts of 'The war's over'. But the other three components of Franchet d'Esperey's 'Army Group North' remained relatively intact. After consultation with Pétain, Franchet concentrated his forces from high ground overlooking Reims and Epernay westwards to the woods on the north bank of the Marne, beyond Château-Thierry. Ludendorff's advance troops had pushed too far too fast, repeating the mistake which made possible 'the miracle of the Marne' forty-five months previously; sustained pressure against the flanks could force them into retreat – provided always that they could not broaden the apex of the salient they had established. That possibility was denied to them by three resolute actions: the initiative of General Mangin, who launched a successful counter-attack from the forest of Villers-Cotterets and, with the help of tanks, threw the Germans back two miles; the American 3rd Division at Château-Thierry, forcing Germans who had crossed the Marne to abandon their bridgehead on 3 June; and the US 2nd Division who defended Belleau Wood, five miles to the west, in bitter fighting from 3 June to 5 June. The momentum of Ludendorff's third thrust was finally checked, though the battle for Belleau Wood continued for three more weeks before the American Marine Brigade forced the Germans back.

Foch was eager to launch a counter-offensive, taking advantage of the new American troops at his disposal and of the arrival on a huge scale of French tanks and aircraft. The Soissons–Château-Thierry road, the one supply route to the German advanced troops in the Marne salient, was a tempting objective. But Pétain urged him to wait until Ludendorff had exhausted all possible means of attack. French and American Intelligence units were decoding German orders; several Alsatians of French descent had deserted, bringing with them confirmation that Ludendorff was planning a fourth attack, though not on this occasion with Paris as the prize; aircraft reconnaissance revealed the concentration of troops behind the lines. Ludendorff's strategic plan called for an enveloping movement south-westwards, with Epernay and Châlons as immediate objectives and the elimination of the French line from Verdun to Nancy as the ultimate goal. The German press no longer referred to the fighting in France as the Emperor's Battle: significantly, they wrote of *Der Friedensturm*, the 'Peace Offensive'; and there were highly placed officials in Berlin who genuinely anticipated Allied requests for an armistice within the next few days.

While the French were celebrating their national festival, the *Quatorze Juillet*, the Kaiser went to an observation post some twelve miles north-east of Reims to see the opening day of the battle. When he returned to the imperial train the following evening, Admiral von Müller thought that his sovereign's 'mood was slightly less ebullient than usual'. And small wonder. For on this occasion the French defenders had not been taken by surprise. Dummy trench lines were ready for the Germans and, from foreknowledge, the French artillery opened up a barrage soon after midnight on 14–15 July, two hours before Ludendorff's concentrated 2,000 batteries were due to begin their preparatory bombardment. East of Reims the Germans failed to make any progress, suffering heavier casualties than on the first day of any other attack since Verdun. But west of Reims, in the wooded hills above the valleys of the upper Marne and the Ardre, the Germans fought with great tenacity against French, American and Italian troops in well prepared defences along the higher ground. They could not break through. Less than sixty hours after the initial bombardment Ludendorff gave orders for the attack to be broken off. The Germans had lost 50,000 men in three days; the Allies and the Americans perhaps as many as 59,000, mostly sustained under the impact of the first bombardment.

Next morning – Thursday 18 July – Foch launched his first counterstroke, an assault by Mangin's Tenth Army against the Soissons road, with troops from French Morocco and sections of the US 1st and 2nd Divisions in the van of the fighting, giving support to 350 French light tanks, recently completed at Renault's Billancourt factory in western Paris. In three days of battle the last threat to the French capital was removed. At Avesnes on that Thursday the Kaiser berated Ludendorff for having gone ahead with an abortive attack which would have a bad influence on opinion at home and abroad. The First Quartermaster-General, though described as 'jumpy', would not think of standing on the defensive. His staff was working on four operational plans, most pressingly in Flanders and for a direct assault on Reims. It was left to Field Marshal von Hindenburg, on the following Monday afternoon, to inform his All Highest War Lord that the last offensive in what had begun as the Emperor's Battle was ending in total failure.

CHAPTER 12

OUTLYING THEATRES

News of Ludendorff's third thrust, the drive from the Chemin des Dames to the Marne, was brought to Lloyd George on 27 May 1918 by the CIGS seven hours after it began. Hankey was present and describes how, on hearing the bad news from the Front, the three men began to look ahead, sombrely assessing the war situation. Two months of 'great anxiety', Sir Henry Wilson predicted, would be followed by two months of 'diminishing anxiety'. If the Allies survived those four months, they ought – by October 1918 – to be at the start of 'a long interval' during which they could prepare for one massive co-ordinated stroke to overcome the Germans in the following year; the interval might also be used for 'striking some blows in the outlying theatres'. It was a gloomy prospect, postponing fulfilment of even the limited expectations outlined in January's Joint Note 12. The outlook did not improve over the following fortnight. Secret discussions on 30 May and 5 June considered what was to be done if the Channel ports had to be abandoned, or if it proved necessary to withdraw from the Continent entirely, should 'the French crack'. The spectre that was to become a reality in 1940 seems almost to have cast a forward shadow as this earlier war reached its climax.

Concern in London and Paris over perils close at hand left the managements in 'outlying theatres' free to mount programmes of their own devising. Allenby, frustrated by the forced abandonment of his spring offensive at Whitehall's demand, sought in early May to establish and retain a commanding position at Es Salt, threatening Amman over the Jordan valley. This second Transjordan raid, which was made by Australians and New Zealanders, with three brigades of the London Division, failed for three reasons: promised local Arab support was not forthcoming; air reconnaissance failed to spot a large Turkish force, concealed in broken scrub; and the relatively few tracks in hilly terrain could easily be covered by defensive fire. The Australians and New

Zealanders, supported by two battalions from the West Indies and by the Jodhpore Lancers, remained in the almost unbearable heat and humidity of the Jordan valley throughout the summer, successfully fending off a German-led counter-attack in July. Meanwhile, at his Bir Salem headquarters in the coastal plain, Allenby studied the lessons of the Transjordan raids. His victory at Gaza had been won by an unexpected thrust inland. Should he follow this strategy in a modified form a year later? The raids showed that progress through the hill country would be painfully slow and costly; ought he to revert to the traditional route up the coast? And how far could he rely on Arab support? The flame of Arab nationalism, which glowed brightly after the capture of Aqaba, could not fire the spirit of sheikhs of the Jordan valley.

Despite the disappointments of the spring Allenby did not intend to remain on the defensive. From Turkish prisoners captured by patrols, and from a steady stream of deserters, he realized that the troops facing him in northern Palestine felt far less committed to fight than the defenders of Gaza and Jerusalem in the previous autumn. Even though his armies were seriously depleted, he began to look ahead confidently to the peak campaigning season, those eight or nine weeks between the passing of high summer and the coming of the early November rains.

There was now little risk of a German–Turkish attempt to recover Jerusalem, although rather curiously Allenby mentioned such a possibility in conversation with the Zionist leader, Chaim Weizmann. The *Yildirim* grand design, which looked so menacing on paper, had proved as insubstantial as a mirage, as Falkenhayn realized once he sought to lead the Turks in the field. After five months in Asia Falkenhayn welcomed a recall to Germany in the last days of February 1918; his war was to end obscurely in Lithuania, protecting German garrisons from the wrath of the Poles and the enticements of the Bolsheviks. But Falkenhayn's departure did not make the task of the EEF any easier, for he was succeeded by Liman von Sanders, head of the military mission to Turkey before the war and commander in defence of Gallipoli. Liman might not possess so brilliant a military mind as Falkenhayn, but he understood the Turks, had built up their army on the eve of war, and was respected by them. Behind Liman in Constantinople, as Chief of the Ottoman General Staff, was General Hans von Seeckt, perhaps the most skilful German staff officer of the twentieth century. Yet neither Liman nor Seeckt could lift the fighting spirit of troops who had served in the front line too long without relief and lived on subsistence rations, receiving no more than 350 grams of bread a day. Liman himself reckoned that, between the start of the war and Falkenhayn's recall, as many as 300,000 Ottoman soldiers had deserted, a figure half as large again as the number of troops currently serving in the field. Despite the leavening of good German and Austro–Hungarian specialist troops still serving in Syria, there was every reason for Allenby to strike hard against the hungry and demoralized Turks as soon as he could replace the divisions sent to France.

Manpower, however, remained his most pressing concern. Increasing use was made of units which might foment discontent among peoples subject to Turkish domination: three specifically Jewish 'Judaean' battalions, mostly recruited from the bigger English towns, were formed within the Royal Fusiliers as a nucleus for the Jewish Legion long envisaged by Lloyd George. The French similarly raised three Armenian battalions, including refugees rescued by French warships in 1915; they formed the nucleus of a *Légion d'Orient* which was intended to win the backing of Armenians in Syria for the French. The 3rd Indian Division arrived from Mesopotamia in April and more reinforcements from India between June and August, replacing Australian and British troops sent to France, but Allenby was uncertain of their effectiveness. As a young man he had sought entry to the Indian Civil Service, but failed the examination; he never visited India and knew little of the Indian Army or its traditions. He saw for himself at Messines in 1914 the appalling casualties suffered by the 57th Indian Rifles, as they encountered trench warfare for the first time; and he was strongly opposed to employing Indian artillerymen in Palestine, apparently from fear of mutiny or sedition. He was worried by problems of religious obligation; almost a third of his Indians were Muslim, and German Intelligence ensured that pan-Islamic appeals printed in Urdu were circulated among the troops arriving in Egypt.

So concerned was Allenby over the risk of Muslim fighting Muslim that on 2 June he even suggested in a telegram to the War Office that three or four Japanese divisions might be brought to Suez, for service in Palestine and Syria; the Japanese were the one ally with a good army unlikely to be swayed by religious sentiment in the Holy Places. Already fourteen Japanese destroyers and a cruiser were in the Mediterranean, regularly escorting convoys between Malta, Alexandria and Port Said. But Japanese military pride made it unlikely that Emperor Yoshihito would have let his troops play the role cast for the Portuguese in France. Moreover, the British were at that time encouraging the Japanese to join the Americans in occupying Vladivostok so as to prevent stores accumulated at the head of the Trans-Siberian railway from being moved westwards for the Bolsheviks to barter with the Germans and their allies. The War Office turned down Allenby's request, apparently without reference to Tokyo.

He also learnt from Whitehall in June that there was little prospect he could receive any troops from France or Italy before the end of the year. Throughout that critical month in the West, he was even uncertain if he would be able to retain three Australian light cavalry brigades and the 54th East Anglian Division. Not until 26 June did the War Cabinet discuss Palestine, and decide that there was now no longer a need to withdraw further forces from his command. The retention of these troops – particularly the Australian horsemen – were essential to the plans Allenby was perfecting during the hot weather. His armies still enjoyed a two-to-one superiority in infantry, cavalry and firepower over their Ottoman and German enemies; and six squadrons of the Royal Air Force, together with an Australian squadron, ensured mastery of the skies. The terrain and the climate imposed more formidable problems on Allenby's planners than likely enemy resistance. And there were political vexations, too: a well founded suspicion that Feisal might be responding to almost secret approaches from the Turks; and constant doubts over the next move of that indefatigable intriguer, the French 'High Commissioner for Palestine and Syria', François Georges-Picot.

Such problems Allenby was content to leave to the Arab Bureau in Cairo and to the experienced Storrs, now his Military Governor in Jerusalem, but their mounting complexity emphasized the need for a decisive victory as speedily as possible. When, on 15 June, Allenby made it clear at GHQ that he wished to resume the offensive, his intention was to advance only as far north as the administrative boundary between Syria and Palestine. Such a plan corresponded to the cautious encouragement he received from London, when Whitehall remembered his existence. But soon the lure of Damascus began once more to appeal to him. By the beginning of July his thoughts were outpacing his planners. A month later his mind was made up. One morning in the first week of August he returned to headquarters from a ride, 'strode into his office' and told his operations staff that his objective was more ambitious: Ottoman power in Syria must be destroyed before the rains came. 'Time is the enemy, rather than the Turks', he was to tell his staff officers more than once during the following weeks.

The War Cabinet's change of heart on 26 June was a direct consequence of good news from Italy, giving hope that General Diaz's armies would soon be able to penetrate central Europe without help from his three British divisions, which could then return to France. On 15 June what was to become the last Austro-Hungarian offensive had been launched, with the customary bombardment of high explosive and gas shells; within six days it could be clearly written off as a failure.

The June offensive was the brainchild of the veteran Conrad and the Croatian-born Field Marshal Svetozar Boroević von Bojna and was more ambitious than Caporetto. Unlike the series of assaults directed by Ludendorff in France, this attack extended along the whole of the Italian Front, from the Tonale Pass, close to the Swiss border with the Tyrol, through the British and French held Asiago plateau and down the Piave to the Adriatic. Conrad would make the main thrust, striking southwards from his headquarters at Trent and breaking through the mountains to Vicenza. Boroević would cross the Piave, take Treviso, isolate Venice and advance on Padua. If by then the Italians had not sued for peace, he would press forward to the Adige and meet Conrad in Verona. It was a reversion to sound, old-fashioned war games strategy, a 'brush-up-your-pincer-movement' exercise. Perhaps in 1914 or 1915 the old Habsburg Army might have pulled it off; but not a tired and hungry army, with some infantrymen going into battle in boots with paper soles.

Throughout the early months of 1918 large sections of the multi-national army were on the verge of mutiny, as Conrad and Boroević knew well. While they were planning the offensive no less than seven army divisions were stationed far from the war zones, for purposes of internal security. On 1 February a mutiny, begun by Czech agitators aboard the *Szent Georg*, flagship of the Austro-Hungarian cruiser squadron at Cattaro in southern Dalmatia, spread through forty warships before it was suppressed. Red flags were flown, but the mutineers' programme called merely for better food, an end to the war and genuine national autonomy; an enterprising junior officer and two petty officers escaped punishment by seizing a seaplane and crossing to Italy. Army mutinies came with the spring. During May, troops ordered to the Front refused to board their trains: there were mutinies of Slovenes in western Syria, Ruthenes in Ljubljana and Czechs at Rumburk, a small garrison town close to the frontier with German Saxony. Returned prisoners of war from Russia had no wish for further battle experience. 'Reliable' guard regiments herded the mutineers into sealed railway waggons for the journey to the Front. The contrast with the meticulous preparations for the Fourteenth Army's attack in the previous October was striking. It is curious that Emperor Charles showed any confidence in Conrad's planning. He was slow to realize how far the privations of the past seven months had blunted old loyalties.

In the Italian war zone itself there was a constant stream of deserters from the *Kaiserlich-und-Königlich* joint Army, particularly in the Trentino. Further south the rivers were a hindrance; a Polish gunner, captured later in the summer, told the Italians that many of his compatriots had wished to desert, 'but were put off by having to swim across the Piave to give themselves up'. Slovaks and Romanians from Transylvania, conscripted into the Hungarian Honved regiments, complained of brutal treatment by Hungarian NCOs and officers. 'The Austro-Hungarian soldier receives more blows than bread', one Slovak deserter told his Italian interrogators. For four days in the second week of April a 'Congress of Oppressed Peoples' met in Rome, attended by spokesmen for the Italian, Czecho-Slovak, southern Slav, Polish and Romanian minorities within Austria–Hungary and affirmed a determination to carry on a common war of liberation from Habsburg rule so as to secure the establishment of 'completely independent national states' in post-war central Europe. The Congress was given great publicity by the Italian press and the British propaganda machine. But shortage of food was a greater incentive to desertion than political manifestos. Most foot soldiers were sent into battle after subsisting for weeks on a daily ration of eight ounces of black bread, three ounces of meat and, occasionally, some thin vegetable soup. Rumour encouraged a belief that behind the Allied Front there were good stocks of food, drink and tobacco, an illusion sustained by leaflets dropped from Italian planes. During the six-day battle 12,000 Austro-Hungarian troops took the opportunity of coming over to enemy lines, painfully conscious that they had, almost literally, no stomach for the fight.

The *Comando Supremo* had long anticipated the June offensive and General Diaz had prepared good defences in depth, especially in the north. Some of the heaviest fighting on 15 June was on the Asiago plateau, where the two French divisions held to their line, while the British recovered within a day a small segment lost under the weight of the first attack. Only on the lower Piave was there any echo of the Caporetto panic among the Italian infantry. There Boroević's troops established bridgeheads along a fifteen-mile front. But the river crossings were immediately bombed with great accuracy by a Royal Air Force squadron; and the swift-flowing river, its water level raised by heavy rain on 16–17 June, swept the pontoon bridges away. Morale among the sapper bridge-building units within the *K-und-K* Army evidently remained high, for engineers made a courageous attempt to save one important bridge from disintegrating in the swirling waters. But, in general, there was little will to fight a protracted battle. By the end of the week, when Diaz felt able to order cautious counter-attacks, the Austro-Hungarian army had lost over 80,000 men as battle casualties or through desertion. When, on 16 June, the Emperor Charles was informed of the failure to break through the Allied defences, he became finally convinced that the war was lost. Over the following months he was to authorize drastic experiments to preserve the integrity of Austria–Hungary, but he could offer little to counter the persuasive appeals of Masaryk, Beneš, Trumbić and the Polish spokesmen abroad. On 28 June – the fourth anniversary of the assassination at Sarajevo – France took the lead in giving official political recognition to a breakaway movement: the Czech-Slovak National Council in Paris, led by Dr Beneš, was accepted as 'supreme organ of the nation and the first basis of a future Czecho-Slovak government'. British recognition followed on 9 August; American on 2 September.

The defeat of Austria's summer offensive convinced the military leaders in London and Paris that Italy need no longer be treated as the Entente's poor relation. The willingness of the *Comando Supremo* to send brigades to France and to help protect the stores accumulated at Archangel in northern Russia seemed to confirm their hopes that the Italian theatre could be left once more to King Victor Emmanuel's officers and men. But Diaz secured the retention of the five British and French divisions as a visible guarantee of Allied good faith should his troops become war-weary when autumn returned. Diaz was also eager for an American presence in Italy, an issue over which he was strongly supported by the Prime Minister, Orlando; every politician from southern Italy knew from personal experience of the warm and deep emotional ties binding Italian peasant families with kinsfolk across the Atlantic. Pershing was unsympathetic but was overruled from Washington. On 25 July the 332nd Infantry Regiment, part of the American 83rd Division newly landed in France, was transferred to Italy; and their arrival was rapturously welcomed by the press. 'They come with rifles and high hearts to defend the freedom of the world wherever it may be threatened', the *Tribuna* declared on 29 July; and in his *Popolo d'Italia* next day, Mussolini – a warm supporter of April's Congress of Oppressed Peoples – wrote that only from America might new men and new ideas be expected to come; he still professed admiration for President Wilson. It was a period of grand, symbolic gestures. Eleven days later – 9 August – the fifty-five-year-old dramatist and poet Gabriele d'Annunzio flew as pamphlet-aimer passenger in an

SVA-5 reconnaissance aircraft escorted by seven fighters, on a 625-mile round trip to drop leaflets over the Austrian capital. The Viennese were praised for their intelligence, told to think dispassionately of the future, and urged to shake off 'Prussian' fetters while they had the opportunity. Had their message been printed clearly in German rather than in the Italian language superimposed on an Italian national flag, the leaflets might have aroused more interest.

D'Annunzio's propaganda mission was acclaimed by the Italian press. But, predictably, the leaflets did not cause any rattling of fetters. In reality, since May, when angry verbal exchanges between Czernin and Clemenceau alerted OHL to the extent of Charles's peace overtures the previous year, the Germans had tightened their grip on Austria–Hungary; a *Waffenbund*, 'armed forces alliance', bound the two armies closely together. Despite the losses in Italy, the Germans insisted that summer on a strengthening of the *K-und-K* contingent on the Western Front. Although some Hungarian punishment troops sent to the Argonne crossed the lines at the first opportunity, there were still 18,000 officers and men serving in France during the autumn as Austria–Hungary faced disintegration.

Defeat brings dismissal, open or disguised, as the recent careers of Nivelle, Gough, Murray, Cadorna and Falkenhayn illustrated. Now, failure in Italy ended Conrad's career; Emperor Charles relieved his most experienced general of his command on 14 July, replacing him by the Habsburg professional soldier, Archduke Joseph. A month previously, among the French on the Western Front, the axe had fallen, too. Clemenceau's first victim, understandably, was General Duchêne of the Sixth Army on the Aisne. He was also tempted to make Pétain a scapegoat for having failed to anticipate the German drive back to the Marne. But he had no faith in any of the corps commanders as a successor to Pétain. Instead, on 6 June, he decided to recall Guillaumat from Salonika and appoint him Military Governor of Paris, ready to take over from Pétain as Commander-in-Chief should the 'saviour of Verdun' fail to rise above the defeatism which seemed often to envelop him. To fill the vacancy in command of the Allied Armies of the Orient, Clemenceau turned at once to Franchet d'Esperey. Six months previously Franchet had declined the post. But now he was himself under a cloud, since it was his Army Group North which was thrown into retreat by the initial attack of 27 May on the Chemin des Dames. Pétain could stay; for Clemenceau astutely judged that Franchet's removal would placate critics among the parliamentary Deputies.

The order to set out for Salonika reached Franchet at his headquarters in Provins on the afternoon of Thursday 6 June. He was received by Clemenceau at the Rue St Dominique next morning; it was a frigidly correct meeting. On the next Tuesday evening he left the Gare de Lyon for Rome and Brindisi. Somewhere south of Dijon, in the small hours of the morning, his train passed the express bringing Guillaumat back to Paris. He reached Salonika the following Tuesday afternoon, 18 June. A group of senior officers greeted their new commander at the railway station. But he was no man for social pleasantry: '*J'attends de vous une énergie farouche*' ('I expect from you ferocious vigour'), he told them bluntly. 'Seems a smart looking little man', General Milne noted non-committally in his diary.

In some respects Franchet d'Esperey's transference to Salonika resembles Allenby's experience the previous June. While neither general had 'failed' on the Western Front, each fell short of expectations raised by former successes. Each projected a forceful character, seeking to conceal sorrow at the loss in battle of an only son, Franchet's at Verdun, Allenby's in Flanders. Both generals, though scrupulously loyal, were critical of their commanders in France: Allenby mistrusted Haig's plans for the Ypres Salient; and Franchet never became reconciled to what a senior British soldier called 'Boche killing'. A few hours before leaving Paris for Salonika, Franchet told a friend: 'I am not angry at being sent there, as I don't approve of the Foch–Pétain way of doing things. It will certainly defeat the Boche, but at the cost of men, of time and of money. These fine fellows [*Ces braves gens*] have no imagination'. Yet there were two important differences between their assumption of the new commands: while Allenby knew little of Palestine in modern times, Franchet was familiar with the Balkans and had preconceived ideas on the strategy he should follow; and, while Allenby's Prime Minister had given him a definite objective within a definite time limit before he left London, neither Clemenceau nor Foch provided Franchet with military or political instructions of any form. His only order was to leave for Salonika 'as soon as you can'.

Allenby had benefited from Murray's legacy of railway and water-pipeline constructions and from Chetwode's considered reflections after the first two battles of Gaza. Franchet d'Esperey inherited abortive projects put forward by Sarrail's staff during 1917 and an operational plan drawn up by Guillaumat in March 1918, providing for a limited offensive up the Vardar valley, between the river and Lake Doiran. He was not attracted by any proposal put before him; each was too restricted in scope, and there was no touch of originality or surprise about them. More to his liking was a scheme put forward by the Serbian

Chief of Staff, Živojin Mišić, the general whose First Army scaled the 'butter churn' mountain, Kajmakcalan, nearly two years before. Mišić had won the support of Prince-Regent Alexander of Serbia for another assault on the mountain chain along the Greek-Serbian frontier, believing that it would be possible to break the Bulgarian defensive line and force the enemy back across the Vardar and into Bulgaria proper.

Ten days after arriving in Salonika, Franchet accompanied Prince Alexander and Mišić to the Serbian headquarters, eighty-five miles north-west of Salonika, in a clearing among the fir trees 5,500 feet up in the Moglena Mountains, beyond Kajmakcalan. Next day they climbed higher still, another 2,000 feet up to a Serbian observation post hewn in the rock. From this eyrie it was possible to see, four miles away, the Bulgarian defensive system, running along the formless ridge known as the Dobropolje. Behind this line of bare summits was a slightly higher peak, the Kozyak, three miles to the north and included by the Bulgarians in their second line of defence. Beyond the crests of the mountains bridle paths and goat tracks led down to valleys which ran towards the upper Vardar, along the natural line of advance for any army seeking to turn the enemy's position and move forward up the main route towards the Danube and the distant goal of the central European plains. The mountain barrier was formidable, the peaks not so high as Kajmakcalan but steeper and forming a broader chain, militarily deeper in defensive depth; the Serbs had planned an attack on the Dobropolje as part of Sarrail's stillborn offensive in the spring of 1917 but had succeeded in capturing only a few outposts among the foothills. Thereafter both Sarrail and Guillaumat dismissed the prospect of making any advance through this region; the mountains seemed unassailable. Franchet, too, hesitated – but for less than twenty-four hours. The enemy would never expect an attack here and might be caught off-balance by a surprise assault. He could see around him evidence of the skill of the Serbs as mountain fighters; he was impressed by their eagerness and by the volunteers in the Yugoslav Division, who had made a journey halfway round the world to fling themselves into the battle. On 30 June he let Mišić and Prince Alexander know that he favoured a major attack in this sector of the Front; the whole Serbian Army would go forward and would be supported by two French divisions, placed under the command of Mišić in the field. A week later Franchet's staff had completed their first draft survey of the projected offensive. Hundreds of navvies – Italians and displaced Russians as well as local Greeks and Albanians – were engaged to open up approach routes to the Moglena Mountains. Enemy Intelligence was, in the early stages, deceived into believing that the principal task of these labourers was to improve communications with Albania's Adriatic harbours.

Franchet d'Esperey did not receive his formal directive from the Ministry of War in Paris until the day after his return from Serbian advanced headquarters. His orders, approved by Clemenceau, prescribed a series of local actions, designed to weaken Bulgarian resistance preparatory to a major offensive in the autumn, which would relieve pressure on the Western Front. But Franchet did not seek merely local gains: they needlessly cost lives and wasted material. His intention was to build up the Serbian and Greek forces before striking hard and swiftly to break the Bulgarian defences and knock aside the weakest of Germany's props. Once that was achieved he could implement that grand design he had outlined to Poincaré during the first months of war, the thrust deep into the heart of Europe.

Lloyd George, once inspired by a similar strategic vision, now showed little interest in Salonika. The Balkans were not on the War Cabinet's agenda. The 13th Black Watch had sailed from Salonika for Taranto and the train to France two days before Franchet's arrival, and even as late as the last week in July the CIGS urged the War Cabinet to withdraw all British regiments from Macedonia and replace them with Indian troops. When the Supreme War Council met at Versailles on 2 July the Prime Minister complained to Clemenceau that he had not been consulted over Franchet d'Esperey's appointment; why, he wished to know, were the French contemplating an offensive in a theatre of operations where the Council had resolved to stand on the defensive? Clemenceau was disarmingly frank: he reminded Lloyd George that he personally always opposed Balkan expeditions and more than once wanted the whole Allied force brought back from Salonika; he would never allow an attack to be made in Macedonia that 'would weaken the strength of the Allies on any other Front'. Clemenceau was not being evasive; at such a critical moment for the armies in France he remained supremely uninterested in Franchet d'Esperey's movements. Over the next two months the staunchest advocate of the Salonika armies was their old commander, General Guillaumat, who became French Military Representative on the Supreme War Council in the second week of July.

The British remained sceptical. The 'smart looking little man' handled Milne badly; for the British commander, though by far the longest-serving general in Salonika, was not consulted over Franchet's proposed offensive. He received the draft general plan on 25 July and found that his staff was expected to develop operational details for the xii and xvi Corps around Lake Doiran and also for six Greek divisions under his command. In the hills above Doiran the Bulgarians had the advantage in numbers and in firepower. Milne would have preferred an advance up the River Struma to the Rupel Pass, a natural route through the fruit-growing region around Kustendil and on to the capital, Sofia. One wonders why this plan was not followed, for the defences along the Struma were much less formidable than around Doiran, or in the Moglena Mountains. It is possible that the new Commander-in-Chief, always inclined to take snap decisions on first impressions, failed to appreciate the value of the Struma route after he visited the Greek Corps there, in company with Milne, on 19 July. It was a fifty-mile journey from Salonika, the temperature reached 101°F in the Struma valley, and in contrast to his experience with the Serbs, Franchet was not impressed by the Greek contingent. (Nor indeed was Milne when he paid a surprise visit to the Greeks three weeks later and found that, though outposts were fully manned, their occupants saw no reason to forgo an afternoon siesta).

If he was to order an assault on the heavily fortified Bulgarian positions above Doiran, Milne needed howitzers and several shipments of shells. He began at once to press a reluctant War Office for these supplies. But, in dealing with London, Milne made a tactical error. His messages back to the cigs showed, as his biographer remarks, not so much a 'cautious optimism' as a 'tempered pessimism'. They also perpetuated the suspicion that French strategy was linked with political and commercial ambitions in the post-war world, practices which stood out so flagrantly during the Sarrail era. Yet was it sensible for Milne to expect a steady supply of arms and ammunition for an offensive which he thought was being fought for French national interests and in the outcome of which he expressed so little confidence? Urgent telegrams to London seeking ammunition and shells were sent on four occasions. They remained unanswered. Eventually, twenty-four hours before his artillery was due to open up on the Doiran positions, Milne received his first shipment of shells, only one-fifth of the number he had requested. As other reinforcements, there arrived some Indian drivers for the ammunition train, and a small consignment of Lewis guns. Haig's needs in France had priority.

To troops manning the defences in Macedonia and other outlying theatres during the first days of August 1918, it would have seemed improbable for the war to end victoriously within three and a half months. The German Empire was still the predominant power in Europe, from the Belgian coast to the Urals. Although Germany was shaken by strikes and violence in January 1918 the peace treaties of Brest-Litovsk and Bucharest (with Romania) gave promise of food, oil and material goods from the East, lifting morale throughout the summer despite the failure of the Western offensives. Expansionist groups in Berlin and Army headquarters at Spa in Belgium continued to develop plans for exploiting their gains from the old Russian Empire. Ludendorff, echoing the views of the nationalist Fatherland Party, sought the creation of puppet states from the Dniester to the southern Caucasus, with the Crimea a German dependency, offering Junker land-owners a Prussian riviera and the Imperial Navy a base from which to dominate the Black Sea. To promote these dreams Ludendorff was prepared to leave forty divisions – one and a half million experienced troops – in the Ukraine and southern Russia while the armies in the West were seeking to break through to the Channel ports or Paris. When, on 23 May, Georgia proclaimed independence and asked Germany for military and political protection, Ludendorff advised immediate acquiescence and recommended to the Foreign Ministry in Berlin that similar appeals from other peoples of the Caucasus should be treated sympathetically. If German ambitions in the East clashed with Enver's dreams of a pan-Turanian empire, the Turks must come to heel; a peremptory order from OHL on 8 June insisted, on grounds of joint general strategy, that the Ottoman armies should seek to advance, not farther into the Caucasus, but southwards into Mesopotamia. Posses-sion of the Baku oilfields was vital for Germany, Ludendorff insisted in July. As late as 9 August a conference of senior representatives of the Army, Navy, Foreign Ministry and the Trade and Industry Ministry emphasized the need for German economic control of the Caucasus and a 'sphere of influence' to include 'the Mesopotamian oil-wells'.

The British had been aware of the German threat in central Asia even before the Brest-Litovsk Peace Treaties were signed. In the War Cabinet both Milner and Curzon stressed the important role of the Mesopotamian Expeditionary Force which, since the death of General Maude in November 1917, was commanded by General Sir William Marshall. Despite having to send the 3rd Indian Division to Egypt for service under Allenby, Marshall sought to satisfy the often confused instructions reaching him in Baghdad from London. The Mesopota-mian Expeditionary Force pursued the Turks up the Euphrates to the ancient town of Hit in March 1918 and pressed further northwards on the long road towards Aleppo, making effective use of light armoured cars. It was a tedious terrain; 'Miles and miles and miles of damned all' was one veteran's succinct comment in his diary. At Khan Baghdadi, on

27 March, a cavalry brigade cut off the Turkish defenders, taking 5,000 prisoners; armoured cars pursued the rest of the garrison up the Aleppo road and captured the Turkish commander and the chief of the German Intelligence mission. But by April both the War Office and the India Office were so alarmed at the activities of German agents along what the Kaiser had called 'the bridge to India' that the CIGS ordered Marshall to shift the main emphasis of his advance away from the Euphrates and across to the Tigris and Kurdistan. He was to stop any German or Turkish attempt to control northern Persia.

Marshall knew, from experience, the limitations imposed by geography and climate in such a distant theatre of war. He was being asked to penetrate much hillier country, where the temperature was more equable than in the plains around Hit but where heavy storms could soon turn gullies into wide torrents. To an even greater extent than Allenby in Palestine, his operational timetable was dictated by rainy seasons and hot weather. Moreover, there was a danger that – like Townshend in 1915 – he might advance so rapidly as to place an impossible burden on supply routes. Marshall's 13th Division – a cavalry brigade with horses and armoured cars, and mobile columns of infantry from Lancashire and Staffordshire in several hundred Ford trucks – set out north-eastwards after nightfall on 26 April, the way ahead illuminated for them by flashes from an electrical storm. They covered 150 miles, to take Kirkup on 7 May; but the strain on Marshall's supply line proved so severe that, two and a half weeks later, he decided to evacuate the city, falling back with his troops protecting some 1,600 Kurdish refugees, fearful of Turkish reprisals. Like Allenby, he would wait until the passing of the hot weather before resuming an offensive against troops who, as on so many other fronts, were showing less and less inclination for sustained resistance.

But this was not what London wanted. The War Office might, in this critical summer in France, treat Salonika and Palestine as sideshow irrelevancies, but the German thirst for Middle East oil ensured that on several days Mesopotamia held centre stage. A telegram from the CIGS on 28 June complained that Marshall 'was not taking full advantage of our opportunities . . . a greater and more sustained effort must be made in north-west Persia . . . Your main attention must be directed against Persia and the Caspian'. Calmly Marshall remained on the defensive. Little action was possible in the summer heat, when the shade temperature in the encampment north of Baghdad had climbed to 125° Fahrenheit. He did, however, shift the spearhead of his forces to cover the northern frontier of Persia; it was cooler in the high plateau.

And, in the strangest of many twists on the road to victory, Marshall hastily improvised 'Dunsterforce'.

There had never been any possibility that Marshall could send a fully equipped army into Persia, across mountains as forbidding as the chain along the Greek-Serbian frontier, so as to secure the Baku oilfields; they were as far from Baghdad as Warsaw from Haig's headquarters in France. In the last week of January 1918, however, a military mission of forty-one Ford trucks and armoured cars set out from Baghdad to establish a British presence in the Caucasus. At their head was Major-General Dunsterville of the Indian Army, who forty years previously had shared a school study with Rudyard Kipling and was the original model for the fictional Stalky. Most of Dunsterville's military career had been along the north-west frontier of India; he was a qualified interpreter in Russian, Chinese, Persian, Urdu and Punjabi and also spoke German and French. His convoy crossed into Persia and covered 345 miles in fourteen days, through the almost snow-blocked Asadabad Pass, to rest at Hamadan on 11 February before following a good, Russian-built road for 150 miles and reaching the more important town of Qazvin on 16 February. Dunsterville was still 150 miles from Persia's Caspian seaport of Enzeli (also known as Bandar-e Pahlevi), and Baku itself was another 200 miles north across the sea. The General was now delayed, partly by hostile action by Persian tribesmen and partly by the complications of shifting loyalties in Russia's protracted civil war. By midsummer – with a mainly Turkish army concentrating in Tabriz, ready to march through Azerbaijan to Baku – the urgency of Dunsterville's needs prompted Marshall to find the men and lorries for the specially designated 'Dunsterforce'. Hence on 1 July – while US Infantry were storming the village of Vaux, outside Château-Thierry, and Britain's Prime Minister was 'motoring' from Dieppe to Versailles to confront Clemenceau over the Salonika Question – four battalions of British infantry left the 39th Brigade camp north of Baghdad for the Caspian Sea, where Dunsterville was already supported by a battalion of the Hampshire Regiment, a squadron of Hussars, some armoured cars and several thousand anti-Bolshevik Cossacks.

The 39th Brigade took five weeks to reach Dunsterville at Enzeli, the first three companies of the North Staffordshire Regiment arriving on Sunday 4 August. While the lorries had carried them for 500 miles, they had covered nearly 150 miles on foot, escorting pack camels through deep forests and two mountain passes. Other troops completed the long trek during the week, though sickness reduced their numbers. By Wednesday they were in Baku, having sailed aboard a commandeered

steamer named in honour of President Kruger. For over a month –
decisive weeks for the war in Europe – infantry from Warwickshire,
Worcestershire, Hamphire and Staffordshire, supported by a battery of
field artillery, armoured cars, two Australian planes, partially trained
Armenians and Russians of varying loyalty resisted a Turkish force of
more than 12,000 men. Dunsterville did not attempt to destroy the
oilfields (though some were damaged by shellfire) because that would
have provoked desperate resistance from the local Tatar oil-workers.
On the night of 14 September three steamers evacuated Dunsterforce,
and many civilian refugees with it.

Next morning the Turks entered Baku and set up an administration
headed by Enver's brother, Nuri. Technically the Dunsterforce 'sideshow of a sideshow' had proved a failure; and, in the mounting drama of
the following weeks, its remarkable achievements went largely un-
noticed at home. But the long resistance paid a negative dividend. For,
by the time the war ended, not a single barrel of oil from Baku had
reached the German or Ottoman armies in Europe or Syria. The
ambitions of Ludendorff and Enver remained pipeline dreams. On 17
November the ss *President Kruger* brought British troops back to the
Baku quayside.

CHAPTER 13

THE FLOWING TIDE

The fourth anniversary of Britain's declaration of war – 4 August 1918 – found the Allied governments bracing themselves for at least another year of war. It was on this Sunday that footsloggers from the English pottery towns reached the Caspian Sea; and in Wadi Rumm, north of Aqaba, an English major wrote admiringly in his diary of the brother officer who, riding 'in spotless white' like 'a Prince of Mecca', set the Camel Corps on its track for one last raid on the Hejaz railway outpost of Mudawara. On the Western Front, Foch's troops on the Aisne – counter-attacking throughout the past fortnight – entered ruined Soissons, historically the most besieged city in France; General Mangin was to claim that his Tenth Army took more than 30,000 prisoners and 700 guns in pushing the Germans from Soissons on that Sunday. In one sense it was a day of portent: in Flanders, on the recommendation of the (Jewish) adjutant of his Bavarian regiment, Corporal Hitler received the Iron Cross, First Class, a rare distinction for a junior NCO; and in Champagne the visiting Assistant Secretary for the US Navy, Franklin D. Roosevelt, fired a shell from an American battery which, so spotter-planes reported, duly hit the railway junction of Bazoches, a full eight miles away.

Across the Channel the weekend once again covered the August Bank Holiday break. People sought as usual to get away to the seaside, though the trains were crowded and the need to preserve coal, and a shortage of footplate-men, precluded the running of excursion 'specials'. Most Londoners made for the coast of Kent and Sussex; the newspapers reported long queues for tickets at London Bridge and Victoria; Charing Cross gave priority to traffic from France, and travellers were accustomed to seeing convoys of ambulances pulling out from the station forecourt, giving grim notice of the coming of hospital trains. It was hard to escape the war in southern or eastern England. On the cliffs and promenades of several resorts the rumble of guns from France could be clearly heard; paddlers on beaches from Deal to Dungeness were

nearer the trenches in France than they were to London. Those who
ventured further afield, up to the Norfolk coast, were disturbed by
searchlights sweeping the skies for Zeppelin raiders on their way to
bomb the Midlands. As twilight fell on 5 August, over the sea off
Cromer and Sheringham, the newest of Germany's airships, *L-70*, was
shot down in flames, killing the most famous Zeppelin commander,
Peter Strasser, and his crew of twenty-one officers and men. No more
Zeppelins or German aircraft approached British shores during the war.

Although newspaper headlines suggested that the Germans were in
retreat in France there was still grave uncertainty over the immediate
future; high hopes would so often end in disillusionment. During June a
new concern had manifested itself in several British cities, an unusually
severe summer influenza epidemic. At home the incidence of illness
receded in July, but commanders overseas continued to report an
extraordinarily high sick list. Milne, Marshall, Allenby, Haig and
Pershing were faced by similar problems; so, too, were the German
forces in France and in Italy. Far worse was to come, for the virulent
pandemic of this inaptly named 'Spanish flu' did not reach a peak in
western Europe until the last weeks of the war, when it found easy
victims among the famished and weary. But even in August it was clear
that the nation's general debility was low. Would a tonic of good news,
prescribed by the newest departmental creation, the Ministry of
Propaganda, be sufficient to sustain the people? Over this Bank Holiday
weekend both Churchill and Lloyd George felt a need of messages to lift
morale. 'This war has got to be won and it is not won yet', Churchill
wrote bracingly to his constituents. 'The *appearance* of power is with the
enemy but the *reality* of power is with us'. In a message to the nation,
which was read aloud in places of entertainment on Bank Holiday
Monday, Lloyd George told the people, 'Hold Fast'; with a million
Americans already come from across the Atlantic and the enemy falling
back, 'Our prospects of victory have never been so bright as they are
today'.

As 4 August was a Sunday, many people heeded the call of the
Archbishop of Canterbury to mark the anniversary with moments
of remembrance and rededication. The Primate himself – Randall
Davidson – preached at a special service in St Margaret's Church,
Westminster, which, following Crimean War precedent, constituted 'a
solemn act of prayer, confession, thanksgiving, commemoration and
resolve'. Earlier in the war some senior churchmen had displayed a
belligerent patriotism, speaking out insensitively, as if they were
consecrated recruiting sergeants. The Archbishop always deplored such

pronouncements. In a noble sermon on that Sunday he emphasized war's 'unspeakable hatefulness', the need to ensure that 'a repetition of its ghastly horrors shall become impossible'. He condemned the 'poisonous hatred running right counter to the principles of a Christian's creed', the mood of 'selfishness and greed of gain'. His congregation included peers and MPs, Cabinet ministers from home and overseas, and King George V and Queen Mary; he charged them to remember that 'As pledged disciples of a living Lord and Master who died upon the Cross for all who hated Him, we have to see to it that the spirit of hate finds no nurture in our hearts'.

On the following Wednesday the King crossed to Boulogne for his fifth visit to the BEF in France; and on Thursday – 8 August – Lloyd George left London to enjoy the Eisteddfod in the land of his fathers. Neither seems to have realized that the war was approaching its climacteric, though chance gave the King a better opportunity than his Prime Minister to keep a rendezvous with history. Preparations for an offensive on the British sector of the Front some twelve miles south-east of Amiens by General Rawlinson's Fourth Army were made in great secrecy: on Rawlinson's orders a slip of paper with 'Keep Your Mouth Shut' printed on it was pasted into the paybook of every officer and man under his command. The crack Canadian Corps, fully fit and well equipped, was moved almost silently southwards from Arras during Tuesday night; 324 heavy tanks were concentrated as a spearhead with ninety-six 'whippet' light tanks and twelve armoured cars in support, the noise of their engines drowned by low-flying reconnaissance aircraft over the German lines; there was to be no preliminary bombardment. Intelligence of the attack never reached the Germans; and had it done so, it might well have misled them, for Haig's original intention of beginning his attack on 10 August was, at Foch's request, advanced by forty-eight hours. Bogus wireless messages suggesting that an offensive near Ypres was imminent confused King Albert of the Belgians, and may therefore have fooled the enemy, too. On the left of the Canadians was the Australian Corps of General Monash, the Melbourne civil engineer who had distinguished himself as a brigade commander at Gallipoli and in leading a division in Flanders for the past two years. The British III Corps comprised the main flank-guard, with cavalry in support. The US 33rd Division stood in reserve, with seven French divisions of General Humbert's Third Army putting pressure on the Germans from the south. A supplementary attack, planned by Haig and Rawlinson in close collaboration with General Débeney of the French First Army, would be made by Débeney's troops on the town and railway junction of

Montdidier. For ten nights and days the RAF bombed German approach roads and base towns, although the total weight of bombs dropped (184 tons) was only the equivalent of four missions by the six plane formations favoured on the eve of the Normandy landings twenty-six years later.

A ground mist covered the chalky plain of Picardy at dawn on Thursday 8 August. 'Glass steady', Haig noted in his diary, after a glance at the barometer, 'An autumn feel in the air'. For once the ground was hard, sun-baked, rather than rain-soaked. A sudden heavy bombardment at 4.20 in the morning sent tanks and men forward. 'The blasts from the guns made our steel helmets jump on our heads', a British infantryman was to recall. 'The whole world heaves, rocks, tumbles', wrote a gunner, describing how his tank was rolling like a tramp steamer in the Bay of Biscay, 'Millions of lights flash and stab and crisscross . . . Lurch, dip, slide down, nose up, heave forward, amble along'. The top speed of the heavy tanks was no more than a steady walking pace, and the Canadians followed them closely, storming through the holes they made in the wire and clearing the trenches. So great was the surprise that the attackers were able to take all their original objectives with two hours to spare.

By 10.30 in the morning the Australians, attacking east of the ruined industrial town of Villers Bretonneux, had reached the rear bivouacs and administrative huts of the German 13th Division facing them. They went on to surprise the divisional staff, eating a hastily scrambled lunch. The French made slower progress, partly because they made no use of tanks and partly because of hillier ground around Montdidier (which was not finally in French hands until Saturday 10 August). But by Thursday nightfall Haig could report that the advance along a ten-mile sector had penetrated the defences between seven and nine miles. The Germans admitted they suffered 27,000 casualties on that day, of whom 15,000 were taken prisoner; they also lost 400 guns. British, Canadian and Australian casualties were under 9,000 – killed, missing and wounded: one-eighth of the appalling losses on the first day of the Somme.

'As the sun set over the battlefield on 8 August the greatest defeat sustained by the German army since the start of the war was an accomplished fact', the German official account of the day records. Ludendorff, who was at field headquarters in Avesnes, received such 'gloomy news' from the sector before noon that he sent a senior staff officer to discover what was happening. When the officer returned his 'report . . . perturbed me greatly . . . whole bodies of our men had surrendered to single troopers or isolated squadrons'. It was this first clear evidence that 'the morale of the German Army was no longer what it had been' that induced Ludendorff, in a much quoted phrase, to write, 'August 8th was the black day of the German Army in the history of this war'. Tactical reversals and the loss of crater-pitted wasteland might be redeemed; the surrender of thousands of Germans to the advancing Allies could not. Ludendorff was deeply shaken. He was still in this state of proxy shell-shock when, on Friday morning, the Kaiser arrived at Avesnes to discuss the crisis with the First Quartermaster-General and with the General Field Marshal, who was much calmer. An offer of resignation by Ludendorff was brushed aside by both William II and Hindenburg. While the three men were in conference a message arrived from the chief German liaison officer at K-und-K headquarters in Baden, south of Vienna. It was clear that the reports from the Western Front, following the failure on the Piave, had strengthened Emperor Charles's desire for an early peace. He wished to confer with his German ally. The Kaiser, unusually calm for a man so prone to self-dramatization, declared: 'We have reached the limits of our strength. The war must be brought to an end.' But he would not be hurried. He proposed to hold an Imperial Crown Council 'in the next day or so at Spa', preparatory to receiving there Emperor Charles and the K-und-K military leaders.

Over the next few days the pace of the Allied advance slackened. Rawlinson's army met stiffer German resistance from troops rushed to the danger zone; it was difficult to move forward rapidly through the hideous obstacles marking the line of old battlefields along the Somme and, as anticipated, it proved impossible to keep the heavy tanks in action for any long offensive. On Friday 9 August only 145 tanks were still mobile and capable of going into action; by Saturday morning that number had fallen to little more than a hundred. But the Germans were allowed no respite. The French Third Army's main attack began on that Saturday; Mangin's Tenth Army followed, further to the south on 17 August; and the British resumed the offensive on 21 August with a fiercely fought battle for the town of Albert which succeeded in turning the German positions on the Somme.

By the end of the month the changes which had been made to the war maps by the 'Emperor's Battle' were eradicated. The 'Backs to the Wall' army of April became a 'Back to the Hindenburg Line' army in August.

Both the British and American press enthusiastically reported the Allied successes. Barely thirty hours after Rawlinson's first attack the

New York Times of 9 August carried three rows of banner headlines:

HAIG BREAKS FOE'S LINE ON 25-MILE FRONT:
GAINS 7 MILES, TAKES 10,000 MEN, 100 GUNS,
GERMAN MAN POWER VISIBLY ON THE WANE

But the British government, perhaps made sceptical by its own propaganda, was curiously slow to realize the magnitude of what was happening in France. Only Winston Churchill, the Minister of Munitions, sensed the significance of that initial breakthrough by the tanks. He flew to France on the afternoon of 8 August, lunched with General Rawlinson at Fourth Army headquarters next day and, though he spent much of the following week at top-level discussions in Paris, it was not until 24 August that he came back to London. He thus acquired a fuller understanding of the changing fortunes of the war than Lloyd George. For the Prime Minister, after returning from the Eisteddfod for several days of talks with visiting imperial statesmen, resumed his Welsh holiday on 17 August. He remained at Criccieth for eleven days, giving much thought to holding a general election so as to strengthen his authority as a spokesman for the country in war and in peace. But before returning to Wales he did at least discuss reports from France with his colleagues on Monday (12 August) and Tuesday morning, showing a certain mistrust of Foch (who had been created Marshal of France a week previously), largely on the ground that he was too inclined to commit troops to operations which would incur heavy losses. As yet Lloyd George seemed unwilling to accept that the German tide was on the ebb. 'The P.M.', Hankey noted in his diary for 13 August, 'does not take a very sanguine view of our military prospects, in spite of recent success'. And he added: 'Nor do I – very'.

But at OHL headquarters in Spa, that most English of watering-places, the Germans saw matters differently. On that same Tuesday, 13 August, Hindenburg and Ludendorff received Chancellor Hertling and the Foreign Minister, Rear-Admiral von Hintze, who had left the Navy some years before the war to hold important diplomatic posts in Russia and Norway. To Hintze's amazement Ludendorff had given up any hope of forcing the Allies to seek a peace. Germany, he argued, would have to fight a strategically defensive campaign which would destroy her enemy's will to continue the fight; at the same time the Foreign Ministry would have to find ways of ending the war advantageously, through diplomacy. The Chancellor was criticized for failing to safeguard food supplies and for not devising means to counter enemy propaganda. There was no doubt that the effective centre of government was not Bismarck's old Chancellery in Berlin but the home of OHL, ironically in this instance Spa's Grand Hôtel Britannique, uphill from the Boulevard des Anglais.

Next morning the Kaiser, the German Crown Prince and the chief executants of government, civil and military, joined the discussions at the Hôtel Britannique, thus constituting an Imperial Crown Council. Ludendorff affected a confidence which he had not shown at Avesnes or in his talks with Hintze on Tuesday. He still had hopes of securing a victorious peace, if not of total and decisive victory. Hindenburg was even more assured 'we shall be able to make a stand on French soil and thus in the end impose our will on the enemy'. Only Hintze, a man of intelligence and broad understanding, doubted the apparent certainty of his colleagues. The Kaiser was clearly wavering; he wanted a vigorous morale-boosting propaganda campaign to stamp out defeatism at home; but he was prepared to authorize 'peace feelers through diplomatic channels', using Queen Wilhelmina of the Netherlands or King Alfonso XIII of Spain as an intermediary. It was also felt that the approach should only be made 'after our next successes in the West'; and it was to be emphasized that any peace in Europe would have to accept both Belgium and Poland as German dependencies.

On Wednesday afternoon the Emperor Charles, his Foreign Minister (Count Burian, who had succeeded Czernin in May) and his Chief of the General Staff (General von Arz) reached Spa. During that evening and next morning the ruling Hohenzollern and Habsburg sovereigns met in conference for the last time. By now Charles wanted a direct appeal made to all belligerent governments, pressing for an immediate armistice pending a peace conference at some unspecified date in a neutral country; no peace terms would be demanded in advance of the conference. But the Germans would have nothing to do with such ideas. They insisted that Austria–Hungary should make no independent peace moves. In the East, as Ludendorff emphasized, the Central Powers remained in a strong position, still capable of reshaping the map of Europe. Even in these critical days at Spa, the discussion ranged around which German princeling should become king of post-war Poland. But the main talk was of military affairs; one more German success on the Western Front before asking for peace, Hindenburg and Ludendorff insisted again and again. Emperor Charles, with Arz and Burian, left for Baden on 15 August: he was prepared to wait for a week before seeking peace; but he would delay no longer.

Briefly, on 21-2 August, OHL thought there was a chance of gaining the face-saving success on which Hindenburg laid such stress. General Byng's Third Army, seeking a route for tanks between the craters of the

Somme and Arras battlefields, went forward on a day when early
morning mist gave way to glorious sunshine – good for support from
aircraft, but creating such intense heat within the heavy Mark V tanks
that some crews lost consciousness. The Germans, mainly Bavarian
units, fell back for more than two miles, and then thought Byng's
advance had ground to a halt. The Bavarians claimed a defensive victory.
On 22 August they even counter-attacked, though at heavy cost. But the
Third Army's halt accorded with the British strategic plan. It enabled
Rawlinson's Fourth Army, on Byng's right, to take control of ruined
Albert. Next day, with the heat so unbearable that even in the light
Whippet tanks guns became too hot to hold, the combined Third and
Fourth Armies resumed their advance, on a front now thirty-five miles
wide. Eight thousand prisoners surrendered that day, 2,000 of them to
the Australians. Several thousand more Germans were passing into
French prisoner of war cages as Mangin's Tenth Army took Noyon.

Among the British troops were newly commissioned officers of
eighteen or nineteen who had been on 'field days' with their school
Officer's Training Corps only a few weeks before and came to the
trenches fresh from the classroom. Hindenburg and Ludendorff also
were counting by now on aid from youngsters born in the twentieth
century. German front-line resistance was as tough as ever, but the will
to continue fighting, the iron resolve of endurance, began to crumble
away. Disappointment prompted dismay. In Hutier's Eighteenth Army
Captain Herbert Sulzbach – who had received his Iron Cross, First
Class, a day after Corporal Hitler – fell back mile by mile with the
German guns from France into Belgium; in his diary, after a fortnight of
the retreat, he wrote on 2 September, 'It is just very bitter that now we
have to clear out of all the ground which we have conquered in those
brilliant victories since 21 March; and we were already dreaming about
being in Paris'.

Exactly a week after Emperor Charles's return from Spa, the Austro-
Hungarian ambassador in Berlin presented Hintze with a draft of his
government's peace appeal to the world. The Germans continued to
play for time. A week later the ambassador was back again, with a
message that no more time should be lost; the Emperor would seek an
immediate end to the war. Still the Germans prevaricated. Hintze
himself made the journey to Vienna insisting, on 3 September, that OHL
was still preparing that 'strategic defensive' of which there had been so
much talk at Spa. Dutifully, Vienna agreed once more to wait; for there
was at least no sign of an attack on the *K-und-K* armies in northern Italy.

On 30 August *The Times* in London carried the most encouraging headline for many months; it read, quite simply, 'The Flowing Tide'. The principal news item was the entry of the New Zealand Division into the town of Bapaume on the previous day, but the whole tone of that Friday's edition was celebratory, almost three weeks of Allied advance. But could it really continue? Before dawn on Saturday two under-strength battalions of the Australian 2nd Division – no more than 550 men – attacked the centre and flanks of the German fortified position on Mont St Quentin, a hill some 140 feet high about a mile south of the town of Péronne. They carried the position by surprise, taking more than seven hundred prisoners. Before nightfall the Germans made fifteen counter-attacks in a desperate bid to throw out the Australians, but without success. Eight of twenty Victoria Crosses won by General Monash's Australians were awarded for the fighting at Mont St Quentin on that last day of August. Two days later the Canadians in the British First Army stormed a heavily wired position south-east of Arras with similar courage, breaking the line at a critical point in a four-hour assault. Seven Canadians received the Victoria Cross in recognition of their valour. There were, in all, fifty Victoria Crosses bestowed during the last hundred days of fighting on the Western Front.

For Germany, Sunday 1 September was 'Sedan Day', a victory anniversary proudly celebrated each year since the proclamation of the Empire. By an oddly prophetic coincidence, the Kaiser was in residence at Wilhelmshöhe, the palace near Kassel which his grandfather designated as a place of internment for Napoleon III after the French Emperor's surrender on the battlefield of Sedan. There was no cause for rejoicing this year. News from the Front remained grave throughout the day, with heavy fighting 'south of Cambrai'. On Monday evening the Kaiser told his military suite that 'The campaign is lost . . . Our army is at the end of its tether.' By the following morning he was in such a state of nervous collapse that, after breakfast, he retired to bed. But within twenty-four hours he had taken a grip on himself and at the end of the week was exuding a confidence he may not himself have felt.

The British, of course, had no perception of this passing despondency at the heart of the imperial circle. Uncertainty persisted in London. There remained a fear that the deep wire entanglements along the Hindenburg Line and the long-since sited artillery positions and machine-gun nests would lead to a second Passchendaele. On Sunday afternoon the CIGS telegraphed to Haig a curious 'personal message'. He was reminded of the anxiety with which the War Cabinet would react to news of 'heavy punishment' being received from the Germans in response to any assault on the Hindenburg Line.

Haig was angry at such a cumbersome off-the-cuff warning. He did not realize the mistrust with which the War Cabinet looked on all proposals for attack in the West, especially now that the long sun-baked days were over; heavy thunderstorms across northern France revived memories of last autumn's mud-clogged immobility. Equally, the policy-makers in London never reflected that Haig, too, was a natural barometer-tapper; by now, experience had made him a cautious commander, convinced that he needed to end the fighting before winter came again, and certain that it was within his power to do so. Every report from Intelligence interrogators stressed that the Germans were badly shaken; they must be defeated in the field before they could pause to regroup their armies. Haig was prepared to leave GHQ and cross to London, even while his troops were attacking the first obstacles of the Hindenburg Line, to emphasize his point in Whitehall. On 10 September Haig spoke at length to the War Secretary (since late April Lord Milner); he urged that all reserves of men, transport and supplies must be sent to France at once, to maintain pressure on a retreating enemy in this new war of movement. Milner seemed sympathetic to Haig, and nine days later crossed the Channel to see conditions at the Front himself. But at heart Milner remained sceptical; he could not convince himself that Haig, so rashly optimistic in 1916 and 1917, was right. Like General Wilson earlier in the month, Milner felt impelled to give a warning: if Haig 'knocked his present army about there was no other to replace it'.

Marshal Foch, like Haig, wished to end the war in the West before the coming of another winter. But, as an Allied generalissimo, he had to tread cautiously. There was no carefully considered grand strategic design issued from his headquarters at the Château de Bombon, twenty miles north-east of Paris. Foch was an inspirational leader, rather than a detailed planner, with a large staff to co-ordinate advances according to a perfect timetable. He would offer laconic generalizations, to which his faithful shadow and Chief of Staff, General Maxime Weygand, would give a certain clarity and precision. Foch expected the national commanders-in-chief (Pétain, Haig, Pershing and King Albert of the Belgians) to adhere to a broad plan of rolling the Germans back with continuous attacks – 'Everyone goes into battle' (*'Tout le monde à la bataille'*). But the specific advance of individual armies, and often individual divisions, owed more to opportunism and flair in subordinate commanders than to directives from the Foch-Weygand partnership at Bombon. At the same time, the Marshal was himself prepared to suggest late adjustments to agreed plans in order to meet changing circumstances – as when, for example, he asked Haig to advance the opening of the Fourth Army's offensive south-east of Amiens by forty-eight hours. Haig had protested successfully on 14 August when Foch wished the Fourth Army to press forward immediately to the line of the Somme, a move which the British generals believed would lead to heavy casualties in men and the loss of many tanks. Thereafter the two commanders worked well in partnership. Even before Haig travelled to London to see Milner, Foch had told him how hopeful he was that 'the German is nearing the end'.

The Foch style did not suit General Pershing. On 24 July, during a conference of commanders-in-chief at Bombon to decide on the general shape of future strategy, it was agreed that the Americans would eliminate the salient at St Mihiel, which the Germans had held since the autumn of 1914. By giving the Germans a bridgehead on the western bank of the Meuse the thirty-two-mile broad salient effectively checked any advance towards Metz and into Lorraine, and it had long hampered communications with Verdun, twenty-three miles north of the town of St Mihiel. Pershing personally assumed command of the US First Army and his staff began planning the battle during the first week of August. Much of the work was supervised by Colonel George C. Marshall, US Chief of Staff throughout the Second World War, and who, as Secretary of State, is remembered for a more beneficent plan. But, while Colonel Marshall and his team were at work, the British and French successes from the Aisne to Flanders made Haig – and later Pétain – question the wisdom of an all-out assault on St Mihiel. For Metz, the ultimate prize of any attempt at a breakthrough in the salient, was the strongest fortified city in western Europe, with a girdle of defences fifteen miles in circumference and capable of resisting assault as determinedly as Verdun; no army of keen and courageous newcomers, seeking a speedy end to the war, should be pitted against Metz. Moreover – and of more immediate concern – a line of advance up the Moselle would be set too far south-eastwards to coincide with the Allied thrust from the Aisne and the Somme and the Yser into Belgium. Haig therefore suggested to Foch that the American drive should be made northwards into the Argonne Forest west of Verdun, with Sedan and Mézières as objectives rather than Metz. On 24 August Pershing visited Foch at Bombon and discussed detailed arrangements for launching the St Mihiel operation on 10 September, with sixteen American divisions and a French Colonial Corps assigned to Pershing's command. But six days later Foch and Weygand travelled up to Pershing's field headquarters, fifteen miles south of St Mihiel, and outlined to him a revised plan: after clearing the St Mihiel salient, the Americans would stand on the defensive across the Woevre plain; Pershing's army would then be divided, with one half joining the French Second Army in an advance through the Argonne Forest while the remaining troops would join the French Fourth Army up familiar fields across Champagne.

By now, however, Pershing was adamant over the need for a strict recognition of the unity and coherence of the AEF. He had agreed to the detachment of American divisions in order to support the French around Soissons and the British in Flanders during the critical months of spring and summer, but he remained determined to develop an independent American army which, while playing a role in Foch's general plans, would assert its character as the military arm of an Associated Power, not an Ally. He therefore told Foch bluntly that 'the American people and the American Government expect that the American Army shall act as such, and not be dispersed here and there along the Western Front'. When Foch asked 'Do you wish to take part in the battle?' Pershing replied, 'Most assuredly, but as an American Army and in no other way'. Foch returned to Bombon, leaving an outline of his proposals in a memorandum drawn up by Weygand.

Pershing's written response to these proposals reveals the difference of approach between a commander who, as yet, had fought no great battles in the West, and veterans like Foch and Haig. For Pershing rejected the generalissimo's basic assumption: he complained that his troops had met such difficulties in serving with the French and British that 'it is inadvisable to consider' their return 'to French and British control'; he proposed to complete the St Mihiel operation and then withdraw the AEF for winter training and the arrival of more divisions and supplies from America in anticipation of the spring offensive of 1919, when his army would take Metz and head for Trier or cross Lorraine to the Saar.

As a grand design, there was much to be said in favour of Pershing's strategy; if the British and French cleared the Germans from Belgium and the Americans advanced up the Moselle, the Allies could converge on the Cologne–Coblenz stretch of the Rhine, though Germany might well surrender before the old frontiers were crossed. But such speculative planning assumed the war must drag on into the following year. At a further meeting with Marshal Foch and General Pétain on 2 September a compromise was reached: the St Mihiel attack would go ahead, but within a fortnight of its completion Pershing's First Army would move to the Argonne where, under Pétain's overall direction, it would advance on the right of the French Fourth Army between the Meuse and the Argonne.

The coming 'first all-American show' received wide press publicity, especially in neutral Switzerland; no censor could trim news reports there. Fortunately predictions over timing and sector varied widely, partly as a result of deliberate misinformation planted in towns near the Swiss border where agents were thought to lie heavily on the ground. The Germans withdrew to a shortened line as the US First Army moved into the assault trenches; and much of the heavy bombardment, which illuminated the intensely dark sky in the small hours of 12 September, fell on empty lines. But the Germans had not anticipated an attack on both sides of the salient simultaneously, nor had they expected the Americans to press forward so rapidly, particularly as low cloud and rain hampered movement on the first morning. As the Americans penetrated the salient they met heavy resistance from machine-gun nests, though an Austro-Hungarian division, giving token support to German allies, felt no obligation to offer long resistance and surrendered almost unscathed. Most second-day objectives were in American hands by nightfall on the first day. So great was the success that Pershing ordered two divisions to continue their advance under darkness; and the IV Corps, from the south-west, and the 26th (Yankee) Division, from the north-west, duly met in the small town of Vigneulles, twenty-five hours after the attack began. Within another five hours the battle was over. The Americans had taken 15,000 prisoners, some 400 guns and a whole ammunition train, as well as clearing the enemy from some 200 square miles of France occupied for four years. Despite the German pre-battle evacuation of front-line trenches, casualties were ominously high. More than 4,500 Americans died and another 2,500 were seriously wounded. Young men, as eager for action as the *poilus* of 1914, lost their lives in moments of tragic recklessness; and competitive rivalry between proud units did not always promote disciplined co-ordination. War was no ball game.

Clemenceau visited the salient on the day after the battle to congratulate Pershing and his men; but he had misgivings over American skills at organization when he found the support road through Thiaucourt hopelessly snarled up. President Poincaré also went to St Mihiel – though his journey may have had a double purpose, since he owned a small château in the newly recovered countryside. Pershing himself came to regret Foch's veto on exploiting St Mihiel; he claimed that, had he been allowed to press forward from the cleared salient, his troops could have advanced 'possibly into Metz'. Many years later

Douglas MacArthur, then a brigade commander, declared that on the evening the offensive ended he had seen through his field glasses the city of Metz; and it did not appear to have especially strong defences. As Metz was at least sixteen miles from the most advanced position reached by MacArthur's 42nd Division that day, he must have possessed remarkable binoculars to be able to make such a deduction ring with confidence. Another great name of the Second World War, Colonel George Patton, had a less satisfactory day, as commander of the pioneer 304th Tank Brigade. His machines ran out of fuel nine miles short of their objective and they were left inactive for thirty-two hours because tankers with gasoline supplies could not penetrate the traffic jams which so irritated Clemenceau.

During the middle fortnight of September the French First Army (Débeney), the British Fourth (Rawlinson) and the British Third (Byng) pressed forward against the outworks of the main Hindenburg Line. By now there was a clear indication of the Central Powers' desire for peace. On the evening of 14 September Austria–Hungary's 'cry to the world' was published: an appeal to all the belligerent governments to 'send delegates to a confidential and non-binding discussion on the basic principles for the conclusion of peace'; the meeting would be held 'in a neutral country and at an early date'. The Emperor Charles – a saintly soul, politically naive – made the offer in good faith; had it been accepted, with an armistice agreed before the end of September, perhaps as many as a quarter of a million lives would have been saved, though precedents from earlier great wars gave no certainty that such a conference would bring a speedy, lasting peace. The Austrian Note, issued officially in Burian's name rather than the Emperor's, was swiftly rejected, by the British Foreign Secretary, Balfour, in a speech forty-eight hours later; by President Wilson next day; by Clemenceau a day later still. It was believed that the Austrian appeal was a trick. 'This is not an attempt to make peace by understanding, but to weaken those forces which are proving too strong for them in the field', Balfour declared. Meanwhile the war continued. The US III Corps of Pershing's First Army had reached its new sector west of the Meuse on the day Burian published the Austrian Note. Though many regiments marched and some 90,000 horses and mules made the journey along the narrow, poplar-lined roads, there were also convoys of French heavy lorries on the move day and night throughout that week, carrying 428,000 men to complete the transference of the Americans from St Mihiel to the Argonne. In retrospect it is clear that too many troops were concentrated in too narrow a corridor. But the actual deployment of the AEF remains a masterpiece of hurried planning.

The first artillery barrage of Foch's great autumn offensive began at half past two in the morning of Thursday 26 September, on the American Front to the east of the Argonne Forest. Three hours later the infantry went forward, following a rolling barrage and supported with bombing raids by several hundred planes. They cut off the fortified hill town of Montfaucon and, as at St Mihiel, reached all their main objectives for the day long before sunset. Next morning they ran into far fiercer opposition and full problems of advance in such difficult wooded country drastically slowed down the tempo of Pershing's attack. This second day of the offensive, 27 September, was marked by the start of the drive of the British First and Third Armies towards Cambrai and, in particular, by the initiative of General Currie's Canadian Corps in crossing that ready-made defensive moat, the Canal du Nord. By Saturday morning the Belgians – with French and American support and with the British 9th Division to their right – were going forward in Flanders. To its own astonishment this 'Flanders group' of armies was able to advance more than five miles on the first day, crossing the notorious crater-splattered battlefields around Ypres. In a matter of hours the Belgians even cleared the Germans from Passchendaele once more, before the heavy rains came yet again and trucks, limbers and waggons were bogged down in water oozing from the churned-up Flanders clay.

The fourth of Foch's concerted drives against the Hindenburg Line began on Sunday 29 September, when the armies of Rawlinson and Débeney resumed their advance between Cambrai and St Quentin. In this region the Canal de St Quentin – linking the rivers Oise, Somme and Scheldt – was an even more formidable anti-tank obstacle than the Canal du Nord, for it was steep-sided and the water was deep. General Braithwaite of ix Corps and General Sir Gerald Boyd, commanding the 46th (North Midland) Territorial Division, devised an audacious plan for crossing the canal near the small town of Bellenglise, some seven miles north of St Quentin. While the Royal Engineers improvised scaling ladders, rafts, collapsible boats and wooden piers, an unknown enterprising officer telegraphed Boulogne with a request for three thousand lifebelts from the cross-Channel steamers, the 'leave boats'. The attack across the canal was launched by two battalions of the South Staffordshires and one of the North Staffordshires – another battalion was, at that moment, with 'Dunsterforce' on the Caspian shore. Fog covered the

canal and its approaches as Sunday dawned, and the infantry with
their cumbersome equipment cleared the trenches on the left bank of
the canal. The further bank was heavily defended by machine-
gunners, but in the fog it was impossible for the Germans to see
what was happening in the canal cutting, where the lifebelts enabled
the infantry either to swim, or be towed, across forty feet of water
before scaling the steep slopes and capturing the German positions.
By midday, when the fog gave way to autumnal sunshine, the canal
banks were cleared and passage created for other troops in the 46th
Division to break into the Hindenburg Line. The Staffordshire
canal-scalers took 2,000 prisoners that morning; and by nightfall the
Division as a whole could claim 4,200 men and seventy guns
captured and over three miles of Hindenburg Line defences cleared,
with less than 800 casualties. The lifebelts were returned to the leave
boats at Boulogne.

Elsewhere along this sector of the Front there were heavy casualties
that Sunday, especially among the two American divisions serving for
the first time alongside General Monash's Australian Corps in
Rawlinson's Fourth Army. They lacked sufficient officers or skilled
NCOs and soon lost contact with each other in the fog. The tanks, too,
had a disastrous day: seventy-five were destroyed, either on a minefield
(apparently laid by the British themselves in 1915) or from field gun fire
once the fog had lifted. News from the Argonne was disappointing, with
the American First Army suffering heavy losses from hidden machine-
gun nests and field guns on its flanks. Back at headquarters that
Michaelmas Sunday, Marshal Foch could see that the tide was not yet
flowing in full victory flood.

A hundred miles behind the farthest trench lines, among the paladins
of Spa, a different mood prevailed. On the previous Wednesday news
came that Bulgaria was seeking an armistice. The Kaiser was told at
Kiel; in the train that evening he remarked resignedly, 'This can bring
the war to an end, but not in the way we wanted it'. On Sunday
morning he arrived at Spa, about the hour that the Staffordshires were
celebrating their triumph on the Bellenglise canal bank. The General
Field Marshal and First Quartermaster-General awaited him with the
Foreign Minister, Hintze, in attendance. Gloomily Hindenburg spoke
of crumbling defences in France and Flanders, of weary troops for
whose relief there were no reserves on hand. In Hintze's mind was
fear of revolution if democratic reforms did not come swiftly; in
Ludendorff's there was dismay at Bulgaria's 'treachery . . . leading
inescapably to the collapse of our allies'. The three men were agreed on

the need for a change of government in Berlin and an armistice appeal to President Wilson. Sadly and silently the Supreme War Lord concurred. But forty-three more days passed before the fighting came to an end.

CHAPTER 14

BALKAN EXPRESS

The collapse of Bulgaria came with all the spontaneity of a diseased elm tree crashing to the ground. After a poor harvest in 1917 occasional deserters had continued to bring tales of falling morale: bread shortage, resentment at German exploitation, a lack of fertilizers for farming, and concern over lost export markets for the most remunerative crop, tobacco. But in June when a liberal democrat, Alexander Malinov, became Prime Minister conditions eased, with a fairer system of bread distribution. There were fewer signs of social disorder than in many Western countries – even than in Britain, where that autumn there were strikes by miners, railway workers, engineers and briefly by the police of central London. Undoubtedly Bulgarian enthusiasm for the war, genuine when the alluring prize of Macedonia seemed on offer, had long since died away; in the six years since the outbreak of the Balkan Wars, successive campaigns had cost the lives of a higher proportion of the actively employable population than in France, Germany or Austria–Hungary. On the other hand, there had been no destructive invasion of the country and few air raids on Bulgarian towns. The Bulgarian General Staff had every confidence in the defensive line along the mountains, as indeed had the regiments manning it. They were supported by the German Eleventh Army, ten Austro-Hungarian battalions and a leavening of Prussian-trained staff officers. Some Bulgarian commanders even still hoped to make a surprise descent on Salonika.

Surprise, however, was Franchet d'Esperey's privilege. German Intelligence knew that an autumn offensive was planned in Macedonia, but did not know where or when; the loop of the River Crna, around the railhead of Brod, seemed the likeliest place. Little attention was given to the inhospitable bastion of the Dobropolje, ten miles to the east of Brod. But on the evening of 13 September 1918 – the Friday on which the Americans and French erased the St Mihiel salient – General Mišić rode

up through the fir trees of the Moglena to spend the night at the
observation post on the Floka mountain from where he had shown
Franchet the panorama of Bulgarian positions eleven weeks previously.
The Serbian *Voivode* had before him a task of great responsibility.
Franchet d'Esperey was not prepared to risk bad weather ruining his
offensive, with rain and mist obscuring targets on the Dobropolje and
the Kozyak after an opening barrage had revealed the concentration of
artillery so carefully concealed from enemy eyes. General Mišić knew
his mountains; he could predict weather better than any meteorologist
at headquarters in the plain. Dawn broke soon after five o'clock, the
peaks on his right pink with the rising sun; a strong east wind dispersed
lingering mist; no clouds, no scent of rain in the air. Mišić was satisfied:
J-Jour had come. From his eyrie on the Floka the *Voivode* sent a signal to
battery commanders west of the Vardar: 'Get going with 14 officers and
8 privates' ('*Mettez en route quatorze officiers et huit soldats*'); decoded, the
message was for the guns to open up in two hours' time, at 8 a.m. on 14
September.

The bombardment was unprecedented in the Balkans: 500 guns along
eighty miles of front, with the greatest concentration on a six-mile
sector along the ridge of the Dobropolje. The shelling continued for six
hours without intermission and resumed in mid-afternoon, the guns
only becoming silent as darkness fell and resuming again in the small
hours of Sunday morning. The mountain ravines magnified the sound
of what a German veteran of the Western Front called the 'iron storm'
of gunfire. Forty miles to the east, it could be heard by British troops
moving into forward positions west of Lake Doiran, even though the
wind was blowing from the opposite direction. And sixty miles to the
north, at the German Army Group von Scholtz's headquarters in
Skopje, the noise could be heard rumbling in the distance all day, like a
brooding thunderstorm. From the direction of the sound General von
Scholtz assumed the attack had been made at the point he anticipated,
between Brod and Monastir. He even ordered a Bulgarian regiment and
a good German battalion to leave Prilep and move southwards in order
to protect the route north-eastwards from Monastir, so certain was he
that he knew which way the Allies would strike.

The Serbian infantry duly went forward on Sunday morning (15
September), supported a few hours later by French colonial troops,
including four battalions of Senegalese and by the Yugoslav Division. It
was a day of intensely fierce fighting, for though the barrage smashed
through barbed wire and destroyed advanced trenches, the shells made
scarcely any impression on nests of machine-guns and the light artillery

Victory 1918; The Props Knocked Away

→ Franchet's proposed advance into Germany

▪▪▪▶ Converging British advances on Constantinople

➤ Western Front advances into Germany

⇦ Allied advances into Bavaria and Austria

0   100   200   300 Miles

Petrograd

altic Sea

Warsaw

Bug

Vistula

HOSLOVAKIA

AUSTRIA-HUNGARY
Prop 3; Padua Armistice,
effective 4 Nov.

nna

apest

TRANSYLVANIA

ROMANIA
Resumed war
with Germany,
9 Nov.

Belgrade

Bucharest

RUSSIA

Odessa

Sevastopol

Black Sea

Danube

BULGARIA
Prop 1; Salonika
Armistice, effective
30 Sept.

Bosphorus

Constantinople

Cattaro

ALBANIA

Brindisi

Salonika

Mudros

Dardanelles

T U R K E Y
Prop 2; Mudros Armistice,
effective 31 Oct.

Mosul

GREECE

CORFU

• Smyrna

Aleppo

Athens

CRETE

CYPRUS

• Damascus

Mediterranean Sea

Port Said

Suez Canal

set in the rock face and often given additional protection by concrete
emplacements. Only direct hits could destroy such positions; the
combination of mountain wall and German defensive engineering had
given the Bulgarians a Hindenburg Line of their own. The French
commander, General Henrys, was forced to bring up flame-throwers to
push forward against fanatical resistance on a plateau broken by ridges,
each fiercely contested. Cavalry waited in reserve around the Greek
town of Florina. Farther west the Italian 35th Division moved against
Hill 1050, another grimly held defensive promontory, which defied
assault for a week. There was as yet no sign of any weakening of the
Bulgarian will to resist along this section of the Front.

By Monday 16 September, the French, the Serbs and the Yugoslav
Division had pushed back the Bulgarians to their second line of defence,
running across the slopes of the Kozyak, a peak even higher than the
Dobropolje ridge. A German reserve battalion – the 13th Saxon Jägers –
was sent into the line to assist the defenders and fought resolutely but,
even as the Saxons were digging in, there were the first hints of panic
among the Bulgarians, who had to bring forward inexperienced troops,
with little training. At Skopje General von Scholtz for the first time
became alarmed. All precedent in Macedonia over the last eighteen
months indicated that the Allies would call off their attack after stiff
resistance on a second day. But by the evening he heard that the
Bulgarian units were breaking off the fight, to fall back indiscriminately.
Scholtz ordered a group of senior German officers to go at once to the
Kozyak; with revolvers in hand they were to check any incipient rout. At
the same time he telegraphed Hindenburg in Spa asking for a German
division to be sent at once to southern Serbia in order to stiffen
resistance to the advancing Serbs and French.

Scholtz's request reached Spa as the Supreme Command was
assessing Foch's realignment of armies preparatory to the assault on
the Hindenburg Line, a time when the worries of an army group
commander in distant Skopje had low priority. The appeal carried a
familiar ring: back in the late autumn of 1916 Hindenburg and
Ludendorff had been forced to send relief from the Western Front to
General von Below in Macedonia, only to find that Sarrail's offensive
petered out in bad weather before any reinforcements crossed the
Balkan mountains. Now, two years later, there could be no question of
sparing troops from France. Scholtz's request was referred to the
Austrians, at Baden. But General Arz, too, was hard-pressed for men
and munitions: already there were 50,000 K-und-K combat soldiers on
the Balkan Front; and he was expecting Diaz soon to open an offensive

in Italy, where the Austro-Hungarian forces were heavily outnumbered. Moreover, now that Emperor Charles had let it be known that he favoured peace talks, reliable troops would have to garrison cities in the Monarchy where subject nationalities were clamouring for independence; there were even doubts over maintaining order in the Austrian capital, not only from fear of radical socialists, but also because greater Vienna formed a metropolis in which as many Czechs were thought to have their homes as in Prague. The unfortunate General von Scholtz heard from Spa that a German composite brigade from the Crimea would be put aboard ship for the Bulgarian port of Varna but would take at least a fortnight to reach Macedonia. Meanwhile, General Arz let Scholtz know that he might expect an Austro-Hungarian division; composition and provenance were unspecified; so too was the date of arrival. But Arz was too courteous and obliging a Habsburg officer to send an outright refusal.

Meanwhile there was a clash of wills between the generals at the Front. Early in the Monday evening (16 September) General von Steuben, commanding the German Eleventh Army, found that Major-General Rusev, the Bulgarian commander in that sector of the Front, had given orders to fall back overnight to the third line of defence, the foothills covering the River Crna. It was difficult for the Germans to keep contact with their ally. During Tuesday morning the French and Serbs found themselves going forward with little resistance, though a composite division, under General von Reuter, inflicted heavy casualties on the Yugoslav Division. Reuter and Steuben were certain that they could halt the retreat and hold the third line of defence; but at three o'clock in the afternoon Rusev pulled the Bulgarians back behind the River Crna, without informing either of the German generals of his decision. Such a move made good sense for the Bulgarians: the Crna was fast-flowing, cutting its way down through rocky defiles impossible to ford and difficult to cross; and the line of retirement was north-eastwards, in the general direction of Bulgaria. But for the Germans it threatened disaster: Rusev was exposing a likely corridor five miles wide, with Steuben's Eleventh Army strongly entrenched west of the river, the Bulgarians falling back to the east, and the Serbs and French striking northwards through the Crna defiles towards its confluence with a smaller mountain stream, the Belasnica, and ultimately to the River Vardar at Gradsko. Through many winters Gradsko had remained a small and silent town unacknowledged by most map-makers. Now, in 1918, it bustled with activity; for in Gradsko were sited the advanced supply depots for the whole of Army Group von Scholtz.

As yet the offensive had been the work of the French, Serbs (and other Yugoslavs) and of the Italians, of whom there were by now 45,000 combat troops in the Balkan theatre. The British and Greeks remained waiting in long expectancy of battle around the shore of Lake Doiran and eastwards to the River Struma: some 140,000 British troops and 130,000 Greeks were spread along a line of slightly more than one hundred miles. Milne, their joint commander, was still desperately short of shells; long preliminary bombardments were out of the question. He had, of course, no tanks – though arguably they would have had a decisive value in the Balkans denied them in waterlogged Flanders. Most worrying of all for Milne was the high incidence of sickness among his men – 'a fever-stricken army . . . worn with three years service in the most unhealthy part of Macedonia', he repeatedly emphasized to the CIGS. During the second week of September a new wave of 'Spanish flu' hit the British contingent, already weakened by malaria. On 7 September the 65th Brigade in General Maitland Wilson's XII Corps had to withdraw from the Doiran sector because of the influenza epidemic; the brigade was replaced by French Zouaves who had no liaison experience with British units. Throughout Milne's army the sick lists became so long that, on the eve of the offensive in the Moglena, almost half his combat troops were ill; in the XII Corps there were several battalions, with nominal strengths of 1,000 men, who mustered less than 400. Milne would have liked to postpone the British and Greek contribution to the offensive by forty-eight hours, partly to give an opportunity for some of his sick to report fit again and partly to ensure that his gunners could draw on the shipment of shells which had at last reached Salonika harbour from England. But Franchet d'Esperey needed the attack east of the Vardar to pin down crack troops in the Bulgarian First Army who might otherwise strengthen their faltering compatriots in the loop of the Crna. On the evening of 15 September, after listening all that Sunday to the rumble of guns from the west, Milne learnt that his army must go forward on Wednesday morning.

The message to attack, sent to all units in the small hours of 18 September, sounded ludicrously inconsequential: '508 bottles of beer will be sent to you'. But the meaning of the code was grimly serious: at eight minutes past five that morning the infantry would go forward. They were to move in the murk before dawn, with an hour and three-quarters to come before a rising sun would penetrate the valleys. There would be no preliminary concentrated bombardment, only a few gas shells during the night, aimed at the enemy's gun emplacements and their 'roomy well-timbered dugouts' (as Milne was to write, a few weeks later). Twice in the spring of 1917 his infantry had attacked in this region, without success and leaving 5,000 men dead or seriously wounded. Fourteen of the battalions which fought over these ridges seventeen months previously were to try again, spurred on now by the French newcomer general dubbed, none too affectionately, 'Desperate Frankie'. For hundreds of these British troops Pip Ridge, the Grand Couronné, the Petit Couronné were already familiar names which had been assigned in earlier fighting to the three hills above the western shore of Lake Doiran, the core of the Bulgarian defence line. Strictly speaking these promontories were not mountains, for their highest point was only some 2,000 feet above sea level, but, as Milne wrote, they 'stand out in conspicuous domination'. To many West Midland soldiers coming up to Kilindir station from Salonika, forty miles to the south, they looked at first glance like the Malvern Hills as seen from the River Severn below Worcester. Long ago the English topped their ridge above Malvern with a warning beacon, but now military science dictated more sophistication; the Bulgarians sank an observation post deep into the rock face of the Grand Couronné, protecting it with twelve feet of concrete. For the British, waiting in gullies south of Lake Doiran, this 'Devil's Eye' was clearly visible as a black dot on the bare uppermost slopes; through field glasses their officers could focus on the steel protective grille from behind which, as the Bulgarian Colonel Damian Nedeff wrote a few years later, 'we gained' such 'a precise idea of movements in the rear of the enemy' that 'we could deduce where we must expect an attack and what, roughly, would be the timing of the operation'.

To be subject to such surveillance from on high was unnerving and before going over the top that Wednesday several company commanders made certain their men were 'well-dosed with rum'. Down by the lakeside Greek troops fought their way into Doiran town, while at the same time the British infantry overran enemy advanced outposts beneath the steep and rugged Petit Couronné. Once in the deep ravines, however, the troops were caught by enfilading machine-gun bursts from the next low ridge, half a mile away, and by heavier fire from the Grand Couronné another mile back. To their right, lingering gas from the British bombardment, blown back on Allied lines by a suddenly strong wind, forced the exposed attackers to pause and put on gas masks. Even so, thirty of fifty-five survivors in the 7th South Wales Borderers inhaled so much gas that they were sent down to hospital that evening. Yet this battalion reached the top of the Grand Couronné; only deadly enfilading machine-gun fire prevented it storming the Devil's Eye. The battalion commander, Lieutenant Colonel Dan Burges, was wounded three times before being taken prisoner. He was awarded the Victoria Cross, and the battalion received the Croix de Guerre from Franchet d'Esperey, who rarely showed such high regard for the courage of foreign regiments. But despite these acts of Welsh valour, the Devil's Eye was not even bruised.

The 66th Brigade – three light infantry battalions from Cheshire, southern Lancashire and Shropshire – attempted to scale Pip Ridge, above the Grand Couronné positions. Like the Welshmen they were caught in machine-gun crossfire and suffered the heaviest casualties of the day; only one in three infantrymen crept back to the ravine outside the village of Doljeli where they had gathered in the hours before the attack. As early as ten o'clock in the morning Generals Maitland Wilson and Milne could see that the Bulgarians were no more likely to be prised from their positions than seventeen months before.

There remained, however, one glimmer of hope. What was happening around the north shore of the lake? For along the dismantled railway track to Serres, hidden from the prying Devil's Eye, Milne brought up by night to a point seven miles north-east of Doiran an Anglo-Greek force, Cretans supported by guns and infantry from the British 28th Division. He hoped that an outflanking movement would isolate the strong Bulgarian garrison. Here the terrain was different: donkey tracks down steep slopes to a flat plain of long grass, broken by stretches of woodland, sometimes little more than copses, and covering more than four miles to Pip Ridge's northern slope. Good progress was made at first, especially by the Cretan Division; but there was hesitation mid-morning, with lack of support from British gunners, and a failure of communication. It was agreed that a co-ordinated advance would be made mid-afternoon. But hardly had this second move into the plain begun than the parched grass erupted in a wall of flame, which spread rapidly through fields tinder-dry from the summer heat. Desperately the assault troops hurried back, placing a ravine between themselves and the sudden inferno. There was certainly no need for flame-flowing fuel canisters in this sector. No one knows if the fields were fired by the defenders, by the belated shelling from the British, or even by sheer mischance. Whatever the cause, the effect of the grass fire on the unfolding plans for the offensive was devastating. The gain from Milne's only tactical innovation of the day proved nil.

Franchet d'Esperey came up to Milne's advanced headquarters in the afternoon and seems to have made little effort to hide his displeasure: 'talks rot' was Milne's terse note in his diary. General Maitland Wilson ordered the 65th Brigade back to the line, whether fit or fever-ridden. They led two assaults on Pip Ridge next morning, with three Scottish battalions in support, and suffered heavy casualties: all the battalion commanders were lost, killed or gravely wounded; an impressive simple cross on the hillside still honours Scottish lives lost 'in action, 19 September'. But in six hours' fierce fighting, no Bulgarian positions were taken and retained. Strategically Milne's men performed the task assigned to them; they made certain that no units of the Bulgarian First Army moved further down the Front. They took over 1,200 prisoners. But, unlike the French and Serbs, they did not break the enemy line. And yet, in the two days of battle, they suffered more than twice as many casualties as the armies which had stormed the Dobropolje and the Kozyak.

General Nerezov, who commanded the Bulgarian First Army, was an able officer, Potsdam-schooled and much respected by the crack troops serving under him. From observing the state of the sick and weary prisoners captured in the first day's fighting, he decided that Milne's army was physically weak and clearly short of men. He therefore began to think of a counter-offensive, coming initially down the Struma and completed by an advance from Doiran so as to take Salonika while the main Allied armies were deep in the mountains to the north and east. His proposal, given over the telephone to Bulgarian GHQ at Kyustendil, was welcomed by the acting Commander-in-Chief, General Todorov, a man of limited skill who had never even visited the Doiran fortifications. At that moment Todorov's standing with his German allies was at rock-bottom. He was about to set off for a potentially embarrassing conference at German Eleventh Army's headquarters in Prilep; he needed to explain not only General Rusev's propensity for hasty retreat but also why he had himself panicked on Wednesday, when without reference to Scholtz he telegraphed to Hindenburg pleading for six German divisions to be sent to his aid immediately. Nerezov's telephone call would enable Todorov to trump any grievances the Germans might raise in conference; for what did a retreat up the Crna matter, if it were followed by a descent on Salonika itself?

The Germans were not impressed. Where, enquired General von Steuben, would Todorov find the transport, supplies and field guns to enable his divisions east of the Vardar to emerge from their fortified positions and engage in a fast-moving campaign? It would be far wiser, Steuben and Reuter thought, to entice the Allied armies deeper into the mountains, until the promised German and Austro-Hungarian reinforcements and a revitalized Bulgarian army on Franchet's right flank could cut off the advance, leaving the French and Serbs isolated as winter descended on them; all that mattered was for the German Eleventh Army and the Bulgarian 3rd Division on its right to remain in contact, so as to check the Franco-Serbian tide before it engulfed the Army Group's supply depot at Gradsko.

Considering the general position of the Central Powers, this strategic design was hardly less of a pipe dream than the offensive which Nerezov had put forward. Todorov, however, accepted it – though with one vital condition. If the defence line west of the Vardar had been abandoned, the Bulgarian armies above Doiran and along the lower River Struma were needlessly exposed. They should gradually pull back to the ranges south of Sofia, good defensive obstacles but with valleys down which they might strike at the French and Serbian right flank. Steuben concurred and Scholtz backed the strategic plan. On returning to Kyustendil Todorov gave orders for Nerezov's First Army to fall back up the Strumica valley and over the Kosturino Pass as part of a general retreat. He failed to realize the devastating effect of the order on the morale of the First Army's finest divisions, elated as they were by their defeat of the Anglo-Greek attacks. Colonel Nedeff describes how corps commanders, gathered at Nerezov's headquarters to consider the next phase of operations, heard the order to retreat in stunned silence. Several had believed they were about to go over to a counter-offensive. They felt a bitterness similar to the mood that Captain Sulzbach had noted a fortnight previously in France among brother-officers robbed of their dream entry into Paris.

For Milne's troops the Friday of Todorov's meeting with Steuben – 20 September – was a quiet day of uneasy expectancy. Wednesday's gains in Doiran and along the Petit Couronné were made secure; ambulance-waggon convoys carried the wounded back to the hospitals outside Salonika; staff officers mournfully totted up the lengthening bill of casualties. There was bright moonlight on Friday, but no sign of enemy patrols, and such tranquillity along the lakeside that the croak of scores of frogs could be heard clearly once again. Even after sunrise on Saturday the stillness persisted, a quiet broken by the metallic urgency of aeroplane engines as RAF biplanes from the Sixteenth Wing's advanced airfield at Yanesh took off to see what was happening over the other side of the hills.

It was an observer in one of the De Havilland 9s from 47 Squadron who sent Milne the news, at 10.40 in the morning: a defile leading out of the Strumica valley towards the old Bulgarian frontier was 'packed with transport', ran his wireless message: around the town of Rabovo, some forty miles north of Doiran, were 'anything up to 500 lorries', while horse-drawn waggons were 'waiting to go up the road'. Further flights showed convoys moving along other routes through the mountains. Over the next five days the RAF took the initiative, pilots sending their planes screaming down at full throttle on the columns time and time again. In a single sortie twenty-five biplanes dropped 5,000 pounds of bombs on packed troops seeking a way across the Kosturino Pass, returning to expend 12,000 rounds of machine-gun fire on the smashed trucks and waggons. The pass was hopelessly blocked, with the survivors scrambling up mountain tracks, away from the road, so as to find cover in the rocks before the next sortie of a relentless onslaught. Later in the week, thirty-five air miles to the east, six De Havillands caught a Bulgarian troop convoy moving up the Kresna Pass, the ravine through which the upper Struma cuts a way down to the sea from Sofia. Forty-four bombs hit the slow-moving column before the planes swooped to less than thirty feet, blazing away with a Vickers machine-gun fired by the pilot and two Lewis guns by the observer in his rear cockpit. Here, too, the carnage among men and animals was appalling, and the pass was blocked with blazing vehicles. There was no sign of Bulgarian or German fighter-planes in defence. The RAF had a free range of sky. Somewhere on the railway near Blagoevgrad an observer spotted a train; bombs fell close, but missed. Aboard the train (so the French later reported) were General von Scholtz and Crown Prince Boris, sent by King Ferdinand to give a royal example of endurance to their wavering First Army.

Milne's troops found the Bulgarian positions against which they had thrown their strength deserted. Both British and Greek divisions pressed forward, following the retreating Bulgarians up to the Kosturino Pass, seeing for themselves the shattered remains of men and horses, stenching entrails intermingled, their vehicles thrust to the side of the road as soon as the bombing raids were over; at Rabovo 700 bodies awaited burial in an improvised mortuary beside the hospital. It was for many a chastening experience, grimly enlightening proof of the new air power. Yet to others the march into Bulgaria became unexpectedly self-liberating. Private Stanley Spencer in the 7th Battalion, Royal Berkshires found himself at one moment trudging along a track covered with camouflage screens, from which 'bits of rag' hung down, 'passing over our heads . . . like bird heralds coming from what I was walking into'. But no enemy followed the birds; instead, he was soon bathing in a river, warmed by long hours of blistering sunshine. 'All felt something extraordinary had occurred', the sensitive twenty-seven-year-old painter was to recall, 'Was the war coming to an end?'

For one French colonial brigade, far to the west around Florina, it was only about to begin in full intensity. The 1st and 4th Chasseurs d'Afrique, six squadrons of Spahis from Morocco mounted on sure-footed barb stallions, had as yet seen little action. But now Franchet d'Esperey decided that 'the hour of the cavalry' had come; in 'unceasing and resolute pursuit' horsemen should press ahead of 'the infantry columns and open the way for them'. The brigade commander was General Jouinot-Gambetta, nephew of the radical statesman Léon Gambetta, who had escaped from Paris by balloon in 1870 to organize resistance to the Prussian invaders in provincial France. On 22 September the General set off with his brigade, under orders from General Henrys to capture the town of Prilep and then wheel westwards to cut off any enemy forces coming down from Kosovo. But while the brigade was watering the horses mid-morning, the Commander-in-Chief's car caught up with them; Franchet told Jouinot-Gambetta that he should have his sights not simply on Prilep, but on Skopje, by road nearly sixty miles farther north.

Prilep was reached early the following afternoon, the enemy having pulled away north-eastwards, and the brigade met no opposition. General von Steuben, who had so recently conferred with Todorov in the town, was by now thoroughly shaken. There could be no more talk of falling on the flanks of the advancing armies, for once the Bulgarians pulled back from their original defences their will to fight evaporated; constant attack from the air was a new and terrifying experience. Only a day after Prilep fell, French and Serbian troops reached the outskirts of Gradsko, the supply base for Army Group von Scholtz. Crack Saxon troops of Steuben's army, and Reuter's combined division, offered stout resistance until faced by an outflanking movement. Stores went up in flames, and General Pruneau's colonial division and the Yugoslavs entered the town the next day, to the sound of exploding munition dumps. Everywhere the Germans retired they blocked roads and blew railway bridges. To Hindenburg, writing his memoirs a year later, it seemed impossible that the enemy should press forwards without rest; 'How would he overcome the difficulty of supplies, for we had utterly destroyed the railway and the roads?' When Franchet eventually read these words, he scribbled in the margin of his book, '*Il ne me connaissait pas*' – 'He did not know me'.

More particularly, at that moment it mattered that the German Army Group commander did not know Jouinot-Gambetta. For it was his colonial cavalry brigade that found the way through the mountains to Skopje, an epic march narrated by their general in his (strangely neglected) book *Üsküb* with a descriptive felicity reminiscent of Lawrence's *Seven Pillars of Wisdom*. He describes how, early on 25 September, he reached the foot of the Babuna Pass, meeting in the moonlight a body of men on whom he nearly opened fire, only to discover that they were escaped Italian prisoners of war seeking a way back to their 35th Division. But at the top of the pass he encountered the Bulgarian rearguard, protecting the town of Veles and the main route up the Vardar. He knew his brigade was not strong enough to force a way up narrow roads covered by light artillery; he therefore decided to leave the armoured cars which had served as outriders for his horsemen, ordering them to assist General Pruneau beside the Vardar. The six squadrons of Spahis were to follow him up into the mountains of the Golesnica Planina, where the peaks were nearly 6,000 feet high; packhorses carried the few light thirty-seven-millimetre guns that formed the brigade's only artillery. They had no wireless and lost all contact with headquarters; they were as isolated as a camel corps deep in the Arabian desert. Jouinot-Gambetta moved, however, far more slowly: eleven miles on the first day and, after a four-hour rest, ten miles by moonlight that night. Most of the Spahis could not keep up with their front column; some riders were left to protect the packhorses which had to be led carefully along winding and narrow tracks. There was no sign of any foe; no planes overhead, friendly or hostile; nothing more menacing than an eagle surprised by this incursion into his realm.

Throughout Friday (27 September) Jouinot-Gambetta rested men and horses in a wooded gorge 5,000 feet up. By Saturday morning the brigade was reunited and on that day moved down from the high ground, to reach the railway, that vital link with central Europe, seven miles south of Skopje. It was unguarded. On Sunday morning, around eight o'clock, as the sun dispersed the mist, the brigade approached the city. The German units resisted stubbornly, using an armoured train in the railway station as an improvised fort. But the Bulgarians were thinking only of falling back on their homeland. They fired ammunition dumps, which exploded with red and black flames; houses were burning, 'cypresses flared up like giant torches'; the railway station, too, went up in flames, and the armoured train pulled away northwards, belching out black smoke, its steel waggons impervious to fire from the machine-guns. Within an hour Skopje was in French hands. At ten in the morning a French aircraft, 'the first we saw since Florina', flew over the city and the General signalled news of his victory. Two more planes flew over in the early afternoon, to confirm what seemed at headquarters improbable news; for General Pruneau, the armoured cars and, indeed, the main column of advance were all still twenty miles away. Despite Friday's rest in the mountains, the Brigade Jouinot-Gambetta had in six days ridden through, or stumbled over, fifty-seven miles of the most difficult mountain country in Europe.

While the French and Serbs were heading for Skopje, the British continued to pursue the Bulgarian Army back across the pre-war borders. The Derbyshire Yeomanry were the first troops to enter Bulgaria, crossing the frontier near Kosturino early on 25 September. They were still 130 miles away from Sofia, and almost eighty miles from Kyustendil where, on that Wednesday, General Todorov's headquarters were attacked by mutinous deserters, unsuccessfully. The mutineers, frustrated in their immediate objective, thereupon commandeered trains to take them to Radomir, a manufacturing town in which a powerful socialist organization had long secretly backed republicanism. Three other towns – Berovo, Pechaev and Tsarevo Selo – asserted their self-importance by setting up local Soviets on the Russian model; but Radomir determined the pace and character of the general rebellion; a short-lived republic was proclaimed in the town two days later. General Lukov, commander of the Bulgarian Second Army, and Prime Minister Malinov met King Ferdinand and emphasized the danger to the dynasty unless the army could be brought home in good order. The King agreed. He would seek an immediate end to the fighting.

The Derbyshire Yeomanry detachments left Kosturino early on 26 September. Before they had covered many miles they saw, coming towards them, a staff car with a large white flag fluttering from a pole beside the driver's window. Major Trianov and another officer wished to come through the British lines to seek General Milne and discuss a two-day cessation of hostilities while armistice negotiations took place. The emissaries were sent on to Salonika for a meeting with Franchet d'Esperey, who rejected any suggestion of a ceasefire but said he would receive properly accredited representatives who sought an armistice. The car made the journey back across the frontier while Franchet telegraphed Clemenceau for instructions. He was answered speedily: he could impose the conditions on Bulgaria most suited to the successful conclusion of the war against her German, Turkish and Austro-Hungarian partners. Any armistice should be a French affair; as commander of the Armies of the Orient Franchet d'Esperey need not consult France's allies.

News of the Bulgarian peace moves only reached Whitehall next morning (27 September). Hankey at once noticed that the Bulgarian envoys approached the British lines rather than the Franco-Serbian; it was therefore assumed that Britain would play a major part in deciding the form of the armistice. Lloyd George was ready to cross to Paris and, along with French representatives, receive Bulgarian emissaries. But such a procedure never entered Clemenceau's mind. He told President Poincaré that he wanted to settle the Bulgarian business as soon as possible and bring back all those British and French divisions from Macedonia to the Western Front. Poincaré demurred; the growing strength of American arms made withdrawal to France superfluous, he insisted. Clemenceau, however, was becoming disenchanted with America; President Wilson's continued treatment of his partners in France as 'associates' rather than 'allies' asserted a disturbing independence.

Such distinctions meant little to Malinov in Sofia. Like Lloyd George he envisaged armistice talks, at some length; and he relied on moral backing from across the Atlantic, for the USA was never at war with Bulgaria, and he was on good terms with American diplomats in Sofia willing to serve as intermediaries. Early on 27 September a British sentry reported that 'a gentleman attired in morning dress' had come to Bogdanci checkpoint, his car carrying a white flag and an oversize Stars and Stripes. 'Mr Walker from the American Legation' was duly guided to General Milne's field headquarters at Yanesh and sent on to Franchet in Salonika. But Walker was no more successful than the two Bulgarian majors the previous day. Franchet d'Esperey would only receive peace envoys authorized to sign an armistice unconditionally. There would be no American mediation.

On 28 September, for the third day running, a 'huge German staff car' passed through Bogdanci. On this occasion the passengers were General Lukov and the Bulgarian Finance Minister, Andrij Liapchev, who was himself a Macedonian by birth. They were given lunch by General Milne, who sent a detailed account of his conversation to the CIGS in London; Milne stressed their wish for an immediate armistice, to forestall tighter German control of the country. Ironically, on that same day, it was the (newly arrived) German troops promised by Hindenburg from the Crimea who, alongside Sofia's military cadets, saved the royal palaces and government buildings of the capital from the poorly organized Radomir republican insurgents. Briefly there was a prospect of German military rule being imposed on central Bulgaria by General von Scholtz. Lukov and Liapchev, both of whom had long opposed the pro-Germans in Sofia, were perfectly sincere in seeking peace terms, as Milne emphasized in his message to London. He pointed out, also, that there was no British senior military or political representative in Salonika to check the French demands, as he was himself at Yanesh and the head of the British Legation was in Athens. By contrast, both Prince Regent Alexander of Serbia and the Greek Prime Minister, Venizelos, were on hand and in frequent talks with Franchet.

The two Bulgarian envoys were received by Franchet d'Esperey with icy politeness at his headquarters in the former Bulgarian consulate at Salonika. There would, he told them brusquely, be no discussion of terms; Bulgaria must face the consequences of making war on the Allies 'without any cause'. After a night's reflection Lukov and Liapchev were conducted to Franchet's villa overlooking the gulf where, soon after 9 a.m., they were presented with an armistice convention of seven clauses: evacuation of Serbian and Greek territory; demobilization, except for a division to defend the frontier with German-occupied Romania and a division to protect the railway system; the handing over to the Allies of arms, ammunition and military transport and horses; restoration to Greece of equipment seized in 1916; all Bulgarians in the German Eleventh Army to lay down their arms immediately; the employment by the Allies of Bulgarian prisoners of war; and all German and Austro-Hungarian troops and diplomatic/consular officials to leave Bulgaria within four weeks. It was agreed that the ceasefire would become effective at noon next day. Nothing was said in writing about the political structure of Bulgaria; but in conversation with Liapchev Franchet indicated that, while 'he would not interfere with your government', the Allies might find it 'easier to deal with Crown Prince Boris' than with the sovereign who had ruled the country for thirty-two years, 'Foxy' Ferdinand of Saxe-Coburg. The Armistice Convention was duly signed by Franchet d'Esperey, Liapchev and Lukov at 'General Headquarters, 29 September 1918, 10.10' (at night). The offensive which forced Bulgaria out of the war had lasted just sixteen days.

Milne's chief of staff woke him up at two o'clock in the morning to say he had heard that an armistice was signed and hostilities with Bulgaria would end at noon. Milne received a copy of the terms later in the day; Franchet never bothered to let the British commanding general know their contents in advance, even though only British and Greek forces under his command were as yet advancing within the frontiers of old Bulgaria. Similarly, Lloyd George did not learn details of the armistice until after the Bulgarian envoys had put their signatures to the Convention in Salonika. Such treatment rankled in London, and was remembered. Franchet's high-handed behaviour, reminiscent of Sarrail's atttitude to Mahon and Milne in earlier days, set a precedent for future peace talks with Turkey – which, it was confidently felt in London, must soon be at hand.

CHAPTER 15

ROADS TO DAMASCUS

General Sir Edmund Allenby stamped the final offensive in Palestine with the power of his personality and all the authority of his fertile military mind. At Luxor in February the grand design agreed with Smuts and his team from London had provided for an advance along the coast, taking Tyre, Sidon and Beirut, before turning inland on Homs so as to isolate Damascus, which would then be attacked by a force advancing from Deraa and the Jordan valley. At the end of March the crisis on the Western Front forced Allenby to abandon such a comprehensive plan and in June he encouraged his staff to develop detailed studies for a limited advance, at least carrying the EEF over the borders of Palestine and into Syria. But by July it was clear that almost every advantage lay with the Entente allies, for the folly of Enver and his associates in pursuing new conquests in central Asia left the armies in Syria short of men and supplies. Allenby accordingly revived, and extensively modified, earlier and more ambitious projects which were intended to force the Ottoman government to sue for peace. He remained, however, cautious over his immediate objectives, especially in messages back to the War Office in London. Although to corps commanders he might speak occasionally of Damascus and beyond, an advance on this oldest city in the world was not mentioned in any orders drafted earlier than the third day of the offensive.

By August 1918 Allenby could call on the equivalent of four cavalry divisions (some 12,000 mounted men) and eight infantry divisions (about 57,000 troops), with over 500 guns with seven squadrons of aircraft; he enjoyed almost total mastery of the skies. His strength lay in the high quality of his Australians and New Zealanders, in the persistence of his veteran Yeomanry and infantry regiments from Hampshire and East Anglia, in the ingenuity of his sappers, and the professional dedication of the Indian Lancers and Gurkhas; the Indian cavalry transferred to Palestine from the Western Front were eager to show their enterprise after the years of frustration in France, although many troopers contracted malaria from service in the Jordan valley. Alongside them in the Desert Mounted Corps was a French colonial regiment of Spahis and Chasseurs d'Afrique, but Colonel de Piépape's impressively named French Detachment of Palestine and Syria (DFPS) was attached to the xxi Corps, with the British infantry regiments. The DFPS comprised two battalions of Algerian infantry, the two Armenian battalions raised as a nucleus for the *Légion d'Orient*, some dismounted Spahis, and three batteries of artillery; it was as much a political presence as a fighting force, though morale was good and the DFPS moved rapidly in the plain. If Allenby advanced up the coast he could rely on gunnery support from destroyers of the Royal Navy. In the desert to his right were Feisal's Arabs, an uncertain quantity; in January the Northern Arab Army had fought a set-piece battle brilliantly under Lawrence's leadership to defend Tafila and take the Crusader fortress at Karak; but they were ejected by the Turks once Lawrence was no longer with them. Gold supplies, filtered to the Bedouin from Allenby by Lawrence, brightened their military ardour. For the ablest Arab soldier, Feisal's Iraqi Chief of Staff, Colonel Nuri al-Sa'id, so too did whisky.

This composite force of Allenby heavily outnumbered Liman von Sanders' three armies, the remnant of the *Yildirim* Group. Liman had nearly twice as many heavy machine-guns as his opponents, but no other advantages. There were still several thousand *K-und-K* troops under his command, nearly all gunners in coastal batteries defending Syria or serving howitzers behind the main front. At his GHQ in Nazareth Liman retained a good, German staff. And other German units remained in Palestine, too. The 'Asia Corps' strengthened the Ottoman Eighth Army (10,000 men), which held a line from the coast to Furqua, some twenty miles inland, with headquarters at Tulkarm. The German 146th Infantry Regiment was attached to Mohammed Djemal Kuçuk's Ottoman Fourth Army, of 8,000 men and only seventy-four guns. Mohammed Djemal Kuçuk – not to be confused with the prominent Young Turk and one-time commander in Syria, Ahmed Djemal – had headquarters in Amman, with responsibility for the vast area east of the River Jordan. Between the Eighth and Fourth Armies, covering twenty miles of front among the hills of southern Samaria, was an entirely Turkish force of some 7,000 men, the Ottoman Seventh Army, with headquarters at Nablus. On 7 August General Mustafa Kemal was given command of the Seventh Army, returning to responsibilities he had held briefly the previous summer, before resigning in protest at Falkenhayn's policies and attitude.

Kemal was not impressed by the situation at the Front. It was painfully clear to him that, with the collapse of Russia, the lure of the Caucasus had induced Enver to treat Syria as a sideshow. He was promised a regiment of two battalions, newly trained and said to be in good order. It arrived with no colonel in command and no staff; they had been posted at the last moment to the Caucasus. Soon after reaching Judaea one battalion, thoroughly demoralized, deserted *en masse*; leaflets had promised food and comfort in a prisoner of war camp while waiting for the war to end, so that they could all go home again. 'The British now think they will defeat us by propaganda rather than by fighting', Kemal wrote to a friend early in September; 'Every day from their aircraft they throw more leaflets than bombs, always referring to "Enver and his gang . . .".'

Kemal soon found that in one important respect he was mistaken; for even while he was travelling south from the Bosporus to Damascus, Allenby was perfecting plans to inflict a 'defeat . . . by fighting'. In these early weeks of August he worked closely with his three Corps commanders: the highly experienced Sir Philip Chetwode, in command of xx Corps, with Brigadier-General Wavell as his Chief of Staff; the Australian Sir Harry Chauvel, commanding the Desert Mounted Corps; and the Irishman Sir Edward Bulfin, in command of the xxi Corps. Allenby proposed to concentrate Bulfin's infantry in the coastal plain, sending it forward after a short heavy bombardment and then wheeling inland, so as to allow three of Chauvel's cavalry divisions to ride rapidly northwards, cross the inner spur of the Mount Carmel Ridge through the Musmus Pass, and, constantly swinging slightly eastwards, push across the Esdraelon plain to reach the River Jordan at Beisan (now Beit Shean). The main Turkish and German forces would then be split, with Djevad's Ottoman Eighth Army falling back into northern Galilee and the Seventh Army trapped, south and east of the new line. Two subsidiary attacks would be made further east, with the largely independent 'Chaytor's Force' of Anzac cavalry and an Indian brigade fighting over the familiar hill country around Es Salt and crossing the Jordan to take Amman, when the Turks began to pull back. There is a curious and totally accidental resemblance between the right-wheeling manoeuvre through the Musmus Pass on the Jordan at Beisan proposed by Allenby in Palestine and the almost concurrent right-wheeling manoeuvre from the Dobropolje on the Vardar between Gradsko and Skopje developed by Franchet d'Esperey in Macedonia. Both commanders-in-chief combined horsemen and aircraft to keep the battle lines moving. But the two campaigns were fought in markedly different terrain.

Allenby was also in touch with Emir Feisal, theoretically a
Lieutenant-General under his command, although proudly asserting a
princely independence as commander of all Arab forces operating
north of Aqaba. In the second week of July Allenby received Lawrence
at GHQ in Bir Salem, at a time when he was beginning to formulate the
plans which only finally took shape a month later. Lawrence records
that Allenby wished to impose a precise timetable so as to co-ordinate
British and Arab moves against the Turks; for it was vital that the
Arabs should cut the Hejaz railway north and west of Deraa so as to
prevent the Ottoman armies receiving reinforcements from the north.
If the Arabs struck too soon their demolition work could be repaired; if
they struck later than GHQ required, their raid would have little effect
on the main offensive. 'Allenby', writes Lawrence in *The Seven Pillars of
Wisdom*, 'wanted us to lead off not more than four nor less than two
days before he did. His words to me were that three men and a boy
with pistols in front of Deraa on September the sixteenth . . . would be
better than thousands a week before or a week after.' Such precision
time-keeping was alien to Bedouin ways. Yet, despite moments of
great uncertainty, Lawrence and his team of British liaison officers
succeeded by 12 September in assembling a force of 1,000 men – Arab
regulars and irregulars, French Algerian gunners, three British
armoured cars and some Gurkhas – at Azraq, 'the blue fort on its rock
above rustling palms', where Lawrence had first found refuge ten
months previously. Azraq is surpassed as an oasis in the Syrian desert
only by Tadmor-Palmyra, far to the north. The surrounding 'fresh
meadows' were firm enough to serve as a base for two RAF aeroplanes.
As Azraq is fifty miles due west of Amman, news of the presence of this
considerable Arab force at the oasis strengthened the Turkish conviction that Allenby would deliver his main autumn attack east of the River
Jordan and secure control of the Hejaz railway route into Syria. A
rumour that Feisal was about to march on Amman was deliberately
circulated among the local Arabs, for Liman's staff to hear and assess.

There was a bumper crop of misinformation ready for harvesting that
autumn. Elaborate measures were taken by GHQ and by the agencies
in Cairo to deceive the enemy. By now the Germans and Turks
understood Allenby better than before Gaza; they knew that, given the
opportunity, he would use his mounted troops; and Allenby for his part
accepted that they had decided he was first and foremost a cavalryman.
He therefore needed not only to convince Liman that he was going to
attack across the lower Jordan, but also to find ways of confirming his
belief by faking evidence of cavalry preparation. Despite the heat of late

summer most of Chaytor's Australasians and some Indian units were retained in the Jordan valley to give a semblance of reality. An illusion of activity was also provided by the British West Indies Regiment, footsloggers who would march by day from camps in the hills down to positions in the Jordan valley, only to be brought back at night by lorries with no lights and sent out again on another day as fresh reinforcements. Bluff was used on a large scale: a Jerusalem hotel was commandeered, turned into a bogus headquarters filled with maps of the Jordan valley and given supplementary telephone wires, their installation easily seen by curious passers-by outside. Fake wireless messages between fictitious commanders in the hotel and notional units around Jericho kept enemy Intelligence intrigued. Orders for fodder, to be held ready for thousands of horses, were placed by trusted agents among Arab merchants of less trusted discretion between Es Salt and Amman. Tents for dummy camps were pitched in the Jordan valley, and sappers seemed to be busy bridge-building. Fifteen thousand canvas horses, suitably painted, were brought down to the camps in the valleys; at watering time, when it was reasonable to expect horses to be led down to the Jordan for a drink, clouds of dust could be seen by enemy observers from afar, who did not realize that it was caused by mules drawing sleighs across the parched ground. By contrast, troops were moved to the coastal plain only at night and were concealed within the orange groves and olive clusters around Jaffa. The cultivation of citrus fruit meant that, beneath the trees, were irrigation channels which could provide some water for the horses. At other times, when the horses had to be exercised, RAF aircraft patrolled the skies, both to discourage aerial intruders and to distract attention from what was happening on the ground. Ten thousand cavalry were concentrated in the Jaffa area. As a final ruse to confuse the enemy it was announced that on Thursday 19 September a race meeting would be held outside Jaffa.

On Tuesday, as though to confirm Allenby's earlier doubts, an Indian sergeant deserted and told his Turkish co-religionists that an offensive would begin within forty-eight hours, with the principal thrust along the coastal plain. The Turks passed on the information to Liman, one experienced colonel suggesting that he should withdraw his advanced troops back from their positions on the coast so that the British would waste their shells on empty trenches. But Liman refused to give credence to the sergeant's information; here, Liman thought, was a shoddy display of British ruse planting, for why should an Indian sergeant be so well informed of his commander-in-chief's intentions? The latest German Intelligence assessments showed activity in the

Jordan valley but nothing of interest down by the coast, though on Sunday a German pilot reported some movement of horses behind Allenby's left flank. Only Kemal, at his headquarters in Nablus, took the sergeant's information seriously and he was at that time ill in bed, racked with pain from a chronic kidney complaint. He alerted his corps commanders and let Liman know of his concern – only to be commended for his precautions, though with the inference that they were the worries of a sick man. On the previous night Lawrence's Arabs had demolished a bridge to cut the Deraa–Amman section of railway and in the small hours of Wednesday another bridge at Tell Arar, north of Deraa, suffered a similar fate, while Nuri al-Sa'id had raided Muzeirib station, west of Deraa. To Liman it seemed obvious that the offensive would come east of the Jordan; and he ordered German troops from the Asia Corps reserve to strengthen the garrison defending Deraa.

The guns – in that sector, 390 of them to Liman's 130 – opened up at 4.30 a.m. on 19 September, concentrating on enemy artillery positions with great effect. A quarter of an hour later the infantry of Bulfin's XXI Corps moved forward, in all the smoke and murk of a battle begun before dawn, like Milne's troops in Macedonia twenty-four hours previously. But while the first day's attack around Lake Doiran was checked by stubborn resistance, in Palestine Allenby's confidence in his plans was soon justified. There was little difficulty in cutting a wide gap in the Turkish wire; the borders of the gap were then staked out with coloured flags. General Barrow's 4th Cavalry Division passed through the wire and over the trenches between nine and ten in the morning, while General Macandrew's 5th Cavalry Division found a way northwards along the beach and in the lee of the cliffs as soon as dawn broke. At the same time the RAF struck, grounding enemy planes by bombing the aerodrome at Jenin in a series of raids and attacking a crucial railway junction, the two Army headquarters at Nablus and Tulkarm and the co-ordinating telephone exchange at Afula. The air raids were so effective that, within three hours of the start of the offensive, Liman's GHQ at Nazareth had lost all contact with Djevad's Eighth Army, which was falling back rapidly up the road through Tulkarm to Jenin. As in Macedonia the airmen turned their attention to the columns beneath them, and the roads were soon blocked with broken, burning vehicles. Seven thousand prisoners and a hundred guns were taken by the 60th Division along the Tulkarm road that day; and the Australian Light Horse Brigade on its left captured many more, too. The Ottoman Eighth Army disintegrated, though the Germans in the Asia Corps kept together as a unit, falling back to the higher ground of upper Galilee in good order.

By the end of the first day Bulfin's infantry had fought their way across fourteen miles of steadily rising country, and were in Tulkarm before darkness fell. The two cavalry divisions were riding far ahead, with General Barrow anxious to clear the narrow defiles of the Musmus Pass before the Germans or Turks could cover the route with machine-gunners. In the darkness the vanguard missed the entry to the pass, a mistake hastily rectified by the General himself. Not until the Lancers were at El Laijun in the early morning, clearing the last hills before the Plain of Esdraelon, did they meet the Turkish battalion sent to defend the pass against them. The cavalry pushed ahead relentlessly. By eight o'clock in the morning General Barrow held the railway junction of Afula, where his division captured not only large stocks of supplies but also several railway engines and three German aircraft on the ground. The pilot of a fourth German plane made a perfect landing, but disconcertingly found himself received with fixed bayonets rather than by his regular mechanics. The Cavalry Division had still not reached its main objective, but this was achieved in the early evening when the Lancers reached the Jordan, tightening the noose around what remained of the Ottoman Seventh and Eighth Armies.

When the 4th Cavalry Division emerged from the Musmus defiles on to the plain it had passed biblical Megiddo, a city captured by Joshua and fortified by Solomon and the site of the battle in 609 BC during which King Josiah was killed by an arrow; and in the last book of the New Testament the hill of Megiddo, *Armageddon*, becomes the apocalyptic setting for the final conflict between good and evil. Although in 1918 there was no more than a skirmish around Tel Megiddo itself, the biblical and symbolic association induced Allenby to revive the name Megiddo and bestow it collectively on the series of battles which were to continue for five more days across Galilee.

While Barrow's men were riding cautiously through the Musmus Pass, early on 20 September farther to the north General Macandrew sent some squadrons from the 5th Cavalry Division on a special mission. At half past four in the morning Liman von Sanders, in bed at his headquarters in the Casa Nuova hospice at the top of the hill at Nazareth, was awakened by the sound of shooting down the main road south of the town. A troop of Gloucestershire Hussars galloped up the main road, with swords drawn, looking for the enemy commander-in-chief's residence. A quarter of a mile down the road from the Casa Nuova they halted, naturally enough, at the Hotel Germania; there they took several hundred prisoners, but not their commander-in-chief. The distraction enabled Liman, still in night attire, to get to his staff car and set out northwards. When a German counter-attack forced the British cavalry to withdraw, Liman returned and had an opportunity to recover his clothes and his dignity before ordering a withdrawal from Nazareth in the early afternoon.

Over the next few days the Turkish hold was loosened one by one from the towns of Palestine and Transjordan. Nablus, Jenin and Beisan fell on 20 September, the same day as Nazareth. On 23 September the Mysore and Jodhpore Lancers rode into the port of Haifa, after charging machine-gunners on the slopes of Mount Carmel; and on that same Monday, across the bay, the cavalry brigade which had so nearly captured Liman made a dash for Acre, and, with support from armoured cars, found little difficulty in securing within two hours the peninsula fortress which in 1799 defied Napoleon for two months. The RAF dived on the Turks retreating up the Wadi Fara, hour after hour, inflicting the heaviest casualties of the whole campaign, causing panic among men and horses.

Across the Front, some sixty miles to the south-east, in the region where Liman had expected the main blow to fall, Chaytor's Force had secured positions commanding the Jordan crossing during 20 September, with two battalions from the British West Indies Regiment making the main infantry attack. On Monday evening (23 September) the New Zealand Brigade secured the town of Es Salt and, unlike in the attacks earlier in the year, were able to consolidate their position and maintain the pressure so as to threaten Amman, which fell in the afternoon of 25 September, after a few hours of stubborn resistance from well led Anatolian troops. By now the Turkish garrison down the railway at Maan was isolated, and it duly surrendered two days later. The main body of Chaytor's Force came from New Zealand and Australia, but it was supplemented by an Indian Brigade and by the two Jewish Royal Fusilier battalions, as well as by the volunteers from the West Indies, who were eager to show their fighting tenacity after the 'marching on' role assigned to them during those pre-offensive weeks of deception. Although the casualties in the week's fighting were mercifully light – 139 men killed or wounded – forty-one were sustained by the 2nd West Indies Battalion. Chaytor's Force took over 10,000 prisoners, and many hundreds of local conscripts seized opportunities to slip away to their homes and lie low until the storm of war passed on northwards. The gravest threat to the Turks in Transjordan came from Bedouin raiders, who showed great rapacity and little mercy.

While Emir Feisal remained at Azraq his principal fighting force was forty miles to the north, with Lawrence at Umtaiye, south-east of Deraa, where it was exposed to frequent air attack from German and Turkish planes. During the first two days of Allenby's offensive neither Feisal nor Lawrence had any clear information of what was happening further west. Lawrence was back at Azraq on 21 September when a De Havilland 4 two-seater plane brought news of the early successes and revised orders for the Emir: the Arabs were to concentrate on raiding Deraa and Turkish units falling back through the Yarmuk valley, down to Lake Tiberias (the Sea of Galilee); under no circumstances was Feisal to 'embark on any enterprise to the north, such as an advance on Damascus' without Allenby's consent. As so often, the Sykes–Picot Agreement was casting a political shadow over military operations.

Lawrence decided to fly back to Palestine in the observer's cockpit, partly to clarify the orders over Deraa and partly to seek protective air cover. The Commander-in-Chief received him at Bir Salem, his 'cool, airy, whitewashed' headquarters 'made musical by the moving of the wind in the trees outside'. Allenby explained that, once Chaytor had secured Amman, he proposed a parallel advance on Damascus: Chauvel, Macandrew and the main body of the Desert Mounted Corps would follow the road from Tiberias through Quneitra, and Sa'sa; Barrow's 4th Cavalry Division would strike due north through Deraa and along the *Haj* pilgrim route to meet Chauvel some ten miles south of Damascus. Allenby required the Arabs to harry the Ottoman Fourth Army, from the desert on Barrow's right flank; again he emphasized that there must be no premature Arab dash for Damascus. In London next morning, like some distant echo of these thunderous events, the French ambassador called at the Foreign Office to remind Balfour that, in making arrangements 'for the administration of the country he was presumably about to occupy' General Allenby should remember that 'Syria . . . was . . . within the French sphere of influence'.

Lawrence returned to the desert with the temporary loan of two Bristol fighters and a De Havilland 9 from the Royal Australian Flying Corps, capable of providing air cover for the Arabs. An RAF Handley Page bomber, the largest aircraft in the Middle East, brought in supplies: 'THE aeroplane', Arabs declared in awesome wonder. For three days the Arabs raided the railway south of Deraa, but on 26 September they switched to the north and destroyed a stretch of newly repaired track. As yet there was no sign of General Barrow and the 4th Cavalry Division, which on that day was checked by Turkish gunners on high ground above the Wadi el Ghafr at Irbid. In Barrow's absence Lawrence prepared for an assault on Deraa town by Northern Arab Army 'regulars'. He established the Arab camp at Sheikh Saad, seven miles west of the pilgrim route and eighteen north of Deraa itself. By now Turkish rearguards were behaving atrociously in the towns and villages through which they retreated. At Tafas, south of Sheikh Saad, women and children were slaughtered with particular bestiality as punishment for alleged support of the Arab Revolt. Such excesses in their turn brought ghastly reprisals from the Arabs over the next few days. Theoretically on 26–27 September the Arabs took more than 2,000 Turkish prisoners, but many more of the enemy were shot or bayoneted after surrender; and even worse was to follow. Arab anger resented the disciplined order of outsiders incapable of understanding their ways.

Over one episode on the following night, 27–28 September, there remains a certain mystery. During the evening Lawrence accompanied Nuri al-Sa'id's patrols down to the approaches to Deraa but he stopped short of entering the town, turning back to Sheikh Saad, which he did not reach until midnight. In his absence the Arabs went on a rampage of slaughter and looting; it was 'one of the nights in which mankind went crazy', Lawrence wrote in *The Seven Pillars of Wisdom*, a night 'when others' lives became toys to break and throw away'. Why did Lawrence turn back? Was it revulsion at entering a town where he had himself briefly been held captive – apparently unidentified – and subjected to a savage beating and homosexual assault ten months ago? Or did he return to Sheikh Saad to protect captured Turks – and, perhaps, to meet one eminent Turk in person? For among the Ottoman officers seeking to escape from Deraa to Damascus that weekend was Mustafa Kemal. More than once after the war Lawrence maintained that 'in September 1918' he held 'conversations' with Kemal in the course of which the Ottoman Fourth Army commander claimed to be the leader of the anti-German section of the Turkish officer corps and affirmed that he was convinced that Turkey should abandon the Levant and the Balkans and concentrate on central Asia. Kemal was, according to this version of events, allowed to make his way up to Damascus because the Arabs felt he was an alternative Turkish leader with whom agreement might be reached (and there had, indeed, already been correspondence between Kemal and Feisal). It is possible that this talk ran only through Lawrence's fantasy mind: there seems to be no record of such a meeting, English or Turkish, nor is Kemal ever known to have mentioned it; but it *could* have taken place during those few hours late on Friday night. If there was a meeting and Lawrence allowed so important an enemy officer to go free, he could hardly mention the incident while the war was in progress. Significantly, one of Nuri al-Sa'id's patrols found, and retained, Kemal's baggage in Deraa that night.

By dawn Lawrence was inside Deraa, riding the eighteen miles from the Arab camp to this least attractive of Syrian towns on Baha, a camel moving 'with piston-strides like an engine'. It was, he admits, a place he hated because 'I had felt man's iniquity here'. He attempted, however, to impose some order and travelled out to meet General Barrow, who was preparing to obey Allenby's orders and take the town by conventional means. Barrow was angry at Lawrence's conduct in allowing the Arabs into Deraa and horrified by what his troops found when they rode in: 'A sight of dreadful misery', unparalleled by anything he had witnessed throughout the war, he was to recall in his memoirs twenty years later. Indian Lancers of the 10th Cavalry Brigade were appalled to see Bedouin looting a hospital train in Deraa station, hacking to death those who were caring for the Turkish wounded. General Barrow had no patience with Lawrence's attempts to set up an Arab administration in the town and roundly rebuked both Lawrence and Nuri al-Sa'id for the bloodshed of the past twenty-four hours. British military rule was imposed. During the following week, as the armies moved northwards across Syria, Barrow had no sympathy with Lawrence, Feisal or the Arab cause in general. He feared what might occur in Damascus. So indeed did his corps commander, General Chauvel, who had felt betrayed by local Bedouin during the abortive second Transjordan raid in May; like most Australians, he was by now mistrustful of all Arabs. The prospect of freeing Damascus from Turkish rule as smoothly as Jerusalem seemed remote. And even after eighty years the events of the next four days seem as intricate and confusing as the alleyways off the city's great souk.

Unlike his subordinate generals, Allenby's breadth of vision enabled him to comprehend the significance of Damascus for Feisal and his army; within the city was Islam's fourth holiest shrine, the Omayyad Mosque, and the tomb of Salah al-Din (Saladin) who, though a Kurd by descent, remained the supreme warrior inspiration of the Arab peoples. It was unthinkable for an Arab army to stand aside while Europeans it had aided marched into a city with almost fourteen hundred years of unbroken Muslim rule. Allenby intended that Damascus should be 'left under its present civil administration'; no national flags were to be flown. When Chauvel asked about the position of the Arabs, worried that they might seek to secure the political administration of Syria, Allenby told him that such questions must 'wait until I come, and, if Feisal gives you any trouble, deal with him through Lawrence, who will be your liaison officer'. Allenby retained confidence in Lawrence as an officer who would ensure that Feisal behaved with political discretion.

On 25 September the Commander-in-Chief changed his mind over the Arab advance on Damascus; he sent a letter to Feisal, by an airborne carrier, letting the Emir know that he hoped the EEF would be in the city within four or five days and that he had no objection to Feisal's entry as soon as he thought he could safely do so. By the time this message reached Feisal Lawrence was no longer with him; he does not seem to have known that Allenby had lifted the ban on an Arab advance until after his stormy encounter with General Barrow in Deraa. Lawrence did not meet Feisal in Deraa until late on Sunday 29 September, several hours after Barrow and the 4th Cavalry Division set out for Damascus, some seventy miles to the north. With Nuri al-Sa'id and the Northern Arab Army committed to a march on Barrow's right flank and the Bedouin 'irregular' tribesmen harrying Turkish detachments that threatened to break off from the retreating fold and into the desert, Feisal was in no position to make an entry into Damascus ahead of the EEF and secure the Syrian capital for the Arabs. A week ago, a dash for the city from Umtaiye, or even Azraq, would have been possible; but by now General Barrow had a day's start on him; and Chauvel's main body of troops was almost clear of the high ground known today as the Golan Heights, following the 'road to Damascus' which Christian tradition assumes Paul travelled when he received his call to become an apostle.

On Monday morning Lawrence joined the race for Damascus, heading out of Deraa at dawn in the relative comfort of a blue Rolls-Royce tender, and accompanied by Major Frank Stirling, the shrewd, level-headed staff officer made responsible for British troops serving the Northern Arab Army. They caught up with General Barrow's cavalry at noon, watering their horses which, by now, were near exhaustion. Chauvel's advance from Quneitra was checked by strong Turkish and German resistance above Wadi ez Zabirani at Sa'as, nineteen miles south of Damascus; but by one o'clock in the afternoon an advanced column of Australian horsemen, New Zealand machine-gunners and the Spahis and Chasseurs d'Afrique of the French colonial regiment were among the hills beside the Barada River, flowing down into Damascus; an order was then received from GHQ to halt the advance and make no entry into Damascus. In fact, this force was far ahead not only of Barrow's cavalry brigade but also of the Northern Arab Army; for the Arabs, regulars and tribesmen alike, were engaged in a merciless battle against the rearguard of the Turkish Fourth Army, the perpetrators of the massacre at Tafas. During the afternoon of 30 September there remained some hesitancy over the final stages of the advance into Damascus. Having imposed his 'no entry' veto Allenby, whose staff car had constantly carried him from one advanced position to another during the early days of the campaign, rather strangely remained at Tiberias, 120 miles away, leaving vital decisions to his commanders in the field; and they were by no means certain whether the Germans and Turks intended to fight for the city or, as seemed more likely, fall back on the mountains of Lebanon and the high ground commanding the road to Homs and Aleppo.

Liman von Sanders himself was by now already in the Lebanon, having set up headquarters in Baalbek on the previous day, Sunday 29 September. He had decided there was no good defensible position protecting Damascus; and his great concern was to get the Turkish and German troops out of Damascus before Allenby's net enveloped them. He hoped to regroup at Riaq, to the south of Baalbek, and on the hills around Maalula above the Homs–Aleppo route. Kemal personally travelled into Damascus with a small bodyguard, found the people coldly hostile to everything Turkish, noticed that the balconies along the narrow streets were already decked with Arab national colours, and accepted that Ottoman rule in the city was at an end; he led his staff westwards towards Riaq. There were, however, still some 10,000 Turks at the barracks within the city; some columns marched out, following Kemal towards the Barada Gorge and the way to the Lebanon, but when they found that way blocked by Australian and French troops they gave up the attempt, returned to barracks and passively awaited a moment to surrender.

By the early hours of Tuesday 1 October there remained one escape route to be cut, the road to Homs. To reach it, however, Major Olden of the 3rd Australian Light Horse Brigade had to bring his men down from the north-west along the lower Barada Gorge and then across the approaches to the crenellated walls of the old city and out again to the north-east. Although, in the spirit of Allenby's no entry order, Holden sought to pass the city gates at the gallop, he was stopped by welcoming crowds and then by desultory rifle fire. With drawn swords the Australians turned towards the Serai (town hall) to establish some form of order, although they met no further resistance. Indeed, at the Serai they were received by a committee with, at its head, an Arab who claimed to be the nominee as Governor of General Djemal Kuçuk and he duly surrendered Damascus to Major Holden and his escort soon after six o'clock in the morning. By seven the cavalry, almost all from

Western Australia, had ridden out of the city to resume their pursuit of the Turks retreating towards Homs.

At about nine o'clock Colonel Lawrence and Major Stirling arrived in the blue Rolls-Royce, preceded by what Stirling describes as 'a patrol of Bengal Lancers'. The Indians had in fact delayed their arrival by arresting and detaining what they assumed to be a Turkish officer wearing Arab headdress and his companion who was 'in full Arab kit'. When this anticlimactic incident was resolved – it is passed over rapidly in *Seven Pillars* – Colonel Lawrence went to the Serai, rejected Djemal's nominees as men without authority, and appointed a local landowner to govern the city in Feisal's name. As at Deraa Lawrence attempted to impose order on Damascus, where the situation was rapidly getting out of hand.

Meanwhile a third claimant to represent the people of the city – Ali Riza Rikhabi, Mayor throughout most of the war – had been taking an early breakfast with General Barrow at Zeraqiye and explaining how, as a good Arab nationalist, he had encouraged the Turks to site all their artillery in unsuitable places; so vigorous was Ali Riza's exposition that he upset the scrambled eggs and cocoa with which Barrow's servants had provided him. Nevertheless, as an Arab not known to be associated with Feisal, he became the nominee of Chauvel and the army for Governor of the city; this arrangement was perfectly acceptable to Lawrence, whom Ali Riza – a man with a belief in leaving no future unexplored – had contrived to meet secretly in the outskirts of Damascus as long ago as June 1917.

That night there was serious looting and, in many parts of the city, a spate of killings in the streets. A semblance of order was restored by the Arabs themselves before noon on 2 October, when a formal parade entry was made by the Australian, New Zealand, Indian, British and French colonial troops of the Desert Mounted Corps, with Generals Chauvel, Macandrew and Barrow at their head. In twelve days they had ridden over 400 miles, farther than from London to Edinburgh, and had taken more than 47,000 Turks, Germans and Austro-Hungarians prisoner. Casualties had been mercifully light for such a massive campaign: 150 killed in action and under 500 wounded.

Already a message of congratulation had reached Allenby's headquarters from King Hussein in Aqaba; 'I ask Almighty God to enable me to kiss you between the eyes', it ran. As yet, the General had not met any member of the Hashemite dynasty, but it was essential for him to see Hussein's third son, the Emir Feisal, and settle the immediate future of Syria. On 3 October Allenby was driven up from Tiberias to Damascus, an eight-hour journey, only to learn that Feisal had just arrived by special train from Deraa and was to make a triumphant entry at three o'clock in the afternoon. But Allenby needed urgent conversations with Chauvel, Lawrence and Feisal and he wished to be back at GHQ in Tiberias that night to assess news of the pursuit of Liman through the Lebanon. There was no time to waste. A car was made ready to fetch the Emir to the conference in the Hotel Victoria. Yet though Feisal's celebrations might be cut short, he was not a man to be upstaged by military formality. Outside the Hotel Victoria he was rapturously welcomed by a waiting crowd. 'He managed to dodge my emissaries somehow', Chauvel wrote later, a little sourly; 'He came not in the Rolls-Royce' but 'at a hard gallop followed by some forty or fifty Bedouin horsemen'.

This first meeting of Commander-in-Chief and Arab Prince was dramatic, but calmly dignified: each man admired the other's qualities. Allenby was more sympathetic to Arab claims than to the French; but political necessity obliged him to impose the basic terms of the Sykes–Picot Agreement. Feisal was told that, as deputy for his father King-Sherif Hussein, he could set up a military administration for all occupied ex-enemy lands east of the Jordan and above, from Aqaba up to and including Damascus. But France, rather than Great Britain, would be the Protecting Power in Syria, and Feisal would have a French officer with him to give advice. He learnt also that Lebanon, where Indian troops had entered Beirut on the previous day, would be directly administered by France (whose warships were, at that moment, bringing troops to secure their prize).

Against all these arrangements Feisal strongly protested, using Lawrence as his interpreter. He had, he maintained, no knowledge of the Sykes–Picot Agreement, and Lawrence denied ever telling Feisal about it – dubious statements, as everyone else in the room knew full well. But Allenby insisted that, for the moment, this settlement must be regarded as a military order, to be obeyed. The black, white and green colours of the Sherifian flag might fly over Damascus as token of Arab victory; but political discussion could only be resumed when the war was over. Politely, but with deep inner bitterness, Lieutenant-General the Emir Feisal complied.

Firmly, and with a confused sense of personal and political betrayal, Colonel Lawrence did not. He told Allenby after Feisal left the meeting that it would be impossible for him to work with the Arabs alongside a French liaison officer. A long spell of accumulated leave was due; might he take it and return to England, he asked? 'Yes, I think you better had',

Allenby conceded. Next evening the blue Rolls-Royce set out again, heading south to Cairo. Twelve days later he sailed from Port Said for Taranto and the long train journey across Italy and France to the Channel coast. Thus within three weeks of entering Damascus Lawrence was home in Oxford. It was two months since his thirtieth birthday. He was the same age, almost to the day, as General Bonaparte on his turn from Egypt in 1799; Marengo, the Imperial Crown, Austerlitz, and Moscow all lay ahead of Napoleon. So, too, did Waterloo and St Helena. And the future for Lawrence?

CHAPTER 16

'EVERY DAY LOST . . .'

Lloyd George welcomed the news that Allenby was in Damascus, with the Sherifian flag flying over the city. But the Prime Minister was far less inclined than the Commander-in-Chief to heed French wishes; 'Britain had won the war in the Middle East and there was no reason why France should profit from it', he told the War Cabinet, speaking at about the same hour that Allenby was in conference with Feisal and Lawrence. As so often during this last year of the war, he was furious with the Foreign Office; why had not Balfour and his mandarins made it clear in Paris that the Sykes–Picot Agreement was a dead letter? A revised settlement would soon emerge. Sykes himself, by now in London, was at work on a new proposal: France could remain in Lebanon, but would forgo other Arab lands in return for a protectorate over 'the whole Kurdo-Armenian region from Adana to Persia and the Caucasus'. Neither the Prime Minister nor his War Cabinet colleagues knew of Sykes's latest ingenious exercise in sphere-defining until the end of the week, and his outline was then seen to contain so many flaws that it was soon back on the drawing board. But the existence of such a scheme, and of others too, emphasized London's mounting conviction that through the victories in Palestine and Mesopotamia, Britain – and Britain alone – now possessed the authority to arbitrate within the nursery world of Arab nationalism. This illusion was to become the most dangerous of all post-imperial fallacies.

Few people in London believed that Turkey could stay at war much longer. Lloyd George was not surprised to hear five days after the fall of Damascus that a Turkish envoy was on his way to Athens to discuss armistice terms. This diplomatic initiative came to nothing, for the envoy lacked proper credentials, but it served to concentrate attention on unresolved questions in the East. It was nearly four years since Lloyd George first pressed for the defeat of Germany by 'knocking away the props', a phrase Hankey recalled when celebrating Bulgaria's plea for an armistice. Bulgaria, however, was not a belligerent in 1914 when the metaphor was coined: Lloyd George was thinking of the Ottoman and Habsburg Empires; he specifically mentioned Syria as an area where Turkey was vulnerable; most of all, he favoured an advance northwards from Salonika to Serbia, the Danube and the heart of Austria–Hungary. By 1918 the strategic balance within Europe had changed completely, especially since the elimination of Tsarist Russia. Now Lloyd George was more interested in the Black Sea than in the Danube basin. As soon as he heard of the Bulgarian armistice he wanted to switch Milne's army eastwards, taking it away from Franchet d'Esperey's command and placing it under Allenby as part of a grand strategic pincer movement on Constantinople.

This latest example of what Sir Henry Wilson regarded as 'amateur strategy' was opposed not only by the CIGS, but by Milner, Balfour and Hankey, too. They still believed it was possible for Germany and Austria–Hungary to concentrate troops in Romania and advance southwards, occupying Bulgaria, even setting up a military administration in Sofia, and securing a firm hold on southern Serbia as well. Reluctantly Lloyd George gave way; the command structure of the Army of the Orient was left intact. No one believed that the war in central and south-eastern Europe would be over before the coming of winter. Even a Balkan military expert as knowledgeable as Amery thought 'we can't really prevent the Germans retaining control of the Danube' and 'we may only be able to hold the line of . . . the old pre-1914 Turkish frontier'. It is hardly surprising that in those early October days, while British troops were storming their way through formidable defences in the Hindenburg Line, the CIGS should cross to France for talks with Foch and Clemenceau; what *is* surprising is that the main topic was not these battles in France, but safeguarding gains in the Balkans. There was a fatalistic acceptance that fighting in the West must pound on, right up to the following spring. A fortnight later – less than a month before Armistice Day – Sir Henry Wilson could still tell the War Cabinet that 'there was nothing to warrant the assumption that the present military situation justified the Germans in giving-in'; he took it for granted that rain and mud would soon bog down the armies in France and Belgium once more.

The weather gave warning of what might be expected on the Western Front when, in the small hours of Tuesday 1 October, heavy rain began to fall after days of fitful autumn sunshine. At OHL's Supreme Headquarters in Spa, beneath the misty birch and pine forests of the Ardennes, the gloom engendered by Bulgaria's 'treachery' intensified.

The Kaiser's sciatica became so acute that he walked with a stick; an equerry's well meant comment that the rain would stop the enemy tanks brought him little comfort. Senior officers were gleaning for straws of good news to clutch: the best they could find was the gravity of the influenza epidemic in France; Ludendorff told Hindenburg, and Hindenburg told Admiral Scheer, and everyone seems to have told the Kaiser. Rather curiously, they forgot that disease can be nobody's ally; within a fortnight it was rampant in the German capital, leaving 1,500 Berliners dead.

But, as October opened, influenza seemed the best hope of curbing the massed divisions which Foch was assembling. Bad news continued to come in from the field headquarters; German troops pulled back from Armentières and Lens, and by 3 October the Navy had moved thirty-one serviceable destroyers, torpedo boats and U-boats from Ostend, Zeebrugge and the Bruges Canal, for the High Command admitted that it could no longer guarantee to protect bases along the Belgian coast. By Tuesday evening, when the German imperial train pulled out of Spa for an overnight journey back to Potsdam, the Kaiser had become almost reconciled to the double programme thrust on him by the OHL paladins: immediate constitutional reform to give Germany a democratic parliamentary system, followed by an appeal to President Wilson for an end to the fighting, pending a settlement based upon his Fourteen Points.

Throughout that night and all next day Germany had no Chancellor. Hertling had resigned at Spa, and there was much scurrying in Berlin to find someone acceptable to the sovereign, to the Supreme Command and to a wide range of parties in the Reichstag. The deputy Chancellor declined the succession, a possible contender fended off the first approaches; and increasingly the liberal royalist, Prince Max of Baden, emerged as the most likely choice. The Prince was a distant cousin of the Kaiser; he had won respect from both sides for recent services to the International Red Cross and prisoners of war; and speeches he gave the previous winter showed a sense of responsibility to Europe as a whole rare among German public figures at that time. These qualities were, as he appreciated, offset by inexperience of political infighting, and he was reluctant to accept the post; but by noon on 2 October, when the Kaiser stepped down from the train at Potsdam's Wildpark Station, the Prince was in Berlin telephoning politicians for their support in a coalition which the Reichstag would back. To form such a government was no easy task. 'Why join a bankrupt enterprise?', was the moderate socialist Philipp Scheidemann's initial response.

Later that Wednesday Prince Max attended a Crown Council. For the first time Hindenburg was present without his partner, but he dutifully transmitted Ludendorff's views, as though from a prepared text: the Army must have an end to the fighting within forty-eight hours. The Prince deplored precipitate action; it would be seen abroad as capitulation, and Germany could hope for no more consideration than Bulgaria. Though he thought the picture less black than OHL, an armistice was clearly needed for the Army to be kept together in good order at the Front and in the garrison cities of the Fatherland. But, he argued, there should be a delay of at least a fortnight, in which to establish parliamentary government on a sound basis and prepare the nation for the ending of the war. Hindenburg, unaccustomed to having OHL's decisions questioned, began to flounder. The Kaiser intervened; there could be no argument over an immediate armistice: 'The Supreme Command considers it necessary, and you have not been brought here to make difficulties for the Supreme Command', he told Prince Max bluntly, reverting to the autocratic style that came naturally to him.

Perhaps at this point the Chancellor-designate should have given up his efforts to form a government and returned to Karlsruhe. But he had a deep sense of duty; to pull out might unleash Red revolution, he feared. Hindenburg, however, could add nothing new to the discussion. Like Kitchener in London at the start of the war, he found it hard to present a reasoned argument in council. Now he only knew that he must consult the First Quartermaster-General. He would provide the Kaiser and the Crown Council with a written, considered report tomorrow, he announced. Making the best speed his bulk would permit, he hurried away to telephone Spa. Meanwhile in the Reichstag building a spokesman for the Supreme Command was telling the astonished leaders of the political parties that OHL recognized that 'We can no longer win'. He explained that, while Germany's reserves of manpower were exhausted, the Entente allies could make good their losses with aid from the United States; the struggle must be brought to an immediate end. The Reichstag Deputies were deeply shocked. Until that day most assumed that the only possible end would be a victory in the West to match the victory won a year ago in the East.

Next morning, 3 October, Hindenburg delivered the formal letter which he had discussed with Ludendorff. It repeated the demand for the immediate despatch of a 'peace offer to our enemies': 'Owing to the breakdown in the Macedonian Front . . . weakening our reserves in the West' and because of 'the impossibility of making good our very heavy losses . . . of the last few days', it explained, 'there no longer exists any prospect . . . of forcing peace upon our enemies'; the German Army was still beating back every attack, but the position was getting so bad that the Supreme Command might have 'to make serious decisions'. An early peace was essential. 'Every day lost cost thousands of brave soldiers' lives', the letter ended. It was signed by Hindenburg; but if, as seems likely, it was dictated by his partner the last sentence carried a poignant sincerity; for the childless Ludendorff, for whom it is so hard to feel sympathy, had recently lost in France a cherished stepson.

Prince Max was, however, determined to make the dangers of a peace appeal evident to the Supreme Command; did Hindenburg realize it was probable that Germany would lose not only Alsace-Lorraine but also the predominantly Polish lands in East Prussia? At the same time, the new Chancellor brought into his government leaders of the SPD (Social Democrats), the largest party in the Reichstag – a sign to the officer corps of the likely power structure in a democratic Germany. No doubts over the political changes were raised by the Hindenburg–Ludendorff partnership; and the Chancellor was grudgingly told that the loss of the Reichsland (Alsace and Lorraine) was acceptable. But the General Field Marshal insisted that Germany must retain the eastern borderlands. Hindenburg himself came from Posen, Ludendorff from a small town in the same region. To be made a foreigner in his birthplace was a humiliation neither General wished to contemplate. 'The independent Polish state' proposed in the Fourteen Points should stop short of East Prussia. OHL assumed that Wilson's programme was negotiable. Prince Max was less sanguine; but, in the early hours of Thursday 4 October, he authorized the legation in Berne to seek Swiss mediation. President Wilson was to be told that the Imperial German Government sought 'the restoration of peace' on the basis of the Fourteen Points and his subsequent explanatory statements. 'To avoid further bloodshed', the German government asked for 'the immediate conclusion of an armistice on land, sea and in the air'. A similar request from Vienna, using Swedish mediators, was sent later in the day.

These peace pleas reached Washington at a difficult moment for the President. American troops were keeping forty German divisions tied down in the Argonne that month, at times fighting from tree to tree in thick forest. The persistence of a 'lost battalion', the endurance of carrier pigeon 'Cher Ami' and the marksmanship of a Tennessee backwoodsman created familiar epic legends of initiative which time does not tarnish. But though press reports from the Argonne might celebrate the heroism of Major Charles W. Whittlesey and Corporal Alvin C. York, local newspapers also carried lists of casualties, often along with photographs of faces familiar to folk back home, in what was still small-town America. Not all the deaths were in battle; in nine weeks 20,000 American troops in Europe died from illness, mostly influenza and pneumonia. These were sad months on both sides of the Atlantic, and, indeed, in much of Asia too. But in America the harsh impact of war heightened rather than blunted patriotic sentiment. There were few peace demonstrations. Through many states, especially down the eastern seaboard, ran a wave of vocal support for the AEF; 'Finish the war soon, but be true to our boys', 'Strike down the mad brutes and open the road to Berlin'. And in Cleveland, Ohio an editor told his readers, 'Germany can have the peace that came to Bulgaria – a peace of utter surrender'.

In Washington and New York party bosses studied the public mood, for on 5 November the mid-term Congressional elections would be held, with a third of Senate seats and all the House of Representatives up for the taking. There was not as yet the frenetic media interest of the television age, but the nature of the US Constitution gave the contest an importance which outsiders in Europe failed to understand, and a significance still neglected in many histories of the war. For Republicans to gain control of Congress, and the chairmanship of its influential committees, would tie the Democrat President's hand more effectively than any verbal knots Clemenceau or Lloyd George might improvise.

During the first year of America's war loyal dedication to 'this land of ours' kept political partisanship muted, but in April 1918 a by-election caused by the death of the Democrat Governor of Wisconsin prompted an attempt by the ruling party to brand all Republicans as pro-German pacifists. This tactic misfired; the Republican won. After a bitter contest, criticism of war prosecution was no longer deemed taboo in the political arena; five investigations into alleged mismanagement of recruitment and arms production were authorized by the Senate, even though it was still under Democratic Party control. Federal regulation of the price of wheat hit the farmers in Midwest states which had backed Wilson two years previously. As the mid-term elections approached, patriotic all-Americanism brought a restored unity to the Republican Party. Ex-President Theodore Roosevelt – whose youngest son, an incipient air ace, had been killed in action on 15 July – launched a 'fight the war to a finish' campaign, urging the imposition of 'unconditional surrender'. In New York's Carnegie Hall, Roosevelt welcomed 'the triumph of the war spirit in America'; an armistice 'must be obtained by machine guns and not typewriters', he declared. After such an apotheosis of belligerency Wilson's dispassionate reliance on 'the moral compulsions of the human conscience' seemed to echo the confident hopes of a distant era.

The President spent thirty-six hours working in his study on the text of a reply. He did not discuss it with his full Cabinet, nor did he take British or French diplomats into his confidence; at times the Chief Executive of the American Republic could be as autocratic in style as one of Europe's hereditary emperors. He did, however, consult Secretary of State Lansing, who mentioned to him the need to remember the mid-term elections; and he called in his constant adviser, Colonel House, who (as he himself writes) said 'with some heat' that to have the elections in mind would make it impossible to reply 'properly or worthily. I thought the elections were not to be considered in thinking of the settlement of this great world tragedy.' House favoured 'no direct reply, but merely a statement that the President would confer with the allies' over the German approach. But Wilson abhorred secret diplomacy; he thought it better for American and world opinion to follow what was happening. Accordingly, on 8 October he made public the response sent that morning to Berlin. Basically he sought to clarify the German attitude, asking three questions: would Berlin accept the Fourteen Points and the President's later elaborations on them as a basis for peace?; would Germany withdraw troops from all foreign soil? and for whom did the Chancellor speak, did he represent 'merely . . . the constituted authorities . . . who have so far conducted this war'? The tone was far too conciliatory for the Republican press and Roosevelt's 'war to a finish' group. Perhaps these critics had a good case. For both at Berlin and at Spa the note was well received: no impossible demands; no timetable for evacuation of territory; nothing about the future of the fleet. 'The note seemed to justify the optimists', Prince Max of Baden wrote later in his memoirs.

Yet while there was relief in Germany, there was intense fury in London. Prince Max's elevation to the Chancellorship had been welcomed in England; he was regarded as an enlightened aristocrat, 'a reformer who quotes Kant and Plato', said *The Times*, which in those days rated philosophical dilettantism more highly than today. But his standing soon fell. The peace note to Washington was regarded as a trick; it would allow the German Army to fall back to a new line without molestation and enable the German people to break free from the stranglehold of blockade during the coming winter. Even so, it was assumed that President Wilson would discuss possible armistice terms with the Allied statesmen. Lloyd George was at Versailles for talks with Clemenceau and Orlando, the Italian Prime Minister, during the weekend that Wilson was considering his reply to the Germans; the European leaders and their representatives began their discussion of armistice terms. No doubt France would play the chief role in settling the military terms and Great Britain the naval. On 9 October, the day after Wilson sent his three queries to Berlin, two joint messages were telegraphed from Paris to Washington: a political demand for a personal envoy who enjoyed the President's full confidence to come to Europe for discussion with the heads of government; and a strongly worded complaint that the message to Berlin had no military safeguards to prevent the Germans from re-forming with their existing equipment in new positions from which the war could be continued. Three days later – 12 October – a second note from Prince Max assured Wilson that he could be certain Germany would satisfy the conditions raised by his three queries; but it asked for a joint commission (from both sides) to negotiate how the evacuation of occupied territories would be carried out. This apparent evasiveness confirmed Lloyd George's darkest suspicions.

Even though peace seemed near, fighting continued in full intensity on almost every front: in the West, where the British took Cambrai on 8 October, the Belgians were seeking a way through the mud to Roulers and Bruges, the French entered Laon and the Americans cleared the Argonne to reach the Meuse; in the Balkans, where French and Serbs took Niš, completing an advance of over 170 miles in three weeks of continuous battle; in Syria, where General Macandrew reached Homs, at the centre of the fertile Orontes plain, on 10 October; in Mesopotamia, where General Marshall was beginning an advance up the Tigris towards Mosul; and in East Africa, where General Lettow-Vorbeck still had more than 300 Europeans with several thousand askaris and other African troops in his lone campaign to tie down the King's African Rifles and Portuguese colonials around the head of Lake Nyasa. Even in Italy a bustle of activity along roads north of Treviso suggested that Diaz and the *Comando Supremo* might soon bid for a victory on the Piave before peace broke out.

At sea, too, the war continued, though for the most part at periscope level. In the Mediterranean *UB-68*, forced to surface off Malta, was sunk by gunfire; most of the crew were taken captive including the commander, *Oberleutnant zur See* Karl Dönitz. Off the American coast *U-152* and *U-155* received orders from Berlin on 11 October to withdraw to the Azores, so as not to prejudice peace exchanges with Wilson. But this precaution came a day too late. On 10 October another U-boat had sunk an unarmed steamer off the Irish coast and a few hours later rekindled angry memories of the *Lusitania*'s loss when it fired two torpedoes to sink the Holyhead mail packet *Leinster*: more than 500 passengers and crew were reported to have drowned in the Irish Sea that day, including Americans crossing from Dublin. Thankfully, the final figure was far less.

The tragic fate of the *Leinster*, and the response of Wilson's Republican critics, strengthened the tone of the President's second note to Berlin, sent on 14 October: U-boat attacks must stop; there was to be no more 'wanton destruction' of towns and villages evacuated by the retreating troops and forcible eviction of their 'very inhabitants'; the German proposal of a joint commission was ruled out, for any armistice would have to include 'absolutely satisfactory safeguards and guarantees of the maintenance of the present military supremacy of the Armies of the United States and the Allies in the field'. In generalized terms, the President returned to what he regarded as the fundamental constitutional problem, calling on the German people to make certain that there would be no future opportunity for the arbitrary authority of a single individual ruler to disturb the peace of the world.

In London it seemed as if Wilson was 'flying from excessive leniency to austere strictness'. The vicissitudes of the President's approach were puzzling, especially to those uninterested in American domestic policies. But no British decision-makers were sure of the next step forward. Even the Prime Minister remained unconvinced that a negotiated armistice was desirable. During the preceding weekend Lloyd George stayed at Danny Park, the home of the newspaper proprietor Sir George Riddell near Hurstpierpoint in East Sussex. After lunch on the Sunday, 13 October, he presided over a meeting of great historical significance. With him were Bonar Law (from the War Cabinet), General Sir Henry Wilson (CIGS), Admiral Wemyss (First Sea Lord), Balfour (Foreign Secretary), Churchill (Minister for Munitions), Lord Reading (ambassador in Washington, but on leave since August) and Philip Kerr (of his secretariat). This unofficial gathering was raised in status when, as Riddell's guests were 'in conference over their cigars', an urgently summoned Maurice Hankey arrived to take minutes – in due course to be filed among the Cabinet papers.

The Danny Conference Minutes make strange reading, eighty years on. It is as if Lloyd George was thinking aloud. His words seem prophetic, yet curiously detached from that autumn's tragedy, the battles across the Channel, those lost days costing 'thousands of brave soldiers' lives'. Any ceasefire would give the German Army a respite in which to reorganize and recover, he argued. 'Was it really worth stopping the fighting unless Germany was badly beaten?', he wondered. What if the democratic government in Berlin on which President Wilson set such store did not last? The German public could then be told that these 'miserable democrats had taken charge and had become panic stricken, and the military party would get to power again . . . If Peace were made now, in twenty years time the Germans would say what Carthage had said about the First Punic War, namely that they had made this mistake and that mistake, and that by better preparation and organization they would be able to bring about victory next time'. He asked his companions to consider 'whether the actual military defeat of Germany and the giving to the German people of a real taste of war was not more important, from the point of view of the peace of the world, than surrender at the present time when the German armies were still on foreign territory'.

The conference continued for three hours, with the participants showing a marked distrust of American policy. President Wilson was reminded by telegram that the British government considered several of the Fourteen Points were in need of further clarification; the President's concept of 'Freedom of the Seas' was unacceptable. It would end the traditional strategy of blockade; and was thus 'a step directed absolutely against the British navy', the First Sea Lord complained that afternoon. Wilson was also to be warned that Britain could never agree to cease-fire terms so binding that they limited the freedom of action of Allied governments at the subsequent peace conference. But to Lloyd George's vital questions over the desirability of an armistice, no clear answers were given. Perhaps they were not expected, immediately.

Yet it is clear that most prominent figures were looking for good reasons to dispel doubts over the wisdom of seeking peace. The Danny Conference stimulated discussions over the following two weeks. Smuts pointed out that if 'peace comes now' it would be a British peace; if the war continued until 1919, the brunt of the fighting would have been borne by American troops, and it would be an American peace imposed on an exhausted Europe. Curzon, who was highly indignant at not being invited to the Danny Park meeting, was more specific. He told the War Cabinet on 15 October that a punitive armistice agreement was desirable, with clauses which guaranteed reparation to Belgium and other invaded countries and a pledge of indemnities to the Allies for 'the colossal expenditure enforced upon them'. Curzon also recommended that 'certain specified and notorious German malefactors' should be surrendered for trial by a specially constituted international tribunal. Haig, in London for talks on 19 October, was pessimistic. He thought that enemy resistance was stiffening along the River Sambre; severe armistice terms would be spurned 'and the war would continue for at least another year'. The CIGS, too, was cautious. It was three days after the talks at Danny Park that he warned the War Cabinet, 'there was nothing to warrant the assumption that the present military situation justified the Germans in giving-in.'

In France there were even stronger differences over the nature of an armistice than in Britain. Clemenceau and the Foreign Minister, Pichon, were more sympathetic to Wilson's policy than was Lloyd George, although the Tiger – still deeply concerned with the military direction of affairs – was critical of 'fine troops' in the AEF being 'mismanaged' by officers who did not understand the limitations of warfare on the Western Front. Foch defended the 'magnitude of the American Army's effort', but he was alarmed by President Wilson's conciliatory political gestures to the *Boche*. He insisted that the Allied armies must occupy the whole of the left bank of the Rhine and three bridgeheads on the right bank. General Pétain took an even tougher line than Foch: he saw no reason to attach any conditions to the armistice; let Germany receive terms as strict as Franchet d'Esperey had imposed on Bulgaria. From Salonika Franchet himself was pressing for permission to carry out his cherished plan to send the enemy crashing down: 'I can with 200,000 men cross Hungary and Austria, mass in Bohemia covered by the Czechs, and march immediately on Dresden', he wrote to an influential friend in Paris. And, to Clemenceau's intense anger, Franchet's consistent champion, President Poincaré, wished to impose his own views on the government. They were not as clear-cut as the General's, but they were harsher than either Clemenceau or Foch envisaged: no armistice at all in 1918; let nothing stand in the way of a victorious Allied advance across Germany to Berlin. So persistent was Poincaré that Clemenceau threatened to resign. Rather than risk plunging France into a political crisis at such a moment, the President agreed to leave decision-making in the hands of his Prime Minister. He continued, however, to press his recommendations on Foch, whom he invariably supported in any conflict with Clemenceau.

On 18 October Marshal Foch at last left his Château Bombon headquarters for Senlis, north of Chantilly. From there next day he issued a general directive for what was to become the final victory offensive of the Allied armies: the Belgian and British armies in Flanders to enter Bruges and advance on Brussels; Haig and the BEF to cross the Sambre, drive the enemy back into the Ardennes Forest and cut the main thirty-five-mile lateral railway route from Hirson to Charleville-

Mézières; and the French and American armies to press northwards towards historic Sedan. At the same time, however, Foch and Weygand were preparing detailed armistice conditions. They assumed that the Rhineland would eventually, in the peace talks, be given a new status: would it be annexed to France or neutralized and given autonomy? Foch sought to clarify the question with Clemenceau in order to include in the armistice conditions preliminary arrangements for the occupation of the prized region. But Clemenceau was not going to allow the Army leaders to dictate future frontier-making. The fate of the Rhineland was a political decision, he told the Marshal. All that a government expected from Army chiefs was sound military advice.

So too, of course, did Germany's new Chancellor. Wilson's second reply, with its tone of 'austere stiffness', caused dismay in Berlin, not least because it indicated that a parliamentary revolution from above was not enough. The monarchical structure itself was seen to be threatened. 'A black day', noted Admiral Müller on 16 October, after reading details of the reply in the newspapers. 'All prospects for peace have been ruined. There remains a life and death struggle. Perhaps a revolution.' At a far lower level of the Navy, among a minesweeper crew at Wilhelmshaven, 'the mood' was 'grave, very grave indeed', a Bavarian, Seaman First Class Richard Stumpf, wrote that Wednesday in his diary. 'Many of our younger men have had their heads turned by Bolshevik ideas . . . What will happen if all our efforts to negotiate a peace should fail and we are left no other choice but to fight it out to the bitter end?' The latest American note 'shamefully demands unconditional cessation of submarine warfare', Seaman Stumpf complained; 'I have the distinct impression that they always spit on our hand whenever we stretch it out in peace.'

The Chancellor persevered. He needed calm and considered counsel from the Army and Navy chiefs. At a meeting of the Cabinet on the Thursday morning Prince Max plied Ludendorff with searching questions. Most of all he wished to know for how long OHL thought it possible to keep the enemy away from Germany's pre-war frontier? And, if war continued through the winter, would Germany's position be better or worse in the spring? By now the First Quartermaster-General had recovered his poise and magisterial evasiveness; nothing more was said of an urgent need for a truce. Traditional Flanders weather had dulled the impact of Haig's offensive; sound defences on the upper Meuse were containing the Americans; 'If the army holds on through the next four weeks, up to the onset of winter, then we shall be on safe ground', he declared. The Minister of War had told him that, by giving priority to Army service and by calling up factory workers and labourers from the fields, 600,000 men would create a new reserve, for training during the winter and front-line service in the spring. The socialist Philipp Scheidemann, now a Cabinet minister, pointed out that such redirection of labour would only increase the numbers of disaffected soldiery within an army allegedly close to mutiny. But Ludendorff was adamant. He would not give precise answers to the Chancellor's questions, only an assurance that 'every effort made at the moment will improve our position'. Admiral Scheer, since August head of the newly created *Seekriegsleitung* (SKL, Supreme Navy Command) voiced similar groundless optimism: 'Our position will get better as the enemy's gets worse', he said, 'That's why they want to finish things off this autumn'. But SKL had one clear demand, with which the Army chiefs fully agreed: there must be no abandonment of the U-boat campaign. Ludendorff returned to Spa, prepared to hold the line of the Meuse and, if possible, the Scheldt; Scheer remained in Berlin.

Max of Baden had no illusions: if he saw no reason for OHL's despair in the last days of September, he could equally see no reason for the bubble of confidence a fortnight later. Personal contacts in neutral capitals emphasized to him the American President's deep concern over submarine warfare, and he was accordingly prepared to defy Scheer over this issue. The Kaiser, however, had imbibed some of that sparkling Spa confidence: he was now scoffing at Wilson's 'unmitigated frivolous nonsense'; he backed OHL and he backed Scheer. Prince Max – like Clemenceau – threatened resignation if he were not allowed to include guarantees over U-boats in his next reply to the White House. The Kaiser, even more than President Poincaré, feared the consequences of a change in government at this time. Weakly he gave way over the U-boat question. On 20 October the third note was sent off to Wilson: it asserted the trust of the German people in the American President's desire for a just peace; it emphasized the continuing character of constitutional reform, though avoiding any reference to the monarchy; and, while defending German troops and seamen against charges of inhumanity, it gave notice that German submarines had been ordered not to attack passenger ships.

The third reply came quickly, for Wilson's Republican adversaries in the mid-term election campaign were making much of his failure to impose terms on the enemy, a complaint also voiced increasingly by the European Allies. On 23 October the German Chancellor was told that the 'powers associated with the United States' would collaborate in drawing up peace terms which would 'make a renewal of hostilities on the part of Germany impossible'. But the note also complained that the constitutional changes in Germany left 'the power of the King of Prussia to control the policy of the Empire unimpaired'. The United States government could only deal with a Germany in which the people were the 'real rulers'; if the 'military masters and monarchical autocrats' retained authority the President would have to 'demand, not peace negotiations, but surrender'.

Ludendorff had been angered by what he called the Chancellor's 'cowardly note'. Wilson's further response seems almost to have unhinged him. He would, he notified Berlin, come to the capital with the General Field Marshal to discuss how the fight should go on. The Chancellor ordered the military leaders to stay at Spa. They ignored him, and came. In an Order of the Day sent to the Berlin newspapers over their joint signatures they declared that the latest message from Wilson was unacceptable to any soldier; 'the fight must continue with all our strength'. Such defiance came close to treason. It was too much for Chancellor and Sovereign. On 26 October the Kaiser demanded and received Ludendorff's resignation. Hindenburg, still the trusted Titan of so many German families, remained in office.

CHAPTER 17

MUDROS, PADUA, BELGRADE

Shortly after midday on 21 October, while the War Cabinet was considering the military and naval requirements of a German armistice, a telegram brought unexpected news from the Aegean. A Turkish tug flying a white flag had approached the anchorage of Mudros on the island of Lemnos and was intercepted by a naval launch. To the surprise of the officer in charge of the launch, aboard the Turkish vessel were General Sir Charles Townshend, still regarded as the hero of Kut, and the aide-de-camp to the Turkish Minister of Marine. Townshend made it clear that he had been released from internment on Prinkipo Island in the hope that he could speedily arrange for the opening of peace talks with the British. After what Hankey calls 'a tremendous discussion' among Cabinet ministers and Service chiefs a signal was sent to Admiral Calthorpe, Commander-in-Chief of the Mediterranean Fleet: he was empowered to open negotiations with accredited Turkish envoys aboard HMS *Agamemnon*, anchored off Mudros; conditions of an armistice would be sent to him the next day. The news was telegraphed from Smyrna to Constantinople. On Saturday 26 October the Turkish Minister of Marine, Hussein Rauf, together with the Deputy Foreign Minister and a colonel from the General Staff were picked up by a British warship off Mytilene and transferred to the *Agamemnon* for peace talks, under the Admiral's chairmanship. Rauf, a distinguished naval officer and close associate of Mustafa Kemal, visited Townshend shortly before he left Prinkipo for Lemnos. 'We are not Bulgarians', Rauf emphasized with characteristic national pride, 'Let England do things quietly and trust Turkey as a gentleman'.

'England' welcomed the opportunity to 'do things quietly'. Once Russia went out of the war, the British Empire had borne the burden of the fighting with the Ottomans almost alone. By Lloyd George's reckoning there could be no better venue for armistice talks than an admiral's day cabin of a British battleship, in immediate telegraphic

contact with London. He had feared worse arrangements. Although the
Turks were still resisting Allenby's cavalry advance in Syria, the loss of
Damascus and Beirut had finally toppled the pro-German Young Turks
in Constantinople; on 14 October Sultan Mehmet VI accepted a 'Peace
Ministry', with General Ahmed Izzet as Grand Vizier. Next day the
Turkish envoy in Washington delivered a note formally asking
President Wilson to arrange for armistice talks as the preliminary to a
peace based upon the Fourteen Points. The United States and the
Ottoman Empire were not at war and there was much admiration for
Wilson among Turkish intellectuals; when political censorship and
restraints were eased in July 1918 a Turkish Wilsonian League was
among the earliest political societies established in the capital. To turn
to the White House for help seemed a natural move for an enlightened
Peace Ministry.

But not by British reckoning. A succession of unofficial approaches,
mainly in Switzerland, had made the Foreign Office assume that the
making of peace with Turkey would be in British hands. If Wilson was
involved, there would be delay; secret agreements would come under his
icy scrutiny; France and Italy would need substantial rewards whatever
the President might say and Venizelos was already in France to advance
Greek interests. Early exchanges in Paris made the British tread warily.
Before Townshend and his companion sailed into the Aegean scene, the
War Secretary had sent a note to the Foreign Secretary: Britain's allies
would be 'suspicious and troublesome', spoiling 'the whole game',
Milner complained; and with echoes of Palmerston – or Gilbert and
Sullivan? – he continued, 'By no possibility can you get any Frenchman
or Italian to believe that if we took on this job alone & at once we were
doing it for the general good. They would be convinced we were doing
it to steal a march upon them, & to collar Constantinople for ourselves,
or some such nonsense'.

Hurried efforts were made in the first week of October to build up
British naval power in the Aegean, where at the time of the Bulgarian
armistice the French had more warships. Their commander, Vice-
Admiral Amet, was the senior naval officer keeping watch on the
Dardanelles until Admiral Calthorpe raised his flag in *Agamemnon*.
With the arrival of two dreadnoughts, sixteen destroyers and an armada
of small craft to augment the existing squadron, the Royal Navy could
trump the French presence by three to one. It was not difficult for Rauf
to convince Izzet and the Sultan that the message to President Wilson
had gone off too hastily; talks with the British at Mudros would better
meet Turkey's needs than lengthy exchanges through Washington;

bargaining was easier across a table than across a transatlantic cable. The Turks' direct naval-officer-to-naval-officer approach simplified matters for Lloyd George, too. The French and Italians were told of the terms proposed by the British four days before the talks opened. When Clemenceau asked angrily why Admiral Amet was not invited to take part in the negotiations, Lloyd George cited the example set by Franchet d'Esperey and the Salonika Armistice; sticklers for diplomatic protocol also pointed out that the credentials of the Turkish envoys permitted negotiations only with the British Admiral.

General Macandrew entered Aleppo with an escort of armoured cars on the morning of 26 October, about the time the peace talks were beginning aboard the *Agamemnon*. Allenby remained in Damascus and Lebanon, where there was mounting tension between the Arabs and the French, who had landed at Beirut a day after its entry by the Indians. Feisal's Northern Arab Army, with Colonel Nuri es-Sa'id still in command, accompanied Macandrew and the 5th Cavalry Division northwards. Macandrew first invited Aleppo to surrender on 23 October but his offer was rejected by Kemal's chief of staff, the General himself being treated at the Armenian Hospital for his chronic kidney trouble. From a sickbed in Baron's, then a recently built luxury hotel outside the city walls, Kemal directed delaying operations; Macandrew, for his part, saw no sense in a frontal attack on the grey-stone city, nestling beneath the triple ramparts of its hilltop citadel. In reality it was less formidable than it appeared, as the Turks had neglected the defences and many of the walls were crumbling. But Macandrew was cautious. His cavalry enveloped the city, forcing Kemal to pull out on the Friday evening (25 October), and the only shooting in Aleppo was the work of Arab irregulars, who were led by Sherif Nasir of Medina, Lawrence's companion on many of the later raids.

Yet, even as the peace talks opened, the Turks continued to show plenty of fight. About an hour after Macandrew entered the city, the Jodhpore and Mysore Lancers came under heavy fire from Kemal's rearguard, holding a ridge at Haritan, five miles to the north-west on the Alexandretta road. Fighting continued until nightfall, when Kemal's force slipped away. There would be no more skirmishes during the campaign. Fittingly, on 29 October it was the Arabs who seized the last and vital railway station at Muslimiya, the junction of the line to Baghdad and the line to Damascus and beyond. At ten o'clock in the morning on 31 October a wireless message reached 5th Cavalry Division headquarters in Aleppo: an armistice had been concluded at Mudros; the fighting was to end at noon.

At Aleppo Allenby's advance troops were 700 miles from Constantinople; but there were British troops much closer than that to the Ottoman capital. On 10 October General Milne ordered the 22nd and 28th Divisions to set out from their old positions east of Doiran for the Turkish frontier, along the Maritza River. Some battalions were fortunate; they had only to footslog for four days, down to the coast at Stavros, where destroyers ferried them along the coast to what was then the open roadstead of Dedeagach. On some days the sea was so rough that they could not land and had to return to Stavros. Hardest hit of all were gunners, engineers, horsemen and muleteers in the 22nd Division, forced to travel for 250 miles through rainswept mountains in which there were virtually no roads. Sometimes the only way forward was along the bed of a stream 'rough and boulder strewn'. If the river became impassable fully loaded gun limbers and ammunition trucks had to be hauled through bushes and scrub before the main route could be found again. 'The wear and tear on men, animals and waggons was severe: horses would jib, poles or traces or axles would break, and vehicles turn over; long traffic jams resulted, and everyone was tired or angry or both', one veteran recalled, forty years later. Another remembered 'toiling on drag ropes' until brought to an exhausted standstill; 'Indian mule drivers sat in miserable huddles by the roadside'; 'no dry men nor dry blankets'; 'we buried many horses'. Patrols had to stand ready for instant action, for no one was sure if the Turks had retired across the Maritza, or whether they were still waiting to sweep down from mountain recesses. By dusk on 30 October the movement was completed. Milne reported that his divisions were 'ready . . . to occupy . . . Adrianople' and 'take part in the general advance on Constantinople', 150 miles away. That night news of the Mudros Armistice reached Dedeagach. There would be no general advance eastwards to the Sea of Marmara. Only one brigade would be needed in the Turkish capital; no field artillery. For horse-drivers and gunners there followed 'three days rest and drying out, and then the long haul back'. The round journey of 500 frustrating miles in six rain-sodden weeks, with no epic moments and no elation of victory, epitomizes the task of the British Salonika Army during three years spent in what their commander called 'this malarious and inhospitable country'.

The telegram received by General Milne from Admiral Calthorpe telling him of the armistice signed aboard the *Agamemnon* ended, 'Please inform the French C-in-C'. No doubt Milne did so with wry satisfaction, after his treatment during the Bulgarian negotiations a month previously. The request may not, however, have been a calculated rebuff to the Allied joint commander in the East. At Mudros Calthorpe can have had little knowledge of Franchet's movements; he was with the French army north of Skopje when he heard that signature of a Turkish armistice was imminent. He then hurried back to Salonika, and was conveniently on hand when the Admiral's message reached Milne.

There was, in fact, little in the terms of the Mudros Armistice of immediate relevance to Franchet's operations. Almost a third of the text covered naval affairs. Other clauses provided for the surrender of Turkish garrisons in Syria, Mesopotamia and outposts of the Arabian peninsula and Libya, evacuation of Persia and the Caucasus, expulsion within a month of German and Austrian personnel, the handing-over to Allied control of port facilities and railways, the release of prisoners of war and Armenian internees, and the immediate demobilization of the Turkish Army. The Dardanelles and Bosporus were to be opened, in order to secure access to the Black Sea, and the forts commanding the Straits would be occupied by British and French troops. To the relief of the Turkish envoys the armistice did not insist on Allied occupation of the capital, nor was any attempt made to impose new forms of government. But there remained an ominous threat in Clause 7: the Allies were accorded the right to occupy any strategic points if a situation arose which might threaten their security. Under authority allegedly emanating from this clause the French landed a battalion at Alexandretta and the British insisted that Marshall's troops, who were still forty miles south of Mosul when the armistice was signed, should press on northwards to occupy the oilfields during the next three days. Moreover, though Constantinople remained under Turkish administrative control, an Allied High Commission operated within the city before the end of November. General Sir Maitland Wilson landed at Stamboul on 13 November, to be received by a guard of honour of 300 British prisoners of war, and General Milne moved his headquarters there a fortnight later. Franchet d'Esperey was eventually to make a triumphal entry into Constantinople; but not for three more months. By then, a palace overlooking the Bosporus, vacated by Enver when he fled to the Caucasus, would be ready to accommodate Franchet and his staff in the style to which they aspired.

For the moment, in the first week of November, Franchet was more concerned with the Danube than the Bosporus. The German Eleventh Army continued to fight a magnificent rearguard action up the Morava valley and across the wooded hills of the Sumadija region, the historic cradle of Serbian independence. But on the day the Mudros Armistice was signed, French and Serbian gunners once again reached the heights south of Belgrade; stretching to the horizon beneath them were the broad, grey trails of the Danube and the Sava, natural river trenches whose waters were dotted with small craft ferrying the enemy back to the Hungarian shore. In a rush of Bonapartism to the head, Franchet declared that 'For the first time since 1809, a French army is marching on Vienna'; this was not such an inflated boast as it seems, for though the army still had 360 miles ahead of it, everywhere in these November days the 'sideshow' troops could move forward with astonishing speed.

Further down the Danube a French mission headed by General Berthelot was in Romania, hoping that with the victory in Serbia and with British troops south of the river and less than forty miles from Bucharest, the kingdom might re-enter the war before the fighting ceased – a move achieved with forty-eight hours to spare. But of more immediate interest to Franchet was what was happening in the lands ahead of his army, to the north and west; for across central Europe newspaper reports of peace moves under Wilsonian auspices had prompted a popular stampede towards independence. 'National Councils' seemed to spring up spontaneously, as had 'soviets' in the towns affected by Bolshevism over the past year. A National Council of Serbs, Croats and Slovenes within the Habsburg Monarchy was set up in Zagreb as early as 6 October, under the presidency of the Slovene priest Anton Korosec; national councils in Split, Sarajevo and Ljubljana came into being later in the month and recognized the authority of Korosec's institution. The Romanians in Transylvania, led by Iuliu Maniu, established a National Council at Oradea on 12 October, moving to Arad a fortnight later. By then the liberal Count Mihály Károlyi had formed a Hungarian National Council in Budapest (25 October); and on 28 October he was recognized as Prime Minister by Emperor-King Charles. On that same day the Prague National Committee proclaimed the 'Czechoslovak State' and contacted Beneš's National Council in Paris, which was already recognized by Britain, France and the USA as the Czechoslovak government. The Slovaks, however, set up a National Council of their own at Turčiansky Sveti Martin on 30 October, while National Councils of Ruthenes (ethnic kin of the Ukrainians, cut off inside historic Hungary by the Carpathian Mountains) flourished in both Lubovna and Khust. Meanwhile, Silesian and Moravian Germans set up a Sudetenland council in Troppau, and in Ruthenia the predominantly Jewish Magyar town of Uzhgorod had a National Council which backed Károlyi's efforts in Budapest. There were also at least three national committees within Galicia, two Polish and one Ukrainian. Experience was to show that these creations did not always embody the general will of the peoples they claimed to represent; but neither did the agreements made in Pennsylvania by Masaryk on behalf of the Czechs with Slovak-Americans in Pittsburgh and with Ruthene-Americans at Homestead.

Each of these dozen or more national councils sprang up within Austria–Hungary while Emperor Charles was still seeking to preserve the integrity of the Habsburg lands, with promises of self-determination. But his final concession, the federalist Imperial Manifesto of 16 October, came too late to rally support. Moreover, it applied only to the 'Austrian' half of the Dual Monarchy: Poles, Czechs, Slovenes and Italians might have benefited; the Slovaks, Ruthenes, Croats, Serbs and Romanians within Historic Hungary could not. In January Wilson's Fourteen Points had accepted the need for an independent Poland, but offered Charles's other subject nationalities merely 'the freest opportunity of autonomous development'. By the autumn this Tenth Point had been modified, largely under the influence of Thomas Masaryk who was in America from 29 April until the end of the war. On 19 October Secretary of State Lansing made it clear to the Austrians that, for President Wilson, autonomy was not enough; the peoples must find satisfaction of 'their aspirations . . . rights and destiny as members of the family of nations'. In effect the Monarchy's Yugoslavs and Czechoslovaks should receive full independence. 'Be worthy of our liberators, Masaryk and Wilson' the Prague National Committee urged its compatriots in proclaiming the new republic's independence on 28 October. At such a moment it was a significant coupling of philosopher-statemen's names. But, although encouragement – perhaps even incitement – might come from across the Atlantic and from influential propagandists in London, the impetus for revolutionary change sprang from within the Dual Monarchy itself. Austria–Hungary was not broken up by outsiders: for good or ill, it fell apart.

That process of disintegration was already well advanced when, on 24 October – the first anniversary of Caporetto – General Diaz's long-promised assault was launched on the Italian Front. He had under his command fifty-one Italian divisions, three British, two French, one Czechoslovak (now accepted as an Allied national fighting unit) and the 332nd US Infantry Regiment. At 5 a.m. the customary artillery bombardment began, high up in the mountains, with no less than 1,400 guns shelling Austrian positions around Monte Grappa, in the central sector, south of Feltre. The first British objective – assigned to the 7th Division, in Lord Cavan's Tenth Army – was to secure a crossing of the

Piave, which could be achieved only by using the large island of Papadopoli as a stepping-stone. At first it was hoped to safeguard the crossing by taking the island in a surprise assault on the night of 23–24 October, before the guns opened up farther north. Over eight hundred men were ferried across in twelve flat-bottomed boats, holding no more than seven 'passengers' each, and two Italian *pontieri* who knew the currents of the Piave, flowing at some ten knots that night after heavy rain. Each boat had to make at least ten return journeys, and yet none was sunk. The island was cleared of Austrian defenders as dawn broke and, over the following twenty-four hours, British and Italian sappers succeeded in anchoring pontoons for a bridge in the river-bed, an astonishing feat of improvised engineering. Not until 27 October was it possible for the Gordon Highlanders to wade, with linked arms, to other smaller islands and so reach the far bank; the Northumberland Fusiliers, following the Scots, suffered heavy casualties. By 28 October the whole river was bridged, covering almost a mile of water in spate. The Tenth Army and the Italian Eighth Army crossed this one vital bridge before the Italian Twelfth Army made another island-hopping crossing, further downriver. Once beyond the Piave it was possible for the three armies to move forward rapidly along twenty-five miles of front. For the first time in Italy there was an opportunity to make effective use of cavalry and armoured cars. Before dusk on 30 October – the Wednesday on which the Mudros Armistice was signed – the Italians were in the small town of Vittorio Veneto, the place name fittingly accorded to the whole battle.

Further north the Italians had met stiff resistance in the Monte Grappa region from well disciplined Austrian regiments, and for the first four days of battle the British and French divisions attached to General Montvori's Sixth Army could only make slow progress across the familiar pitted battlefields of the Asiago plateau. Some French troops crossed the upper Piave fifteen miles above Papadopoli Island, but their attempts to complete pontoon bridges were frustrated by the rush of flood water down the river from the mountains.

As early as 26 October three Hungarian divisions formally requested to be moved from the Italian Front to the homeland, so as to protect their families from the Serb invaders and their allies. The request was granted. This fear of what was happening at home while they were fighting on the edge of the Alps inevitably weakened resistance in Italy. On the day after the Piave was crossed, the Emperor Charles made an urgent appeal to President Wilson for an armistice within twenty-four hours, hoping that American mediation would lead to a more generous agreement than he might expect from the Italians. But, like Rauf some days earlier in Constantinople, the Austrian military commanders suspected that any response from Washington would come slowly; they therefore persuaded the Emperor to authorize a direct soldier-to-soldier approach on the Italian Front. It would be made, however, not in the plains around the Piave, where the command structure was in confusion, but closer to Army headquarters at Trent and the main rail and road route from Venetia to the Tyrol. At daybreak on 29 October an Italian-speaking Austrian staff officer, Captain Ruggera, climbed a railway embankment above Serravalle all'Adige, thirty-six miles north of Verona. Under the protection of a white flag, and escorted like a medieval herald by two trumpeters, he sought a safe route across No Man's Land.

It was half past eight on Tuesday morning when Captain Ruggera reached the outposts of an Italian infantry division in the Val Lagarina. Yet, despite the Emperor's wish for a speedy ceasefire, hostilities did not formally end until the following Monday at three in the afternoon. For this delay there were three main reasons: Austrian muddle-headed casualness, the traditional *Schlamperei*, which failed to give Ruggera correct credentials and misunderstood the timing of the ceasefire; Italy's territorial appetite, which led General Badoglio, the *Comando Supremo*'s representative, to seek as much ethnically disputed land as possible before America's high-minded President noticed what was happening; and contact with the Supreme War Council at Versailles, where the Allied military spokesmen wished to dictate terms so precise that it would be possible to advance speedily into southern Germany through the North Tyrol. One telephone call from Paris to Padua lasted four hours and twenty-five minutes, mainly through difficulties in noting down and identifying on the map place names often different in Italian from German.

The armistice was signed in the Villa Giusti at Mandria, a village in the hills nine miles east of Padua, in the afternoon of Sunday 3 November. It required the evacuation of all occupied lands, of the South Tyrol up to the Brenner Pass, Istria, fifteen islands in the Adriatic and the whole of Dalmatia. Withdrawal of Austro-Hungarian forces would be followed by Allied occupation of these regions. Railway track and equipment was to be surrendered and the Associated Powers were given rights of free movement over all Austro-Hungarian territory and of occupying strategic points, both for internal security and for 'the conduct of military operations'. German troops were to quit within fifteen days. The Austro-Hungarian Army was to be demobilized, though up to twenty peacetime divisions could be kept to maintain order outside the Allied occupation zones. Austro-Hungarian naval dockyards were to be handed over jointly to the Allied powers, as also were three battleships, three cruisers, six Danube monitors, fifteen submarines and twenty-two other surface vessels. But before the armistice was concluded Emperor-King Charles ordered the last Commander-in-Chief, Admiral Horthy, to surrender the fleet at Pola to Korosec's Yugoslav National Council in Zagreb. On 1 November the flagship *Viribus Unitis* was sunk by two Italian naval officers in a 'leech' (*mignatta*), a propelled torpedo-like adhesive mine, as she lay at anchor, flying the red, white and blue ensign of the Serbs, Croats and Slovenes. A new contest for control of the Adriatic was manifesting itself even before old rivalries were finally settled.

Although the Padua Armistice treated Austria–Hungary as a single entity, the imperial-royal bond had already been broken. Charles absolved his newly appointed Hungarian Prime Minister, Károlyi, from his oath of allegiance on 1 November; and Károlyi's War Minister, Colonel Béla Lindner, at once ordered all Hungarian officers and men to lay down their arms. The Padua Armistice terms virtually ignored Hungary; the only region of the Kingdom to receive a mention was the port of Fiume, coveted alike by Italians and Croats. But Károlyi was alarmed at the imminent invasion of Hungary from the south by the Serbs and the French. He sought talks with Franchet d'Esperey, hoping he might win the Frenchman's support for a Hungary which would soon become a republic.

Their meeting was not the happiest of encounters. Károlyi and a small delegation from the Hungarian National Council travelled downstream to Belgrade from Ujvidek (Novi Sad) in a Danube steamer, flying a table-cloth from the dining saloon in lieu of a white flag. Franchet came up by train from Salonika, a three-day journey broken by triumphant entries into Sofia and Niš and culminating on 7 November in an enthusiastic welcome at Belgrade station. An hour and a half later, at 7.30 in the evening, the Hungarians awaited Franchet in one of the city's finest mansions, fittingly in the Rue du Théâtre. 'His entrance was that of a victorious General on the stage; I felt he had rehearsed it beforehand', Károlyi wrote in his memoirs. The General declined Károlyi's outstretched hand and listened impatiently to his verbal manifesto of Hungarian democratic ideals, making depreciatory gestures when the name 'Wilson' was reverently intoned. It was then Franchet's turn to declaim; after treating Károlyi's companions with studied (and anti-Semitic) incivility, he denounced fifty years of

Hungarian collaboration with Germany and told the delegates that Hungary must expect similar punishment ('*elle sera châtiée comme elle*'). True to form, he stalked out, leaving his staff to distribute typed copies of eighteen armistice terms after his dramatic exit. The demands authorized the Allies to occupy the eastern and southern regions of the old Hungarian Kingdom and any other strategic points they might wish.

After a vain appeal by telegram to Clemenceau, Károlyi accepted that he was beaten. He had hoped that, if parts of Hungary were to be occupied, at least the troops should be British, French, Italian or American; no Czechs, Serbs, Romanians or 'colonial troops'. But Franchet had no sympathy with Hungarian national pride; Károlyi must realize that Hungary was a vanquished state, in no position to bargain. Sadly, at midnight, he signed a military convention – not technically an armistice, as the Hungarians had already ceased to offer armed resistance. By daybreak the river steamer was carrying the Hungarian deputation back to Novi Sad, wretchedly disillusioned. Some had even come with postcards which they were hoping the great Frenchman would autograph as souvenirs of so historic an occasion. The postcards remained unsigned in their pockets.

So long as there was a considerable German army under Field Marshal von Mackensen in Romania, Franchet d'Esperey was justified in seeking to control all strategic routes westwards through Transylvania and southern Hungary. The Romanians declared war on Germany once more on 9 November but were too busily engaged in containing Mackensen's troops to attempt any moves across the frontier; the lead for the union of Transylvania and old Romania (the *Regat*) was taken by Maniu's National Council at Arad, with Romanian troops only crossing the frontier two days after the Armistice was signed in the West. But Franchet's policy also favoured the Serbs, with whose military leaders he was on the closest of terms. When, during 1917, the exiled Serbian government was hard-pressed and almost forgotten in the West, Prince Regent Alexander and his chief minister, Pašić, had necessarily curbed ambitions for a Greater Serbia and supported Croat and Slovene hopes for a federated Yugoslavia. Once back in Belgrade, however, the Serbs reverted to old habits of mind. They cited the Franchet–Károlyi 'armistice' to occupy southern Hungary and Slavonia and sent troops not only to Zagreb but also into Slovenia, allegedly to prevent the Italians from taking Ljubljana. So grave was the tension between Serbs and Italians in southern Dalmatia that early in November American troops – the 2nd Battalion of the 332nd Infantry Regiment – were hurriedly sent to Cattaro to keep the two Allies apart. This first US peacekeeping mission to the troubled Balkans continued until the following spring.

Yet, though these disputes showed how peacemaking could expose weakness among the Allies, the immediate significance of the Padua Armistice and the Belgrade Military Convention was their potential impact on the principal enemy, Germany. At last the grand strategic projects of the first winter of war, that search for 'some other outlet' than the Western Front, had come to fruition. Germany's survival was now threatened by an advance into Bavaria and on to Munich from the Tyrol and Salzkammergut, and by an advance into Saxony and on to Dresden and Leipzig from the ambitious Franchet d'Esperey's armies. It is doubtful if any of Germany's allies was a supportive 'prop' in 1918, though the route down the Danube and across the Black Sea might still have provided OHL with oil had the Habsburg and Ottoman Empires remained in the war. What had been knocked away were not so much the props of Lloyd George's metaphor as the bolts on Germany's two side doors.

CHAPTER 18

'HOSTILITIES WILL CEASE
AT 11 A.M.'

General Wilhelm Groener was in Kiev when, to his surprise, he was summoned to Spa to succeed Ludendorff as First Quartermaster-General. Ten years before he had been one of the most gifted instructors at the *Kriegsakademie* and a brilliant future seemed to beckon. But fate played a strange trick on him. In July 1914, as Chief of Transport on the General Staff in Berlin, it was his hand that unlocked the safe containing the directives for mobilization, while his clear mind and organizational skill ensured that the troop trains moved smoothly east and west. He was so efficient that opportunities for field command passed him by; from control of strategic railways he was promoted in 1916 to mobilizing industry as part of the German war machine, with the rank of Major-General. Briefly in 1917 he commanded an army corps on the Western Front, but before he could be tested in battle Russia collapsed and his particular gifts were required in the East. At Kiev it was his responsibility to speed up the supplies of Ukrainian grain for the Fatherland. He seemed as unlikely a choice as First Quarter-master-General as Prince Max of Baden as German Chancellor. Being a shrewd realist, he may have suspected that he owed the appointment to the happy circumstance of south German origins. For Groener was a Swabian, born at Ludwigsburg in Württemberg, the son of an Army sergeant. To a Prussian officer corps facing defeat, Groener seemed a God-given fall guy, an outsider who could fail and leave their collective reputation intact. But they underestimated him.

Groener completed the 1,300-mile train journey to Spa on the morning of 30 October, and found Hindenburg morose and confused at the thought of accustoming himself to a new partner after four years of joint billing with Ludendorff. Within a few hours the soldiers were unexpectedly joined by their sovereign. The Kaiser had left Potsdam by the imperial train an hour before midnight, never to return. He set out without consulting his Chancellor, who was in bed with influenza; but during the journey a telegram was sent to Prince Max, explaining that he was making the journey in order to bolster up a Supreme Command shaken by Ludendorff's departure; the Chancellor would realize that he wished to make certain the 'replacement' fitted in well at Spa. This was at best a half-truth. For the Kaiser, aware of mounting pressure in Berlin for his abdication, had decided at his wife's prompting to run for cover in the Ardennes. To the officers who received him at Spa he complained that, in order to please the Americans, 'Prince Max's government is trying to throw me out. At Berlin I should be less able to oppose them than in the middle of my troops.'

He could not, of course, go to ground in this way. Telegrams from the capital pursued him into Belgium. The Chancellor urged him to return, in case his presence at OHL made it appear that he was planning to use troops to reimpose autocracy: even the rumour of such action would jeopardize the moves towards peace. In Berlin the Cabinet ministers were divided over the abdication question: General Scheuch, the War Minister, thought that if the Supreme War Lord signed away his obligations it would be impossible to rely on the loyalty of the Army; and Matthias Erzberger, leader of the (Catholic) Centre Party, saw abdication as a step towards Bolshevism. Not even the SPD socialists were republicans as yet; a regency for one of the Kaiser's grandsons was suggested. But it was clear that somebody would have to go to Spa and talk sense to William II. Prince Max had the tact and status to succeed in such a task, but he was genuinely too ill to leave Berlin; instead, he sent the Prussian Minister of the Interior, Wilhelm Drews. Having taken that decision the Chancellor, exhausted and feverish, returned to his sickbed; he accepted sedatives on the Friday evening, 31 October, which knocked him out for thirty-six hours of unbroken sleep. By Sunday afternoon, when he awoke, Drews's mission had already failed. No successor of Frederick the Great would abdicate, he was told by the Kaiser; and both Hindenburg and Groener rallied stoutly to the defence of the Crown.

One rumour so bolstered the Kaiser's confidence in these critical days that he began to weave around it the last of his fantasy policies. Reports from neutral countries reaching OHL, the Chancellor's private office and some leading businessmen all suggested that 'the English are at loggerheads with the Americans'. The Kaiser proposed to anyone who would listen to him in Spa and by telegram to Berlin that Germany should exploit this breach in the enemy's ranks and secure a separate peace with England. His imagination went further still: the two naval powers, Britain and Germany, must then form an alliance against the United States and proclaim for Europe a Monroe Doctrine in reverse.

All this was great nonsense, advanced by a failed autocrat with no idea of the hatred his person and title aroused in so many lands. Even if it had been possible to realign confronting armies, public opinion would never accept such a sudden turnabout of purpose: to many millions across Europe, Woodrow Wilson remained the visionary prophet of permanent peace. The rumours of Anglo-American friction were much exaggerated. Undoubtedly there were several instances of personal antagonism; thus the chief of US naval operations, Admiral Benson, mistrusted Britain's seamen and his coolness was reciprocated. Nor was the people's prophet held in reverent esteem; after spending several weeks in America the First Lord of the Admiralty, Sir Eric Geddes, arrived home scornful over Wilson's ignorance of the war and complaining unfairly of a President who 'golfs every morning, motors every afternoon and goes to a picture palace every evening'. The ideal of 'Freedom of the Seas' was an unpopular concept, as Admiral Wemyss made clear during the discussions at Danny Park. The jingoistic retired admiral, Lord Charles Beresford, told a packed meeting of the Navy League that the second of the Fourteen Points 'means that the British fleet was going to be under international control. That would never be allowed.' Beresford's speech was given unexpected publicity in *The Times* on 1 November.

There is, however, an artificial touch of contrivance over the way in which, during a conference at the Quai d'Orsay on 29 October, Lloyd George used 'Freedom of the Seas' as a basis for general criticism of the Fourteen Points. He goaded Colonel House into a threat that the USA might make a separate peace, which may well have been the Prime Minister's purpose. For both the British and French leaders were able to respond to this blackmail by the Associated Power with firm statements that their country would fight on against Germany even without America – a possibility which, on analysis, seems almost as impracticable as the Kaiser's belated 'European Monroe Doctrine'. In the event, this heated exchange cleared the air: House agreed that the 'Freedom of the Seas' issue could be set aside for discussion at a peace conference and also accepted Clemenceau's persistent demand for an armistice to include compensation from Germany for the damage to occupied territories. The Allied statesmen recognized that, however much bluff might call bluff around a conference table in Paris, realistically the ending of the war depended on the President in Washington DC, where the mid-term elections on 5 November were fast approaching.

All that remained in Paris and Versailles was to fix military and naval clauses that Germany would accept, for there was still some danger that humiliating terms might be proudly rejected. Pershing, with little regard for his President's wishes and by politics a Republican rather than a Democrat, wanted stiff terms which were almost tantamount to unconditional surrender. Haig's proposals were moderate, and did not seek the military occupation of any German territory east of Alsace-Lorraine; Pétain's, on the other hand, provided for the occupation of the whole of the left bank of the Rhine, with substantial bridgeheads on the right bank. Foch, as generalissimo, finally settled for terms close to those of Pétain and stronger than Lloyd George would have wished. The naval conditions proposed by Wemyss and Beatty seemed at first too severe not only to the French but to Lloyd George as well. The Prime Minister had to be persuaded by his colleagues that Germany would not continue the war simply to preserve the Kaiser's one-time 'luxury fleet'. By 5 November the armistice terms were ready for presentation. It was accepted by the Supreme War Council that Foch should speak for all the armies and the British First Sea Lord, Wemyss, for the navies.

In preparing the naval terms Admiral Beatty, Commander-in-Chief of the Grand Fleet, insisted that the German High Seas Fleet had to be eliminated 'either by surrender or as a result of Fleet action'. In the two years since Jutland there had been no major naval confrontation, though by coincidence the German fleet had made a sortie in the upper North Sea in a vain search for a Scandinavian convoy on 23 April 1918, the night of the famous raid on Zeebrugge by Sir Roger Keyes's Dover Patrol 500 miles to the south. After so many months in port a 'fleet action' in November seemed improbable. But the recall of Germany's U-boats on 21 October had prompted Admiral Scheer to consider a revised strategy for offensive action to strengthen Germany's bargaining position during the proposed armistice negotiations. Without inform-ing either the Kaiser or the Chancellor he at once sent his chief of staff from Berlin to Kiel with a verbal order for the fleet commander, Admiral Hipper: 'The forces of the High Seas Fleet are to be made ready for attack and battle with the English fleet'. Scheer hoped that the Imperial German Navy would accomplish what was now beyond the Army's powers – a surprise attack on the enemy. Success could save Germany from a dishonourable peace. A noble failure, if pressed home valiantly, would create a legend for the future. As Hipper's chief of staff commented, 'An engagement, even if it means dying in honour is still worthwhile, because it would inflict a severe wound on England'.

Hipper's plans were completed by 24 October. Four days later twenty-five U-boats left home waters to take up positions in the North Sea, between the Orkneys and the Frisian Islands; and the naval airship division at Nordholz was put on the alert, for Hipper hoped for seven Zeppelins to act as distant scouts for the fleet. Attacks on the Thames Estuary by cruisers and destroyers would draw the Grand Fleet south from Scottish waters, across minefields newly created by U-boats, and eventually into battle with the main High Seas Fleet, off Terschelling. Officially there was strict security but, as soon as the U-boats sailed it was suspected aboard the capital ships that some operation was contemplated; too many excited junior officers spoke too freely to ratings of the glorious prospect of battle. Ashore, in Wilhelmshaven, Seaman Stumpf noted in his diary, 'One rumour follows another'. There was an Anglo-American fleet at sea off Heligoland, it was said. There was not; but the mere possibility of a call to action stations when all the talk was of peace proved sufficient to turn resentment at poor food and irksome duties into mutiny and incipient revolution.

Trouble among the stokers on the light cruiser *Strasburg* on 27 October spread to the battleships on the following day. When Hipper gave sailing orders on the early evening of 29 October he was forced to cancel them within two hours because the crews refused to make the vessels ready for sea. He tried again next day, after assuring the men that they would only be taking part in defensive actions to safeguard the Fatherland. Once more sailing orders were cancelled; infantry units stood ready on shore to arrest troublemakers. On 1 November Hipper finally gave up all idea of a fleet action; foolishly he dispersed his squadrons among the three ports of Wilhemshaven, Cuxhaven and Kiel, thus giving a helping hand to the dedicated left-wing activists eager to spread revolution in as many ports as possible. When the Third Squadron reached Kiel some mutineers were placed under arrest, an action which only increased the tension. Protest marches through Kiel on 2 November and 3 November attracted support from dockers, shipyard and factory workers. Sailors' councils sprang up and, for the first time, the wave of unrest became overtly socialist. Nevertheless, some control was reasserted in Kiel itself, by the arrival of an SPD moderate, Gustav Noske, who was elected chairman of the Sailors' Council and appointed Governor of Kiel by his colleagues in the Berlin Cabinet. There was not, however, a Noske on hand to send to every city that flew the red flags that day. On 6 November Hamburg and Bremen were in the hands of Workers' and Soldiers' Councils. Cologne, barely eighty miles from OHL at Spa, was infected, despite the attempts of the

Centre Party Lord Mayor (*Oberbürgermeister*), the forty-two-year-old Konrad Adenauer, to safeguard its loyalty as the second largest city in the Kingdom of Prussia.

By Tuesday 5 November General Groener had completed his first tour of inspection of the Western Front. There seemed no weakening of the army's fighting spirit: the New Zealanders were forced to scale the ramparts of Le Quesnoy, a walled town near the Belgian frontier, in order to persevere with their advance in the Sambre–Scheldt sector; but, thanks to their ingenuity in overcoming medieval defences by the medieval device of escalades, 2,500 Germans were taken prisoner, along with a hundred guns. These were losses Groener found hard to accept. As yet, the German line was dented but not broken, despite relentless American pressure down the left bank of the Meuse, a fifteen-mile thrust in four days. Groener was a realist. Even apart from mounting uncertainty within Germany itself, he was convinced that the Army would find it impossible to resist any determined offensive Foch might launch. In Berlin he told the Chancellor on 6 November that 'We shall have to cross the lines with a white flag . . . by Saturday at the latest'. Still he refused to press the Kaiser to abdicate: no 'honourable soldier' could do that, he insisted.

While Groener was at Berlin a message was received from President Wilson, indicating that Foch would receive a German armistice delegation. At Groener's suggestion the Chancellor cajoled a reluctant Matthias Erzberger to be the principal government representative in the armistice delegation. He was, like Groener, a Swabian. More importantly he was a Catholic conservative who, because of his consistent support of peace moves in the past two years, was respected alike by his socialist colleagues and by Prince Max. Erzberger travelled back to Spa with Groener. A former military attaché in Paris, General von Winterfeldt, a Foreign Ministry official, Count Oberndorff, and Captain Vanselow of the Admiralty completed the Armistice Commission, who were accompanied by two General Staff captains, Geyer and von Helldorf. At 2.30 a.m. on 7 November a wireless telegraph message from the Eiffel Tower gave instructions from Marshal Foch for the plenipotentiaries to advance to French outposts on the Fourmies–Guise road. But it was noon before the five-car delegation left Spa. 'Go with God's blessing and try to obtain as much as you can for our homeland', Hindenburg told Erzberger as he set out. At 8.20 p.m. a Prussian cavalry trumpeter from the running-board of the first car blew a few notes of the call 'Cease Fire' to let the French, waiting in mist and drizzle, know that peace was almost in sight.

While the peace convoy drove slowly from Spa to the Fourmies road – two cars broke down – London editors received a welcome message for the evening editions: 'Reuter's Agency is informed that according to official American information the armistice with Germany was signed at 2.30'. Swift denials from the Foreign Office and the US embassy soon doused the fire of excitement in the City, but across the Atlantic the rumour persisted. 'The equilibrium of Washington was upset as never before by any such celebration', *The Christian Science Monitor* reported haughtily in distant Boston. The Administration was curiously slow to react, due perhaps to the intrusion of domestic political affairs. For that morning's papers carried the mid-term election results: the Republicans had captured both houses of Congress, though only by one seat in the Senate. Later analysis showed that the decisive issue was the price of wheat in the Midwest prairie states, but the results were a blow to the President's prestige; they ensured that, over the next two years, he would be faced by Republican chairmanship of the Foreign Relations Committee. As the 'Armistice signed' rumour spread through Washington a crowd gathered outside the White House; Mrs Wilson urged her husband to come out on the portico and respond to his well-wishers. He declined; that day he had no wish to meet the people – not even to deny that an armistice had been signed.

Meanwhile, on the eastern outskirts of La Capelle, Captain Lhuillier of the 171st French Infantry Regiment received the German delegates, replaced the trumpeter on the running-board by a French bugler, and led the envoys to the Villa Pâques, in the centre of the small town, where staff officers from Débeney's Sixth Army awaited them. The room was dominated by a portrait of Napoleon III; by a strange twist of historical irony, forty-eight years previously, General von Winterfeldt's father had escorted Napoleon's emissary to the King of Prussia outside Sedan with the Emperor's message of surrender. Soon the envoys were on their way again; two hours to Débeney's headquarters for a late supper; and eventually at 1.30 a.m. to the ruined railway station at Tergnier. A train awaited them. They were not told their destination. Their saloon car was venerable; green satin drapes with the monogram 'N' and an imperial crown left General Winterfeldt in little doubt of its origin.

The train finally stopped at seven in the morning, of what was now Friday 8 November. The French escorts unsealed the windows: no station platform to be seen, only rain-dripping bare branches in a forest glade and, through the mist, the outline of other carriages on a parallel track. Marshal Foch had decided that, for reasons of security, the armistice talks would be held in isolation; he chose a spur of railway at

Rethondes, in the Forest of Compiègne, on lines laid for heavy artillery, concealed in a wooded glade. Shortly before nine o'clock the Germans were led across duckboards to the converted wagon-lit restaurant car which served Foch as a carriage-office. Erzberger introduced the German delegation to Foch, who reciprocated by presenting his companions: Admiral Wemyss, Rear-Admiral Hope, General Weygand. The Marshal sought an assurance that the Germans were asking for an armistice and recognized that the conditions were not negotiable. When Erzberger remarked 'But President Wilson . . .', he was cut short by Foch. There would be no discussion. Erzberger saw that he had little chance of fulfilling Hindenburg's charge to him. He had no choice but to concur; 'Yes', Germany sought an armistice. Weygand began reading out the detailed conditions. The Germans looked pale; Foch was totally impassive; Wemyss played with his monocle.

The terms were severe, though less harsh than those presented to France in 1871. The immediate evacuation of Belgium, northern France, Luxembourg and Alsace-Lorraine was to be expected, together with the repatriation of deportees from these lands; so, too, was the return of German troops from Russia, the stragglers still caught in the Balkans and the few hundred European soldiery still in East Africa. Wilson's messages had made it clear that Germany would be required to offer compensation for the destruction caused in Belgium and France. There was a formidable list of material possessions to be surrendered, mostly within a month: 2,500 heavy guns; 2,500 field guns; 25,000 machine-guns; 3,000 trench mortars; 1,700 aeroplanes; 5,000 railway engines; 5,000 lorries; 150,000 railway waggons. All U-boats were to be handed over, together with ten battleships, six battlecruisers, eight cruisers and fifty destroyers; other warships would remain, disarmed, in German ports. American, Belgian, British and French troops would occupy all of western Germany up to the River Rhine and three bridgeheads beyond the river, in Coblenz, Cologne and Mainz. A neutralized zone six miles deep was to be established along the Dutch and Swiss frontiers. The upkeep of the armies of occupation would be Germany's responsibility. The Armistice would last for five weeks, but was renewable.

Captain von Helldorf was sent off to Spa with the text of the terms, leaving Rethondes at one o'clock that Friday afternoon. While he was absent, Winterfeldt and Vanselow held talks with Weygand and Hope, seeking relief of the blockade so as to get food through to Germany before winter set in. At the same time they complained that the terms would so reduce the effectiveness of the rump German Army that it would not be able to stamp out Bolshevism in the cities. No concessions could be obtained, although it was pointed out that Clause Twenty-six did at least stipulate that the occupying powers would make certain Germany was 'provisioned as necessary' during the Armistice.

The war continued on land and at sea. Belfort, France's unassailed citadel between the Jura and the Vosges and only nine miles from the German frontier, had its 701st air raid warning of the war, but no attack followed; the German pilots seemed to be making one last flight before being permanently grounded; not a life was lost. It was otherwise in those historic waters off Cape Trafalgar where, in a final thrust at British naval pride, *UB-50* torpedoed HMS *Britannia* on 9 November: forty officers and ratings were drowned, though more than 700 of the battleship's crew were saved. In the traditional war cockpit of Europe, battle place names evoked historic memories: Haig's troops passed Malplaquet and captured Maubeuge while the French passed Rocroi and entered Mézières, the Americans approached Sedan and the Belgians reached Ghent. The fighting lost none of its intensity. Around Fourmies the peace courier Captain Helldorf was unable to cross the lines and bring details of the Armistice to Spa for nearly twenty-four hours. When at last a ceasefire by his compatriots enabled him to complete his journey, the German Empire no longer existed.

By 8 November the Kaiser had become more concerned with the spread of Red revolution than with the military terms of an armistice. Groener found him wildly sabre-happy that evening: a Supreme War Lord should lead his troops back into the Fatherland and strike down revolution wherever it rose its head, he insisted. Prince Max, on the other hand, still urged William to abdicate, even telephoning him at some length to explain the danger of civil war if he remained in Germany. There was now a separatist threat as well as the menace of 'Spartacist' revolutionary communism: in Munich King Ludwig III had already stepped down and the 'Democratic and Socialist Republic of Bavaria' came into being on 8 November, with Kurt Eisner as chief minister. The Kaiser was contemptuous of all politicians, from Prince Max down to Eisner. Germany would be engulfed by the 'rising flood of Bolshevism', he told his aide-de-camp, Major Niemann, 'It is my sacred duty to build a dam against this madness'.

Groener, though exasperated by his sovereign's behaviour, sought to gauge the mood of the troops who would form the dam. Overnight, field officers from the three Army Groups in the West were summoned for an urgent early-morning conference at OHL headquarters in the Grand

Hôtel Britannique. Thirty-nine officers made the journey. Hindenburg addressed them, though without expressing any opinion on the merits of a march into Germany. After he left, the officers were asked for their views on the loyalty of the troops they commanded. Most were non-committal. Only one major thought his regiment would follow the Kaiser personally if he marched against the Reds; eight officers were certain that their men would not take part in a civil war, in whoever's name it was waged. The lack of enthusiasm confirmed Groener's doubts.

Shortly before eleven in the morning the General was driven out to La Fraineuse, the small château a mile and a half from Spa which served as an imperial residence. He insisted that William must give up all notions of a military counter-revolution. Bluntly Groener told him, 'The army will march home in peace and order under its leaders and commanding generals, but not under the command of Your Majesty, for it no longer stands behind Your Majesty'. The Crown Prince arrived, to strengthen his father's resolve. Every good soldier would remain loyal to his oath to the colours, the Crown Prince's chief of staff claimed. Groener's patience was running out. 'Today oaths of loyalty count for nothing' ('*Der Fahneneid ist jetzt nur eine Idee*'), he remarked cuttingly, before returning to headquarters. At La Fraineuse, father and son lunched privately.

In Berlin Prince Max of Baden was finding the task of holding together a coalition Cabinet impossible. 'Either the Kaiser goes or we resign', the SPD leaders said in effect. Mob rule seemed close at hand; a red blanket was draped over the balcony of the Imperial Palace. At half past one in the afternoon, without consulting Spa again, Prince Max issued a formal decree which he sent to the official German news agency: 'The Kaiser and King has decided to renounce the throne'; he would himself remain Chancellor until matters concerning the sovereign's abdication and the Crown Prince's renunciation of his rights were resolved; Friedrich Ebert would then become Chancellor and would summon a constituent assembly to decide on the future form of government for the German people. Independently, at about two o'clock, the SPD Deputy Philipp Scheidemann, from the steps outside the Reichstag, called down to the crowd below 'Long Live the Republic'. With two acts of solely personal initiative the revolution from above was completed, and Germany moved from empire to republic.

Shortly after lunch the head of the Hohenzollern dynasty discovered by a message from Berlin that he was now the ex-Kaiser. Angrily he

denounced Max of Baden's 'treachery', his fire and fury fed by
sycophantic officers around him. At last Hindenburg, who had been
present at the proclamation of the German Empire in January 1871,
came out to La Fraineuse for its interment. There could be no more
imperial play-acting. Even Aachen, the nearest German city to Spa, had
gone over to the socialists. He could no longer guarantee his Imperial
Majesty's safety, he told William. He should abdicate and seek
sanctuary in the Netherlands. Soon afterwards Admiral Scheer arrived
and backed Hindenburg's advice. At five o'clock in the afternoon
William accepted the inevitable; he would abdicate as German Emperor
but not as King of Prussia. In twelve hours' time he would set out for the
Dutch frontier; it was only forty miles away.

Across the North Sea this second Saturday in November was a
traditional day of celebration for the City of London, with the Lord
Mayor's Show in the morning and a banquet at the Guildhall, at which
the Prime Minister was a speaker. Already during the afternoon there
were rumours that the Kaiser had abdicated, but the news was only
confirmed publicly by Lloyd George in a triumphant speech that
evening, warmly cheered. Germany was 'headless and helpless', the
Prime Minister declared; 'Empires and kingdoms and kings and
crowns were falling like withered leaves before the gale'. But
'Germany, the most formidable of our foes', was not his only theme.
He defended 'sideshows' as the means of opening up Germany's
'vulnerable flank'. He explained, so the *Sunday Times* reported next
day, that 'We thought it better to begin knocking the props from
under their feet. It is an old policy some of us have advocated for years,
and it has come off at last. [Laughter and cheers].' His wizardry of
words was, as so often, beguiling. Archbishop Davidson, conversing
with Arthur Balfour between the cheering and applause, reflected on
the change in Lloyd George's popularity in the ten years since he was
the radical Chancellor of the Exchequer whom so many mistrusted.
'But you have to admit that the beggar deserves it', his old adversary
Balfour insisted.

Yet, if it was an evening of triumph for Lloyd George, it was not yet
an evening of victory, as he had at one time hoped. Not until Sunday
evening (10 November) did Erzberger receive a telegram from Berlin
accepting the armistice terms handed over to Hellsdorf some fifty-five
hours before; a further message confirmed his authority to sign the
Armistice. There was, too, a long cipher telegram from Hindenburg
pressing 'for an end to the fighting . . . as soon as the signing has been
completed . . . in order to save human lives'. The Armistice Commis-

sion returned to Foch's carriage-office at 2.10 on Monday morning. For three hours there were explanatory discussions over points in the text. Erzberger read out a statement of protest, especially at the continuance of the blockade, but ending with a certain resilience: 'A people of seventy million are suffering, but they are not dead', he affirmed. '*Très bien*' Foch responded, for he was not a man to waste words. Finally at 5.10 a.m. the text of the Armistice was signed by Foch and Wemyss for the Allied and Associated Armies and by Erzberger, Oberndorff, Winterfeldt and Vanselow for Germany. The Marshal would carry the news to Paris. 'Hostilities will cease at 11 a.m. today' ran the message sent to all commanders at ten minutes to seven; 'Defensive precautions will be maintained. There will be no intercourse with the enemy until receipt of instructions from GHQ.'

There was some bitter fighting and needless deaths on that last Monday morning; British and American commanders sought to seize vital bridges before the retreating Germans could demolish them. At Mézières a fanatical artillery commander shelled the town with incendiaries and gas; there was a desperate struggle to evacuate wounded from the burning hospital. Outside Mons, which the Canadians had re-entered even as the Armistice was being signed, three veterans of the retreat of 1914 were caught in a burst of machine-gun fire as they waited for the war to end where, for the BEF, it had begun. At last, as watches showed the eleventh hour on the eleventh day of the eleventh month, a mantle of silence suffused the shell-cratered war zone. Cheers of relief followed, but not of triumph; too many sad memories, too much uncertainty ahead for that. Here and there Verey pistols fired silver balls of light into a misty sky, though few found satisfaction in pyrotechnics. In some towns recently freed from occupation buglers sounded the 'Stand Fast'. It seemed a wise injunction.

In London, despite a steady drizzle of rain, there was more noise of revelry, though no Mafeking hysteria. A maroon fired from the roof of the Air Ministry, at the Hotel Cecil, prompted a senior official to order an 'Air raid – take cover' warning. Most celebrations caused less alarm: church bells, river-tug hooters, patriotic singing, cheers for public figures and the King and Queen on the Palace balcony. A few minutes after eleven, outside the Mansion House, 'a crowd swelled until it filled the heart of London'. 'Heartful' cheering 'was followed by a mighty burst of song, of sacred song, the swelling glorious chords of the Doxology – "Praise God from whom all blessing flow".' The *Daily Express* (from which all these reports of religious observance are taken) duly reminded its readers that Armistice Day was also 'Martinmas, the feast-day of the great soldier-saint of France'.

Throughout Britain there was a genuinely religious sense of thankfulness. In the Essex village of Great Easton the rector, The Revd Percy Widrington, thought a peal of bells insufficient: he held an Armistice Day thanksgiving service before noon. At St Paul's Cathedral 'men and women came to pray in their own way in their hundreds all the morning, in the heart of the cheering business world'. In the Commons Lloyd George, having informed MPs of the end of 'the cruellest and most terrible war that has scourged mankind', moved the adjournment of the House 'to give humble and reverent thanks' in St Margaret's Church; Asquith seconded the motion. The Commons followed the Lords across the road for a simple service of two hymns, Psalm 46, prayers, a reading from Isaiah Chapter 61 and a Te Deum. The *Daily Express* praised the congregational singing, 'peers and MPs joining in with full-hearted unison . . . It was Parliament at its best'.

The House of Lords, though not the Commons, resumed its sitting; and Archbishop Davidson, who had conducted the service in St Margaret's, was speaking later in the day to his fellow peers on a Teachers' Superannuation Bill. But for most people it was a holiday, though for some so sad and empty that they wished to spend it alone. The 'Spanish flu' pandemic had recently hit Britain's cities with particular virulence; over two thousand families in London were mourning deaths from influenza in the past fortnight. Telegrams with sorrowing news from the Admiralty and War Office plunged homes into grief on this day as on others. Stoically the Dean of Rochester led a service of Armistice thanksgiving in his cathedral within hours of learning his seaman son was dead.

Police and Army had agreed that, on Armistice Day, existing bans on bonfires and fireworks would be lifted. After dusk, the people of Hythe in Kent were therefore able to burn the Kaiser in effigy – though, in reality, 'the most hated man in England' was on that evening dining as a guest of his Dutch host, Count Bentinck, at Amerongen. Restraints had also been lifted on domestic lighting and the big cities were brightened for the first time since 'dim glimmer' was imposed with the onset of Zeppelin raids. A crowd of Londoners and servicemen on leave filled Trafalgar Square, often linking hands, singing and swaying. To Captain Osbert Sitwell of the Grenadier Guards 'they moved . . . as in a *kermesse* painted by Breughel the Elder'. Captain Sitwell, accompanied by the impresario Diaghilev and the dancer-choreographer Massine, joined a party at the Adelphi, between Trafalgar Square and the Thames. Fellow guests included Bloomsbury intellectuals and artists and D. H. Lawrence and his wife, the cousin of the German air ace Baron von Richthofen, who had been killed seven months before. Close by, in the Union Club overlooking Trafalgar Square, T. E. Lawrence was at a quieter celebration, dining with two archaeologists, pre-war friends now in uniform. What Captain Sitwell, both Lawrences and so many celebrants that night shared in common was a revulsion from the war, a delight in talking of other things, a desire to reach out and resume as swiftly as possible the avocations of a peaceful life.

Across the Channel, Clemenceau would have recognized that mood. Like Lloyd George he had been cheered by his fellow parliamentarians but, old atheist that he was, there had been no religious thanksgiving. He welcomed back 'Alsace-Lorraine to France, one and indivisible'; he spoke of 'gratitude to our noble dead'; and, as the ceremonial guns thundered outside the Chamber, he reached his peroration: 'France, yesterday the soldier of God, today soldier of humanity, for ever the soldier of the ideal will recover her place in the world, to carry forward her magnificent and unending quest for human progress'. The Assembly then voted an Order of the Day to be placarded throughout metropolitan and overseas France: 'Citizen Clemenceau and Marshal Foch have deserved well of their country'. Then the Tiger returned to his lair in the Rue St Dominique. Crowds spilled across the Seine bridges and converged on the narrow road, calling his name. He opened the window, held up a hand for silence, shouted *Vive la France* and went back to a favourite chair. Later, when there was calm outside, he sought the companionship of his old friend, the great painter Claude Monet. He told Monet of his relief that the dark days of war were over. 'Yes', Monet replied, 'And now we shall have time to get on with that monument to Cézanne.'

Not yet, however. Metz and Strasbourg were to be entered. The army was to follow the Germans to Mainz, as the British were to Cologne, the Belgians to Duisburg and the Americans to Coblenz. A watch must be kept, not simply on the Rhine, but also on the new republican Germany of Chancellor Ebert further to the east, on its close links with General Groener and its handling of the Spartacist/communist challenge, especially in Berlin. Moreover, ultimately an armistice was only an extendable ceasefire. 'We have won the war; now we have to win the peace', Clemenceau remarked to his military secretary General Mordacq on Armistice Day; and he added reflectively, 'That may prove harder'.

The British had two outstanding and pressing problems. The first was how to stop Imperial Germany's colonial war and implement Clause Seventeen of the Armistice, which required German forces in Africa to surrender within one month. In late October General Paul von Lettow-Worbeck's 3,000 mixed troops had invaded Northern Rhodesia (now Zambia), crossing the border from German East Africa between Lakes Nyasa and Tanganyika. Contact was made with them on 13 November at the rubber factory of Chambesi: they were told of the Armistice and ordered to Abercorn (now the Zambian town of Mdabal) 180 miles to the north. There they surrendered, but in recognition of a 'gallant fight' the European officers and ranks were allowed to keep their personal arms. A guard of honour from the Ugandan battalions of the King's African Rifles paraded at Abercorn on 25 November as the last German imperial flag of war was handed over.

At home in the United Kingdom the topic of greatest interest was the fate of the German fleet. There had already been satisfaction at detailed reports of the passage of Admiral Calthorpe's Allied squadrons through the Dardanelles to lie off the Golden Horn on 13 November, sixteen miles of sea-power riding at anchor in the heart of the Ottoman Empire. But Germany had been the pre-eminent naval rival for the past twenty years. The Armistice provided for seventy-four German surface vessels and all submarines to be interned in neutral ports pending the rulings of a peace treaty. But no neutral country was willing to act as host-jailer. Perhaps they were never expected to be. For within sixty hours of signing the Armistice, the First Sea Lord won Allied consent for all surface warships to be interned at Scapa Flow and submarines at Harwich. On 15 November the light cruiser *Königsberg* moored in the entry to the Firth of Forth; arrangements for the surrender were discussed with Admiral Beatty with as much detail as the making of the Armistice itself.

The submarine surrender was a straightforward affair. Admiral Tyrwhitt met the first twenty U-boats at sea on 20 November and escorted them to Harwich with no cheering, no humiliating incidents, no arrogance of victory. The White Ensign was run up over each vessel and the crews repatriated almost immediately. By the end of the month another ninety-four U-boats had been brought into Harwich, without fuss or publicity. Other U-boats were to be found in German shipyards over the next few months. By the coming of the New Year the weapon of greatest threat to Britain's survival during the whole war had, with quiet efficiency, been rendered harmless.

Admiral Beatty, on the other hand, had Franchet d'Esperey's sense of theatre, and magnificent stage props on which to exercise it. There was, too, a purpose in the drama he produced: Britannia should be seen to rule the waves, especially by the representatives of a President who sought to proclaim the freedom of the seas. On the other hand, there was a genuine sense of gratitude to Admiral Sims for the aid he had brought so rapidly in the worst weeks of the war in the Atlantic. Sims was given a role to play: five dreadnoughts from the US 6th Battle Squadron could accompany the Grand Fleet as it sailed out from Rosyth to a rendezvous some forty-five miles out into the North Sea. Rear-Admiral Grasset of the French Navy was allowed a sailing-on part in Beatty's grand production: an old armoured cruiser with two destroyers came up from Brest.

But 21 November 1918 was Sir David Beatty's Day. Some 90,000 seamen in 370 warships steamed out of the Firth of Forth in a single file to receive the surrender of the High Seas Fleet. The armada then divided, so as to form two columns of thirteen squadrons, six miles apart. It was as spectacular as a Spithead Review, but on this occasion Beatty had ordered his captains to fly their battle ensigns and keep their crews at action stations in case of some desperate act of defiance by the old enemy. The light cruiser HMS *Cardiff* and a destroyer escort went ahead to meet Admiral von Reuter's flagship, SMS *Friedrich der Grosse*, and the eight battleships and five battlecruisers that followed in line ahead, with more than sixty other vessels in their wake. It was, a German officer wrote, an 'endless funeral procession . . . over 50 kilometres in length'. Shortly before ten in the morning *Cardiff* led the German fleet between the two columns in total silence. 'A pitiable sight, in fact I should say it was a horrible sight . . . to see these great ships . . . come in . . . with their old antagonists, the battle cruisers, gazing at them', Beatty wrote. To Seaman Ludwig Freiwald, in SMS *Nassau*, the processional surrender seemed 'the most shameful deed in all the history of the sea'.

Reuter's warships were then escorted to an anchorage off Inchkeith, pending a series of voyages up to Scapa Flow. Beatty and the Grand Fleet passed under the Forth railway bridge to moorings off Rosyth. It was then that the cheering began, from shore and from the assembled ships' companies as the flagship, HMS *Queen Elizabeth*, steamed up the Firth in the full majesty of a victory won through the power of silent guns. At 11.00 hours Admiral Beatty approved a general signal to Admiral von Reuter: 'The German flag will be hauled down at sunset today, Thursday, and will not be hoisted again without permission'. Four and three-quarter hours later, the sun set behind heavy clouds.

The ensigns were lowered. Aboard Beatty's flagship a thanksgiving service was held 'for the victory which Almighty God has vouchsafed to His Majesty's arms'.

CHAPTER 19

PEACEMAKING?

Three weeks after Beatty's Day in northern waters an unimpressive two-funnelled passenger ship was battling with heavy Biscayan seas as she steamed towards Finisterre. Aboard ss *George Washington*, once a German luxury liner, were members of 'The Inquiry', a team of several hundred American experts, mostly young, omniscient in Europe's history, economics, financial affairs and political institutions. With them came the five members of the United States Peace Commission: Secretary of State Robert Lansing; Colonel House; General Tasker M. Bliss; Henry White, a retired Republican diplomat; and Woodrow Wilson in person. Never before had a President absented himself from the United States during his term of office, and several prominent figures in both political parties felt that he should have remained in the White House, especially after his electoral rebuff a week before the Armistice. 'Our allies and our enemies and Mr Wilson himself should all understand that Mr Wilson has no authority whatever to speak for the American people at this time', warned ex-President Theodore Roosevelt on 4 December as the *George Washington* began her slow voyage from New York. But Wilson believed that, even if denied popular endorse-ment of his leadership, he possessed a preordained clarity of vision. All he asked now was precise and accurate information from the seaborne brain trust. 'Tell me what's right and I'll fight for it; give me a guaranteed position', he invited members of The Inquiry in the main saloon of the *George Washington*. To youthful idealists, genuinely convinced that what was morally wrong must never be politically right, his appeal came as a fine challenge. They had, so they assumed, just a few months in which to enlighten war-weary Europe.

Gun salutes echoed off Brest's ramparted boulevard as the *George Washington* brought the President to Brittany on 13 December; it was a Friday, as the supersititious ominously noted. Wilson was expected to spend a month touring France, Britain and Italy before a peace conference opened in the French capital. His arrival in Paris later that day boosted the President's confidence. Two million people packed the Bois de Boulogne, the avenues around the Arc de Triomphe and the Champs-Elysées cheering and shouting '*Vive Wilson, Vive l'Amérique*' as he rode, beamingly content, beside President Poincaré in an open carriage. But thereafter his behaviour was odd. During the fortnight he was free to tour France he never visited any of the battlefields where American troops had so recently won honour at such high cost; the Meuse–Argonne battles had left 150,000 Americans dead or gravely wounded. The AEF paraded before their President in review at Langres; yet he did not stay afterwards to share their dinner of victory celebration. Clemenceau urged him to see for himself the war devastation in northern France. He refused. Did he fear that once he stepped down from his pedestal he would lose the mantle of impartiality and the moral authority that went with it? That was certainly the impression of General Bliss.

On Boxing Day (26 December) Wilson crossed to England. Yet, though greeted warmly at Victoria Station, he was in general received with more restraint; the first Christmastide of peace was a poor time to come, anyhow. Lloyd George seems early to have appreciated that the President was obstinate, but hoodwinkable. Already he perceived that Wilson's chief concern was to see a League of Nations firmly established; a suggestion that 'freedom of the seas' should become a League matter at once postponed the most vexing of Anglo-American questions for later settlement. The President's condescension of manner irritated British imperial statesmen, especially Australia's Prime Minister, William Hughes. Wilson recognized Canada's contribution to the war, with 60,000 dead, 12,000 more than the United States. But he knew little about the Australasian war effort: New Zealand had lost 16,000, one in thirty-three of the total male population; Australia 59,000 dead, one in twenty-five. These proportions were grievously high for young nations, far from the battlefield. 'If we are not very careful we shall find ourselves dragged quite unnecessarily behind the wheels of President Wilson's chariot', Hughes warned the Imperial War Cabinet a few days later.

An ungracious speech on 27 December at a Buckingham Palace banquet, in which the President omitted any tribute to the King's armed forces, went down badly. 'I could not bear him, an entirely cold academical professor – an odious man', George V confessed to an old friend, speaking as one robbed of the delights of Sandringham at Christmas. Two days later, however, Wilson had greater personal success among the Presbyterian community at Carlisle, where he preached a short sermon in the chapel his mother's father had served as minister. And enthusiasm was back on the streets of Rome when, in the first week of January, he spent four days in Italy: he came, after all, from the great land of refuge and opportunity; the promises attributed to him were believed. Parish priests found newspaper photographs of the President beside holy images in family shrines.

On 7 January Wilson returned to Paris, ready to study and digest the detailed information which 'The Inquiry' had collated for him. By then the Foreign Office 'peace staff', trained for their task intermittently for eighteen months, were also in Paris, for a month previously Clemenceau had suggested that the Conference should begin in the first week of January, though the opening was postponed. Other delegations could not count on such good Intelligence back-up as the Americans and British. It did not worry them. The French already possessed the finest diplomatic service in the world; the Italians saw no need to bother about such matters. Nor did the smaller countries, many of whom had knowledgeable advocates in their own statesmen: Venizelos for Greece; Brătianu for Romania; Beneš for the Czechs. The Arabs, whom the French were reluctant to recognize as legitimate claimants for any representation at a peace conference, had to rely on the complementary Intelligence of Feisal and of Lawrence; their partnership was resumed when Feisal reached Marseilles in a British cruiser during the last days of November.

Preparatory meetings to settle the form and composition of the Peace Conference began on 12 January, under Clemenceau's chairmanship. By then nine weeks had passed since the guns fell silent in Europe. Sombre assessments were beginning to show the awful cost of the war in human lives, although it would be many years before final figures were published, and even then for Russia and Turkey they could be no more than estimates. Throughout November and December, prisoners of war arrived home. In Britain some brought with them tales of ill-treatment, mostly in Turkey, though with harsh punishments for malcontents in Germany too. With feelings running high, it was a poor time to expect good sense from public opinion. But Lloyd George was eager to make sure of popular backing. He could scarcely wait to go to the polls; even on Armistice night his table talk at dinner in Downing Street had been of electioneering.

The snap election campaign which began on 22 November brought credit to no one. It released the vindictive passions against which the Archbishop had warned his congregation in St Margaret's on 4 August.

Lloyd George was carried along on a wave of jingoistic hysteria. Although he opened the campaign with appeals against any spririt of greed or revenge, he was soon following the Northcliffe press in its demands to put the Kaiser on trial and make Germany 'pay for the whole cost of the war'. The General Election – the first in which women, over the age of thirty, might vote – was held on 14 December but the declaration of results was delayed for a fortnight, so that servicemen's votes could be counted. Lloyd George gained overwhelming popular backing; his Coalition Government was confirmed in office with a majority of 262. On the last Saturday of the year a jubilant headline in Northcliffe's *The Times* declared 'Pacifists Routed'. Among former MPs who lost their seats were such wise advocates of a just peace as the Liberal Asquith and Labour's Ramsay MacDonald.

While the British election campaign was in progress, Europe and the Middle East were changing rapidly. There was unfinished business from the days of conflict to settle, and new political leaders wished to present the forthcoming conference with accomplished objectives which it would be hard to contest. In Vienna on Armistice Day itself Emperor Charles had signed a message to his peoples renouncing participation in the affairs of state; he did not abdicate but retired with his family to the shooting-lodge of Eckartsau, in the Marchfeld to the north-east of the capital. Next day a provisional national assembly declared Austria a republic, specifically 'a constituent part of the German Republic'. A Greater Germany, substantially larger than the pre-war Reich, was an aspect of self-determination not envisaged by the draughtsman of the Fourteen Points. Here was an early and direct challenge to the coming peacemakers.

Charles had already lost Hungary, where President Károlyi was trying to establish a social democracy under the vigilant scrutiny of Colonel Vyx, Franchet d'Esperey's nominee as Armistice Commissioner. Freedom of the press and of political assembly were guaranteed, an extended franchise introduced and land reforms begun, with Károlyi taking the lead by breaking up and distributing one of his own family estates. But, though the Hungarian people welcomed the reforms, there was deep resentment at Vyx's interference with policy-making, especially his support for the Czechs. Károlyi had to withdraw the last Hungarian militia from the Slovak territories, under pressure from Vyx in early December. At the same time the French military authorities allowed the Romanian Army to advance in Transylvania. These incursions stirred patriotic indignation; and Károlyi, arguably the most dedicated and sincere Wilsonian politician in Europe, was discredited at home even before the Peace Conference opened. Many Hungarians felt that, if the West would not support Károlyi, they would have to look to the East and hope for backing from the Russia of Lenin and Trotsky. The released communist prisoner of war, Béla Kun, was a persuasive agitator and as anti-Romanian as any Hungarian nationalist of the political right, for he had been born at Szilagycseh, in Transylvania. When, on 20 March 1919, Colonel Vyx put further pressure on the Hungarian authorities to allow the Romanians to occupy territory some 250 miles west of the pre-war frontier, Károlyi was swept aside by a coalition of the extreme left. Béla Kun established a Hungarian Soviet Republic, and the peacemakers in Paris suddenly found that, through Vyx's high-handedness, the Danube in Budapest was Red.

Fear of Bolshevism was strongest in Germany. Friedrich Ebert, the social democrat who succeeded Max of Baden as Chancellor on 9 November, found the Army's Supreme Command ready to help the new republican government maintain order and check anarchy. General Groener telephoned Ebert from Spa on his first evening in office and struck a political bargain: provided that Hindenburg remained at the head of the Army and that the Provisional Government co-operated with the officer corps to ensure the troops were well provisioned and their lines of communication unhindered by strikes, Ebert might rely on support from the generals. A telephone hotline linked the private offices of Ebert in Berlin and Groener in Spa (and later Wilhelmshöhe), enabling the two men to hold nightly discussions over the following months. The army came back from France and Belgium in perfect order, mainly on foot. On 11 December – two days before the Parisians cheered Wilson as he drove along the Champs-Elysées – Berliners lined Unter den Linden to greet the troops from the Western Front, marching in column behind regimental colours and regimental bands. Chancellor Ebert waited at the Brandenburger Tor to greet them; 'I salute you who return undefeated from the field of battle', he declared with pride and the emotions of a good German patriot who had lost two sons fighting for the Fatherland.

Many moderate socialists, as well as the communist extremists in the Spartacist League, were dismayed by Ebert's attitude. They were also concerned at the growth of volunteer Free Corps (*Freiwilligenkorps*), nationalistic political paramilitary forces, for which enlistment was secretly authorized by the Supreme Command twelve days after the Armistice. In the absence of an elected German political assembly, a Congress of Soldiers' and Workers Councils met in Berlin on 16 December and demanded not only the dismissal of Hindenburg and the surrender of control of the armed forces to the Councils, but also the replacement of the Army by locally raised militia. The refusal of Ebert's Provisional Government to accept these demands led to street clashes in Berlin between 23 December and 17 January. After Christmas the regular Army backed out of this incipient civil war, leaving the Free Corps to crush the people's militia of the Spartacists mercilessly; at least 1,200 'Reds' were killed. The most notorious atrocity, the murder on 15 January of Europe's two great independent communists Karl Lieb-knecht and Rosa Luxemburg, was the work of officers from the élite Guard Cavalry.

Four days after these murders elections were held for a German National Assembly, which would gather not in Berlin but in peaceful and enlightened Weimar, once the home of Goethe. When the Assembly met in mid-February the Social Democrats emerged as the largest single political group and their leader, Ebert, was elected as Reich President. But the Social Democrats could retain office only through a succession of improvised coalitions. Over the following months there was no strong and cohesive government in Germany to face the challenge of peace terms dictated from Paris.

The smoothest revolutionary transition occurred in Prague. A National Assembly was convened in the city on 14 November and elected Masaryk as President, even though he was still in America. He left New York aboard the liner *Carmania* six days later, but it was not until 21 December that he made an official entry into the capital of the new Czechoslovak Republic. Masaryk was himself of part-Slovak ancestry and he had more sympathy with the non-Czech Slavs in the republic than had the Foreign Minister, Beneš, or the Prime Minister, Kramář. Unfortunately the Slovak representative on the wartime National Council in Paris, the War Minister and charismatic aeronaut, Milan Stefanik, was killed when his plane crashed as he was coming home to Slovakia's regional capital, Bratislava. There was no other spokesman for the Slovaks – still less among the Ruthenes – who carried such influence with the Czechs who thus, inevitably, became the master nationality in the newly created state.

At first the Slovak people treated the political upheaval of late 1918 with total indifference. Around Bratislava they were mainly Protestants and, if their pastors favoured a unitary state in partnership with traditionally Protestant Prague, so be it. But in the foothills of the Carpathians the peasants were Catholic; virtually the only political group – the Slovak People's Party – was led by a priest, Monsignor Andrej Hlinka; and, except in a few cussedly obstinate western

Carpathian villages, the Slovak faithful accepted Hlinka's teaching that the people of Prague were secularist and avaricious. An invasion of Slovak lands by minor officials and teachers from the Czech provinces seemed to confirm Hlinka's warnings. When, early in the Peace Conference, Hlinka and a fellow priest brought a petition to Paris critical of their compatriots' limited opportunities for 'self-determination', the French police discovered 'passport irregularities' and hustled them out of the country. The petition never reached the 'Commission on Czechoslovak Affairs', which President Wilson assumed was ensuring that the spirit of government in central Europe's model democratic republic fulfilled the ideals of the Fourteen Points.

There were other changes, too, in Eastern Europe before the New Year came in. General Josef Pilsudski, a staunchly anti-Russian Polish socialist revolutionary who had led the Polish Legion within the *K-und-K* Army until the Germans imprisoned him in 1917, was able to return to Warsaw on Armistice Day and was accepted as 'Chief of State' three days later. Pilsudski's military skills were needed by the resurrected state, surrounded as it was by potential enemies. In Paris the French Army – Marshal Foch in particular – backed him. Foch insisted that, under the terms of the Armistice, the Germans were bound to allow unmolested passage home for the Polish units who had been serving in the French army on the Western Front. A force of veteran combatants was thus able to augment Pilsudski's army with modern French guns and equipment. The threat from Bolshevik Russia cast a long shadow over the Peace Conference, and by Foch's reckoning a strong Poland would serve as a bastion against both Bolshevism and a revival of Prussian militarism. But, when in January 1918 Wilson had pledged support for an independent Poland, he never envisaged helping a military dictator come to power in Warsaw.

A 'Kingdom of the Serbs, Croats and Slovenes' was officially proclaimed in Belgrade on the evening of 1 December 1918. Though there had long been a sentiment of shared affinities among Yugoslav peoples, there had never been any enthusiasm in Zagreb or Ljubljana for absorption by Serbia. The unitary kingdom did indeed give some protection against Italy, but at a cost of subservience to pan-Serb interests which the Corfu Pact had sought to avoid. Stephen Radić, leader of the Croatian Peasant Party, was impeded even earlier than the Slovak, Monsignor Hlinka; for he was detained in Zagreb while still preparing a memorandum which he wished to take to Paris, complaining of the denial of Croatia's rights to self-determination. On several occasions in the winter of 1918–19 the Italians and Yugoslavs seemed close to war; and Pašić, the new kingdom's principal spokesman in Paris, complained that the Italians were preventing food shipments from being landed in Dalmatia for the relief of shortages in the towns of both Serbia and Croatia. To discomfort the Yugoslavs, the Italians also championed the lost cause of the kingdom of Montenegro, Serbia's first ally in 1914 but in 1915–16 overrun by the Austrians. On 26 November 1918 a National Assembly was convened in the Montenegrin town of Podgorica, which voted with suspicious enthusiasm for union with Serbia. Assessors sent from Paris decided that the Assembly was packed but that the Montenegrins were satisfied with their shotgun marriage. Even Franchet d'Esperey put in an appearance, travelling up to Cetinje from Dubrovnik in the last days of January 1919, to the intense fury of the Italians who regarded this stretch of coast as their stamping ground and mistrusted Franchet's close contacts with the Prince Regent of Serbia. Franchet seems, predictably, to have assured Paris that the Podgorica vote was an instance of self-determination, expressed indirectly. The Italians, however, continued to protest. So did the fallen King of Montenegro, who moved into the Hotel Meurice in Paris with his bodyguard and was eventually allowed to state his case. A compromise was reached. At each plenary session of the Peace Conference a gilt chair was placed behind the table; no plenipotential posterior ever occupied the chair, but on the blotting pad on the table facing it was a white card labelled 'Montenegro' so as to maintain notional representation. Eighty years on, the bond linking Serbia and Montenegro survives the dissolution of a federal Yugoslavia.

Further east, there was a strange anomaly. The whole of the Levant and Mesopotamia formed a political vacuum, but the institution which had provided cohesion remained in existence. For though Kaiser William, Emperor Charles and King Ferdinand had lost their thrones, Sultan Mehmed VI was still in the Dolmabache Palace, facing Asia across the Bosporus. When the war ended he possessed little effective power and, as he admitted, he hated looking out of the palace window, for all he could see before his eyes was the long line of Allied warships at anchor off the Golden Horn. But, rather oddly, Mehmed VI recovered some of his lost authority during the early months of the Allied occupation. On 21 December the Sultan dissolved parliament and, for the first time in ten years, reverted to a system of government by decree. This suited the Allied High Commissioners, for they feared that a political forum might show socialist inclinations. Moreover, the Sultan made good use of his spiritual authority as Caliph to maintain order and discipline in a city prone to alarming rumours. When a menacing mob of Muslims swept down on the mosque which was once Byzantium's basilica of Holy Wisdom because they heard the Greeks were going to restore Christian symbols, it was the Sultan-Caliph's Ottoman guards who kept the peace, preventing a riot which would have brought French troops to the heart of the city.

Allied High Commissioners kept watch on Turkey's political life; and Allied commanders on each other. When reports reached Franchet in Montenegro that Allenby was expected in Constantinople, he made as much haste eastwards as possible in a vain attempt to get there first. Allenby, a massive bull seated beside a frail Milne, rode in the back of an open Rolls-Royce; Franchet entered the city two days later astride a grey without reins, as had the Ottoman conqueror of Byzantium according to tradition. The two Allied generals, so similar as architects of victory but so different in their self-esteem, met cordially. 'I am especially glad that I was lucky enough not to miss Franchet d'Esperey', Allenby wrote to his wife; 'He might have had an idea otherwise that I was trying to steal a march on him.'

But Allenby had graver concerns than ensuring that the feathers of a French peacock stayed preened. He came to Constantinople displeased at the response of Ottoman commanders on the Tigris to the Mudros Armistice terms. In the capital he found that the Allied Commissioners knew of societies 'for the Defence of the Rights of Turks' and had protested against them to the Sultan's ministers; but they took no firm action. Defiance of the occupying powers ran deeper than the Commissioners thought. They do not seem to have identified the 'Outpost Society', a group of highly placed Turks who smuggled arms along the Black Sea coast to eastern Anatolia or southwards to Smyrna; and they were only mildly interested in the activities of General Mustafa Kemal, who was secretly creating the nucleus of a Turkish Nationalist Army. Allenby, on the other hand, knew from Intelligence reports that a resistance movement was being built up in Cilicia. He found Turkish generals slow to fulfil armistice conditions, especially in the Mosul region; and he was convinced that non-compliance was being co-ordinated from Constantinople itself. While he was in the capital Allenby summoned to his presence the Ottoman War Minister and the Foreign Minister and read out a list of demands. On this occasion, action followed swiftly. Not only was the Turkish General at Mosul dismissed; his Sixth Army was also disbanded. And soon afterwards Mustafa Kemal found himself deprived of his status as an aide-de-camp to the Sultan, and of the official car that went with the post.

Vigilance was not maintained. Three months later, when Allenby was back in Cairo, the British High Commission approved a visa allowing Kemal to sail off along the Black Sea coast as Inspector General of the Ottoman army in eastern Anatolia. Kemal's departure to the Turkish heartland marked the start of the great national revolution which ended both sultanate and caliphate. Before the end of the year 1919 the erstwhile Inspector General was in Ankara at the head of an insurgent Nationalist Army ready to defy the Sultan, the British and the French. But the outstanding enemy of all Turkish nationalists was Greece – and especially the Greek force which, on 15 April 1919, had landed at Smyrna covered by Allied warships, to secure the segment of Asia Minor which Venizelos's persuasive tongue was winning from the peacemakers in Paris.

The Greeks in Anatolia were Lloyd George's concern, rather than Allenby's. Throughout the first quarter of 1919 he was deeply worried over the heightening conflict of rival nationalities within the lands his armies had occupied. The worst clashes came between the local Muslim population and the Armenians, some of whom continued to seek and kill ex-Turkish officers whom they held guilty of acts of genocide. At the same time, Armenian women and girls released from Turkish harems were singled out for maltreatment in Aleppo, where over a hundred Armenians were killed by local Muslims. The Arabs looked on Armenians as agents of the French, especially in the exploitation of the coveted port of Alexandretta, where Allenby had to offer British troops to help the French and Armenian forces defend their base. Further south there was trouble between the Australians and the Palestinian Arabs, which increased as Anzac units became impatient at what they regarded as the slow rate of repatriation.

Allenby became convinced that, throughout large areas under his command, the French were deliberately seeking to provoke the Arabs, in order to be given an excuse for ejecting Feisal's troops and bringing Syria fully under French control. There were personal affronts: an order to remove the Hejazi flag from Feisal's car in Beirut as he set out for the Paris Peace Conference, for example. And there were political affronts, notably the refusal to allow the Arabs special privileges at any port in Syria and Lebanon. In November Sir Mark Sykes and François Georges-Picot, whose partition plans had caused such a conflict of interests at the height of the war, toured Aleppo, Damascus and Beirut in the hopes of encouraging reconciliation. Sykes, back in Paris, continued to prevent the gap between French and British interests widening. He was present on 6 February 1919, when Feisal and Lawrence put their cases before the Council of Ten – the heads of government and foreign ministers of the Big Five (America, Britain, France, Italy and Japan) who served as the Conference's presiding executive. But already Sykes's health was failing. He succumbed to influenza; pneumonia soon followed; and he died in his Paris hotel room ten nights later.

Experience had brought Sykes wisdom and comprehension, and his restraining influence and knowledge were missed in Paris. Specialists continued to plead their causes. Feisal contended that self-determination justified the creation of independent Arab states south of the Taurus Mountains. Maronite Christian delegations emphasized the need for protection from France and supported a French mandate, as also did a Catholic deputation of Syrians, mostly resident in Europe. On 27 February Chaim Weizmann and a Zionist delegation impressively made a good case for the implementation of the Balfour Declaration. But the gravest assessment of future danger came from Allenby himself, who was summoned to Paris a fortnight later. On 19 March he gave the Council of Ten a blunt warning that if Syria became a French mandate, there would be a war with Feisal's Arabs which might involve the British in Palestine and extend as far south as the Hejaz.

Lloyd George's policies remained devious. From his secretary's diary it is clear that Allenby spoke out at the Prime Minister's prompting. Yet he did not want to lose French friendship for the sake of Syria; the Bull might be encouraged to snort with fury, but there must be no risk of a head-butting charge. On the day after Allenby gave his warning, his services were rewarded with the Kitchener prize posting of High Commissioner in Egypt. The appointment elevated him from military command in Palestine to an imperial proconsulship; it also moved him well away from any French sphere of influence. In practice, however, Allenby's staff-work left French feelings ruffled for many months to come. Commissions of enquiry were sent out to Syria and Palestine, thus slowing down decision-making in Paris. Over another Middle Eastern problem, Wilson indicated in May that he believed he might eventually gain Congressional backing for a United States mandate for Armenia. But, with so much uncertainty in the region, none of these questions could be resolved speedily. Accordingly, as Lloyd George and Clemenceau had always wished, the settlement of the Near East was put in cold storage, until after the German treaty was signed.

The first formal meeting of the Peace Conference, held at the Quai d'Orsay on 18 January 1919, fell either by chance or by design on an already historic date. For that Saturday was the anniversary of a French humiliation, the proclamation of the German Empire in 1871 in the palace of Louis XIV at Versailles. With Clemenceau in the chair the mood seemed set to become strongly anti-German. Pleas to lift the Allied blockade to ease the acute famine in Germany and Austria were rejected – even, in the first week of March, a plea from General Plumer with the Second Army in the occupied Rhineland which urged the swift sending of food as his troops 'cannot stand [the] spectacle of starving children'. There was a general feeling among the main delegates that, as Germany was the principal enemy, the terms to be imposed on her should be agreed first; and then the blockade could be lifted.

Wilson, however, expected priority to be given to the League of Nations, whose Covenant (constitution) he wished to see included as the first clause of each peace treaty. The dispute over the nature of the Covenant continued for a month, further delaying the German settlement. There were then deep divisions among the British and French, with Foch complaining that the proposed terms were too lenient, and Lloyd George – in what is known from its place of origin as the Fontainebleau Memorandum – suddenly expressing alarm that harsh terms might perpetuate a spirit of revenge. He was opposed, in particular, to excessive reparations and the loss by Germany to Poland of Prussia's eastern frontiers. Clemenceau, though less acquisitive than Foch, was unimpressed. He suggested that if the British wished to ease the burden on Germany, they should look overseas and make colonial concessions or modify the naval conditions.

The Germans, assuming that the Peace Treaty would be the subject of discussion, had prepared counter-proposals. But they found that all negotiation was ruled out. At the end of the first week in May their delegates were summoned to Versailles, where they were presented with terms far harsher than they had anticipated: Alsace-Lorraine was to be returned to France; Poznania, parts of East Prussia and Upper Silesia to go to Poland, with Danzig as a 'free city'; Belgium to receive Eupen-Malmédy; Czechoslovakia to receive the Hultschin district; Lithuania to gain the port of Memel; the Danish frontier in Schleswig-Holstein to be readjusted on lines of nationality after a plebiscite; all colonies to be surrendered, passing under League of Nations mandated protection; the Saar basin to be under League control until 1935, with the French having compensation rights on its minefields; the Rhineland to be demilitarized and under Allied occupation for up to fifteen years; a ban on the union of Germany and Austria; heavy demands for reparations; limitation of the German Army to 100,000 men, with no General Staff, no conscription, no heavy guns, no poison gas, no aircraft, no tanks; the German Navy to be limited to vessels under 10,000 tons, with no air arm and no submarines; provision to be made for the trial of the Kaiser and other war leaders; and a clause admitting Germany's guilt for causing the war. On 9 May the German delegates formally complained to Clemenceau that the terms were 'intolerable for any nation'. Meetings across Germany complained of international deceit; the earliest peace notes in October 1918 assumed that the settlement would correspond to Wilson's published principles, not to the dictates of victors over vanquished. In reality only three of the Fourteen Points had referred to Germany directly: the evacuation and restoration of Belgium; the return of Alsace-Lorraine; and the creation of 'an independent Polish state' with 'free and direct access to the sea'. Each of these was included in the proposed treaty; but so, too, was much else besides.

President Ebert wished to reject the terms. He seriously contemplated a renewal of the war and duly consulted both Groener and Hindenburg. By now, the growth of the Free Corps volunteer movement meant that, on paper, Germany could mobilize an army of 400,000 trained and experienced troops. As at Spa, Groener again methodically sought the views of regimental commanders; the response was discouraging. They believed that in particular regions local resistance was possible, but the people as a whole would not accept renewed hostilities. The Allies would advance, not only from the Rhine but through Bavaria as well, while Pilsudski could re-establish an Eastern Front, and Franchet d'Esperey carry out his cherished plan of entering Saxony and striking for Berlin through Dresden. Never before had Germany faced such tight encirclement. Groener, ever a realist, knew that Germany must accept the terms. On 17 June Hindenburg told Ebert that the Eastern frontier could be defended against the Poles but that it would be impossible to resist an offensive in the West. Even so the General Field Marshal thought it would be 'better to perish honourably than accept a disgraceful peace'. Two days later Groener and the Minister of War, Noske, presided over a virtual Council of War attended by the leading generals, senior staff officers and an admiral. Overwhelmingly the meeting urged rejection of the peace terms; the generals seemed to have expected Noske to become Chancellor, denounce the Armistice and head a military dictatorship which would renew the war. They were wrong; but throughout that weekend the German government was engulfed in deep crisis. Ebert felt obliged to summon the National Assembly to gather in Weimar on Sunday 22 June, where it would take the crucial decision on acceptance or rejection of the peace terms. From Paris Clemenceau telegraphed one small concession: the Armistice was due to expire at noon (German time) on Saturday 21 June; he would allow the Germans another forty-eight hours' grace.

Up in the Orkneys that Saturday was a delightful summer's day. Some 400 pupils from Stromness Academy were enjoying what one boy was to remember as 'the strangest school journey ever made', a trip across the waters of Scapa Flow in the Admiralty auxiliary support vessel, *Flying Kestrel*, to see Admiral von Reuter's interned fleet at close quarters. The British battleships normally at anchor in the Flow were at sea that morning, for Admiral Fremantle had decided to order a tactical exercise. Only three destroyers kept watch on the Germans. Reuter's seventy vessels made an impressive sight for the boys and girls. Yet those who came from naval families and knew about such things were surprised to spot that on this Saturday each vessel was flying close-up the ensign of the Kaiser's fleet. An artist sketching the scene became puzzled; it was difficult to get the perspective right; the line of the nearest battleship's stern seemed nearer the water each time he looked up. A destroyer guardship, too, noticed something odd; and at 12.20 Admiral Fremantle, eight miles out to sea in the Pentland Firth, was surprised to receive the signal 'German battleship sinking'. By half past two, when his squadron returned to Scapa, the captive fleet was effectively scuttled. There had been some shooting by the guardship, uncertain what was happening; and the captain of the battleship *Markgraf* and nine crewmen were killed. By five in the afternoon fifty-one warships lay on the seabed of Scapa Flow. Admiral Reuter, not knowing that the Armistice had been extended, maintained that he had every right to order the scuttling of the fleet, since otherwise the warships would have been seized immediately by the Royal Navy.

The events in Scapa Flow were treated with patriotic satisfaction by German newspapers next morning. Deputies could read the news as they awaited the opening of the National Assembly in Weimar: a protest had been made against the iniquitous peace terms. After a three-hour debate the Assembly decided that a renewal of the fighting was out of the question; the peace terms must be accepted. Even so the Assembly insisted on one assertion of national pride: the delegates in Paris were authorized to sign, but without acknowledging the war-guilt clause or accepting the need to put on trial the Kaiser and the war leaders. Once again there came a firm refusal from Clemenceau; unconditional signature it must be.

Ebert telephoned Groener and Hindenburg at OHL's headquarters in Kolberg, Pomerania. The decision to sign or not must be taken by the

Army leaders. He gave them until four o'clock to make up their minds. 'You know as well as I do that resistance is out of the question', Hindenburg told Groener at a quarter to four, and added, 'There is no need for me to stay. You can give the answer to the President.' Thus it was not a member of the Prussian officer corps who advised the civilian authorities to sign the treaty, but a Swabian from south Germany. In Paris, Clemenceau was informed of Germany's acceptance by one of the German delegates twenty minutes before his 'ultimatum' expired.

The German treaty was signed in the Hall of Mirrors at Versailles on 28 June 1919, the fifth anniversary of the murders at Sarajevo which had formed a tragic prelude to the full tragedy of all Europe. It was four years and 328 days since the Germans had declared war on Russia, the 'lost' Great Power – for whom no one signed. Some participants in the conference remained uneasy: Foch, and a group of French senior officers, thought the terms too lenient; on the other hand General Smuts, who was one of the two South African plenipotentiaries, nearly refused to sign and, in the end, did so only under protest, for he thought the terms far too vindictive. In a statement to the newspapers Smuts argued that, though the treaty marked the end of Prussian militarism and held out the promise of a better future through the League, it was 'simply the liquidation of the war situation'. 'The real peace of the peoples ought to follow, complete, and amend the peace of the statesmen', he declared. There was doubt whether a defeated Germany could pay reparations. President Wilson consoled his conscience with the thought that, once the bitter passions of the war years receded, the League of Nations could right the injustices done at Versailles. Everyone now accepted that the war was over. The blockade of Germany was lifted on 12 July; a Victory Parade was held in London on 19 July. The French had celebrated victory on the greatest festival of the republican calendar five days previously.

Peacemaking, of course, continued in Paris. But with much less participation from heads of state. President Wilson returned to the United States, where he found he had to fight, not merely for acceptance of the idea of a League of Nations, but for ratification of the Peace Treaty itself. In his obstinacy during the Peace Conference he had cut himself off from Lansing, General Bliss and even from Colonel House. Warnings of the American people's swing towards 'isolation' went unheeded. Wilson's health, precarious in Paris during April, deteriorated rapidly as he fought political battles against the Senate Foreign Relations Committee. He found his conviction that the American people should underwrite the new world order aroused opposition not

only among the Republicans, but from two influential Democrats as
well, Senators Gore of Oklahoma and Walsh of Massachusetts. At this
point – as the experts in Paris were drawing up final terms for the
Austrians and the last US combat division was two days out from Brest
on its homeward voyage – the President determined on a grand appeal
to the American people. He left Washington by train on 3 September,
to spend three weeks crossing the continent. His speeches were both
messianic and emotional; at times he was in tears; at least once he spoke
of the dead spirits who haunted the Flanders trenches, crying out for a
just world society to honour their sacrifice. His sense of deep personal
commitment led the President to increase his speaking engagements to
two and sometimes three addresses each day. Inevitably the strain was
too much for him. In Kansas on 26 September he suffered a grave
stroke, and could campaign no more. On 19 November the vote to ratify
the Treaty of Versailles came before the Senate. Press reports recall the
gasp that went through the galleries when the result was made known:
thirty-nine Senators voted for acceptance; but fifty-five rejected the
Treaty. Wilson's failure was complete.

No bilateral peace treaty between the USA and Germany was
contemplated. On paper America's 48,000 war dead had brought the
republic no tangible gain, apart from some enemy assets confiscated
during the war. The Senate's action ended American political involvement in Europe's affairs for twenty-two years, although great
humanitarian relief work was undertaken. The League of Nations,
legally constituted eight weeks later, began its work without any backing
from the American patron who, by the terms of the Covenant, had been
designated convenor of the first session.

Yet the task of peacemaking had to continue, though final maps
would be drawn with no reference to American wishes. Originally it was
assumed that all the treaties would be signed before the end of the year
1919, once Germany accepted the terms imposed on her. The treaty
with the Austrian Republic was concluded in the Palace of St Germain
on 10 September. The new state was forbidden to call itself 'German
Austria' or to unite with Germany; the Trentino, the South Tyrol and
Trieste went to Italy; Dalmatia, Slovenia and Bosnia-Herzegovina
to the new Yugoslav State; Bohemia and Moravia became part of
Czechoslovakia; Galicia went to Poland; the Bukovina to Romania. The
new republican army was limited to 30,000 men; reparations would be
required. Once again the terms were harsh. Before 1914 there had been
28 million people in the non-Hungarian part of the Dual Monarchy;
post-war Austria had a population of slightly under 8 million, with a

huge capital city built up for an empire of 50 million. Most sentiment was provincial rather than national; one province – the Vorarlberg – sought to secede and join the Swiss Confederation; but this instance of local self-determination was rebuffed at every level. The people of the Tyrol deeply resented a frontier carried to the Brenner Pass for strategic reasons rather than on any ethnographic grounds; over 200,000 German Austrians passed under Italian rule. The people of Carinthia, in the Klagenfurt basin, were most fortunate; plebiscites kept the region within Austria despite Yugoslav incursions while the Peace Conference was in session. Many of the villages were indeed Slovene, as also were some in Styria. This difference between the ethnic composition of towns and villages was common to much of eastern and central Europe.

Two months later Bulgaria was presented with her bill for having joined the Central Powers in 1915 and was forced to pay heavily, despite the influence of prominent British sympathizers. The Treaty of Neuilly (27 November 1919) ceded the whole of western Thrace to Greece, thereby cutting off Bulgaria from the Aegean Sea and the Mediterranean waters beyond. Two districts ceded to the Yugoslavs were relatively small, but Serbia retained the gains in Macedonia made in the Balkan Wars, which had already aroused deep resentment in Bulgaria. Romania, too, recovered the southern Dobruja, ceded after the Second Balkan War. Like the earlier treaties, Neuilly insisted that Bulgaria should pay reparations and restricted the army to 20,000 men. The largest minority in Bulgaria was Turkish, some ten per cent of the population – a proportion which has remained constant throughout most of the century.

The signing of the treaty with Hungary was delayed by the intrusion of Béla Kun's Soviet Republic. For four and a half months in 1919 a primitive experiment in a form of communism was imposed by Kun's regime in Budapest. Almost all the details of the Hungarian peace settlement had been agreed in Paris by the early summer of 1919, but none of the Powers wished to strengthen Kun's position by recognizing his government; there was, accordingly, no acknowledged authority to whom peace terms could be presented. Kun did not gain Bolshevik backing to sustain his Soviet. Rashly he attacked the Romanians along the Carpathian divide in July; by early August the Romanian counter-attack had reached Budapest, and Kun fled to Vienna and eventually Russia. So cruel had been the conduct of many of his henchmen that even those Hungarians who once thought Kun might successfully defy the Entente swiftly abandoned him. Support went to the last commander of the Austro-Hungarian fleet, Admiral Horthy, who organized a counter-revolutionary army at Szeged, and made a triumphant entry into Budapest in November. Four months later, on 1 March 1920, Horthy became Regent of the Hungarian Kingdom, an office he held for twenty-four years; but his arrival in power in November was accompanied by so many executions and by mob attacks, especially on Jews, that the Entente allies were at first as reluctant to accept his regime as they had been to recognize Kun. Only after elections were held in January 1920 was it accepted that stable government had returned to Budapest and that progress might be made on a peace treaty.

This long period of uncertainty enabled Hungary's neighbours to consolidate gains around the frontiers of the old kingdom. In many respects the treaty signed under considerable protest by Horthy's delegates at Trianon on 4 June 1920 merely confirmed the existing situation. Almost three-quarters of what had formed the Kingdom of Hungary from 1867 to 1918 was detached from the new Regent's realm. In acquiring the whole of Transylvania and part of the Banat (down to within fifty miles of Belgrade) Romania gained territories larger than the area left to Hungary. Czechoslovakia was confirmed in possession of the Slovak provinces (except for a small northern enclave, which went to Poland) and of Ruthenia. Yugoslavia absorbed Croatia–Slavonia and the rest of the Banat. The Yugoslavs would also have acquired Hungary's only port on the Adriatic, Fiume, had it not been seized on 12 September 1919 by Italian irregular troops led by Gabriele d'Annunzio, who for sixteen months defied every effort of the peacemakers to eject him; Italian possession of Fiume was recognized by the Yugoslavs in 1924, and three years later Mussolini allowed the Hungarians special rights in the port they had themselves created. The Treaty of Trianon also permitted most of Hungary's most Germanized western province to join Austria, as the 'Burgenland'; reparations were again imposed and army restrictions, no more than 35,000 men. Over the following twenty years the Trianon Treaty prompted a sustained campaign for frontier revision inside and outside Hungary which was even more vociferous than Germany's much publicized resentment of the Versailles terms.

The last of the five Peace Conference treaties was presented to the Sultan's delegates a week after the signing ceremony at the Trianon. Once again the terms were harsher than expected. The Turks had been resigned to the loss of all the Arab lands; they were shocked by the awards to Venizelos's Greece: a frontier in Europe advancing the Greek border to within twenty-five miles of Constantinople; eight islands in the Aegean; and Smyrna to be under Greek control but Ottoman sovereignty until 1925, when a plebiscite would decide if it was to remain Turkish or Greek. The treaty also ceded the islands of the Dodecanese and Rhodes to Italy, imposed demilitarization of the Dardanelles and the Bosporus, and placed the Straits under an international commission (of which Japan was a member). An independent Armenia was to be created, which would include Russia's Armenian provinces in the Caucasus and also the fortress of Erzerum and the port of Trebizond, though the exact boundaries were left to American arbitration (although President Wilson's hopes of a United States mandate had soon been dashed after his return to face the realities of isolationist sentiment). An army of 50,000 men was permitted and a coastal defence navy. The Ottoman plenipotentiaries signed the treaty at Sèvres on 10 August 1920 under protest – and with a near-certain conviction that the treaty would never be ratified.

For Sèvres achieved for the peacemakers what earlier treaties had narrowly avoided: the coming of a new war, even before signature. Marshal Foch had feared the worst when he saw the first draft of the terms in April. He warned the French Foreign Minister that to impose these terms on a reluctant Turkey the Allied powers would need an army of twenty-seven divisions, some 325,000 men, in and around Constantinople. On investigation there were found to be 8,000 British soldiers available to defend the city and the Straits. Kemal's growing nationalist forces around Ankara advanced down the Sea of Marmara as soon as the terms were known, meeting no opposition from troops loyal to the Sultan; the nationalist army was only halted by gunfire from Allied warships, which forced Kemal's men to pull back out of range. In June Greek troops already ashore in Smyrna began a campaign in Anatolia which was to continue for more than two years before Kemal's Nationalists exhausted the Greeks in a twenty-two-day battle along the River Sakarya, barely fifty miles fron Ankara. The Sèvres Treaty was destroyed in a succession of blows struck by Kemal between 26 August and 11 October 1922: the Greeks' line was broken; the invaders were forced back on Smyrna, which was left in flames on 13 September. Fighting with British troops seemed imminent at Chanak a fortnight later, but was avoided by the good sense of the commander on the spot, General Harington. All power thereafter rested with Kemal, who proclaimed the abolition of the sultanate on 1 November 1922 – almost exactly eight years after the Ottomans first entered the war as Germany's ally. Another twelve months elapsed before Kemal became President of a Turkish Republic.

During that period a new peace settlement was reached – through negotiation and not dictation. The Treaty of Lausanne of 24 July 1923 tore up Sèvres. The Turks recovered fire-gutted Smyrna (they called it Izmir), the islands of Imbros and Tenedos and the whole of eastern Thrace. They accepted, however, the continued demilitarization of the Straits and the loss of the Arab lands, although Deputies in Ankara's Grand National Assembly deplored the failure at Lausanne to secure the return of Mosul and the inclusion within French-mandated Syria of Alexandretta and the Gulf around the port. The worst losers by the Treaty of Lausanne were the Greek families forced to migrate from Turkish Anatolia to new settlements in their ethnic homeland, and also the Armenians and Kurds, of whose national hopes for self-determination nothing was put on paper.

The system of mandates, authorized by the League of Nations, was formalized for the Middle East at the San Remo Conference of 1920. As anticipated, the British received mandates for Palestine and Transjordan (treated together) and for Iraq. At the same time France received a similar mandate for Syria and Lebanon, from where the last British troops were withdrawn in November 1919. So long as Georges-Picot remained in Damascus Feisal made some attempt to co-operate with the French, but Picot was soon recalled to Paris and was succeeded by a military High Commissioner, General Gouraud, a staunch champion of French colonialism. At this point Feisal's loyal Arabs seem to have played into French hands, for on 10 March 1920 the Arabs proclaimed Feisal King of Syria and Palestine. This action induced Gouraud to mount a full-scale military operation, advancing from the coast on Damascus and, unlike Allenby, entering the city as an arrogant conqueror. He is said to have gone immediately to the tomb of Salah al-Din; 'We are back, Saladin! The Cross defeats the Crescent', Gouraud was heard to boast, exultantly.

Feisal's reign in Damascus thus ended ten weeks after it began. The British were in a quandary. They had no desire for an Arab to claim kingship in Palestine, where military rule continued for two years after the fighting ended, and where early in 1920 the first Arab riots against Jewish immigration threatened life and property in Jerusalem. But British officials continued to respect the Hashemite dynasty. At the Cairo Conference of March 1921 – attended *inter alia* by Churchill, Sir Herbet Samuel, Gertrude Bell and T. E. Lawrence – it was decided to offer the kingship of mandated Iraq to the deposed Feisal. At the same time an Emirate of Transjordan was created for Feisal's elder brother Abdullah – Kitchener's contact in that distant summer of 1914 when the first stirring of Arab revolt against the Ottomans was perceived in Cairo.

Both brothers were serving as British subsidized rulers by August 1921, Feisal having received by plebiscite a popular vote so overwhelming as to seem suspect to the cynical. About all these arrangements there was an air of probationary improvisation: Abdullah's first subsidy was guaranteed for only six months, optionally renewable. Yet seventy-seven years later his grandson, King Hussein, who was beside his grandfather when he was assassinated in 1951, still reigns in Amman, despite the chronic turbulence of the Arab world.

By 1921 peacemaking was virtually complete. The achievement fell far short of the Wilsonian ideals espoused aboard the ss *George Washington*. A genuine attempt was made to base the settlement on self-determination to a greater extent than after any previous war. But such was the complexity of the ethnic map in east-central Europe that, during the years 1920 to 1938, one person in five living in the lands between Germany and the Soviet Union remained a member of a national minority. The frontiers were so drawn that, between 1919 and 1991, the Yugoslav State comprised nine nationalities; in much maligned pre-1918 Historic Hungary there were seven nationalities. Territorially the most spectacular beneficiaries of the peacemaking in Paris were the governments in Warsaw, Prague, Bucharest and Belgrade. Yet it is often forgotten that the peace treaties allowed both the French colonial empire and the British Empire – 'Imperial Commonwealth' was a term first used in 1917 – to attain their fullest extent. Briefly in 1920–21 it would have been possible to travel overland in a great arc from Capetown to Singapore by way of Cairo and Baghdad, either through lands directly under George V's sovereignty, or held as British mandates, or under British protection (Egypt), or in a special treaty relationship (Persia, Siam). Asquith's Liberal government in 1914 had not gone to war for territorial aggrandizement overseas, but the victorious campaigns in the Middle East and Africa inevitably brought to Asquith's successor responsibilities of imperial trusteeship which he was fully prepared to accept.

But, despite the territorial changes in Europe and the wider world, by 1920–1 the peoples of all the countries at war and their governments had begun to see sombrely the terrible cost of the victory which in 1918 the Allies had celebrated. Reports returned to Paris showed that across northern and eastern France eight thousand square miles of good farmland and nearly two thousand square miles of forest were laid waste; one and a half thousand schools were wrecked, along with twelve hundred churches or other places of worship. The greatest British material losses had been in merchant shipping, with nearly 8 million tons sunk; the second largest sufferer from torpedoes and mines being Norway, careful to cherish her neutrality throughout the war. But it was the cost in human life that marked off the First World War from its predecessors. In the Napoleonic Wars the military loss of life had stood at an average of ten deaths in each hour that the conflict lasted; in the Crimean War that figure had risen to forty-four an hour, dropping to thirty-six for the Franco-Prussian War but ominously rising to slightly over eighty an hour in 1912–13 for the Balkan Wars. During what survivors were by 1920 calling 'the Great War', from all the belligerent nations, 'Allied' and 'enemy' combined, 230 soldiers, airmen or seamen perished for each hour of the four and a quarter years it continued.

The terrible nature of the fighting, and in particular the concentrated power of artillery barrages, established for this conflict a gruesome record. In no previous war had it become necessary to bury so many broken remains of those killed in battle unidentified, nor to list so many casualties as 'place of burial unknown'. As the second anniversary of the Armistice approached it was suggested that one of these shattered bodies should be brought home to Britain for burial in a national shrine. The earliest public proposal seems to have come from J. B. Wilson, the news editor of the *Daily Express*, who in a leader on 16 September wrote, 'Shall an unnamed British hero be brought from a battlefield in France and buried beneath the Cenotaph in Whitehall?' The Revd David Railton, an Army chaplain who had become Vicar of Holy Trinity, Margate, thought Westminster Abbey more appropriate. The idea was taken up by Sir Fabian Ware of the War Graves Commission and by Dean Ryle of Westminster who, in early October, contacted Buckingham Palace. King George V was, at first, doubtful; might not a funeral now seem belated and 'reopen the war wound which time is gradually healing', he wondered? But the Prime Minister and the CIGS welcomed the proposal. The coming Armistice Day seemed appropriate, because on that morning the King would unveil, a few hundred yards from Westminster Abbey, the permanent Cenotaph in Whitehall, designed by Sir Edwin Lutyens.

On 10 November 1920, a grey and misty Wednesday, a modern destroyer approached a Dover Harbour much changed since Kitchener's non-departure on the eve of the war. HMS *Verdun* would have been an unlikely name for a warship then; but now it was selected to honour the great sacrifices made in 1916 by Britain's French ally. Aboard the destroyer in a coffin made from royal oak from Hampton Court was the body chosen by a blindfolded officer from five unknowns selected from Britain's war cemeteries in Flanders and France. Marshal

Foch had stood at the salute as the coffin was handed over by a French cavalry escort to the Royal Navy at Boulogne. But though the broken body came from the Western Front, it represented the sacrifice of lost lives in every land campaign and at sea and in the skies. Six other destroyers escorted the *Verdun*. A field marshal's salute of nineteen guns was fired from Dover Castle. Six officers, chosen from the Royal Navy, Royal Marines, the Army and the Royal Air Force, bore the coffin along the quayside of Dover's Admiralty Pier to a train which would carry it to London.

Next morning, with a steel helmet and a crusader's sword on the coffin, the Unknown Warrior was brought on a gun carriage into Whitehall, soon after the symbolic eleventh hour. The cortège paused at the Cenotaph; King George V placed a wreath on the coffin, with assistance from Earl Haig. Then, between a double line of holders of the Victoria Cross, the coffin was carried into Westminster Abbey for a short service. The practice of having a symbolic burial of this nature became general; France's Unknown Soldier was interred beneath the Arc de Triomphe on the same day. Each nation accepted the need to honour collectively the sacrifice of the ordinary warrior, somebody's son who had been willing to fulfil his duty with no thought of public recognition.

Less than twenty years later Europe was at war once again. The Second World War brought lasting renown to Churchill but discredited three other survivors: Pétain, Weygand and Lloyd George were all, in different ways and to a different degree, regarded as defeatists. Pietro Badoglio, the chief Allied signatory of the Padua Armistice with Austria–Hungary, took a leading part in the downfall of Mussolini in 1943 and signed Italy's unconditional surrender to the Allies later that same year. But few of the leading soldiers from the First World War were still active when the Second broke out. Field Marshal Earl Haig had died in 1928, spending much of the last ten years of his life helping ex-servicemen in the British Legion. Viscount Allenby of Megiddo survived until May 1936, a year after T. E. Lawrence was killed riding his motorcycle. Marshal Foch died in 1929; he became the only French soldier honoured by a statue in London, erected in 1930 in Grosvenor Gardens, close to Victoria Station. General Sarrail, frustrated in his hopes of making Greece a French commercial satrapy, again provoked controversy in 1925 when he served as High Commissioner in Syria and stamped out a Druse revolt with sustained severity; he died in 1929, a few days after Marshal Foch. Franchet d'Esperey, who received his Marshal's baton in 1921, was seriously injured in a motorcar accident in

Morocco in 1933, but lived on for another nine years, for much of them confined to a wheelchair. He settled in the unoccupied zone of France in 1940. On his desk in these last years Franchet placed a loaded revolver, which he said he would fire at any German who crossed the threshold of his study. None came near him. General Milne became CIGS for seven years, was promoted Field Marshal and, on retirement from active duty in 1933, was raised to the peerage. By a curious freak of history his only son was taken prisoner by the Germans in Greece in the Second World War, and at one time found himself detained in his father's old headquarters in Salonika. The Field Marshal died in March 1948, having as Patron of the Salonika Reunion Association interested himself in his later years in the well-being of the men who fought under him.

Eighty years after the final victory of 1918 the First World War seems almost as remote as the battles of the Crimea. The last Australian Gallipoli veteran died in the closing months of 1997, to be followed within weeks by the last New Zealander. Yet survivors remain. In *The Times* of 16 April 1998 Alan Hamilton described how one veteran, Henry Wells of Bournemouth, who had been gassed near Arras at the age of eighteen, was able to return to the old battlefield for the funeral service and interment in Monchy-le-Preux military cemetery of two privates of the 13th Battalion, Royal Fusiliers, killed on 11 April 1917. Private King and Private Anderson had been buried in an unmarked shallow grave; their bodies, and the unidentifiable remains of twenty-five of their comrades, were discovered by building contractors laying the foundations for a new housing estate. They were accorded the rites of Christian burial eighty-one years after the battle which cost them their lives. For how much longer will the bugle call of the Last Post sound out across newly dug graves in the slaughter fields of the Western Front?

ALTERNATIVE
PLACE NAMES

Abbreviations used: Alb Albanian; Ar Arabic; B Bulgarian; Cz Czech or Slovak; Ger German; Gk Greek, or from Greek; H Hungarian; It Italian; P Polish; Ro Romanian; Rus Russian; T Turkish; S-C Serbo-Croat; Sl Slovene; U Ukrainian.

If no abbreviation is given the name is traditional and of ancient origin.

Adrianople (Gk)	Edirne (T)		
Aleppo	Halab (Ar)		
Alexandretta (Gk)	Iskanderun (T)	Isakandaroon (Ar)	
Ankara (T)	Angora (Gk)		
Bratislava (Cz)	Pressburg (Ger)	Pozsony (H)	
Caporetto (It)	Karfreit (Ger)	Kobarid (Sl)	
Cattaro (It)	Kotor (S-C)		
Chanak (Gk)	Çanakkale (T)		
Constantinople (Gk)	Istanbul (T)		
Corfu (It)	Kerkyra (Gk)		
Damascus	Dimashq (Ar)		
Danzig (Ger)	Gdansk (P)		
Dedeagach (T)	Alexandroupolis (Gk)		
Dubrovnik (S-C)	Ragusa (It)		
Fiume (It)	Rijeka (S-C)		
Gallipoli (Gk)	Gelibolu (T)		
Gorizia (It)	Görz (Ger)	Goriska (Sl)	
Lemberg (Ger)	Lwow (P)	Lvov (Rus)	Lviv (U)
Ljubljana (Sl)	Laibach (Ger)		
Louvain (French)	Leuven (Flemish)		
Monastir (T)	Bitola (S-C)		
Mudros (Gk)	Moudoros (T)		
Novi Sad (S-C)	Ujvidek (H)	Neusatz (Ger)	

Pola (It)	Pula (S-C)	Pulj (Sl)
Posen (Ger)	Poznan (P)	
Ruse (B)	Ruschuk (T)	
Salonika	Thessaloniki (Gk)	
Serres (T)	Serrai (Gk)	
Skopje (S-C)	Üsküb (T)	
Smyrna (Gk)	Izmir (T)	
Split (S-C)	Spalato (It)	
Struma (T)	Strimon (Gk)	
Tarvisio (It)	Tarvis (Ger)	Trbiz (Sl)
Temesvar (H)	Timisoara (Ro)	
Tenedos (Gk)	Bozcaada (T)	
Teschen (Ger)	Tesin (Cz)	Ciesyjn (P)
Tolmino (It)	Tolmein (Ger)	Tolmina (Sl)
Valona (It)	Vlore (Alb)	
Vardar (T)	Axios (Gk)	
Ypres (from French)	Ieser (Flemish)	
Yukyeri (T)	Besika Bay	
Zagreb (S-C)	Agram (Ger)	

NOTES AND SOURCES

Full details of publication of books and periodicals will be found in the Select Bibliography. Abbreviations used in the Notes: FO, Foreign Office papers in the Public Record Office; MEC, Middle East Centre, St Antony's College, Oxford; PRO CAB, Cabinet Papers in the Public Record Office; WO, War Office Papers in the Public Record Office.

PROLOGUE: DOVER, 3 AUGUST 1914
Details of Bank Holiday activities in 1914 are from G. H. Cassar, *Kitchener, Architect of Victory*, pp. 172–7; *The Times*, 3, 4 and 5 August 1914; M. Rudkin, *Inside Dover, 1914–1918*, pp. 26–37; personal family reminiscence. Kitchener not to go back to Egypt: M. Gilbert, *Churchill*, vol. 3, p. 12. For the Kitchener–Abdullah contacts see J. Wilson, *Lawrence of Arabia*, p. 165. Grey's speech of 4 August: Hansard, 5th ser., vol. 65, pp. 1809–27; Asquith's attitude: M. and E. Brock (eds), *H. H. Asquith, Letters to Venetia Stanley*, pp. 148–9 and 152–3; Grey on Kitchener: Grey, *Twenty Five Years*, vol. 2, pp. 68–9. On pre-war Russian arrest of Wavell: *The Times*, 18, 20 October 1913. On Kitchener's views in 1914 see Cassar, op. cit., p. 192–270, G. H. Cassar's contribution to H. Cecil and P. Liddle (eds), *Facing Armageddon*, pp. 37–48, and D. French, *British Strategy and War Aims, 1914–1916*, pp. 20, 24.

1: WIDENING THE WAR
Calculations on length of war: 'not less than six months', General Staff note of 12 March 1912, cited from PRO CAB 16/18B by French, *British Strategy*, p. 115; Grey's comment, Grey, *Twenty Five Years*, vol. 2, p. 68. Defeat of Germany prime task: FO 371/2171/39446, Grey to Buchanan, 13 August 1914, reporting Nicolson–Benckendorff conversation. Kaiser's directive to Liman von Sanders: F. Fischer, *War of Illusions*, pp. 334–5. Djemal in France 1914: A. Palmer, *Decline and Fall of the Ottoman Empire*, pp. 222–3 citing French diplomatic documents. Churchill and Enver: Gilbert, *Churchill*, vol. 3, p. 196; Turkish–Germany treaty, Palmer, op. cit., p. 224. Coming of war with Turkey: ibid., pp.

225–6; Brock (eds), *Asquith Letters*, p. 309. The Kitchener–Hashemite exchanges are cited by J. Wilson in his *Lawrence of Arabia*, p. 165 and pp. 1002–3, which provides a more convincing analysis than E. Kedourie's *In the Anglo-Arab Labyrinth*, pp. 17–20, the main source for the lengthy survey by D. Fromkin in chapter 10 of his *A Peace to End all Peace*. For conditions in Egypt see P. J. Vatikiotis, *History of Modern Egypt*, pp. 252–3. Maxwell's 'marvellous carelessness': M. R. Lawrence (ed.), *The Home Letters of T. E. Lawrence and his Brothers*, p. 302, letter home of 12 February 1915. Kitchener and India Office: see French, op. cit., p. 48, including letter to Duff of 24 September 1914 cited from Mesopotamian Commission papers. Origins of Mesopotamia campaign: F. J. Moberly, *Campaign in Mesopotamia*, vol. 1, pp. 89–106; B. C. Busch, *Britain, India and the Arabs, 1914–1921*, pp. 3–10. Convoys of troops to Egypt and Europe: P. G. Halpern, *Naval History of World War I*, p. 86. 'No anxiety about Egypt': Gilbert, *Churchill*, vol. 3, *Companion*, p. 280. Commission in Aleppo: Lawrence to Mrs Fontana (wife of ex-consul at Aleppo), 4 December 1914, D. Garnett (ed.), *Letters of T. E. Lawrence*, p. 189. Germany running short of men: French, op. cit., p. 65. Kitchener and Alexandretta: ibid., p. 49; Gilbert, *Churchill*, vol. 3, p. 222, quoting Churchill's testimony to the Dardanelles Commission in 1916. Hankey's 'Boxing Day Memorandum': PRO CAB 37/122/194, dated 28 December 1914, printed in M. Hankey, *Supreme Command*, vol. 1, pp. 244–50; Gilbert, *Churchill*, vol. 3, *Companion*, pp. 337–43 and see also S. Roskill, *Hankey: Man of Secrets*, vol. 1, pp. 149–50. Lloyd George Memorandum, 1 January 1915, PRO CAB 42/1/8, extensively printed in D. Lloyd George, *War Memoirs*, vol. 1, pp. 219–24, with 'knocking the props' reference on p. 222. Gilbert, *Churchill*, vol. 3, *Companion*, pp. 350–6 also prints the Memorandum (version dated 31 December), as well as Churchill's memorandum of same date, ibid., pp. 347–9. Churchill's 'volatile mind' and 'heroic adventure': Asquith to Venetia Stanley, 5 December 1914, Brock, p. 327. Cigar butt strategy: A. J. P. Taylor, *The First World War*, p. 72. Balfour's criticisms: his letter to Hankey, 2 January 1915, Gilbert, *Churchill*, vol. 3, *Companion*, pp. 363–4. Alternative objectives: Brock, p. 360. Gilbert's *Churchill*, vol. 3, *Companion*, has extracts from the minutes of War Council meetings of 7 and 8 January (pp. 384–90 and pp. 391–6), Carden's plan telegraphed on 11 January 1915 (pp. 405–6) and the extracts from the minutes of the important War Council meeting on 13 January (pp. 407–11). See also Hankey, op. cit., vol. 1, pp. 265–7; Roskill, p. 153 and R. Rhodes James, *Gallipoli*, pp. 30–4. For Kress and the Suez Canal: G. Macmunn and C. Falls, *Egypt and Palestine*, vol. 1, pp. 28–9, 34–6, 40–3, 48–49; U. Trumpener, *Germany and the Ottoman Empire*, pp. 111–12; Halpern, p. 108; J. L. Wallach, *Anatomie einer Militärhilfe*, pp. 133–5; and F. Kress von Kressenstein, *Mit den Türken zum Suezkanal*, especially pp. 140–52. For naval bombardment: Rhodes James, pp. 39–70; Gilbert, *Churchill*, vol. 3, pp. 351–80. For American ambassador and panic reaction in Constantinople: H. Morgenthau, *Secrets of the Bosphorus*, pp. 100–20; A. Moorehead, *Gallipoli*, p. 59. Peace almost in sight: Violet Bonham Carter, *Winston Churchill As I Knew Him*, p. 369. Hankey Memorandum 'After the Dardanelles': printed in full in Gilbert, *Churchill*, vol. 3, *Companion*, pp. 592–602, with Minutes of War Council discussion of 3 March 1915, ibid., pp. 610–18; Roskill, pp. 163–4. Admiralty and the Danube 1914–15: C. Fryer, *Royal Navy on the Danube*, pp. 21–90; Halpern, pp. 261–74; for the Amery mission, J. Barnes and D. Nicholson (eds), *Leo Amery Diaries*, vol. 1, pp. 112–13. Bribing the Turks at Dedeagach: Roskill, pp. 159–60; fullest details, C. R. G. Allen, 'A Ghost from Gallipoli', in RUSI *Journal*, vol. 108, no. 630, pp. 136–9. Minutes of War Council of 19 March 1915: PRO CAB 42/2/14, partly printed in Gilbert, *Churchill*, vol. 3, *Companion*, pp. 710–16; for the proleptic carving up of the Ottoman Empire see also Gilbert, *Churchill*, vol. 3, p. 355 and for Harcourt and possible American mandate, p. 37. The finest historical account of the Gallipoli landing is Rhodes James, pp. 101–31. Kitchener and danger of rising in Moslem world: Gilbert, *Churchill*, vol. 3, p. 432.

2: PARIS, ATHENS, ROME

Coming of war in France: E. L. Spears, *Liaison 1914*, pp. 3–29, with Joffre's background; also A. Horne, *The Price of Glory*, pp. 27–31. Franchet d'Esperey described his pre-war journeys in an introduction to P. Larcher, *Le Grande Guerre dans les Balkans*, a book which includes part of Franchet's November memorandum as an appendix. For the fate of the plan see P. Azan, *Franchet d'Esperey*, pp. 139–40. For French financial interests in the Ottoman Empire see the chapter by L. Bruce Fenton in M. Kent (ed.), *The Great Powers and the End of the Ottoman Empire*, pp. 141–69 and, in great detail, J. Thobie, *Intérêts et impérialisme français dans l'Empire Ottoman, 1895–1914*. On Briand: D. Dutton, 'The Balkan Campaign and French war aims in the Great War' in *English Historical Review*, vol. 94, no. 370, pp. 100–2. For Poincaré and the consultation with Joffre: R. Poincaré, *Au service de la France*, vol. 6, pp. 7–9; Azan, p. 143. Millerand and Augagneur in London: Brock (eds), *Asquith Letters*, p. 391; French, *British Strategy and War Aims*, pp. 71–3; G. H. Cassar, *The French and the Dardanelles*, pp. 34–45 and 51–60. Lloyd George's trip to Paris: J. Grigg, *Lloyd George: From Peace to War*, pp. 204–6; A. G. Lennox (ed.), *The Diary of Lord Bertie*, pp. 107–9; Brock, p. 393. Delcassé's visit to London and War Council of 9 February: Poincaré, vol. 6, p. 58; Gilbert, *Churchill*, vol. 3, pp. 278, 281–2. Greek affairs, 1914–15: A. Palmer, *Gardeners of Salonika*, pp. 18–19; E. S. Forster, *A Short History of Modern Greece*, pp. 73–9; J. Mavrogordato, *Modern Greece*, pp. 99–101; G. B. Leon, *Greece and the Great Powers*, pp. 108–16. On

Russia, the Allies and Constantinople in March 1915: chapter on 'Russia and the Straits' by M. G. Eckstein in F. H. Hinsley (ed.), *British Foreign Policy under Sir Edward Grey*, especially pp. 433–4; E. David (ed.), *Inside Asquith's Cabinet: From the Diaries of Charles Hobhouse*, pp. 225–7; A. Pingaud, *Histoire diplomatique de la France*, vol. 1, pp. 241–56; C. A. Macartney and A. W. Palmer, *Independent Eastern Europe*, pp. 49–50. On the Treaty of London, 1915: ibid., pp. 50–1; Hinsley, p. 421. Entry of Italy into the war and early campaigning: A. Salandra, *Italy and the Great War*, pp. 335–40; J. E. Edmonds and H. R. Davies, *Military Operations, Italy 1915–1919*, pp. 11, 27–31. Dardanelles and Gallipoli reinforcements in summer of 1915: Rhodes James, *Gallipoli*, pp. 216–18; Churchill speech of 5 June, Gilbert, op. cit., pp. 488–91; Hankey, *Supreme Command*, vol. 1, pp. 338–45 can be supplemented by his diary entries in Roskill, *Hankey*, pp. 185–91, with Kitchener's explanations of 19 July on p. 189; Cassar, *Kitchener*, pp. 366–81. Hankey at the Dardanelles: Roskill, pp. 191–204 (with telegram 'surprise attack definitely failed', p. 198); Hankey, op. cit., vol. 1, pp. 376–404. Appointment of Sarrail: A. Palmer, op. cit., pp. 29–30; J. K. Tanenbaum, *General Maurice Sarrail, 1856–1929*, pp. 52–64; J. C. King, *Generals and Politicians*, pp. 36–79. Calais Conference of September 1915: Hankey, op. cit., vol. 1, p. 411, including 'bit of a poseur' remark and Kitchener's impression; Roskill, p. 216; conference note of 11 September 1915, PRO CAB 28/1; Cassar, *The French and the Dardanelles*, pp. 100–5. Germany and Bulgaria: Macartney and Palmer, op. cit., p. 57; Pingaud, vol. 2, pp. 56–7; K. Robbins, 'British diplomacy and Bulgaria, 1914–1915' in *Slavonic and East European Review*, vol. 49, no. 117, pp. 579–83. Poincaré and Franchet, June 1915: Azan, p. 144. Britain, Serbia and Greece in September 1915: Leon, pp. 207–24; Hankey, op. cit., vol. 1, pp. 418–22; Roskill, pp. 220–22. C. Falls, *Military Operations, Macedonia*, vol. 1, chs 2 and 3; arrival of British troops at Salonika: ibid.; Palmer, op. cit., pp. 9–14.

3: 'IF WE LOSE EGYPT, WE LOSE THE WAR'

Kitchener's visit to the Dardanelles: Cassar, *Kitchener*, pp. 420–2; Rhodes James, *Gallipoli*, pp. 328–32; Hankey, *Supreme Command*, vol. 2, pp. 449–50. Ayas Bay (Alexandretta) project: Rhodes James, loc. cit.; Cassar, *The French and the Dardanelles*, pp. 212–16' G. MacMunn and C. Falls, *Military Operations, Egypt and Palestine*, vol. 1, pp. 76–85; material from French archives cited by J. Wilson, *Lawrence of Arabia*, p. 1017. Kitchener, Egypt and Poincaré: Cassar, *Kitchener*, p. 429; Poincaré, *Au Service de la France*, vol. 7, p. 289. Kitchener's return to London: Violet Bonham Carter, *Winston Churchill As I Knew Him*, p. 431; Kitchener and War Committee of 1 December: PRO CAB 42/6/1, Minutes of committee meeting, with discussions resumed on 2 December PRO CAB 42/6/2. Calais Conference: PRO CAB 37/139/15, Notes on conference,

4 December 1915; D. Dutton, 'The Calais Conference of December 1915' in *Historical Journal*, vol. 21, no. 1, pp. 143–53; Hankey, op. cit., vol. 2, pp. 453–4; Falls, *Macedonia*, p. 63. Chantilly Conference: PRO CAB 28/1, Formal report, 6–8 December 1915; Falls, op. cit., pp. 49–50; French, *British Strategy and War Aims*, p. 164. Paris talks of Grey, Kitchener, Briand and Galliéni, reported PRO CAB 37/139/24. On all three conferences, Palmer, *Gardeners*, pp. 48–9. Evacuation of Gallipoli: Rhodes James, pp. 333–47. The fullest treatment of the Mesopotamian campaign in its successive stages is A. J. Barker's *The Neglected War: Mesopotamia 1914–1918*, supplementing the detailed, discreet official history, F. J. Moberly, *Campaign in Mesopotamia 1914–1918*; General Moberly's more critical *Operations in Persia* was written and printed in 1928 but remained confidential until 1987. See also French, op. cit., pp. 144–6; M. Fitzherbert, *The Man who was Greenmantle*, pp. 169–81; J. Wilson, pp. 253–76, with Kitchener's bribery offer discussed on p. 270. On the river gunboats, Halpern, *Naval History of World War I*, pp. 126–30. 'Air black with flies': Aubrey Herbert's diary for 28 April, cited J. Wilson, p. 272. The most moving narrative account of events in Kut is R. Braddon, *The Siege*. Quotation saluting Townshend and his heroic band: *Sunday Times*, 30 April 1916, p. 8. Robertson as CIGS, and reform of the command structure: French, op. cit., pp. 160–3. Supply problems when Salonika Army was dependent on Egypt as a base: Falls, *Macedonia*, pp. 101–2. For the Paris Conference of 27–8 March 1916: report of conclusions to the Cabinet, PRO CAB 28/1; Falls, *Macedonia*, p. 110; Ministère de la Guerre, *Les Armées françaises*, vol. 7(i), pp. 417–28. Robertson on mingling of finance and politics in French attitude: letter to Murray, 5 April 1916, cited by Dutton, 'Balkan Campaign and French War Aims', loc. cit., p. 98; for Kitchener's views, ibid., pp. 99–100, and R. Blake (ed.), *The Private Papers of Douglas Haig*, p. 137. Briand and Marie Bonaparte: C. Bertin, *Marie Bonaparte*, pp. 122–4. For the McMahon–Hussein correspondence: texts as given in British government bluebook *Correspondence between Sir Henry McMahon . . . and the Sherif Hussein* (Cmd 5957) published in 1939; the judicious assessment by Marian Kent in F. H. Hinsley (ed.), *British Foreign Policy under Sir Edward Grey*, pp. 444–7; Fromkin, *A Peace to End All Peace*, pp. 182–6, who makes extensive use of the numerous studies by Elie Kedourie; J. Nevakivi, *Britain, France and the Arab Middle East, 1914–1920*, pp. 25–40. For Faruqi, Fromkin, pp. 176–80 and J. Wilson, pp. 205–9, 222–3, 227–9. Sykes–Picot Agreement: E. L. Woodward and R. Butler (eds), *Documents on British Foreign Policy 1919–1939*, Series 1, vol. 4, pp. 241–51; M. Kent's contribution to Hinsley, pp. 447–5; E. Kedourie, *England and the Middle East*, pp. 4–5, 65–5, 107–13. See also R. Adelson, *Mark Sykes*, pp. 196–200. On Kitchener's role J. Nevakivi, 'Kitchener and the Partition of the Ottoman Empire', in K. Bourne and D. C. Watt (eds), *Studies in International History*. For Briand and Picot:

C. M. Andrew and A. S. Kanya-Forstner, 'French Colonial War Aims, 1914–1918' in *The Historical Journal*, vol. 17, no. 1, pp. 84–5. Grey's belief that Hussein's proposed uprising was hypothetical: Minutes of War Committee, 23 March 1916, PRO CAB 42/11. Chapter 28 of Fromkin's *A Peace To End All Peace* is a good account of the start of the Revolt. For Kitchener's death and the wreck of the *Hampshire*, Cassar, *Kitchener, Architect of Victory*, p. 476–80. Rumour of Kitchener's survival 'ran like wildfire': *Daily Mirror*, 7 June 1916, p. 5. 'Kitchener can never die': Sykes as reported by Hankey, op. cit., vol. 2, p. 509.

4: ORGIES OF SLAUGHTER

Background to the Somme: French, *British Strategy and War Aims*, pp. 200–1, 204; Hankey, *Supreme Command*, pp. 510–16; M. Middlebrook, *The First Day on the Somme*; B. Liddell Hart *History of the First World War*, p. 303. 'Orgy of slaughter': Hankey diary entry for 2 May 1916 in Roskill, *Hankey*, p. 266. Lloyd George and Boxing Day Memorandum: Hankey diary, 3 July 1916, ibid., p. 286. Brusilov's offensive and Romania: G. E. Torrey, 'Rumania and the belligerents 1914–1916' in *Journal of Contemporary History*, vol. 1, no. 3, pp. 187–8. For the situation in Macedonia in the summer of 1916: Palmer, *Gardeners*, pp. 72–3. Exchanges between Milne and the CIGS in June and July: G. Nicol, *Uncle George: Field Marshal Lord Milne*, pp. 93, 103–4; with Milne's first assessment of Sarrail on 20 July, ibid., pp. 88–9. For Sarrail and Briand in 1916: D. Dutton, 'The Balkan Campaign . . .' in *English Historical Review*, vol. 94, no. 370, pp. 103–5. The Bulgarian offensive: D. Nedeff, *Les Opérations en Macedonie*, p. 45–83. The account of the storming of the Kajmakcalan and the advance to Monastir is based on *Les Armées françaises*, vol. 8 (ii), pp. 1–327 and the annexes 1 and 2 which include the directives for, and reports from, the Serbian army. The British attacks around Machukovo and on the Struma Front are covered by Falls, *Macedonia*, vol. 1, chs 8 and 9. See also, for the Allied offensive as a whole, Palmer, op. cit., pp. 80–92. A German account, highly critical of the Bulgarians, is in G. Strutz, *Herbstschlacht in Mazedonien*. For German reaction to Romanian entry into the war: M. Kitchen, *The Silent Dictatorship*, p. 40; for the impact of Sarrail's offensive on German GHQ Reichskriegsministerium, *Der Weltkrieg*, vol. 9, pp. 195–6 and pp. 345–6; the fullest account of the Romanian campaign is in E. Kabitsch, *Die Rumanienkriege*, but see also N. Stone, *The Eastern Front*, ch. 12. The Milne and Robertson exchanges of November 1916 are in Nicol, pp. 108–10. Sarrail, Zymbrakakis and Salonika's revolution: Falls, op. cit., vol. 1, pp. 208–9 and Sarrial's own version in ch. 12 of his memoirs, *Mon Commandement en Orient*. Dudden's diary consists of a typescript with attractive drawings and watercolours and is in the Imperial War Museum Library; the reference to the excitement of the revolution is on p. 11. Events in Athens in August and September and

Venizelos' flight from the city: Compton Mackenzie, *Greek Memories*, pp. 230–70 and 278–9; and D. Alastos, *Venizelos*, pp. 171–2. Mackenzie, op. cit., pp. 376–408 vividly describes the tragic misunderstandings in Athens on 1–2 December 1916; see also Palmer, op. cit., pp. 105–8, and Falls, op. cit., vol. 1, pp. 225–30.

5: A VICTORY WHILE YOU WAIT

For the emergence of a unified central war command among the Central Powers see Kitchen, *The Silent Dictatorship*, and J. Wheeler-Bennett, *Hindenburg*, p. 82. There are many works on the supersession of Asquith by Lloyd George, but see especially: Grigg, *Lloyd George*, pp. 435–74; R. Jenkins, *Asquith*, pp. 474–519 (paperback edition); Hankey, *Supreme Command*, vol. 2, pp. 553–70; Roskill, *Hankey*, vol. 1, pp. 307–33. For events in France: D. Dutton, 'The Fall of General Joffre in *Journal of Strategic Studies*, vol. 1, no. 3, pp. 338–51; G. Suarez, *Briand*, vol. 4, ch. 3; G. Bonnefous, *Histoire Politique de la 3ème République*, vol. 2, pp. 213–21. B. Bond (ed.), *Fallen Stars*, pp. 52–63 provides an important reassessment of 'Robert Nivelle and the French Spring Offensive, 1917' by A. Clayton. Nivelle's favourable impression on Cabinet: Hankey diary 15 January 1917, Roskill, p. 361. 'A victory while you wait', Repington, *First World War*, cited by D. French, *The Strategy of the Lloyd George Coalition*, p. 40. Lloyd George's first prime ministerial speech: Grigg, p. 502. 'Were we celebrating a glorious victory?': V. Brittain, *Testament of Youth*, p. 271. For Maude's campaign in Mesopotamia see Barker, *The Neglected War*, especially pp. 350–77. Major Crowdy's description of the weariness of his men on entering Baghdad is on p. 60 of his letterbook in MEC DS 461; Barker, p. 377 gives a more traditional account of the entry of British troops. For the reactions of the Prime Minister and of Hindenburg see Lloyd George, *War Memoirs*, vol. 2, pp. 1454–5. Lloyd George's doubts over defeating the Germans in France in 1917: French, op. cit., pp. 51–2. On the Rome Conference: Roskill, pp. 350–2; Lloyd George's account, vol. 2, pp. 838–50; Sarrail's, *Mon Commandement*, pp. 214–17; the CIGS's, W. Robertson, *Soldiers and Statesmen*, vol. 2, pp. 135–7 and the biography of Robertson by Victor Bonham Carter, *Soldier True*, pp. 200–3. Milne's rueful comments are in Nicol, pp. 118–20. See also; Falls, *Macedonia*, vol. 1, pp. 253–5; *Les Armées françaises*, vol. 8 (ii), pp. 377–80 and annexes 1441 and 1442; and the conference notes printed in J. Edmonds and H. R. Davies, *Military Operations, Italy*, pp. 25–6. The Vardar Blizzards: the reminiscences of B. Livermore, *Long 'Un – A Damn Bad Soldier*, pp. 71–4 based on his own diary and citing the diary of Colonel Warde-Aldham from W. R. Elliot's history of the Second Battalion of the 20th London Regiment. Lloyd George's support for Nivelle's plan: French, op. cit., pp. 54–6; D. R. Woodward, *Lloyd George and the Generals*, pp. 146–7. Calais Conference of 26–7 February 1917 and its effects

on Sarrail: *Les Armées françaises*, vol. 8 (ii), p. 397 and report printed as annex no.
1585; E. L. Spears, *Prelude to Victory*, p. 157; Robertson, vol. 2, pp. 136–7;
Victor Bonham Carter, pp. 212–18; Sarrail, pp. 402–3; Larcher, *La grande
Guerre dans les Balkans*, p. 194; Roskill, pp. 362–5. On effects of German
submarine warfare see Halpern, *Naval History*, pp. 335–43, with figures for
April 1917 cited from p. 341. Imperial War Cabinet in 1917: Hankey, op. cit.,
vol. 2, pp. 526–7; Barnes and Nicholson (eds), *Leo Amery Diaries*, vol. 1, pp.
146–8 ('platform bunkum', p. 146). Milner mission to Russia: E. E. Wrench,
Alfred, Lord Milner, pp. 322–6; French, op. cit., pp. 57–8. Press reports of first
Russian revolution: *Manchester Guardian*, 16 March 1917, p. 4 (with German
retreat in France, p. 5); French press, D. R. Watson, *Georges Clemenceau*, p. 259
and footnote. Hindenburg Line retreat: E. Ludendorff, *War Memoirs*, vol. 1,
pp. 305–8; C. Falls, *Military Operations, France and Belgium, 1917*, pp. 87–9. For
Nivelle's offensive see Clayton's contribution to Bond, cited above: Spears, op.
cit., pp. 333–80; Blake (ed.), *Private Papers of Douglas Haig*, pp. 209–18. Fall of
Lyautey and the political crisis in France: Watson, pp. 258–62. On Allenby at
Arras: L. James, *Imperial Warrior*, pp. 92–108; A. P. Wavell, *Allenby*, pp. 171–
82; the British contribution is considered in the context of Nivelle's general
plan by Liddell Hart, *First World War*, pp. 407–17. Extracts from the memoirs
of French soldiers in R. Thoumin, *The First World War: History in the Making*,
pp. 383–7 and 389–92 give a good impression of Nivelle's attack. Painlevé
downhearted; Hankey diary, 18 April 1917 in Roskill, p. 377. St Jean-de-
Maurienne conference: ibid., pp. 377–8; Hankey, op. cit., vol. 2, pp. 633–4;
French, op. cit., pp. 107–8. Robertson's memorandum urging withdrawal from
Salonika: PRO CAB 224/9 of 2 April 1917. Murray and the first two battles of
Gaza: A. P. Wavell, *The Palestine Campaign*, pp. 80–101; a good brief account is
in C. Cruttwell, *A History of the Great War*, pp. 355–8. British night attack
around Lake Doiran: Falls, *Macedonia*, vol. 1, pp. 302–16, with operational
order as Appendix 7; Bulgarian version in Nedeff *Les Opérations en Macedonie*,
pp. 108–18. For the combined Allied spring offensive in April and May in
Macedonia see Palmer, *Gardeners*, pp. 120–31. The fullest treatment of the
French mutinies may be found in the two works of G. Pedroncini, his narrative
of events, *Les Mutineries de 1917* and the collection of primary sources in his *Les
Mutineries des Armées Françaises*. Pétain and waiting for the Americans: R.
Griffiths, *Marshal Pétain*, pp. 48–9.

6: ASSOCIATED POWER

The patriotic incident in New Jersey was reported in the *New York Tribune* of
28 March 1917, p. 3. For the reaction of the USA and of President Wilson to
the coming of war in 1914: A. S. Link, *Woodrow Wilson* vol. 3, pp. 8–56. On
American public opinion and Louvain see Mark Derez, 'The Flames of

Louvain' in Cecil and Liddle (eds), *Facing Armageddon*, p. 621. On House in Europe in 1915: C. Seymour (ed.), *The Intimate Papers of Colonel House*, vol. 1, pp. 340–404. Wilson's first reaction to *Lusitania* sinking; Link, vol. 3, pp. 379–80. 'Too proud to fight': ibid., p. 382. Bryan succeeded by Lansing: ibid., pp. 424–8. House's mission to Europe in 1916: ibid., ch. 4; W. Görlitz (ed.), *The Kaiser and his Court*, p. 132; C. M. Mason, 'Anglo–American Relations: Mediation and "Permanent Peace"', in Hinsley (ed.), *British Foreign Policy under Sir Edward Grey*, pp. 476–80; Mason cites (p. 477) the 'sheep-faced gentleman' comment from the Hardinge papers; Hankey, *Supreme Command*, vol. 2, pp. 478–80, including 'humbug' comment in diary entry for 16 March. Presidential election campaign of 1916: A. M. Schlesinger, F. L. Israel and W. P. Hansen, *History of American Presidential Elections*, vol. 6, pp. 2253–350, including extract from Governor Glynn's speech; for Wilson and the election returns: Link, vol. 5, pp. 155–8. Wilson as peace broker in January 1917: ibid., pp. 190–240; S. Kernek, 'The British Government's reaction to President Wilson's "peace note" of December 1916' in *Historical Journal*, vol. 13, no. 4, pp. 721–66; C. A. Macartney and A. W. Palmer, *Independent Eastern Europe*, pp. 66–8. For pre-1917 American war plans, see J. A. S. Grenville, 'Diplomacy and War Plans in the United States' in P. Kennedy (ed.), *The War Plans of the Great Powers* especially pp. 36–7; and H. H. Herwig and D. F. Trask, 'Naval Operations Plans between Germany and the USA', ibid., especially pp. 60–4. Wilson's reaction to Villa's raid on Columbus: R. S. Baker, *Woodrow Wilson, Life and Letters*, vol. 6, pp. 66–70. Appointment of Pershing to Mexico: Link, vol. 4, p. 208. The two excellent biographies of Pershing, F. Vandiver, *Black Jack* and D. Smythe, *Pershing: General of the Armies* may be supplemented by the evidence from Dr Bevan Steadman's 1995 'psychiatric assessment' of Pershing, used by Vandiver in his chapter comparing Haig and Pershing in Cecil and Liddle (eds), *Facing Armageddon*, especially p. 68. On US reaction to unrestricted submarine warfare see the scrupulously careful reassessment in E. R. May, *World War and American Isolation*, pp. 336–40. Barbara Tuchman's highly readable *The Zimmerman Telegram* may be supplemented by May's ch. 19 and by P. Beesly, *Room 40: British Naval Intelligence 1914–1918*, ch. 13. For Wilson's reaction: Link, vol. 5, pp. 345–6; Baker, op. cit., vol. 6, pp. 474–7. Zimmermann's 'It is True' affirmation: Tuchman, p. 183. British press comment: *The Times*, 5 March 1917. First War Department operational plans in 1917: Grenville in Kennedy (ed.), *War Plans*, p. 37. German High Command, and Major Wetzell's assessment: F. Fischer, *Germany's Aims in the First World War*, p. 307. Admiral Sims's mission to Europe: W. S. Sims, *The Victory at Sea*, pp. 3–8; E. E. Morison, *Admiral Sims and the Modern American Navy*, pp. 339–41. Wilson's war message and the reaction of the Congress: Link, vol. 5, pp. 421–40. Balfour's visit to the USA: French, *Strategy* . . .

Coalition, pp. 65–6; E. C. B. Dugdale, *Arthur James Balfour*, vol. 2, pp. 194–208. Pershing's powers: D. R. Beaver, *Newton D. Baker and the American War Effort*, pp. 65–75. Balfour and 'sphere of influence': *Foreign Relations of the United States; 1917*, Supplement 1, p. 48. Pershing's crossing from New York to Liverpool: Vandiver, vol. 2, pp. 691–704; Pershing and George V, ibid., pp. 706–7. American destroyers at Queenstown: Halpern, *Naval History*, p. 359. Capelle in the Reichstag: Fischer, op. cit., p. 308. AEF arrives in France June 1917: Vandiver, vol. 2, p. 717. 'Lafayette we are here': ibid., p. 724; J. Pershing, *My Experiences in the World War*, vol. 1, p. 93.

7: A BULL AMID THE CAMELS

British military authorities' assessments of probable American assistance: French, *Strategy . . . Coalition*, pp. 102 and 108, citing in particular the Bridges Committee report of 14 June 1917 in PRO CAB 23/3/WC164. For low Italian morale in April 1917: John Gooch's 'Morale and Discipline in the Italian Army' in Cecil and Liddle (eds), *Facing Armageddon*, p. 441. For Brusilov's abortive offensive see his *A Soldier's Notebook*, pp. 300–15. On the change of monarch in Greece: D. Dutton, 'The Deposition of King Constantine' in *Canadian Journal of History*, vol. 12, no. 3, especially pp. 340–4; Hankey diary, 17 June 1917, printed in Roskill, *Hankey*, p. 402. War Policy Committee, ibid., pp. 401–5; and Hankey, *Supreme Command*, vol. 2, pp. 670–86. The most detailed study of the origins of the Flanders offensive is in D. French's *Strategy . . . Coalition*, especially pp. 110–21, with Wilson's diary entry for 5 June cited on p. 111. Attack not to be drawn out like the Somme: Hankey diary entry 16 July, *Supreme Command*, vol. 2, p. 683. Lloyd George finds Palestine 'interesting': Sanders's *High Walls of Jerusalem*, p. 493, cited by Fromkin, *A Peace*, p. 287. Picot alarmed by Murray's projected invasion of Palestine: L. J. Stein, *The Balfour Declaration*, p. 388; and compare Andrew's and Kanya-Forstner's article on French colonial war aims, *Historical Journal*, vol. 17, pp. 94–5. For the Downing Street meeting when Sykes received his instructions: PRO CAB 24/9/GT372 of 3 April 1917, extensively quoted by French, op. cit., p. 134; Adelson, *Mark Sykes*, pp. 317–32; supplementary material in Box 2 of the Sykes Papers, MEC. On Smuts's rejection of the Palestinian command: J. C. Smuts Jnr, *Jan Christian Smuts*, pp. 184–5. Allenby appointed to succeed Murray: Lloyd George, *War Memoirs*, vol. 2, p. 1089; Wavell, *Allenby*, pp. 184–5; L. James, *Imperial Warrior*, pp. 106–7, and 114. Chetwode's military appreciation: Falls, *Egypt and Palestine*, vol. 3 (i), pp. 7–11. Allenby's first impressions and requests, L. James, pp. 115–18; Robertson's replies: D. R. Woodward (ed.), *Military Correspondence . . . Robertson*, 27 July and 10 August 1917, pp. 209–10 and pp. 213–14. For the 60th Division's movements: Palmer, *Gardeners*, p. 149; Livermore, *Long 'Un*, p. 87. Fate of the 10th Division: Falls, *Macedonia*, vol. 2, pp. 13, 14, 15, 17. Salonika's Great Fire: Palmer, op. cit., pp. 152–4. On German–Turkish plans for the *Yildirim* offensive: Falls, *Egypt and Palestine*, vol 3 (i), pp. 5–7: O. Liman von Sanders, *Fünf Jahre Türkei*, pp. 230–42; Trumpener, *Germany and the Ottoman Empire*, pp. 311–33. Falkenhayn's tour of inspection: F. von Papen, *Memoirs*, pp. 70–2. Jeremy Wilson's authorized *Lawrence of Arabia* is one of the finest biographies of the century, distinguishing judiciously between fact, fable and polemic: Wilson on the early phases of the Arab Revolt, pp. 279–358, covered by Lawrence in chs 6 to 37 of his *Seven Pillars of Wisdom*. Clayton's comment on the importance of Aqaba 'after the war' is printed by J. Wilson, p. 397; the memorandum is also in the Sykes Papers at the MEC, Oxford (Box 2, DB244.4, dated 29 May 1917). Lawrence cannot have known of this memorandum when he attacked Aqaba. For Newcombe's pessimism in May 1917; J. Wilson, pp. 418–19. Lawrence's long journey to El Ain Barida is covered by J. Wilson, pp. 412–13; a contemporary report of the expedition, written for Clayton on 10 July 1917, is printed in Garnett (ed.), *Letters of T. E. Lawrence*, pp. 225–30. On the capture of Aqaba: *Seven Pillars*, ch. 57; J. Wilson, p. 417. First meeting of Allenby and Lawrence: James, op. cit., pp. 124–6; Wavell, *Allenby*, p. 193. Lawrence's talks with Hussein, July 1917: J. Wilson, pp. 430–2 and p. 1078.

8: JERUSALEM BEFORE CHRISTMAS

Death of Michael Allenby: James, *Imperial Warrior*, pp. 126–7; B. Gardner, *Allenby*, pp. 145–7; Wavell, *Allenby*, p. 196. On the first phase of the Flanders offensive ('Third Ypres'; 'Passchendaele'): J. E. Edmonds, *History of the Great War . . . France and Belgium, 1917*, vol. 2, pp. 130–233; L. Wolf, *In Flanders Fields*, pp. 113–31, with Gough's morale-boosting remarks quoted p. 129; J. Terraine, *Douglas Haig: the Educated Soldier*, pp. 339–53. See also for Haig's role in the whole offensive: Blake (ed.), *Private Papers . . . Haig*, pp. 250–8 and French, *Strategy . . . Coalition*, pp. 124–32. Eleventh Battle of the Isonzo and its consequences for Allied policies: Edmonds and Davies, *Italy, 1915–1919*, pp. 31–42. Lloyd George's enthusiasm for Italian offensive: Hankey diary entries for 15 July and 15 August, 1917, Roskill, *Hankey*, p. 414 and p. 422; ibid., p. 429; Amery diary for 29 August 1917, Barnes and Nicholson (eds), *Leo Amery Diaries*, vol. 1, p. 169. Guns for Italy, Hankey, *Supreme Command*, vol. 2, pp. 694–5. The Menin Road attacks: Edmonds, op. cit., pp. 250–98; Wolf, *In Flanders Fields*, pp. 143–56. Hankey diary for 16 September on concentrating against Turkey: Hankey, op. cit., vol. 2, p. 697. For the 'moneybags' affair over Turkey: R. Warman's article on 'The erosion of Foreign Office influence' in *Historical Journal*, vol. 15, no. 1, pp. 143–4. Support for Allenby from London in late September and early October: Falls, *Egypt and Palestine*, vol. 3 (i), p. 27. On the preparations for the offensive: ibid., pp. 28–33; Wavell, *Palestine Campaign*, pp. 101–7. Extract on Allenby and Western Front, from von Papen's *Memoirs*, p. 70. For Meinertzhagen's ruse see use made of his diary by James, *Imperial Warrior*, p. 131. Attack on Beersheba: Falls, op. cit., pp. 54–7, with attack on Gaza and its capture pp. 58–76. Wavell, *Allenby*, pp. 207–22 gives a vivid account of the first eleven days of the offensive. For Australian aspects see H. S. Gullett, *Australian Imperial Forces in Sinai and Palestine*, especially pp. 380–99. German concern over Newcombe and his 'camelry', Steuber *Yildirim*, p. 114, cited in Falls, op. cit., p. 83. For the Huj attack by the Yeomanry, see L. James, p. 136, citing the memoirs of a Yeomanry medical officer. On Austro-Hungarian activity in Palestine see Peter Jung's contribution on 'Austria's desert war' in M. Wrba (ed.), *Austrian Presence in the Holy Land*, pp. 194–214. Bombing raids by the Royal Flying Corps: H. A. Jones, *The War in the Air*, vol. 5, pp. 240–4. Capture of Ramleh, Lydda and Jaffa: Falls, op. cit., pp. 181, 184; Wavell's *Allenby*, p. 222. Rain and sleet: Livermore, *Long 'Un*, pp. 124 and 125. On the Balfour Declaration see the specialist study by L. J. Stein; Fromkin, *Peace to End All Peace*, pp. 274–300; Roskill, pp. 350–1. Clayton's warning to Sykes of the 'dismay' caused by the Declaration was given in a letter of 28 November 1917, extensively printed by J. Wilson, *Lawrence of Arabia*, pp. 468–9; a version of the original is in MEC, Sykes Papers. For Bolshevik Declaration of Peace on 8 November 1917 and intention of publishing secret treaties: J. Wheeler-Bennett, *Brest–Litovsk*, pp. 68–70 and 375–6. Djemal revealed to the Arab world some of the secret treaties from Bolshevik sources in a speech at Beirut on 6 December 1917, cited by Kedourie, *England and the Middle East*, p. 107. For Bishop Neshanian's diary, see the contribution by Georg Hintlian, 'The First World War in Palestine and Msgr Franz Fellinger' in Wrba, pp. 179–91; 'dynamite removed', p. 188; 'requisition of carpets for the trenches' and 'fog on Jerusalem', p. 190. War Office directives to Allenby: James, p. 140, citing WO 33/946, 8583–5 of 21 November 1917. Chetwoode's orders of 5 December: ibid., p. 240; fighting of 8 December; ibid., pp. 246–50; see also Wavell's *Allenby*, pp. 228–9. There are several accounts of the almost farcical surrender of the city; I have followed the 'official history' version in Falls, op. cit., vol. 1, pp. 252–3, supplemented by the reminiscences of Bernard Livermore (who was serving in the 60th Division) as given in his *Long 'Un*, pp. 126–8 and in a conversation with me, of which I made notes, in July 1975. Entry into Jerusalem: Falls, op. cit., vol. 1, p. 259; 'imagination of Sykes' comment in Lawrence, *Seven Pillars*, p. 453. (Wilson prints on p. 1084 of his biography the original, extended version of Lawrence's paragraph.) Wavell's account is in his *Allenby*, p. 230; in a note in the collection of Allenby Papers at MEC (DR 588) Wavell suggests that Allenby drafted the Jerusalem proclamation himself and sent it home to London for approval before reading it at the ceremony. The same collection of papers (DR 588) includes a copy of

Allenby's telegram to Robertson on 14 December on the need for advance northwards to be 'step by step'. Reaction to the fall of Jerusalem is extensively covered by James, pp. 142–3.

9: CAPORETTO AND AFTER

Conditions in Germany: Peter Loewenberg on 'Germany, The Home Front' in Cecil and Liddle (eds), *Facing Armageddon*, p. 555. Austrian conditions: G. Brook-Shepherd, *The Last Habsburg*, pp. 121–2; F. Fellner (ed.), *Tagebuch . . . Redlichs*, vol. 2, p. 226. Background in Russia: Vladimir Buldakov on the Russian national experience of war in Cecil and Liddle, especially p. 541, adds to more familiar accounts. Paris and Clemenceau's premiership: Poincaré, *Au service de la France*, vol. 9, p. 368; Bonnefous, *Histoire politique*, vol. 2, pp. 337–46; Watson, *Clemenceau*, pp. 268–76, citing on p. 270 quotation 'not having Clemenceau against him' from *L'Opinion* of 24 November 1917. For London weariness see letter extracts in V. Brittain, *Testament of Youth*, pp. 392–5. Battle of Cambrai: M. Gilbert, *The First World War*, p. 378–83; D. French, *Strategy of . . . Lloyd George*, p. 166–7; Roskill, *Hankey*, p. 461; Liddell Hart, *First World War*, pp. 435–48. For Russian events: Wheeler-Bennett, *Brest-Litovsk*, pp. 63–96. Fate of Russian warships: Halpern, *Naval History*, pp. 250–2 and 255–9. Romania: Macartney and Palmer, *Independent Eastern Europe*, p. 77. For the replacement of Conrad by Arz, Falls, *Caporetto*, pp. 27–30, citing and assessing Austrian sources. Caporetto background: geographical, K. Baedeker (ed.), *Austria–Hungary*, p. 262; Falls, op. cit., pp. 31–9. Main battle is covered ibid., pp. 40–62; Edmonds and Davies, *Military Operations, Italy*, pp. 40–58. On General Below, Görlitz, *The Kaiser and his Court*, p. 47. Approach march of Germans: E. Rommel, *Infantry Attacks*, pp. 169–70. News of Caporetto in London: Roskill, pp. 448–9; Hankey, *Supreme Command*, vol. 2, pp. 716–18. Foch in Italy and agreements with Cadorna and Robertson: M. Weygand, *Foch*, pp. 165–7; J. Marshall-Cornwall, *Foch as Military Commander*, pp. 206–8; Victor Bonham Carter, *Soldier True*, pp. 299–300. Rapallo Conference: Hankey, *Supreme Command*, vol. 2, pp. 719–26, with establishment of Supreme War Council. Effect of Caporetto on the Italians: Gooch contribution to Cecil and Liddle, *Facing Armageddon*, pp. 440–2, and formation of *Arditi*, pp. 444–5; F. Speranza (ed.), *Diary . . . Italy 1915–1919*, vol. 2, pp. 96–103. Last phase of the Caporetto campaign: Falls, op. cit., pp. 76–108; Edmonds and Davies, op. cit., p. 87.

10: PLANS FOR PEACE AND FOR WAR

Smuts's secret mission to Geneva: J. C. Smuts Jnr, *Jan Christian Smuts*, p. 197; M. Gilbert, *Sir Horace Rumbold*, pp. 167–8; Roskill, *Hankey*, pp. 470, 472, 502. Allies to re-state their war aims: K. J. Calder, *Britain and the Origins . . . New*

Europe, p. 122; Brook-Shepherd, *Last Habsburg*, pp. 150–1. For the Austrian peace exchanges in general, ibid., chs 6 and 7; and W. B. Fest, *Peace or Partition*, especially pp. 64–5, 171–3. Kerr and the Turks: his report printed in Lloyd George, *War Memoirs*, vol. 2, pp. 1504–9. On Poland: Calder, pp. 145–74; Macartney and Palmer, *Independent Eastern Europe*, p. 72. Lenin and Peace: Wheeler-Bennett: *Brest-Litovsk*, pp. 69–72. Lansdowne letter and its effects: D. French, *Strategy . . . Coalition*, pp. 199–200. Inter-Allied discussions in Versailles and Paris: Barnes and Nicholson (eds), *Leo Amery Diaries*, p. 182–6; Hankey, *Supreme Command*, pp. 725–31; Seymour (ed.), *Intimate Papers of Colonel House*, vol. 3, pp. 280–2; Clemenceau and Britain's free hand over Turkish terms: Hankey diary, 28 November 1918, printed in Roskill, p. 466. Asquith, Supilo and the 'smaller nationalities': Asquith's letter to V. Stanley, 14 January 1915, Brock (eds), *Asquith Letters*, p. 378; A. Palmer, *The Lands Between*, pp. 124–5, with Trumbić and the Pact of Corfu, pp. 136–7. Pichon's speech of 27 December 1917: Macartney and Palmer, *Independent Eastern Europe*, p. 78. British statements on war aims in winter of 1917–18: Lloyd George, *War Memoirs*, vol. 2, p. 1490–2, with text of his speech of 5 January 1918, pp. 1510–17; textual ambiguity over Thrace is examined in Macartney and Palmer, p. 78 and footnote; see also *Foreign Relations of the United States*, 1918, Supplement 1, vol. 1, p. 6. War Cabinet background: French, op. cit., pp. 203–4, citing PRO CAB 23/5/WC312 and WC313 of 3 January 1918. President Wilson's reactions to British war aims: Baker, *Woodrow Wilson, Life and Letters*, vol. 7, p. 141. Fourteen Points speech: ibid., p. 142; first London reports, *Evening News*, 9 January and *The Times*, 10 January 1918. Austrian reaction: Brook-Shepherd, *Last Habsburg*, pp. 136–8; German reaction, Fischer, *Germany's Aims*, p. 494, and p. 509. Clemenceau, Caillaux and Malvy: King, *Generals and Politicians*, pp. 182–3, 186, 202–3; Bonnefous, *Histoire politique*, pp. 303–4, 313–18, 354–5 and 370–1; Lennox (ed.), *Diary of Lord Bertie*, vol. 2, pp. 170–2, 175, 184–7, 236. Recall of Serrail: Poincaré, *Au Service de la France*, vol. 9, pp. 402–3; Falls, *Macedonia*, vol. 2, pp. 46–7; Sarrail, *Mon Commandement*, pp. 290 and 293–4. For Pogradec and Jacquemot's victory, *Les Armées françaises*, vol. 8 (ii), pp. 513–25. Essad Bey: Palmer, *Gardeners*, pp. 158–9. Versailles conference and Sarrail: Falls, loc. cit., and Alastos, *Venizelos*, pp. 183–4. Franchet declines Salonika command: Azan, *Franchet d'Esperey*, pp. 163–4. Appointment of Guillaumat: Larcher, *Grande Guerre dans les Balkans*, p. 280; *Les Armées françaises*, vol. 8 (ii), pp. 563–4. Milne's comments on Guillaumat: Nicol, *Uncle George*, pp. 148–9. King Alexander and the Greek mutinies: *Les Armées françaises*, vol. 8 (ii), pp. 578–9, with footnotes. Yugoslavs from Russia reach Salonika: L. Villari, *Macedonian Campaign*, pp. 192–3 and Palmer, *Gardeners*, pp. 175–6, which used material from Ante Mandic's *Fragmenti za Historiju Ujedinjenja*, published in 1956 in Zagreb. Haig suggests bringing back

Macedonian army to Western Front: Lloyd George, *War Memoirs*, vol. 2, pp. 1633–4. Allied war plans and Joint Note 12: Barnes and Nicholson, pp. 195 and 199–201; French, op. cit., pp. 190–1. Supreme War Council at Versailles, Jan–Feb. 1918: ibid., pp. 191–2; Hankey, *Supreme Command*, vol. 2, pp. 764–73; Roskill, pp. 489–92; Lloyd George, *War Memoirs*, vol. 2, pp. 1635–64. Robertson's position at this time: Victor Bonham Carter, *Soldier True*, pp. 322–30. Robertson's warning to Allenby, 2 February, 1918: Woodward (ed.), *Military Correspondence . . . Robertson*, p. 282. Advance into Judaean Hills and capture of Jericho: Falls, *Egypt and Palestine*, vol. 3 (i), pp. 362–3. Smuts's visit to Palestine and the Luxor plans: James, *Imperial Warrior*, p. 149; Barnes and Nicholson, pp. 205–7. The 'after tea, concocted plan' diary entry for 18 February is not in the printed extracts but was quoted by Amery in a letter to Wavell in March 1939, filed in the Allenby Collection at MEC, DR 588. Allenby's corps commanders' conference of February, 1918: J. Wilson, *Lawrence*, p. 485; Lawrence, *Seven Pillars*, pp. 503–4. A copy of the CIGS telegram to Allenby of 7 March over the Western Front's precedence in aircraft is in the Allenby Collection at MEC, DR 588. Aborting of Allenby's March expedition against Amman: Falls, *Egypt and Palestine*, vol. 3, (i), pp. 335–45.

11: THE EMPEROR'S BATTLE

Haig's optimism on 2 March: Blake (ed.), *Private Papers . . . Haig*, p. 291. Smuts and Hankey visit the Western Front: Hankey, *Supreme Command*, vol. 2, pp. 756–60; Roskill, p. 485 prints Hankey's letter of 22 January in which he told Lloyd George, 'the army is tired of war'. The account of Haig and Gough's preparations to meet the offensive in C. Cruttwell's *History of the Great War*, pp. 501–3 is admirably clear and concise, and cites the GHQ Intelligence report of 16 March. For German preparations: Reichkriegsministerium, *Der Weltkrieg*, vol. 14, p. 85 and pp. 107–24. First day of the German offensive: J. Terraine, *To Win a War*, pp. 59–60; Cruttwell, pp. 506–7; Gilbert, *Churchill*, vol. 4, pp. 77–82; Hankey, op. cit., vol. 2, pp. 785–8. OHL, Machaelis and Hertling: Fischer, *Germany's Aims*, pp. 400, 439–40. On the Kaiser's activities: Palmer, *The Kaiser*, pp. 196–7 and 202. On Crown Prince Rupert: G. Ritter, *The Sword and the Sceptre*, vol. 4, p. 95. Imperial headquarters during the battle and reference to the *Kölnische Zeitung*; Görlitz (ed.), *Kaiser and his Court*, pp. 343–5. Bombardment of Paris; see the American ambassador's account included in Thoumin (ed.), *First World War*, pp. 462–4 and p. 478. Pétain 'much upset': Blake, p. 297. Doullens Conference; ibid., p. 298; Foch, *Memoirs*, p. 300; Poincaré, *Au Service de la France*, vol. 10, pp. 86–90; French, *Strategy of . . . Lloyd George*, pp. 226–7. German surprise at British rations: H. Sulzbach, *With the German Guns*, p. 156; also Captain Rudolf Binding, cited by Terraine, op. cit., p. 64. Germans halted outside Amiens; ibid., p. 65. Captain Ritter's 'crushing disappointment'; Ritter, vol. 4, p. 232. Rawlinson's diary entry of 26 March on 'back to the wall', quoted by Gilbert, *First World War*, p. 409. Battle of the Lys: Cruttwell, pp. 514–18; Terraine, op. cit., pp. 66–7. Portuguese 'not stopped running': M. Hammerson (ed.), *No Easy Hopes or Lies*, p. 251. Difficulties of Gordon Highlanders in taking over the Portuguese position: C. Falls, *First World War*, p. 321. A facsimile of the original draft of Haig's Order of the Day, with a deleted last sentence ('But be of good cheer, the British Empire must win in the end'), is in W. S. Churchill, *The World Crisis*, vol. 2, facing p. 1302. 'Despairing cry': Taylor in his *English History, 1914–1945*, p. 202, but Taylor's comments in his *First World War*, p. 222 show greater perception. Freyberg's experiences around Bailleul: P. Freyberg, *Bernard Freyberg VC*, pp. 128–9. First battle between tanks: Cruttwell, p. 523. Abbeville conferences, May 1918: Hankey, op. cit., vol. 2, pp. 795–6, with diary entry for 2 May given more fully in Roskill, *Hankey*, pp. 536–8. Wilson to Allenby on battle casualties in four weeks: Falls, *Egypt and Palestine*, vol. 3 (ii), pp. 413–14. Search for reinforcements from Macedonia and Italy: Nicol, *Uncle George*, p. 161; Edmonds and Davies, *Military Operations, Italy*, p. 151. 'Peace awaits Wilson's armies': Speranza, *Diary*, p. 134. US infantry in France less than 55,000: French, *Strategy . . . Coalition*, p. 236, citing PRO CAB23/5/WC319 of 9 Jan. 1918. Pershing and US independence of command: Beaver, *Newton D. Baker*, pp. 118–20; Smythe, *Pershing*, pp. 75–8. Bavarians raid Barthelémont: Gilbert, *First World War*, p. 372; Movements of US 2nd Division artillery: Amos N. Wilder, *Armageddon Revisited*, pp. 65–81. Lloyd George appeals to President Wilson, March 1918: Hankey, op. cit., vol. 2, pp. 786–8; Roskill, p. 512; Smythe, pp. 103–4, 108–11; Beaver, pp. 134–5. Pershing's 'when the war ends' message: ibid., p. 124. Pershing and Foch at Abbeville: Smythe, pp. 113–17, with 'Loire' question on p. 115; Hankey, op. cit., vol. 2, pp. 796–7. Chemin des Dames German breakthrough: Falls, *First World War*, pp. 327–8; Cruttwell, pp. 524–7; Terraine, op. cit., pp. 70–2. Cantigny victory for Americans: Smythe, pp. 126–7; *Evening News*, 30 May 1918. Americans at Château-Thierry and Belleau Wood: Smythe, pp. 129–41; Vandiver, *Black Jack*, vol. 2, pp. 895–9. Last phase of the German offensive, and Mangin's counter-attack: Terraine, op. cit., pp. 93–9. Mood at German headquarters: Görlitz, pp. 371–3.

12: OUTLYING THEATRES

General Wilson's gloomy assessment: Hankey's diary of 27 May in *Supreme Command*, vol. 2, p. 808 and Roskill, *Hankey*, p. 555. Danger the French might 'crack': ibid., p. 556. Allenby's second raid into Transjordan: Wavell, *Allenby*, pp. 250–5; Falls, *Egypt and Palestine*, vol. 3 (i), p. 364. Decision to retain troops in Jordan valley, ibid., vol. 3 (ii), p. 423. Liman succeeds Falkenhayn: ibid., vol. 3 (i), p. 310; Liman von Sanders, *Fünf Jahre*, pp. 254–70; Trumpener, *Germany and the Ottoman Empire*, pp. 167–90. Allenby and manpower: Falls, op. cit., vol. 3 (ii), pp. 414–18; Wavell, op. cit., pp. 262–3; James, *Imperial Warrior*, pp. 158–9. Japanese troops: ibid; and also in Allenby to War Office of 2 June 1918, copy in Allenby Collection, MEC, DR 588, Ds 43, 1AS. For Japanese naval escort duties in Mediterranean: Halpern, *Naval History*, p. 393. Evolution of Allenby's offensive plans in June and July 1918: Falls, op. cit., vol. 3 (ii), pp. 447–9; Wavell, op. cit., pp. 265–8. Conrad's June Offensive: E. Glaise von Horstenau and R. Kiszling (eds), *Österreich-Ungarns letzter Krieg*, vol. 7, pp. 228–74; Edmonds and Davies, *Military Operations, Italy*, pp. 201–39; Falls, *Caporetto*, ch. 13. Mutinies and desertions in *K-und-K* Army: Z. Zeman, *The Break-Up of the Habsburg Empire*, pp. 140–5; Palmer, *Lands Between*, pp. 138–9; Geoffrey Wavro's chapter on 'Morale in the Austro-Hungarian Army' in Cecil and Liddle (eds), *Facing Armageddon*, especially pp. 407–8. The Rome 'Congress of Oppressed Peoples'; Zeman, pp. 192–6; Calder, *Britain and . . . New Europe*, pp. 180–1; Macartney and Palmer, *Independent Eastern Europe*, pp. 82–3. American troops reach Italy: Speranza, *Diary*, vol. 2, pp. 177–8, with press references cited; d'Annunzio's leaflet raid on Vienna, ibid., p. 182. On Franchet's transference from Provins to Salonika: Azan, *Franchet d'Esperey*, 176–8 (including note on 'not being angry'); R. d'Harcourt, *Le Fauteuil du Maréchal Franchet*, p. 43; Palmer, *Gardeners*, pp. 182–6. Milne's first impressions: Nicol, *Uncle George*, p. 166. Franchet's reconnaissance with Mišić and Prince-Regent Alexander: Azan, pp. 182–3; *Les Armées françaises*, vol. 8 (iii), pp. 75–6. Clemenceau's directive to Franchet: ibid., pp. 7–82; Larcher, *Grande Guerre dans les Balkans*, annexes 18 and 19. For discussions over Salonika at the Versailles Supreme War Council meeting: Lloyd George, *War Memoirs*, vol. 2, p. 1917; Falls, *Macedonia*, vol. 2, p. 105; Hankey, op. cit., vol. 2, p. 819. CIGS proposes Indian rather than British troops in Salonika: Falls, *Macedonia*, vol. 2, p. 110. Milne's difficulties over men and material: ibid., pp. 112–17; Nicol, pp. 168–73. Inspections of the Greek Army: ibid., p. 168. Ludendorff's eastern ambitions in the summer of 1918: Fischer, *Germany's War Aims*, chs 20 and 22. General Marshall's advance in Mesopotamia: Barker, *Neglected War*; Moberly, *Campaign in Mesopotamia*, vol. 4, with the CIGS's telegram of 28 June on p. 186. Diary entry on tedious nature of terrain: Major Crowdy's 1918 letterbook, p. 40 in MEC/DS 461. For the expedition into Persia and to the Caspian, see L. C. Dunsterville, *The Adventures of Dunsterforce* and C. H. Ellis, *The Transcaspian Episode*, pp. 35–44.

13: THE FLOWING TIDE

'Prince of Mecca': R. V. Buxton's letter-diary of 4 August 1918, Wilson, *Lawrence of Arabia*, p. 534 and p. 1099. Hitler's Iron Cross: Gilbert, *First World War*, p. 447; F. D. Roosevelt, ibid. Churchill's message to his constituents:

Gilbert, *Churchill*, vol. 4, pp. 128–9. Lloyd George's message: Brook-Shepherd, *November, 1918*, pp. 30–1. Archbishop Davidson's sermon: G. K. A. Bell, *Randall Davidson*, vol. 2, pp. 903–4. King George V's fifth visit to France: H. Nicolson, *King George V*, p. 423. Lloyd George to Eisteddfod on German Army's 'black day': Roskill, *Hankey*, p. 589. Events of 8 August: Terraine, *To Win A War*, pp. 110–15; description of tanks going forward, from L. G. Morrison in Thoumin, *First World War*, p. 494. Ludendorff's 'black day' remark is in his *War Memoirs*, vol. 2, p. 679. Response to attacks at German headquarters: Martin Kitchen's chapter, 'Ludendorff and Germany's Defeat' in Cecil and Liddell (eds.), *Facing Armageddon*, pp. 51–66, especially pp. 56–7; Görlitz (ed.), *Kaiser and his Court*, pp. 377–9; Ritter, *Sword and Sceptre*, vol. 4, pp. 323–4. Development of the offensive: Terraine, op. cit., pp. 116–34. Churchill's reaction to the offensive: Gilbert, *Churchill*, vol. 4, pp. 131–2; Lloyd George's response, Hankey, *Supreme Command*, vol. 2, p. 831, with expanded diary entry for 13 August in Roskill, p. 589. Spa conferences of 13–14 August: Ritter, loc. cit.; Fischer, *Germany's Aims*, pp. 627–9; Brook-Shepherd, *Last Habsburg*, pp. 168–9; R. Lorenz, *Kaiser Karl*, p. 484. The German retreat: Sulzbach, *With the German Guns*, p. 226. Hintze in Vienna and Austrian peace note: Lorenz, pp. 485–6. Australasian and Canadian attacks: Terraine, op. cit., pp. 128–9. Sedan Day 1918: Görlitz, p. 383. The CIGS's 'personal message' to Haig and its consequences: K. Jeffery (ed.), *Military Correspondence . . . Wilson*, p. 56; Terraine, op. cit., p. 139, and p. 144 for Haig's visit to London and exchanges with Milner; for Haig and Foch see Blake (ed.), *Private Papers . . . Haig*, pp. 323–4. Foch and Pershing: ibid., p. 325; Pershing, *My Experiences*, pp. 568–78; Smythe, *Pershing*, pp. 170–7; Foch, *Memoirs*, pp. 450–68. The Battle of St Mihiel: Smythe, pp. 179–89; Vandiver, *Black Jack*, vol. 2, pp. 935–41. MacArthur and Metz: see Gilbert, *First World War*, p. 459. Austria's 'cry to the world' and its reception: Brook-Shepherd, *November, 1918*, pp. 88–91. Foch's autumn offensive: see his memoirs, pp. 470–80; and general accounts: Cruttwell, *History of the Great War*, ch. 34; Falls, *First World War*, ch. 8; and especially Terraine, op. cit., pp. 154–74, with a particularly good account of the St Quentin Canal crossing (p. 167) based on Major R. E. Priestley's account in *Breaking the Hindenburg Line*. German reaction to news of defeats: Görlitz, pp. 394–5; Fischer, op. cit., pp. 634–5; Wheeler-Bennett, *Hindenburg*, pp. 161–3.

14: BALKAN EXPRESS

For the Bulgarian background to the Macedonian campaign: Nedeff, *Les Opérations en Macedonie*, pp. 178–9; Villari, *Madedonian Campaign*, p. 209 and p. 246; Palmer, *Lands Between*, p. 142. Mišić and signal to open the campaign: Falls, *Macedonia*, vol. 2, p. 147. D. Dieterich, *Weltkriegsende an der*

Mazedonischen Front, pp. 26–8, for Scholtz's reaction. For the first phase of the offensive, Palmer, *Gardeners*, pp. 200–2, based mainly on *Les Armées françaises*, vol. 8 (iii), pp. 315–17, supplemented by annexes 964, 973, 975–81, 985, 999–1000, 1003–17, 1031. Scholtz's request to OHL: Dieterich, p. 48; Falls, op. cit., vol. 2, p. 194 and appendix 16; Hindenburg, *Aus meinen Leben*, p. 370 and p. 372. Rusev's withdrawal: Dieterich, p. 37. Milne's difficulties: Nicol, *Uncle George*, pp. 171–2. Code message to attack: H. A. Jones, *Over the Balkans*, p. 111. Bulgarians' 'well-timbered dugouts': Milne's final official despatch of 1 December 1918, of which an abridged version is in G. Willis (ed.), *Salonika Memories*, pp. 4–9 (with passage quoted, p. 6). The despatch gives a meticulous account of the battles of 18–19 September; it may be supplemented by extracts from Milne's diaries in Nicol, p. 174 and p. 175; and by Falls, op. cit., vol. 2, pp. 159–72 and 178–86. See also Nedeff, pp. 233–42 and pp. 245–55; H. Collinson Owen, *Salonica and After*, pp. 248–58; C. Packer, *Return to Salonika*, pp. 248–53. Franchet 'talks rot': Milne diary, 18 September; Nicol, p. 173. For Nerezov, the conference at Prilep and dismay among Bulgarian troops: Nedeff, p. 225 and pp. 283–6; Dieterich, pp. 47–9. Air reconnaissance and bombing in the Balkans: Jones, op. cit., pp. 122–4. Stanley Spencer's hopes for the war ending; M. Collis, *Stanley Spencer*, p. 57. Jouinot-Gambetta's meeting with Franchet: Jouinot-Gambetta, *Üsküb*, p. 28; Prilep's fall, ibid., p. 32. On Gradsko see comments of Dieterich, pp. 94–8; he commanded the defence of the town. Franchet and Hindenburg's comment: Azan, *Franchet d'Esperey*, p. 289. For the 'epic march' on Skopje: Jouinot-Gambetta, pp. 48–82; Thoumin's *First World War*, pp. 498–9, gives a translated extract on the entry into Skopje. For events inside Bulgaria and the Derbyshire Yeomanry's encounters with Bulgarian peace emissaries: Palmer, *Gardeners*, pp. 223–6; Falls, op. cit., vol. 2, pp. 228, 230, 233 and 250. Azan, pp. 196–200 gives an account of Franchet's handling of the peace talks. Lloyd George's expectancy of crossing to Paris to meet Bulgarian delegates: McEwen, *Riddell Diaries*, p. 239. The Salonika Armistice terms are printed in full in Falls, op. cit., vol. 2, pp. 251–3 and Lloyd George, *War Memoirs*, vol. 2, pp. 1946–7. For Franchet's casual treatment of Milne over the armistice terms: Nicol, pp. 178–9. For reception of news of Bulgarian surrender in London: Hankey diary, *Supreme Command*, vol. 2, pp. 839–40.

15: ROADS TO DAMASCUS

On Allenby's preparations for his final offensive: Wavell, *Palestine Campaigns*, pp. 190–6; Falls, *Egypt and Palestine*, vol. 3 (ii), pp. 449–55. Arabs at Tafila: ibid., p. 402; J. Wilson, *Lawrence of Arabia*, pp. 475–6, 480–3, 491–2. German, Austro-Hungarian and Ottoman strength: Liman von Sanders, *Fünf Jahre Türkei*, pp. 270–4; Trumpener, *Germany and the Ottoman Empire*, pp. 103–4.

Kemal's reaction: Kinross, *Ataturk*, pp. 117–18. Allenby and Lawrence: J. Wilson, p. 523: Lawrence, *Seven Pillars*, p. 539. Plans of deception: Gullett, *Australian Imperial Forces*, pp. 685–7; Jones, *War in the Air*, vol. 6, p. 210; Wavell, *Allenby*, p. 269; James, *Imperial Warrior*, p. 162. Indian desertion: Wavell, p. 271. Opening attack on 19 September: Falls, op. cit., vol. 3 (ii), pp. 472–90. RAF attacks: Jones, op. cit., vol. 6, pp. 214–5. Passage of the Musmus Pass: Falls, op. cit., vol. 3 (ii), pp. 517–18. Macandrew's raid on Nazareth: ibid., pp. 525–7; Liman von Sanders's account of his escape, *Fünf Jahre Türkei*, pp. 284–5. Capture of Haifa and Acre: Falls, op. cit., vol. 3 (ii), pp. 534–6. Chaytor's Force, capture of Amman and securing of Transjordan: ibid., pp. 552–5. Lawrence flies from Azraq and meets Allenby: J. Wilson, pp. 550–1. Lawrence's Arabs encamp at Sheikh Saad: ibid., p. 554 and p. 556; possible contacts with Kemal: ibid., pp. 557–8 and 1104–5. The Arabs at Deraa: ibid., pp. 557–9; Lawrence, *Seven Pillars*, pp. 635–6. General Barrow appalled at conditions at Deraa: Falls, op. cit., vol. 3 (ii), p. 583; G. W. Barrow, *The Fire of Life*, pp. 209–15. Chauvel ordered to advance on Damascus: Falls, op. cit., vol. 3 (ii), p. 560 and J. Wilson, p. 556 and p. 1103, citing Allenby's special instructions for control of Damascus from WO 95/4551. For messages to Feisal and Lawrence's movements: ibid., pp. 561–2; W. F. Stirling, *Safety Last*, pp. 94–6. For German-Turkish movements, Liman von Sanders, pp. 285–96; and on Kemal, Kinross, pp. 120–1. Falls, op. cit., vol. 3 (ii), pp. 570–93 gives a judicious account of the events leading up to the fall of Damascus, including General Riza's breakfast (p. 586) and the Australian Light Horse entry (p. 589). There is also a fine account in Gullett, pp. 751–75. J. Wilson (p. 1107) admits from the evidence of the Australian war diaries that the 3rd Light Horse Brigade passed through Damascus early on 1 October. Stirling's account is in his *Safety Last*, pp. 98–9. A copy of King Hussein's greeting to Allenby is in MEC, Allenby Collection, DR. 588. The meeting of Allenby, Feisal, Lawrence and Chauvel: J. Wilson, pp. 566–8; A. J. Hill, *Chauvel of the Light Horse*, pp. 242–3; Wavell, *Allenby*, p. 286; Lawrence's brief account shows a rare tact of omission, *Seven Pillars*, p. 660.

16: 'EVERY DAY LOST . . .'

Lloyd George on France not profiting in Middle East: D. French, *Strategy of the Lloyd George Coalition*, p. 262, citing PRO CAB 23/14/WC482A. Sykes's activities: ibid., p. 263 and Adelson, *Mark Sykes*, pp. 267–8. Lloyd George and realignment of Milne's army: his *War Memoirs*, vol. 2, pp. 1947–50; Hankey, *Supreme Command*, vol. 2, pp. 840–3; Nicol, *Uncle George*, p. 180. Amery's predictions: Barnes and Nicholson (eds), *Leo Amery Diaries*, p. 237 (2 October 1918); and the same entry for CIGS's visit to France. Henry Wilson's doubts over the Germans 'giving in': D. French, op. cit., pp. 270–1 (War Cabinet, 16

October). Events at OHL in Spa and in Berlin: Palmer, *The Kaiser*, pp. 207–8; Görlitz (ed.), *Kaiser and his Court*, pp. 399–400; Brook-Shepherd, *November, 1918*, pp. 211–12, including Scheidemann's rhetorical question; Wheeler-Bennett, *Hindenburg*, pp. 164–9 (with Kaiser's no 'difficulties for Supreme Command' remark, p. 165 and Reichstag meeting, p. 166); Max of Baden, *Memoirs*, vol. 2, p. 15ff. Hindenburg's letter, with 'every day lost' remark: Wheeler-Bennett, op. cit., pp. 166–7. First peace messages sent to Wilson: G. Michaelis (ed.), *Die Ursachen des deutschen Zusammenbruchs*, vol. 2, pp. 378–9. Americans in the Argonne battle: Smythe, *Pershing*, pp. 190–211; Vandiver, *Black Jack*, vol. 2, pp. 956–84. Cleveland, Ohio, editor and general mood in USA: Brook-Shepherd, op. cit., p. 231ff. For the mid-term elections and T. Roosevelt, Charles E. Neu's article 'Wilson's Electoral Defeat', in Purnell's *History of the First World War*, vol. 7, no. 15, pp. 3102–6. Wilson's response to first peace message: Seymour (ed.), *Intimate Papers*, vol. 4, p. 75–6; Baker, *Woodrow Wilson, Life*, vol. 8, pp. 461–2; Lloyd George, *War Memoirs*, vol. 2, pp. 1956–7. Allied reaction: ibid., pp. 1958–9; Hankey, op. cit., vol. 2, pp. 853–5. Wilson's second note: Seymour, vol. 4, pp. 82–6; long extract in Terraine, *To Win a War*, pp. 199–200. Danny Park Conference: Minutes, PRO CAB 24/66/ GT5967; Hankey, op. cit., vol. 2, p. 856; Roskill, *Hankey*, pp. 612–13. Smuts note of 24 October, cited from PRO CAB 24/67/6091 by D. French, op. cit., pp. 276–77. General Wilson on 16 October, ibid., pp. 270–1. Haig on 19 October: Blake (ed.), *Private Papers . . . Haig*, pp. 332–4. Views of French leaders: G. Clemenceau, *Grandeurs et misères d'une victoire*, pp. 60–75; Foch, *Memoirs*, pp. 504–12; Poincaré, *Au Service de la France*, vol. 10, pp. 377–86; Terraine, op. cit., pp. 216–8; Azan, *Franchet d'Esperey*, p. 211. Reception of Wilson's second note in Germany: Görlitz, p. 408; D. Horn (ed.), *The Private War of Seaman Stumpf*, p. 410 and p. 415. German Cabinet meeting of 17 October: Wheeler-Bennett, op. cit., pp. 172–3; Ludendorff memorandum, dated 31 October 1918, Michaelis, vol. 5, pp. 366–7; Brook-Shepherd, op. cit., pp. 245–6, with third note to Wilson, pp. 250–1 and third response extensively quoted on p. 253. For this exchange see also Lloyd George, op. cit., vol. 2, pp. 1966–7. Fall of Ludendorff: Wheeler-Bennett, op. cit., pp. 174–7.

17: MUDROS, PADUA, BELGRADE

News of Townshend's mission reaches London: Hankey diary, 21 October in Roskill, p. 619. For Rauf and Turkish background: Kinross, *Ataturk*, pp. 125–8. For the making of the armistice: G. Dyer's two-part article, 'The Turkish armistice of 1918' in *Middle East Studies*, vol. 8; see also Falls, *Egypt and Palestine*, vol. 3 (ii), p. 618. For Turkish admiration of Wilsonian principles: Palmer, *Decline and Fall of the Ottoman Empire*, pp. 241–2. Milner and

Constantinople's future: Milner to Balfour, 21 October, FO 800/206/355, extract printed in D. French, *Strategy . . . Coalition*, p. 264. British naval build-up: Halpern, *Naval History*, p. 401. Disputes with French over exclusiveness of armistice talks: French, op. cit., pp. 265–6 and second part of Dyer's first article. Capture of Aleppo: Kinross, pp. 122–3; Falls, op. cit., vol. 3 (ii), pp. 612–13. End of the campaign at Haritan and Muslimiya: ibid., pp. 613–16. Advance of Milne's army to Turkish frontier: Falls, *Macedonia*, vol. 2, pp. 262–71. The description of the mountain march of the 22nd Division's gunners is by E. A. Armstrong; it appeared in the Salonika Reunion Association's *The Mosquito* for 1963; for 'toiling on drag ropes' see G. J. Davidge, 'The Dedeagatch Trail' in Willis (ed.), *Salonika Memories*, p. 57. For Calthorpe, Milne and Franchet: D. Nicol, *Uncle George*, p. 183. Terms of the Mudros Armistice: Falls, *Egypt and Palestine*, vol. 3 (ii), p. 625ff. The French and Serbian advance to the Danube and the rearguard action of the German Eleventh Army: *Les Armées françaises*, vol. 8 (ii), pp. 376–93 and 440–68; Dieterich, *Weltkriegsende*, pp. 164–75. Franchet's 1809 comparison: Larcher, *La Grande Guerre*, p. 253. Spread of 'National Councils' across central Europe: Macartney and Palmer, *Independent Eastern Europe*, pp. 89–96; Zeman, *Break-up of the Habsburg Empire*, pp. 222–9, 231–2, 242–5. Emperor Charles's Imperial Manifesto: ibid., pp. 222, 227, 228, 229, 241; Lorenz, *Kaiser Karl*, pp. 510–11; Brook-Shepherd, *Last Habsburg*, pp. 170–81. Diaz's offensive and Austria–Hungary's defeat at Vittorio Veneto: Edmonds and Davies, *Military Operations, Italy*, pp. 264–325; L. Villari, *War on the Italian Front*, pp. 248–67; E. von Horstenau and R. Kiszling (eds), *Österreich-Ungarns Letzer Krieg*, vol. 7, pp. 560–665; Falls, *Caporetto*, pp. 170–7. For the crossing of the Piave at Papadopoli Island see also the eyewitness account in Crosse, *The Defeat of Austria*, pp. 21–30. For *K-und-K* Army condition: I. Deak, *Beyond Nationalism*, pp. 202–4. For Captain Ruggera's movements, Brook-Shepherd, *November, 1918*, pp. 292–3 and 298–300. Brook-Shepherd's account of the Padua armistice talks (ibid., pp. 300–10) contains information unavailable elsewhere. The fullest English-language account (including the protracted telephone call from Paris) is in Villari, op. cit., pp. 280–98. A summary of the terms forms Appendix C of Brook-Shepherd's book. For the sinking of the *Viribus Unitis*: Halpern, p. 177. General Azan (who was present) gives a French version of the Franchet–Károlyi Belgrade meeting in his *Franchet d'Esperey*, pp. 228–32; Károlyi wrote two accounts: seven years later in his *Fighting the World*, and, less fully and more wryly, in 1956 in *Faith without Illusion*, pp. 130–7. Incipient Italo-Yugoslav conflict and US peacekeeping: Palmer, *Gardeners*, p. 238.

18: 'HOSTILITIES WILL CEASE AT 11 A.M.'

On Groener's career: J. Wheeler-Bennett, *A Wreath to Clio*, pp. 134–6, 137–9, 148–51. William II leaves Berlin and travels to Spa: Palmer, *The Kaiser*, p. 209; Ritter, *Sword and Sceptre*, vol. 4, pp. 374–6; Görlitz (ed.), *Kaiser and his Court*, p. 417; Wheeler-Bennett, *Hindenburg*, pp. 182–3. The Drews mission: ibid., p. 185. Anglo–American friction: French, *Strategy . . . Coalition*, p. 279. Geddes's criticisms of Wilson: Hankey diary for 24 October in Roskill, p. 621. The Navy League's activities: Brook-Shepherd, *November, 1918*, p. 295; *The Times*, 1 November 1918, p. 6. Lloyd George and House's separate peace threat: Hankey, *Supreme Command*, vol. 2, pp. 860–1; Roskill, p. 623; Seymour (ed.), *Intimate Papers*, vol. 4, p. 170. On Pershing's attitude to armistice terms: ibid., p. 124. Admirals Scheer, Hipper and the possible German naval sortie: A. J. Marder, *From the Dreadnought to Scapa Flow*, vol. 5, pp. 171–2; Halpern, *Naval History*, pp. 444–6; Holger H. Herwig, '*Luxury Fleet*', pp. 247–50. Stumpf on rumours at Wilhelmshaven: Horn (ed.), *Private War*, p. 417. On the spread of the mutinies from Kiel to Berlin and Cologne: Herwig, pp. 250–2; D. Horn, *The German Naval Mutinies of World War I*, pp. 220–65. Groener's visit to the Front and 'need to cross the lines with a white flag' Wheeler-Bennett, *Wreath*, p. 152. Hindenburg and Erzberger: Wheeler-Bennett, *Hindenburg*, pp. 188–9. German delegates journey to Rethondes: Brook-Shepherd, op. cit., pp. 246–8, based on Erzberger's reminiscences; M. Weygand, *Le 11 Novembre*, pp. 24–5. On US mid-term election results: C. Neu's article on 'Wilson's Electoral Defeat' in Purnell's *History of the First World War*, vol. 7, no. 15, p. 3106. Premature peace celebrations: Reuter's confusion reported in *Daily Chronicle* and *The Times*, 8 November; account of American reaction, Gilbert, *First World War*, p. 495. Discussions at Rethondes: Foch, *Memoirs*, pp. 546–68; Codeville, *Armistice 1918*, pp. 7–9. Events of 8–9 November at Spa and William II's departure for Holland: Wheeler-Bennett, *Hindenburg*, pp. 190–203; Palmer, op. cit., pp. 210–11. Guildhall banquet celebrations in London: *Sunday Times*, 10 November and *The Times*, 11 November; Bell, *Randall Davidson*, p. 915. Signature of the Armistice: Foch and Codeville, as cited above; Brook-Shepherd, op. cit., pp. 377–8; Terraine, *To Win a War*, pp. 254–5. Armistice terms are printed: ibid., appendix C; and as appendix D in Brook-Shepherd, op. cit. Final fighting on the morning of 11 November: Gilbert, op. cit., pp. 500–2; Smythe, *Pershing*, pp. 231–2; B. Pitt, *1918: The Last Act*, p. 454; P. Freyberg, *Bernard Freyberg V.C.*, p. 138; Falls, *First World War*, p. 395; Wilder, *Armageddon Revisited*, pp. 148–51. Account of Armistice Day in England: *Daily Express* and *The Times*, 12 November 1918; Bell, p. 916 (with extracts from the Archbishop's diary); O. Sitwell, *Laughter in the Next Room*, pp. 1–4; Wilson, *Lawrence of Arabia*, p. 580. Clemenceau's Armistice Day: Watson's biography, p. 327. Lettow-Vorbeck: Gilbert, op. cit., pp. 505–6. German U-boat surrender at Harwich: Halpern, p. 448. Beatty and the surrender of the High Seas Fleet: ibid., p. 449; Herwig, pp. 254–7; Marder, vol. 5, pp. 190–4.

19: PEACEMAKING?

Several books used for this chapter (notably S. Bonsal's *Suitors and Suppliants* and works by Goldstein, Mamatey and Mayer) are not given specific references, but are acknowledged in the bibliography. Voyage to Brest of the *George Washington*: Shotwell's diary entry of 13 December 1918 in his *At the Paris Peace Conference*, pp. 79–83. Problems over Wilson's departure for Europe: H. Nicolson, *Peacemaking 1919*, pp. 56–64; S. Bonsal, *Unfinished Business*, pp. 118–19. His brief Christmas visit to AEF: Smythe, *Pershing*, p. 247. His visits to London and Scotland: M. Hankey, *Supreme Control . . . Peace Conference*, pp. 15–20; unfavourable impression on the King, K. Rose, *King George V*, p. 232; his visit to Rome, Speranza (ed.), *Diary*, pp. 237–9. Preparatory work by Inquiry and other staffs; Bonsal, op. cit., pp. 21–4; Nicolson, op. cit., pp. 20–2. Feisal and Lawrence as envoys; J. Wilson, *Lawrence of Arabia*, pp. 588–9. General election campaign: Hankey, op. cit., p. 20; Nicolson, op. cit., pp. 14–19; Sitwell, *Laughter in the Next Room*, pp. 63–7; Barnes and Nicolson (eds), *Amery Diaries*, p. 244 and p. 248; *The Times*, 28 December 1918. Events in Vienna: Brook-Shepherd, *The Last Habsburg*, pp. 191–225. Hungary: Károlyi, *Faith without Illusion*, pp. 152–7; Macartney and Palmer, *Independent Eastern Europe*, pp. 120–1 and 163; Palmer, *Lands Between*, pp. 160–1. Ebert, Groener and 'undefeated' army: J. Wheeler-Bennett, *The Nemesis of Power*, pp. 21–2, 27–8, 31. German Free Corps and Spartacist murders: ibid., pp. 33, 36, 41, 42; E. O. Volkmann, *Revolution über Deutschland*, pp. 69–70, 136–72. Events in Prague and Bratislava: Macartney and Palmer, pp. 91 and 116; Palmer, op. cit., p. 154 and p. 187. For Stefanik's death, see also: Nicolson, op. cit., p. 267. Pilsudski: Macartney and Palmer, pp. 109–10 (with Foch's plan). Unity of Yugoslav peoples and misfortune of Radić: ibid., pp. 96 and 116. Montenegro and the Podgorica Assembly: H. W. V. Temperley (ed.), *History of the Peace Conference*, vol. 4, pp. 201–4; Nicolson, op. cit. pp. 121–5 ('white card'); Azan, *Franchet d'Esperey*, p. 244 (with Franchet's visit to Constantinople on same page). Situation in Turkey: Palmer, *Decline . . . Ottoman Empire*, pp. 243–5; Kinross, *Ataturk*, pp. 136–42. Allenby's visit: ibid., p. 143; Nicol, *Uncle George*, photograph 20, but visit not mentioned in text. Meeting with Franchet: Gardner, *Allenby*, p. 214; letter to Lady Allenby, undated (? Feb. 1919) in Allenby Collection MEC (as DR 588, DS 43, 1AS). Allenby's mounting difficulties with Arab unrest and his suspicion of the French: James, *Imperial Warrior*, pp. 179–84. Lawrence and Feisal at the Peace Conference: J. Wilson, pp. 604–9. Death of Sykes: Nicolson, op. cit., p. 214; Hankey, op. cit., p. 64. Allenby in Paris: James, p. 186; A. J. P. Taylor (ed.), *Lloyd George: A Diary by Frances Stevenson*, p. 174. On Armenian mandate: Fromkin, *Peace to End All Peace*, p. 398. Formal Conference opening: Nicolson, op. cit., p. 197; Hankey, op. cit., pp. 42–3. Fontainebleau Memorandum and its reception: ibid., pp. 98–102; Gilbert, *First World War*, p. 513. Presentation of treaty terms to the Germans; Hankey, op. cit., pp. 150–5. Response summarized from German sources, Wheeler-Bennett, op. cit., pp. 46–51. Possible armed resistance by Germany: J. Benoist-Méchin, *Histoire de l'Armée allemande*, vol. 1, pp. 384–8; Volkmann, pp. 377–82. 'Better to perish honourably': Wheeler-Bennett, *Hindenburg*, p. 217–18. Events at Scapa Flow: D. Van der Vat, *The Grand Scuttle*, p. 21 and pp. 171–4, including extracts from J. Taylor, 'The Strangest School Journey Ever Made' in *Teacher's World* for June 1940; Herwig, '*Luxury Fleet*', pp. 255–6. German attempts to have war guilt clause and war crimes trial clauses deleted: D. Hunter Miller, *Diary*, vol. 18, pp. 528–33. German Army chiefs and advice to sign treaty: Wheeler-Bennett, *Hindenburg*, pp. 219–21; Volkmann, pp. 302–3. Signing ceremony of Treaty of Versailles: among many accounts Nicolson, op. cit., pp. 300–4 and Hankey, op. cit., pp. 186–9. Smuts's protest: J. C. Smuts Jnr's biography of his father, pp. 227, 231, 234. For Wilson's failures and misfortunes see Lansing's *The Big Four* and the final section of his *Peace Negotiations . . . Narrative*. Treaty of St Germain: Temperley (ed.), *Peace Conference*, vol. 4, pp. 368–96; and Lutz and Almond's book specifically on the Treaty. For the Klagenfurt dispute: H. M. Wutte, *Kärntens Freiheitskampf*, pp. 61–5. On Bulgaria and the Treaty of Neuilly: Temperley, vol. 4, pp. 448–60. On Béla Kun and Hungary: ibid., vol. 4, p. 160; Nicolson, op. cit., pp. 240–9; Bonsal, pp. 115–20; Macartney and Palmer, pp. 120–1 and pp. 163–7. On the Treaty of Trianon: Temperley's article on how the Hungarian frontiers were drawn, in *Foreign Affairs*, April 1928; C. A. Macartney, *Hungary and her Successors*, pp. 48–60, 106–17, 214–21, 251–3, 337–9, 390–2. On Fiume: Macartney and Palmer, pp. 128–9. On the Treaty of Sèvres and its consequences: ibid., pp. 134–6; Palmer, *Decline . . . Ottoman Empire*, pp. 253–8; Kinross, pp. 230–301; Fromkin, pp. 403–4. Lausanne Conference and Treaty: D. Gilmour, *Curzon*, ch. 35; Palmer, *Decline . . . Ottoman Empire*, pp. 262–4; Kinross, pp. 354–73. The Syrian crisis of 1920: Fromkin, pp. 435–40. Cairo Conference of 1921: Gilbert, *Churchill*, vol. 4, pp. 544–57; Wilson, *Lawrence of Arabia*, pp. 647–51. War casualties and destruction: Gilbert, *First World War*, pp. 540–1; for comparative figures I have used several different sources and would not regard mine as more than rough calculations, but they correspond closely with some diagrams printed in Purnell's weekly *History of the Twentieth Century*, no. 32, pp. 881–3. For the Unknown Warrior: *Daily Express*, 16 September and 11–12 November 1920. For Franchet's 'loaded revolver', d'Harcourt, *Le Fauteuil*, p. 39 and p. 47. The second Lord Milne told me of his Second World War coincidental misfortune in conversation at a commemorative meeting of friends of the Salonika veterans on 7 October 1989. Alan Hamilton's account of the funeral at Monchy: *The Times*, 16 April 1998, p. 3.

SELECT BIBLIOGRAPHY

BOOKS

Only works consulted in the preparation of *Victory 1918* are listed here. If no other place name is given, the book was published in London.

Abbott, G. F., *Greece and the Allies* (1922)

Adelson, R., *Mark Sykes: Portrait of an Amateur* (1975)

Alastos, D., *Venizelos* (1942)

Albrecht-Carrié, R., *Italy at the Paris Peace Conference* (New York, 1938)

Azan, Paul, *Franchet d'Esperey* (Paris, 1949)

Baedeker, Karl (ed.), *Austria–Hungary; Traveller's Handbook* (Leipzig, 1911, edn.)

Baker, R. S., *Woodrow Wilson and the World Settlement, 3 vols (1923)*
Woodrow Wilson, Life and Letters, vols 4, 5 and 6 (New York, 1937–9)

Barker, A. J., *The Neglected War: Mesopotamia 1914–1918* (1967)

Barnes, J. and Nicholson, D. (eds), *The Leo Amery Diaries, 1896–1929* (1980)

Barrow, Sir George W., *The Fire of Life* (n.d., ?1941)

Beaver, D. R., *Newton D. Baker and the American War Effort, 1917–1919* (Lincoln, Nebr. 1966)

Beesly, P., *Room 40: British Naval Intelligence 1914–1918* (1982)

Bell, G. K. A., *Randall Davidson, Archbishop of Canterbury* (1935)

Beneš, E., *My War Memoirs* (1928)

Benoist-Méchin, J., *Histoire de l'armée allemande depuis l'armistice*, vol. 1 (Paris, 1936)

Bertin, C., *Marie Bonaparte: A Life* (1982)

Blake, R. (ed.), *The Private Papers of Douglas Haig 1914–1918* (1952)

Bond, B. (ed.), *Fallen Stars: Eleven Studies of Twentieth Century Military Disasters* (1991)

Bonham Carter, Victor, *Soldier True: The Life and Times of Field Marshal Sir William Robertson* (1964)

Bonham Carter, Violet, *Winston Churchill as I knew him* (1965)

Bonnefous, Georges, *Histoire politique de la 3ème République*, vol. 2 (Paris, 1957)

Bonsal, S., *Unfinished Business* (1944)

   Suitors and Suppliants, the Little Nations at Versailles (New York, 1946)

Bourne, K. and Watt, D. C. (eds), *Studies in International History* (1967)

Braddon, R., *The Siege* (1971)

Brittain, Vera, *Testament of Youth* (1933)

Brock, M. and E. (eds), *H. H. Asquith, Letters to Venetia Stanley* (Oxford, 1982)

Brook-Shepherd, G., *The Last Habsburg* (1968)

   November, 1918: The Last Act of the Great War (1981)

Brown, M. (ed.), *The Letters of T. E. Lawrence* (Oxford, 1991)

Brusilov, A., *A Soldier's Notebook* (1930)

Busch, B. C., *Britain, India and the Arabs, 1914–1921* (Berkeley, Cal., 1971)

Calder, K. J., *Britain and the Origins of the New Europe 1914–1918* (Cambridge, 1976)

Callwell, C. E., *Field Marshal Sir Henry Wilson: His Life and Diaries*, 2 vols (London, 1927)

Cassar, G. H., *The French and the Dardanelles* (1971)

   Kitchener, Architect of Victory (1977)

Cecil, H. and Liddle, P. H. (eds), *Facing Armageddon: The First World War Experienced* (1996)

Churchill, W. S., *The World Crisis 1911–1918*, 2 vols. (1939 edn)

Clemenceau, Georges, *Grandeurs et misères d'une victoire* (Paris, 1930)

Codeville, Colonel, *Armistice 1918, The signing of the Armistice in the Forest Glade of Compiègne* (Compiègne, n.d.)

Coffmann, E. M., *The War to End All Wars, The American Military Experience in World War I* (New York, 1968)

Collis, Maurice, *Stanley Spencer* (1962)

Crosse, E. C., *The Defeat of Austria as seen by the 7th Division* (1919)

Cruttwell, C. R. M. F., *A History of the Great War* (1934)

Dalbiac, P. H., *History of the 60th Division* (1927)

Dalton, Hugh, *With British Guns in Italy* (1919)

David, E., *Inside Asquith's Cabinet: From the Diaries of Charles Hobhouse* (1977)

Day, H. C., *Macedonian Memories* (1930)

Deak, F., *Hungary at the Paris Peace Conference* (New York, 1942)

Deak, Istvan, *Beyond Nationalism: A Social and Political History of the Habsburg Officer Corps 1848–1918* (Oxford, 1990)

Dieterich, D., *Weltkriegsende an der Mazedonischen Front* (Berlin, 1926)

Djemal Pasha, *Memoirs of a Turkish Statesman 1913–1919* (1922)

Dugdale, E. C. B., *Arthur James Balfour*, vol. 2 (1936)

Dunsterville, L. C., *The Adventures of Dunsterforce* (1920)

Edmonds, J. E., *History of the Great War: Military Operations France and Belgium, 1918*, 5 vols (1935–47)

    History of the Great War: Military Operations France and Belgium, 1917, (ii) (1948)

Edmonds, J. E. and Davies, H. R., *History of the Great War: Military Operations, Italy 1915–1919* (1949)

Ellis, C. H., *The Transcaspian Episode* (1963)

Falkenhayn, E. V., *General Headquarters and its Crucial Decisions* (1919)

Falls, Cyril, *History of the Great War: Military Operations, Egypt and Palestine*, vol. 3 (1930)

    History of the Great War: Military Operations, Macedonia, 2 vols (1933–5)

    History of the Great War: Military Operations, France and Belgium, 1917 (1940)

    The First World War (1960)

    Armageddon 1918 (1964)

    Caporetto 1917 (1966)

Fellner, F. (ed.), *Schicksalsjahre Österreich, 1908–1919; Das Politische Tagebuch Josef Redlichs*, 2 vols (Graz, 1953–4)

Fest, W. B., *Peace or Partition; the Habsburg Monarchy and British Policy 1914–1918* (1978)

Fischer, F., *Germany's Aims in the First World War* (1967)

    War of Illusions: German Policies from 1911 to 1914 (1975)

Fitzherbert, M., *The Man who was Greenmantle: A Biography of Aubrey Herbert* (1983)

Foch, F., *The Memoirs of Marshal Foch* (1931)

Foreign Relations of the United States, 1918 (Washington, 1941–3)

Forster, E. S., *A Short History of Modern Greece* (1941)

French, David, *British Strategy and War Aims, 1914–1916* (1986)

    The Strategy of the Lloyd George Coalition, 1916–1918 (Oxford, 1995)

Freyberg, P., *Bernard Freyberg VC: Soldier of Two Nations* (1991)

Fromkin, David, *A Peace To End All Peace* (1989)

Fryer, C. E. J., *Royal Navy on the Danube* (Boulder, Colo., 1988)

Gardner, Brian, *Allenby* (1965)

Garnett, David (ed.), *Letters of T. E. Lawrence* (1938)

Gilbert, Martin, *Sir Horace Rumbold: Portrait of a Diplomat 1869–1941* (1973)

    Winston S. Churchill, 1914–1916, vol. 3 (1971); *Companion*, 2 parts (1973)

    Winston S. Churchill, 1916–1922, vol. 4 (1975); *Companion*, 3 parts (1978)

    The First World War (1994)

    Atlas of the First World War (rev. edn., 1995)

    A History of the Twentieth Century, vol. 1 (1997)

Gilmour, David, *Curzon* (1994)

Giolitti, G., *Memoirs of My Life* (1923)

Glaise von Horstenau, E. and Kiszling, R. (eds), *Österreich-Ungarns Letzer Krieg 1914–1918*, 7 vols, with 10 supplements (Vienna, 1930–8)

Goldstein, Erik, *Winning the Peace; British Diplomatic Strategy, Peace Planning and the Paris Peace Conference, 1916–1920* (Oxford, 1991)

Görlitz, W. (ed.), *The Kaiser and his Court: the First World War Diaries of Admiral Georg von Müller, Chief of the Naval Cabinet, 1914–1918* (2nd edn, 1961)

Gottlieb, W. W., *Studies in Secret Dipolmacy* (1957)

Grey of Fallodon, Viscount, *Twenty Five Years, 1892–1916*, 2 vols (1925)

Griffiths, R., *Marshal Pétain* (1970)

Grigg, J., *Lloyd George: From Peace to War, 1912–1916* (1985)

Groener, Wilhelm, *Feldherr wider Willen* (Berlin, 1931)

Gullett, H. S., *Australian Imperial Forces in Sinai and Palestine* (Sydney, 1939)

Halpern, Paul G., *A Naval History of World War I* (1994)

Hammerson, M. (ed.), *No Easy Hope or Lies, The World War I Letters of Lt Arthur Preston White* (1991)

Hankey, M., *The Supreme Command 1914–1918*, 2 vols (1961)
    The Supreme Control at the Paris Peace Conference 1919 (1963)

Harcourt, Robert d', *Le Fauteuil du Maréchal Franchet* (Paris, 1947)

Herwig, Holger H., *'Luxury Fleet', The Imperial German Navy, 1888–1918* (1980)

Hill, A. J., *Chauvel of the Light Horse* (Melbourne, 1978)

Hindenburg, Paul von Beneckendorff und von, *Aus meinen Leben* (Berlin, 1920)

Hinsley, F. H. (ed.), *British Foreign Policy under Sir Edward Grey* (Cambridge, 1977)

Horn, Daniel, *The German Naval Mutinies of World War I* (New Brunswick, NJ, 1969)
    (ed.), *The Private War of Seaman Stumpf* (1969)

Horne, Alistair, *The Price of Glory, Verdun 1916* (1962)

Hunter Miller, D., *My Diary at the Conference of Paris*, 14 vols (New York, 1924)

Ingamells, F. G., *On the Salonika Front, 1916–1918* (Norwich, 1944)

James, L., *Imperial Warrior, The Life and Times of Field Marshal Viscount Allenby, 1861–1936* (1993)

Jeffery, K. (ed.), *Military Correspondence of Field Marshal Sir Henry Wilson, 1918–20* (1985)

Jenkins, R., *Asquith* (1964)

Johnson, J. H., *1918, The Unexpected Victory* (1997)

Jones, H. A., *Over the Balkans and South Russia* (1923)
    History of the Great War: The War in the Air, vols 5 and 6 (Oxford, 1935–7)

Jouinot-Gambetta, F. L., *Üsküb* (Paris, 1920)

Kabitsch, E., *Die Rumanienkriege* (Berlin, 1928)

Károlyi, Mihaly, *Fighting the World* (1925)

Faith without Illusion (1956)

Kedourie, Elie, *In the Anglo-Arab Labyrinth* (Cambridge, 1976)
England and the Middle East: The destruction of the Ottoman Empire (rev. edn. 1987)

Kennedy, P. (ed.), *The War Plans of the Great Powers, 1880–1914* (1979)

Kent, Marian (ed.), *The Great Powers and the End of the Ottoman Empire,* (2nd edn, 1996)

King, J. C., *Generals and Politicians: Conflict between France's High Command, Parliament and Government 1914–1918* (Berkeley, Cal., 1951)

Kinross, Lord, *Ataturk, The Rebirth of a Nation* (1964)

Kitchen, M., *The Silent Dictatorship: The Politics of the German High Command under Hindenburg and Ludendorff, 1916–1918* (1976)

Komarnicki, T., *The Rebirth of the Polish Republic* (1957)

Kress von Kressenstein, F., *Mit den Türken zum Suezkanal* (Berlin, 1938)

Lansing, Robert, *The Big Four and Others of the Peace Conference* (Boston, Mass., 1921)
The Peace Negotiations, A Personal Narrative (Boston, Mass., 1922)
The Lansing Papers (Washington, 1939)

Larcher, P., *La Grande Guerre dans les Balkans* (Paris, 1929)

Lawrence, M. R. (ed.), *The Home Letters of T. E. Lawrence and his Brothers* (Oxford, 1954)

Lawrence, T. E., *The Seven Pillars of Wisdom* (1935 edn)

Lawson, J. C., *Tales of Aegean Intrigue* (1920)

Lennox, Lady A. G. (ed.), *The Diary of Lord Bertie of Thame, 1914–1918*, 2 vols (1924)

Leon, G. B., *Greece and the Great Powers* (Salonika, 1974)

Les Armées françaises see under Ministère de la Guerre

Liddell Hart, B. H., *History of the First World War,* (2nd edn 1972)

Liman von Sanders, O. K. V., *Fünf Jahre Türkei* (Berlin, 1920)

Link, A. S., *Woodrow Wilson,* vols 3, 4, 5 (Princeton, 1963–5)

Livermore, Bernard, *Long 'Un – A Damn Bad Soldier* (Batley, 1974)

Lloyd George, D., *War Memoirs,* 2 vols (1938 edn)
The Truth about the Peace Treaties, 2 vols (1938)

Lorenz, R., *Kaiser Karl und der Untergang der Donaumonarchie* (Vienna, 1959)

Ludendorff, Erich, *My War Memoirs 1914–1918*, 2 vols (1929)

Lutz, R. H. and Almond, G., *The Treaty of Saint Germain* (Stanford, 1935)

Macartney, C. A., *Hungary and her Successors* (Oxford, 1937)

Macartney, C. A. and Palmer, A. W., *Independent Eastern Europe* (1962)

Mackenzie, Compton, *Greek Memories* (1919)
Gallipoli Memories (1929)

MacMunn, Sir George, and Falls, C., *History of the Great War: Military Operations, Egypt and Palestine*, 2 vols (1928)

Mamatey, V. S., *The United States and East Central Europe, 1914–1918* (Oxford, 1958)

Marder, A. J., *From the Dreadnought to Scapa Flow*, vol. 5, *Victory and Aftermath* (Oxford, 1970)

Marshall-Cornwall, J., *Foch as Military Commander* (1972)

Masaryk, T. G., *The Making of a State* (1927)

Mavrogordato, J., *Modern Greece, 1800–1931* (1931)

Max, Prince of Baden, *Memoirs*, vol. 2 (1928)

May, E. R., *World War and American Isolation* (Cambridge, Mass., 1966)

Mayer, Arno J., *Politics and Diplomacy of Peacemaking* (1967)

McEwen, J. M., *The Riddell Diaries, A Selection, 1908–23* (1986)

Michaelis, G. (ed.), *Die Ursachen des deutschen Zusammenbruchs*, vol. 2 and vol. 6 (Berlin, 1928–9)

Middlebrook, Martin, *The First Day on the Somme, 1 July 1916* (1971)

Ministère de la Guerre, État-Major de l'Armée, Service Historique, *Les Armées françaises dans la Grande Guerre*, vol. 8 and annexes (Paris, 1925–34)

Moberly, F. J., *History of the Great War, Military Operations; Campaign in Mesopotamia 1914–1918*, 4 vols (1923–7)

Operations in Persia, 1914–1919 (1987)

Moorehead, Alan, *Gallipoli* (1956)

Morgenthau, H., *Secrets of the Bosphorus* (1918)

Morison, Elting E., *Admiral Sims and the Modern American Navy* (Boston, 1942)

Nedeff, D., *Les Opérations en Macedonie: l'Epopée de Doiran* (Sofia, 1927)

Nevakivi, J., *Britain, France and the Arab Middle East, 1914–1920* (1969)

Nicol, G., *Uncle George: Field Marshal Lord Milne of Salonika and Rubislaw* (1976)

Nicolson, Harold, *Peacemaking 1919* (1933)

King George V; His Life and Reign (1951)

Owen, H. Collinson, *Salonika and After* (1919)

Packer, Charles, *Return to Salonika* (1964)

Palmer, Alan, *The Gardeners of Salonika* (1965)

The Lands Between (1970)

The Kaiser (1978)

The Decline and Fall of the Ottoman Empire (1992)

Papen, Franz von, *Memoirs* (1952)

Pedroncini, G., *Les Mutineries de 1917* (Paris, 1967)

(ed.), *Les Mutineries des Armées Françaises* (Paris, 1968)

Pershing, J. J., *My Experiences in the World War*, 2 vols. (New York, 1931)

Pingaud, A., *Histoire diplomatique de la France pendant la Grande Guerre*, 3 vols (Paris, 1938–41)

Pitt, Barrie, *1918: The Last Act* (1962)

Poincaré, Raymond, *Au Service de la France*, vols 2–10 (Paris, 1926–33)

Price, G. Ward, *The Story of the Salonica Army* (1917)

Reichkriegsministerium, *Der Weltkrieg, 1914–1918*, vols 9, 11, 13 (Berlin, 1933–7)

Rhodes James, R., *Gallipoli* (1965)

Riddell, Lord, *War Diary, 1914–1918* (1933)

Ritter, G. *The Sword and the Sceptre*, vol. 4 (1968)

Robertson, W., *Soldiers and Statesmen, 1914–1918*, 2 vols (1926)

Rommel, Erwin, *Infantry Attacks* (1972)

Rose, Kenneth, *King George V* (1983)

Roskill, S., *Hankey: Man of Secrets*, vol. 1 (1877–1918) (1970)

Rudkin, Mabel, *Inside Dover, 1914–1918, A Woman's Impressions* (1928)

Salandra, A., *Italy and the Great War* (1932)

Sarrail, M., *Mon Commandement en Orient*, (Paris, 1920)

Schlesinger, A. M., Israel, F. L. and Hansen, W. P., *History of American Presidential Elections*, vol. 6 (New York, 1985)

Seton-Watson, R. W., *History of the Roumanians* (Cambridge, 1934)
Masaryk in England (Cambridge, 1943)

Seymour, C. (ed.), *The Intimate Papers of Colonel House* (New York, 1928)

Shotwell, J. T., *At the Paris Peace Conference* (New York, 1937)

Sims, W. S., *The Victory at Sea* (Garden City, NY, 1921)

Sitwell, O., *Laughter in the Next Room* (1949)

Smith, R. S., *A Subaltern in Macedonia and Judea* (1930)

Smuts, J. C., Jnr, *Jan Christian Smuts* (1952)

Smythe, D., *Pershing: General of the Armies* (Bloomington, 1986)

Spears, E. L., *Liaison 1914* (1930)
Prelude to Victory (1939)

Spector, S. D., *Rumania at the Peace Conference* (New York, 1962)

Speranza, F. (ed.), *The Diary of Gino Speranza, Italy 1915–1919*, 2 vols (New York, 1941)

Stein, L. J., *The Balfour Declaration* (1961)

Stirling, W. F., *Safety Last* (1953)

Stone, N., *The Eastern Front 1914–1917* (1975)

Storrs, R., *Orientations* (1937)

Strutz, G., *Herbstschlacht in Mazedonien* (Berlin, 1921)

Suarez, G., *Briand: Sa Vie, son Oeuvre avec son Journal*, vol. 4 (Paris, 1939)

Sulzbach, H., *With the German Guns, Four Years on the Western Front* (1973)

Swire, J., *Albania, The Rise of a Kingdom* (1921)

Tanenbaum, J. K., *General Maurice Sarrail, 1856–1929: The French Army and Left-wing Politics* (Chapel Hill, 1974)

Taylor, A. J. P., *The First World War* (1963)
  (ed.), Lloyd George; A Diary by Frances Stevenson (1971)
Taylor, A. J. P., and Pares, R. (eds), *Essays Presented to Sir Lewis Namier* (1958)
Temperley, H. W. V. (ed.), *History of the Peace Conference of Paris*, 6 vols (1920–2)
Terraine, J., *Douglas Haig: the Educated Soldier* (1963)
  To Win a War: 1918, Year of Victory (1986)
Thobie, J., *Intérêts et impérialisme français dans l'Empire Ottoman, 1895–1914*, 3 vols (Paris, 1973)
Thoumin, Richard (ed.), *The First World War: History in the Making* (1963)
Trumpener, U., *Germany and the Ottoman Empire 1914–1918* (Princeton, 1968)
Tuchman, Barbara, *The Zimmermann Telegram* (1958)
Vacalopoulos, A. P., *A History of Thessaloniki* (Salonika, 1963)
Van der Vat, Dan, *The Grand Scuttle; The Sinking of the German Fleet at Scapa Flow in 1919* (1982)
Vandiver, Frank, *Black Jack; The Life and Times of John J. Pershing*, 2 vols (College Station, Texas, 1977)
Vatikiotis, P. J., *The History of Modern Egypt* (1991)
Villari, L., *The Macedonian Campaign* (1922)
  The War on the Italian Front (1932)
Volkman, E. O., *Revolution über Deutschland* (Oldenburg, 1930)
Wallach, J. L., *Anatomie einer Militarhilfe* (Berlin, 1928)
Watson, D. R., *Georges Clemenceau, A Political Biography* (1974)
Wavell, A. P., *The Palestine Campaigns* (1931)
  Allenby: A Study in Greatness (1940)
Weygand, M., *Foch* (Paris, 1947)
  Le 11 Novembre (Paris, 1947)
Wheeler-Bennett, J., *Hindenburg, The Wooden Titan* (1936, rev. edn. 1967)
  Brest-Litovsk, The Forgotten Peace March 1918 (1938)
  The Nemesis of Power (1954)
  A Wreath to Clio (1967)
Wilder, A. N., *Armageddon Revisited, A World War One Journal* (New Haven and London, 1994)
Williams, Ian (ed.), *Newspapers of the First World War* (Newton Abbot, 1970)
Willis, G. (ed.), *Salonika Memories 1915–1919* (Newbury, 1969)
Wilson, A. T., *Mesopotamia, Loyalties 1914–17* (1930)
Wilson, J., *Lawrence of Arabia: the authorised biography* (1989)
Woodward, D. R., *Lloyd George and the Generals* (Newark, NJ, 1983)
  (ed.), *Military Correspondence of Field Marshal Sir William Robertson . . . December 1915–February 1918* (1990)

Woodward, E. L. and Butler, R. (eds), *Documents on British Foreign Policy 1919–1939*, series 1, vols 2 and 4 (1947–62)

Wolf, Leon, *In Flanders Fields* (1960 edn)

Wrba, Marian (ed.), *Austrian Presence in the Holy Land in the 19th and early 20th Century* (Tel Aviv, 1996)

Wrench, E. E., *Alfred, Lord Milner: The Man of No Illusions* (1958)

Wutte, H. M., *Kärntens Freiheitskampf* (Klagenfurt, 1922)

Zeman, Z. A. B., *The Break-Up of the Habsburg Empire* (1961)

ARTICLES IN PERIODICALS

The following list gives details of the articles included in the reference notes.

Allen, C. R. G., 'A Ghost from Gallipoli', *Journal of the Royal United Services Institute*, vol. 108 (1963), pp. 137–40

Andrew, C. M. and Kanya-Forstner, A. S., 'French Colonial War Aims, 1914–1918', *The Historical Journal*, vol. 17, no. 1 (1974), pp. 79–106

Dutton, D., 'The Balkan Campaign and French war aims in the Great War', *English Historical Review*, vol. 94, no. 370 (1979), pp. 97–113

Dutton, D., 'The Calais Conference of December 1915', *Historical Journal*, vol. 21, no. 1 (1978), pp. 143–56

Dutton, D., 'The Deposition of King Constantine of Greece, June 1917', *Canadian Journal of History*, vol. 12, no. 3 (1978), pp. 325–45

Dutton, D., 'The Fall of General Joffre', *Journal of Strategic Studies*, vol. 1, no. 3 (October 1978), pp. 338–51

Dyer, Gwynne, 'The Turkish armistice of 1918', *Middle East Studies*, vol. 8, no. 2 (May 1972), pp. 143–69 and vol. 8, no. 3 (October 1972), pp. 314–89

Kernek, S., 'The British Government's reaction to President Wilson's "peace note" of December 1916', *Historical Journal*, vol. 13, no. 4 (1970), pp. 721–66

Neu, Charles E., 'Wilson's Electoral Defeat', Purnell's *History of the First World War*, vol. 7, no. 15, pp. 3102–6

Robbins, Keith, 'British diplomacy and Bulgaria, 1914–1915', *Slavonic and East European Review*, vol. 49, no. 117 (1971), pp. 565–74

Temperley, H. W. V., 'How the Hungarian Frontiers were Drawn', *Foreign Affairs*, vol. 6 (April 1928), pp. 432–47

Torrey, G. E., 'Rumania and the belligerents 1914–1916', *Journal of Contemporary History*, vol. 1, no. 3 (1966), pp. 171–91

Warman, Roberta, 'The erosion of Foreign Office influence 1916–1918', *Historical Journal*, vol. 15, no. 1 (1972), pp. 133–59

INDEX